VAX-11
Assembly Language
Programming

Sara Baase

San Diego State University

PRENTICE–HALL, INC., Englewood Cliffs, New Jersey 07632

Library of Congress Cataloging in Publication Data

Baase, Sara.
  VAX-11 assembly language programming.

  Includes index.
  1. VAX-11 (Computer)—Programming. 2. Assembler
language (Computer program language) I. Title.
II. Title: V A X-eleven assembly language programming.
QA76.8.V37B3 1983   001.64′2   82–18101
ISBN 0–13–940957–2

Editorial/production supervision
  and interior design: Linda Mihatov
Cover design: Edsal Enterprises
Manufacturing buyer: Gordon Osbourne

**To all the students I've enjoyed
having in my classes**

Prentice–Hall Software Series
Brian Kernighan, Advisor

Printed in the United States of America

10   9   8   7   6   5   4

ISBN   0-13-940957-2

Prentice–Hall International, Inc., *London*
Prentice–Hall of Australia Pty. Limited, *Sydney*
Editora Prentice–Hall do Brasil, Ltda., *Rio de Janeiro*
Prentice–Hall Canada Inc., *Toronto*
Prentice–Hall of India Private Limited, *New Delhi*
Prentice–Hall of Japan, Inc., *Tokyo*
Prentice–Hall of Southeast Asia Pte. Ltd., *Singapore*
Whitehall Books Limited, *Wellington, New Zealand*

Contents

Preface   vi

Chapter 1:   **Introduction**   1

1.1 What Is Assembly Language and Why Study It? *1;*
1.2 Some Terminology *5*

Chapter 2:   **Machine Organization**   7

2.1 Memory and Data Organization *7;*
2.2 The Central Processing Unit *12;*   2.3 Input and Output *14;*
2.4 Summary *14*

Chapter 3:   **Binary and Hexadecimal Numbers and Integer
Representation**   16

3.1 The Binary and Hexadecimal Number Systems *16;*
3.2 Integer Representation *26;*   3.3 Summary *32;*   3.4 Exercises *32*

Chapter 4:   **Introduction to Assembly Language**   35

4.1 Symbols and Labels *35;*   4.2 Operators *37;*
4.3 Operand Addressing *39;*   4.4 Reserving and Initializing Data Areas *45;*
4.5 Beginning and Ending a Program *50;*   4.6 Statement Formats *53;*
4.7 Summary *53;*   4.8 Exercises *55*

Chapter 5:   **Simple I/O Macros**   **58**

5.1 The Macros *58;*
5.2 Summary and Commands for Running Programs *66;*
5.3 Exercises *70*

Chapter 6:   **Integer Instructions**   **72**

6.1 An Overview *72;*   6.2 Arithmetic *73;*
6.3 A Simple Loop Instruction (SOBGTR) and Array Addressing *78;*
6.4 Moving and Converting *83;*
6.5 Conversion Between Character Code and Two's Complement *86;*
6.6 Summary *92;*   6.7 Exercises *94*

Chapter 7:   **Branching and Looping**   **99**

7.1 Condition Codes and Branching *99;*   7.2 Example: Binary Search *110;*
7.3 Loop Control Instructions *115;*
7.4 Example: Converting Character Code Input—Horner's Method *122;*
7.5 Summary *125;*   7.6 Exercises *126*

Chapter 8:   **Machine Code Formats, Translation, and Execution**   **131**

8.1 An Overview *131;*   8.2 Some Register Modes *135;*
8.3 Literal Mode *140;*   8.4 Branch Mode *141;*
8.5 Some Program Counter Modes: Relative Mode and Immediate Mode
     144;   8.6 An Assembly Listing *151;*
8.7 More Addressing Modes: Deferred and Indexed Modes *154;*
8.8 Exceptions, or Execution-Time Errors *160;*   8.9 Summary *165;*
8.10 Exercises *167*

Chapter 9:   **Procedures**   **172**

9.1 Advantages of Procedures—and Implementation Problems *172;*
9.2 The Stack *175;*
9.3 An Overview of the VAX Procedure-Calling Standard *179;*
9.4 The .ENTRY Directive *181;*   9.5 Argument Lists *183;*
9.6 Calling and Returning from a Procedure *192;*
9.7 Linking with High-Level Languages and Library Routines *197;*
9.8 Example: Linked List Manipulation *200;*   9.9 Summary *215;*
9.10 Exercises *216*

Chapter 10:   **Some Assembler Features**   **220**

10.1 Program Sections *220;*   10.2 Terms and Expressions *226;*
10.3 Symbol and Expression Types *229;*
10.4 Restrictions on Expressions *233;*
10.5 Summary *234;*   10.6 Exercises *235*

Chapter 11: **Macros**   **237**

11.1 Introduction *237;*   11.2 Macro Definitions and Some Examples *241;*
11.3 More on Macro Arguments *248;*   11.4 Local Labels *251;*
11.5 User-Friendly Macros *256;*   11.6 Conditional Assembly *261;*
11.7 String Functions *270;*   11.8 Summary *273;*   11.9 Exercises *273*

Chapter 12: **Bit and Bit Field Operations**   **276**

12.1 Introduction *276;*   12.2 Simple Bit Operations *277;*
12.3 Rotate and Shift Instructions *282;*   12.4 Example: Sets *287;*
12.5 Variable-Length Bit Fields *290;*   12.6 Summary *297;*
12.7 Exercises *299*

Chapter 13: **Floating Point and Packed Decimal**   **304**

13.1 Floating Point Data Representation *304;*
13.2 Floating Point Operations *309;*
13.3 Floating Point Immediate and Literal Operands *316;*
13.4 Example: Computational Accuracy in Computing Variance *318;*
13.5 Example: Converting Between Floating Point and Integer *323;*
13.6 Packed Decimal Data *325;*   13.7 Packed Decimal Instructions *327;*
13.8 Summary *330;*   13.9 Exercises *332*

Chapter 14: **Character Strings**   **335**

14.1 Overview *335;*   14.2 The MOVC and CMPC Instructions *336;*
14.3 Character-Search Instructions *340;*
14.4 Translating Character Strings: the MOVTC and MOVTUC
     Instructions *350;*   14.5 The EDIT Instruction *354;*   14.6 Summary *364;*
14.7 Exercises *364*

Chapter 15: **Input and Output Using RMS**   **368**

15.1 Input and Output *368;*
15.2 An Introduction to VAX-11 Record Management Services *369;*
15.3 Exercises *378*

Appendix A **Index of Instructions**   **379**

Appendix B **Hex Conversion Table and Powers of 2**   **387**

Appendix C **ASCII Codes**   **389**

Appendix D **I/O Macro Definitions and Procedures**   **390**

Appendix E **Answers to Selected Exercises**   **394**

            Index   **404**

Preface

This book is intended as a text for an assembly language course such as CS 3: Introduction to Computer Science in the ACM's Curriculum '78. It is also for anyone who wants to learn about the instruction set and assembly language for the VAX-11. The book is written primarily for readers who do not already know any assembly language; the VAX-11 is used partly as a vehicle for teaching about features and principles common to many large modern computers and assembly languages. The book should be suitable for readers who are already familiar with assembly language if some sections are skimmed. The summary sections at the ends of the chapters include reference tables that should be helpful to both the novice and those experienced in assembly language who want to learn about the VAX. It is assumed that the reader is familiar with a high-level language.

The book has been organized to make the chapters easy to cover in sequence in a class where the students begin programming early and write programs regularly on the material as it is encountered. With this aim in mind, I introduce some topics and instructions informally as needed before they are covered in complete detail, and I intersperse chapters on topics that would be the subject of programming assignments (e.g., branching, procedures) with chapters on topics that would not be (e.g., machine code, assembler expressions). Topics are not divided up in precise, logically distinct chunks as they are in manuals. For example, although loop control instructions "belong" in Chapter 7, "Branching and Looping," one loop instruction is introduced early in Chapter 6 so that students can write a nontrivial program.

In our one-semester course we have covered almost all of the text. A few addressing modes (Chapter 8), packed decimal instructions (Chapter 13), Chapter 14, and some of the examples were skipped. (Some topics were skimmed.)

Chapters 1 and 2 are very short introductory chapters and should be covered quickly. Chapter 3 on hexadecimal numbers and two's complement representation may be skimmed if that material has been covered in an earlier course.

Chapter 4 begins the presentation of machine instructions and assembly language. The VAX has a very large set of operand addressing modes. Some of the simpler ones are described in Chapter 4, while some more complex and less commonly available ones are left for Chapter 8.

To allow students to do simple I/O at a terminal, I have defined some I/O macros that can be used quite easily. The VAX Run-Time Library contains procedures that do terminal I/O, but the macros are simpler for students to use. The macros are READLINE, READRCRD, PRINTCHRS, and DUMPLONG. Their functional characteristics and argument formats are described in Chapter 5, and the macro definitions are given in Appendix D.

Students should be able to run simple programs after Chapter 5 and programs with loops after Chapter 6. While Chapters 1 through 5 are being covered in class, the students may be doing an assignment to gain familiarity with their timesharing system and editor. If the first few program assignments use primarily character data and if hex output from DUMPLONG is acceptable for a small amount of numeric output, the somewhat complex conversion between two's complement and character code for input and output, covered in Section 6.5, may be delayed in order to cover sooner some material on conditional branching from Chapter 7.

In some ways Chapter 8, "Machine Code Formats, Translation, and Execution," is the most important chapter, even though it has little to do with programming. Here, probably for the first time, students will begin to see how a computer actually executes instructions and how assembly language statements are translated.

Chapter 8 follows the chapter on branching and looping so that students can begin writing nontrivial programs early in a course. However, since they will see machine code on their program listings and will need to understand a little about instruction formats and execution to interpret and correct errors, it would be a good idea for the instructor to present some material from Chapter 8 (particularly Section 8.8, which explains some of the execution-time error messages) before completing Chapter 7. This is what we do in class, but it seemed awkward to break these chapters up into smaller, intermingled pieces.

Chapter 9 considers the problems involved in communicating between procedures and the programs that call them. It describes several techniques used for solving those problems but focuses mainly on the VAX procedure calling standard. A short section is included on the VAX conventions for linking assembly language with other languages. The information in this section should suffice for many straightforward situations, but it does not cover all argument types.

Chapter 10 presents more about the assembler (and linker): mainly the treatment of expressions and the distinction between absolute and relocatable expressions.

The VAX macro facility is not a particularly powerful or elegant one, but it does include many of the standard features such as argument concatenation, local labels, and a variety of conditional assembly directives. Some of these features and some general points about writing macros are presented in Chapter 11.

Chapter 12 presents the bit and logical instructions and includes a section on the VAX variable length bit field data type and instructions.

The floating point and packed decimal data types and instructions are presented in Chapter 13. The accuracy problems in floating point computations are illustrated.

Chapter 14 describes the character string manipulation instructions, including search, translate, and edit instructions.

Chapter 15 is a brief introduction to the VAX-11 Record Management Services. It will enable the reader to do some I/O without using the macros presented in Chapter 5. A more detailed discussion of I/O devices and operations would involve a lot of discussion of operating systems, so I have chosen not to include that in this book.

The book does not describe all the instructions in the VAX instruction set or all the assembler directives. Some instructions (e.g., quadword arithmetic) are introduced only in the exercises. The VAX instruction set includes some powerful and unusual machine instructions that are designed specifically to efficiently implement some high-level language constructs (e.g., CASE). These are not covered. (All machine instructions are included in the instruction table in Appendix A.) It is expected that students will be able to intelligently consult the relevant manuals to look up additional instructions and directives. The two main reference manuals are:

VAX Architecture Handbook
VAX-11 MACRO Language Reference Manual

The following manuals may also be helpful.

VAX-11 MACRO User's Guide
VAX-11 Linker Reference Manual
VAX-11 Command Language User's Guide
VAX-11 Symbolic Debugger Reference Manual
VAX-11 Record Management Services Reference Manual

This book contains several hundred exercises, ranging from short answer questions to problems that are suitable for programming assignments. Appendix E contains answers to some of the exercises from each chapter.

The type style in which the programming examples in this book were set uses the same symbol for the capital letter "oh" and for the digit "zero." It should be clear from the context which is meant.

Several people helped me, in small and large ways, in the preparation of this book. I would like to thank my colleague Richard Hager for suggesting the idea of writing the book, the many students who gave me lists of typos and errors in the manuscript when it was being used as the text for our assembly language course, instructors Tom Teegarden and John van Zandt for using the manuscript in their classes, and Jack Revelle for writing the editing and formatting software I used to prepare the manuscript, for the use of his computer, and for advice and suggestions throughout the project. Though their contribution to this project was for the most part indirect, several of my colleagues in the computer science group at San Diego State helped out by being such a good bunch of people to work with, and I thank them.

Sara Baase

Chapter 1

Introduction

1.1 WHAT IS ASSEMBLY LANGUAGE AND WHY STUDY IT?

An assembly language is a programming language in which instructions correspond closely to the individual primitive operations that are carried out by a particular computer. These primitive operations, encoded in a form the computer can act on directly, comprise the machine language of the computer. These are partial, informal descriptions, not rigorous ones. Along with the following discussion and examples, they are intended to give the reader a general idea of what assembly language "looks like," what kinds of instructions it has, and how it differs from high-level languages and machine language. In this book we will be studying the assembly language of the VAX-11 made by Digital Equipment Corporation (DEC for short). Each example shows a statement in a high-level language and possible translations of it into the VAX assembly language (called VAX-11 MACRO) and VAX machine language.

Perhaps the most glaring difference among the three types of languages is that as we move from high-level languages to lower levels, the code gets harder to read (with understanding). The major advantages of high-level languages are that they are easy to read and are machine independent. The instructions are written in a combination of English and ordinary mathematical notation, and programs can be run with minor, if any, changes on different computers. Each computer has its compiler to translate high-level language programs into its machine language.

Some parts of the assembly language instructions are decipherable: in Example 1.1 the variable names appear, and one may guess from their names what some of

EXAMPLE 1.1

FORTRAN

COST = BASE + NUM*VAR

ASSEMBLY LANGUAGE		*MACHINE CODE*
COST:	.BLKF 1	
BASE:	.BLKF 1	
VAR:	.BLKF 1	
NUM:	.BLKL 1	
	.	
	.	
	.	
CVTLF	NUM,R3	53DBAF4E
MULF2	VAR,R3	53D3AF44
ADDF3	BASE,R3,COST	C4AF53CBAF41

EXAMPLE 1.2

PASCAL

IF DIR < 0 THEN SUM := SUM + AMNT[I]

ASSEMBLY LANGUAGE		*MACHINE CODE*
TSTB	(R2)	6295
BGEQ	NEXT	0418
ADDL2	(R4)[R5],R6	566445C0
NEXT:	<next instruction>	

the instructions do. MULF2 does multiplication and ADDF3 does addition. The machine code is totally unintelligible without further explanation, and one can see that even knowing all the translation rules wouldn't make reading or writing in machine language an easy or enjoyable task.

The second most visible difference among the different types of languages is that several lines of assembly language instructions are needed to encode one line of a high-level language program. Early computers had very few instructions. The instruction sets included such operations as integer addition and subtraction, sign tests, branching, certain logical operations, input and output, and movement of data. Each instruction performed one operation. (Many modern microprocessors have similarly limited instruction sets.) Integer multiplication and division and floating-point arithmetic had to be programmed using the primitive operations. Now large computers have machine instructions that do integer multiplication and division, floating-point arithmetic, and many more complex logical and data-manipulation operations.

Execution of the Fortran statement in Example 1.1 requires several operations: conversion of the integer datum NUM to floating-point, a multiplication, an addition, and an assignment of the result to COST. In many modern computers the conversion would require a long sequence of instructions, and each of the other operations would be performed by a separate instruction. The VAX has a very powerful set of instructions, though; the conversion is done in one instruction (CVTLF), and the add instruction adds and stores the result. In the second example, the Pascal **if** statement is translated to a sign test (TSTB), a conditional branch (BGEQ, branch if greater than or equal zero), and an addition. On other computers more instructions might be required to reference the array AMNT, but the VAX has very powerful and flexible ways to refer to data.

The machine code for a whole program segment would be one continuous sequence in the computer's memory; it is broken up into separate lines in each example to show the correspondence between sections of the machine code and the assembly language instructions. Actually, machine code is slightly worse than shown here; it consists of a long string of bits—i.e., 0's and 1's. What we see in the examples is a shorthand notation; each digit and letter represents a group of four bits. The notation used is the hexadecimal number system. Hexadecimal numbers are used extensively for machine code, memory addresses, and data, and will be discussed in Chapter 3.

The assembly and machine language sequences in the examples are not the only possible translations of the Fortran and Pascal statements shown. They depend on some assumptions about the context of the statements. In Example 1.1, for instance, the first four lines allocate memory space for the variables, but similar lines do not appear in Example 1.2. In assembly language, all variable names must be defined; i.e., roughly speaking, a position in memory must be assigned to them. In many cases it is possible to refer to variables by name as in Example 1.1 and in high-level languages. For Example 1.2, we assumed that the statement is in a subroutine or procedure, and DIR, SUM, and AMNT are arguments. Space must be allocated elsewhere for the data the routine acts on, but the variable names (if any) are not available for use here. We may not even use formal argument (i.e., dummy argument) names as in high-level language procedures or subroutines.

The machine code contains no declarations, variable names, or statement labels (like NEXT in Example 1.2). It contains only executable instructions; references to data and instructions are encoded in ways to be described in Chapter 8.

In situations where programming in a high-level language is not appropriate, it is clear that assembly language is to be preferred to machine language. Assembly language has a number of advantages over machine code aside from the obvious increase in readability. One is that the use of symbolic names for data and instruction labels frees the programmer from computing and recomputing the memory locations whenever a change is made in a program. Another is that assembly languages generally have a feature, called macros, that frees the user from having to repeat similar sections of code used in several places in a program. Assemblers do many bookkeeping and other tasks for the user. Often compilers translate into assembly language rather than machine code.

If one has a choice between assembly language and a high-level language, why choose assembly language? The fact that the amount of programming done in assembly language is quite small compared to the amount done in high-level languages indicates that one generally doesn't choose assembly language. However, there are situations where it may not be convenient, efficient, or possible to write programs in high-level languages. The first compiler, for example, could not be written in the high-level language it translates because there would be no way to run the compiler. (Actually, nowadays, compilers are usually written in high-level languages.) Programs to control and communicate with peripheral devices (input and output devices) are usually written in assembly language because they use special instructions that are not available in high-level languages, and they must be very efficient. Some systems programs are written in assembly language for similar reasons. In general, since high-level languages are designed without the features of a particular machine in mind and a compiler must do its job in a standardized way to accommodate all valid programs, there are situations where to take advantage of special features of a machine, to program some details that are inaccessible from a high-level language, or perhaps to increase the efficiency of a program,[1] one may reasonably choose to write in assembly language.

Although assembly language programs must be translated into machine code, the translation task is simpler than for a high-level language because of the close correspondence between the assembly and machine language for a particular computer. A program that translates assembly language into machine language is called an *assembler.*

Some of the major reasons for studying assembly language have little to do with its practical use as a programming language. Consider that Fortran was developed in the 1950s when computers were made of vacuum tubes. The same Fortran program that ran on such a machine could also run on a computer in the 1960s made of transistors, on a computer today with integrated circuits, and on a future computer that uses some new technology. Clearly, learning Fortran (and other high-level languages) teaches one virtually nothing about what a computer is and how it actually works. We won't be studying computer hardware here, but the point—that there have been dramatic changes over the years, all virtually invisible to high-level language programmers—is equally true about computer architecture, that is, the conceptual structure and functional characteristics of a computer. A major purpose of studying assembly language is to learn something about computer architecture; in fact, part of Digital Equipment Corporation's definition of architecture is "the attributes of a system as seen by the assembly language programmer." Thus, along with learning how to write programs in assembly language, we will study the structure of the computer, its instruction set, how it decodes and executes instructions, how data are represented, what schemes are used to reference memory locations, and how arguments are passed to and from procedures, or subroutines. All these topics and others covered in assembly language texts help us understand how the computer really works and indirectly help us understand more about the task performed by the compilers that must translate high-level language programs.

---

[1] Optimizing compilers may eliminate this last reason, as some very good ones produce code that rivals for efficiency the work of experienced assembly language programmers.

Computer architecture and assembly languages differ very much from what they were thirty years ago. There are also significant differences among computers available today from different manufacturers, but of course they also have many features and characteristics in common. Why study the VAX assembly language rather than some other one? To be honest, the choice of what assembly language to learn is usually determined by what computer is available at one's university or place of work, and the decision to acquire that particular machine probably depended on many factors having little to do with the merits of its assembly language. If a programmer must use a VAX and intends to write in assembly language, then he or she will probably write in VAX-11 MACRO.[2] On the other hand, if one's purpose is to learn about the architecture of a modern computer, then there are several to choose from that would serve the purpose. The VAX is not the only choice, but it is a very good one. As we indicated in the examples, the VAX has some instructions and ways of accessing data that are more powerful and flexible than those of other computers. The VAX and its assembly language also have many features that are typical of modern machines. It has, as computer people would put it, a nice architecture. Throughout this book we will often mention similarities and differences between the VAX and other computers.

1.2 SOME TERMINOLOGY

In this section we give definitions and brief explanations of some commonly used terms, many of which should be somewhat familiar to the reader. This is not intended as a complete glossary, but rather as a review of some general terminology.

Data are pieces of information of some kind, often numbers or character strings. The singular form of data is *datum.*

A *bit* is often defined as a binary digit, i.e., a 0 or a 1. It also may mean a place (in a computer memory, for example) where a 0 or a 1 may be stored. In many computers, including the VAX, bits are organized in groups of eight called *bytes.* In such machines the byte is considered the basic unit of memory. Half a byte is defined by some computer makers, including DEC, as a *nibble.* (Yes, computer scientists have a sense of humor.) To *complement* a bit means to reverse its value, i.e., to change a 0 to a 1 and change a 1 to a 0. To complement a bit string means to complement each bit in the string.

A *compiler* is a program that translates a high-level language into assembly language. Compilers usually provide a program listing and error messages for syntax errors in the program being translated.

An *assembler* is also a translation program; its purpose is to translate assembly language into machine language. The input to a compiler or assembler is a program written by a programmer; it is called a *source program* (or *source file* or *source module*). The primary output from the compiler or assembler is called an *object*

---

[2] PDP-11 assembly language programs may be run on the VAX in what is called compatibility mode, but we will not consider that here.

module (or *object file*). Like a compiler, an assembler also provides error messages and a program listing. The listing shows the machine code produced by the assembler.

Because a program may consist of several modules or procedures assembled separately, and because the assembler doesn't know where in memory a program will be when it runs, the object file is not the final machine-code translation. Another program, called a *linker,* combines the various object modules and puts them in executable form. The output of the linker is called an executable image or execution file.

An *executable instruction,* in assembly language or a high-level language, is an instruction that gets translated into one or more machine language instructions. Other instructions appearing in a program, such as declarations and header statements, provide information or instructions to the assembler or compiler.

As suggested above, a program goes through three stages: assembly, linkage, and execution. When learning and programming assembly language, it is often important to understand which operations take place in which of these stages. Thus we will talk about an operation, or perhaps an error, occurring at *assembly time* or at *execution time. Assembly time* does not mean the amount of time used to translate the program, but the time span, or stage, when assembly takes place. The same is true for *execution time.*

A procedure is a program section that performs a particular task on (zero or more) arguments that are given to it when it is called by another routine. A procedure can be assembled (or compiled) as an independent unit. (In Fortran, procedures are called subroutines.)

We have used the term *module* several times. Since it is used in many contexts, its definition is fairly vague. A *module* is a section of a program, as an abstract entity or in some representation such as source or object code, treated as a unit for some purpose. When we use the term, we will most often mean a section of assembly language source code assembled as a unit. A module would generally be either a main program or a procedure.

Multiprogramming means concurrent execution of several programs. The computer's CPU (central processing unit) executes only one instruction at a time, but it is so fast that, to avoid wasting this valuable resource, several programs are kept available in memory at once so that while one is waiting for a relatively slow operation (maybe one that takes a few dozen milliseconds) to finish, another program may be executing. The slow operation may involve reading data from a disk, or something really slow: a person sitting at a terminal deciding what to do next.

An *operating system* is a collection of programs that controls and allocates the resources of the computer system. It handles the scheduling of all the jobs in the system, the communications necessary for doing input and output, and record and file management. The standard VAX-11 operating system is called VAX/VMS. The letters stand for Virtual Address eXtensions/Virtual Memory System.

Chapter 2

Machine Organization

A computer system generally consists of three subsystems (as illustrated in Fig. 2.1): the memory, the central processing unit, and the I/O subsystem. In this chapter we present an overview of their architecture, or logical structure.

2.1 MEMORY AND DATA ORGANIZATION

Physical Memory

The *physical memory,* also called *main memory* or *main storage,* of a computer is where instructions and data that the processor can directly fetch and execute or manipulate are stored. The VAX uses MOS (metal oxide on silicon) memory, which consists of chips containing thousands of tiny electric circuits each of which may be open or closed at any time. One state is taken to represent 0 and the other to represent 1. In the past, computer memories have been made of other materials, including, for example, magnetic rings, called cores, that could be magnetized in one of two directions, and thus also could represent one bit. In the VAX (and many other computers) the bits are logically grouped in units of eight called *bytes.*

On the VAX-11/780 it takes an average of a little under 300 nanoseconds to transfer an operand from memory to the central processor. On the VAX-11/750 it takes about 400 nanoseconds. (One nanosecond is 10^{-9} second.) To achieve access times this low, both the 780 and the 750 use a special high-speed memory, called a *cache,* where they store what they are currently working on.

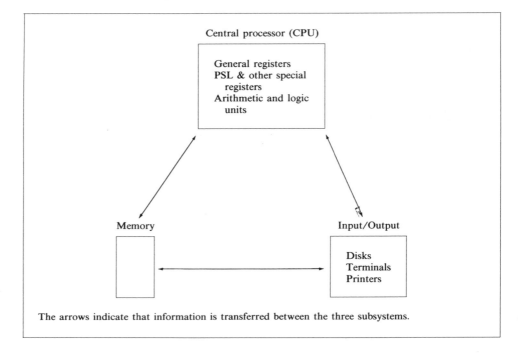

Figure 2.1   The subsystems of a computer

A VAX-11/780 may have up to eight megabytes (roughly eight million bytes) of main memory; a 750 may have up to two megabytes.

The Logical Structure of Memory

Conceptually, memory consists of a sequence of bytes numbered from 0 to the maximum available in the given installation. The number of a byte is called its *address.*

The bits in a byte are numbered right to left, beginning with 0. Thus the rightmost, or least significant, bit is bit number 0 and the leftmost, or most significant, bit is bit number 7. The bits are numbered right to left so that the bit number is the power of 2 represented by that bit when the datum is interpreted as a binary number.

Since each bit may have one of two values, 0 or 1, 256 (2^8) configurations are possible in one byte. A byte may be used to store a character or a small integer. (Characters are encoded in seven bits; the eighth, or leftmost, is always zero.)

Bytes are too small a unit of memory for storing large integers or floating-point numbers. They are grouped in various ways to provide larger units of storage for data that require more space. Each such unit has an address in memory: the address of its first, or lowest-numbered, byte.

A *word* consists of two contiguous bytes, or 16 bits. The bits of a word are numbered from 0 to 15 starting with the rightmost, or least significant, bit. Words are used to store signed integers in the range −32,768 to 32,767 and unsigned integers in the range 0 to 65,535. When a word, or one of the larger memory units described below, is used to represent an integer, the least significant bits of the datum are in the first byte, i.e., the one with the lowest address. In order to read a number in the natural way, with the most significant bits or digits at the left, we must show the bytes of memory in right-to-left order as illustrated in Fig. 2.2. Often this may cause some confusion, so be forewarned! (Alas, to compensate for this backwardness, machine code on program listings and dumps is printed out showing memory contents from right to left on a line, so, while integers may be read easily, data that are stored in the natural way appear backward. This takes some getting used to.)

A *longword* consists of four contiguous bytes, or 32 bits. The bits are numbered from 0 to 31, right to left. Longwords may be used to store very large signed or unsigned integers. They may also be used to store single-precision floating-point numbers.

A *quadword* consists of eight contiguous bytes, or 64 bits, numbered 0 to 63, right to left. Quadwords may be used to store extremely large integers or double-precision floating-point numbers. An *octaword* consist of 16 contiguous bytes, with bits numbered 0 to 127. The VAX provides a complete set of integer arithmetic instructions for byte, word, and longword integers, but not (at the present time) for quadwords or octawords.

Figure 2.3 shows a word, a longword, a quadword, and an octaword to emphasize the bit numbering and the way in which these memory units are addressed.

Bytes may be grouped in other ways for other types of data. For example, one byte can hold the character code for one character, so a contiguous sequence of bytes may be grouped together to store a character string. The number of bytes used will depend on the length of the character string.

The more significant bits of a multibyte datum are in the higher-numbered bytes. Thus in diagrams of memory we show the bytes numbered from right to left, as in this illustration of the word that begins at the byte numbered A.

This word contains the binary representation of 558.

Figure 2.2 An integer in a multibyte memory unit

A word, longword, or quadword may start at any byte in memory, but processing is more efficient if they are aligned as if all of memory were neatly divided up into units of the same size. That is, a word should always start with a byte whose address is divisible by 2, a longword with one whose address is divisible by 4, and a quadword, by 8.

Different computer systems have different word sizes, generally in the range of 16 to 60 bits; 16 and 32 are very common sizes. In some the basic unit of memory is the word, not the byte, and only words have addresses.

For storing very small numbers or a lot of numbers that don't require an integral number of bytes, it may be an inefficient use of space to think of bytes as the basic unit of memory. Arbitrary strings of (at most 32) contiguous bits anywhere in memory (ignoring byte boundaries) may be treated as a unit, called a *variable-length bit field*, by the VAX assembly language programmer.

The notation for referring to a range of bits within a byte, word, longword, or quadword specifies the numbers of the first and last bit in the range, separated by a colon. Since the lower-numbered bits are to the right of the higher-numbered ones, the lower number is written on the right. For example, the bits of the second byte of a longword may be referred to as bits 15:8. (This notation is for descriptive or documentation purposes; it is not the way bit fields are referenced in instructions.)

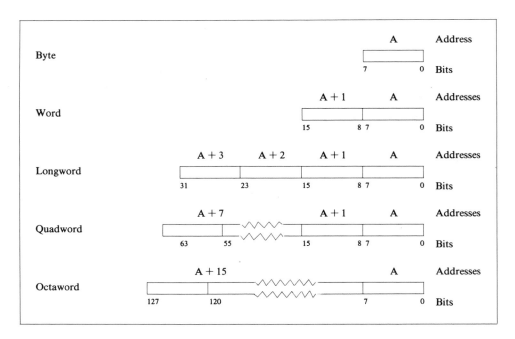

Figure 2.3   Units of memory

Virtual Memory

In a multiprogramming system like the VAX, parts of many different users' programs and their data are in main memory at the same time. However, a programmer may write a program that requires more space than there is in main memory. The VAX uses a *virtual memory* system. One definition of *virtual* is "being functionally or effectively, but not formally, of its kind." With virtual memory the user may imagine that (and program as if) the computer has a much larger amount of main memory than it really has. Since only a small part of a program and its data is being used at any time, that part can be kept in main memory and the rest stored on a disk. Programs are divided into segments, called pages, of 512 bytes each. When a page that is not in main memory is needed, the hardware and the operating system detect this and load the required page from the mass storage device. On the VAX the virtual memory can contain up to approximately 4.3 billion bytes. The limit on the size of virtual memory comes from the fact that addresses are 32-bit integers, and the largest integer that can be represented in binary in 32 bits is 4,294,967,295. The actual amount available depends on the mass storage devices at a particular installation.

The memory locations we refer to when writing assembly language programs are virtual locations. The hardware and the operating system translate these references into references to physical memory. The discussion above about the various units of memory applies to both virtual and physical memory.

Representation of Data in Memory

It should be clear that since memory contains only 0's and 1's, all the data types that we wish to use—integers, floating-point numbers, character strings, etc., as well as machine instructions—must be encoded as strings of 0's and 1's. For some data types, integers for example, there are some fairly standard encodings used by many different computers. For other types there is more variation. As we consider each of the data types, we will describe its representation, or encoding. We will also describe the encoding of instructions.

Since many different types of data may be stored in the same place in memory at different times, how can we, or the computer, tell if a particular location contains a signed integer, a floating-point number, an instruction, or something else? The answer is that we can't tell just by looking at the string of bits; we, and the computer, must know what type of datum is supposed to be there before we can interpret it properly. The type is generally determined from the context in which the datum is used. To emphasize the necessity of knowing the context or the data type in order to decode data, we show below six different valid interpretations of the same longword.

Contents of the longword in hex:	63654440
Longword integer:	1,667,580,992
Two word integers:	17472 and 25445

Four byte integers: 64, 68, 101, and 99
Instruction: ADDF2   (R5)[R4],(R3)
Characters: @ Dec
Floating-point number: 192.38826

This is not an exhaustive list of the valid interpretations of the longword. The datum could be an address, part of a packed-decimal number or a double-precision floating-point number, or various other things.

In many places throughout this book we will diagram or list the contents of memory locations to illustrate the effects of instructions. We will show the data in memory units of a size appropriate to the topic being considered. (If the size of the units used is not explicitly stated, the reader should be able to figure it out from the amount of data shown.) It is important to remember that to the computer, memory is one long sequence of consecutively numbered bytes. The amount of data it will use for a computation, or store as a result, depends on the instruction used, not the diagrams drawn as a conceptual aid for people.

2.2 THE CENTRAL PROCESSING UNIT

The central processing unit (CPU) is responsible for decoding and executing machine instructions. Decoding instructions includes determining what operation is to be performed and computing the addresses of the operands. After the operands are fetched, the CPU performs the operation using its arithmetic and logical units. The CPU also keeps track of its place in the program it is executing and keeps other status information about the program.

The standard machine instruction set on the VAX has more than 240 instructions, including some that do arithmetic and logical operations on integer and floating-point data of various sizes, arithmetic and logical operations on packed-decimal data (another format for numbers), manipulation of character and bit data, program flow control (i.e., testing and branching), manipulation of special data structures called stacks and queues, other special operations such as editing data to be printed, and various others.

A *general register* is a special storage location in the CPU rather than main memory. It takes much less time to access and modify data in registers than it takes for data in memory. The VAX has 16 general registers, each of which has 32 bits, numbered 0 to 31, right to left. The first 12 registers, named R0, R1, . . . , R11, are used by assembly language programs for temporary storage of addresses, intermediate results from computations, and the like. The remaining four registers play special roles. Their names are AP (argument pointer), FP (frame pointer), SP (stack pointer), and PC (program counter). AP, FP, and SP are used for procedure and subroutine linkage. The details of how they are used will be discussed in Chapter 9. The stack pointer has other uses that will be described later.

In many computers the program counter is a special register that is used to keep track of the address of the next instruction to be executed; as each instruction is fetched, its length is quickly determined by the CPU and the program counter is automatically incremented by that amount, so that when the execution of the current instruction is completed, the program counter already points to the next one. The principle is the same for the VAX's PC, but, because the VAX has an extremely flexible instruction format, making it difficult to determine the length of an instruction, the PC is usually incremented several times while processing one instruction. It first points to the beginning of the instruction, where the operation code is, then is incremented to point to the parts of each operand specifier in turn, and finally will point to the beginning of the next instruction.

In machine instructions, register references are encoded by the numbers 0 through 15; AP, FP, SP, and PC are encoded as 12 through 15.

The notation for referring to a range of bits within a register is the same as for bits within a unit of memory, i.e., by specifying the numbers of the first and last bit in the range, separated by a colon.

Although general registers R0 through R11 are available to the assembly language programmer, some instructions have side effects that change the contents of these registers. Some I/O instructions use R0, and several other instructions use R0 through R5. Thus it is good practice for the programmer to use R6 through R11 most of the time. The lower-numbered registers may be used, carefully, for very temporary data.

A general register contains as many bits as a longword. When instructions that act on bytes or words use data in general registers, they use the rightmost byte or word in the register.

Table 2.1, in the chapter summary (Section 2.4), summarizes the uses of the general registers.

The VAX has many special-purpose registers that are used by the CPU and the operating system to execute instructions, manage the resources and programs in the system, and do input and output. Most of these registers are not accessible by the user and their uses are so far "behind the scenes" that they will not be discussed in this book. Parts of one of the special registers, however, can be affected and accessed by assembly language instructions, so it is of importance to the assembly language programmer. This special register is the processor status longword (PSL). The PSL contains a variety of status flags. Those that are available to the user are in the low-order half of the PSL, called the processor status word (PSW); the other half is reserved for the system. An example of the first kind of flag is the *overflow condition code*, which is set when the result of an arithmetic operation is too large to fit in the space designated in an instruction. This condition code may be tested by a program and appropriate action taken. An example of the second kind of flag is one that specifies the level of privilege of the program. The operating system has a higher privilege level than an ordinary user and can execute some instructions that the user can not, including instructions that change the privilege level. The PSL contains some of the critical information that must be saved when a program is interrupted to give another program a chance to use the CPU. The PSL is automatically stored in memory and reloaded when execution of the program continues. We will add more detail about the PSW as we cover instructions that affect and access it.

2.3   INPUT AND OUTPUT

Input and output are very complex operations, much more so than the arithmetic and logical operations that are carried out by the CPU. I/O is complex because it involves communicating with devices external to the computer, such as disks, terminals, tape drives, and printers. Since a variety of different devices may be attached to a computer at any installation and each type has its own rules for formatting and transmitting data, numerous parameters must be specified to describe how and where I/O will be done. For several reasons, the user has neither the privilege nor the responsibility to program I/O directly. Most of the necessary work is done by systems programs that the user can access. Details about physical characteristics of I/O devices and the physical location or format of data files are handled by the systems programs and are invisible to the user, who may think of data as being organized in whatever way is most appropriate to the application. The user is responsible for specifying this logical structure.

Aside from eliminating the need to know and program many, many I/O details, there is another reason for not allowing the user to directly control I/O devices in a multiprogramming system: to prevent interference among different users. Imagine, for example, two programs running concurrently that are both writing data out on the same printer; the data from the two programs would be intermingled—and not particularly useful to either user. Thus the operating system manages and schedules the I/O operations requested by a program.

The VAX has a utility called Record Management Services (RMS) that handles file organization and input and output operations for the user. Even though RMS allows the user to do I/O without considering all the many details inherent in such operations, it still requires a fair amount of background. We will describe some of the capabilities of RMS in Chapter 15. In Chapter 5 we will provide some very easy-to-use instructions that do simple I/O.

2.4   SUMMARY

A computer has three subsystems: memory, the central processing unit, and the I/O subsystem.

The bits in the main memory of many computers are grouped in units of eight, called bytes. The bytes may be further grouped for storing large data. Some of the units that instructions can act on as a whole on the VAX are words (two bytes), longwords (four bytes), quadwords (eight bytes), and octawords (16 bytes). (Octaword instructions are not available on all VAXs.) These memory units may begin at any byte in storage (except of course at the very end, where there is not enough room), but processing is more efficient if they begin at a byte whose address is divisible by the size of the unit. The bits within a byte, word, longword, or quadword are numbered consecutively from zero beginning at the right, or least significant, end. Bytes may be grouped in other ways for character strings and packed-decimal data. Up to 32 bits may be grouped without regard to byte boundaries to form a unit called a variable-length bit field.

Bytes are numbered consecutively from zero to one less than the number of bytes in memory. The number assigned to a byte is called its *address*. When bytes are grouped to form larger memory units, the address of the unit is the address of its lowest-numbered byte.

The VAX uses a virtual memory system; that is, the programmer may program as if the memory were much larger than it really is. The system stores part of the program on a disk and fetches segments, called pages, as they are needed. The system handles the translation of virtual addresses used by the program into the physical addresses where the data and instructions have actually been stored in main memory.

Since all data is encoded in 0's and 1's, we and the computer must know the context in which data are used to interpret them.

The CPU decodes and executes machine instructions.

A *register* is a special storage location in the CPU that can be accessed faster than main memory. The CPU has 16 general registers, 12 of which, R0 through R11, may be used by the assembly language programmer for "scratch work," i.e., temporary storage of addresses and intermediate results of computation. The other four general registers, AP, FP, SP, and PC, have special roles. The first three are used primarily for procedure and subroutine linkage. PC is the program counter; it contains the address of the next instruction to be executed or the address of the next segment of the current instruction. The roles of the registers are summarized in Table 2.1.

The CPU has a special register called the Processor Status Longword. It contains various flags and condition codes that provide information about the status of the program.

Input and output are very complex operations because they involve communicating between the computer and the outside world. Many of the details of I/O programming are handled by the operating system.

TABLE 2.1 General Registers

Registers	Uses
R0–R5	General use; affected by side effects of some instructions
R6–R11	General use
AP (R12)	Argument pointer (for procedures)
FP	Frame pointer (for procedures)
SP	Stack pointer (for procedures and other uses)
PC	Program counter (not used directly by the programmer)

Chapter 3

Binary and Hexadecimal Numbers and Integer Representation

3.1 THE BINARY AND HEXADECIMAL NUMBER SYSTEMS

Since all data are stored in memory encoded in 0's and 1's, it seems natural to store positive integers in their binary representation. To examine and interpret data and instructions in memory, we could read long binary strings or frequently convert back and forth between binary and decimal. Both of these choices would lead to many errors and wasted time. The hexadecimal system is very convenient to use as an intermediate notation between binary and decimal. Conversion between binary and hexadecimal (called hex for short) is simple, but hex is much more compact than binary; only about one-quarter as many digits are needed to represent a number. We will find that in many cases where we would usually use the decimal system, we can use hex almost as easily, so we won't have to convert between hex and decimal very often. In this section we review the principle underlying all these positional representation number systems, and we present algorithms for converting between them and algorithms for doing arithmetic in hex.

To say that a number system uses *positional representation* means that the value represented by a digit depends on its position in the representation of a number. For example, the 3 in 437 represents the value thirty, while the "3" in 3692 represents three thousand. An example of a different kind of number system is the Roman numeral system where, for example, X always represents ten (or negative ten). The value represented by a digit in a positional representation system is the digit's own value multiplied by a power of the base, or radix, of the particular system being used. Thus if a number is written as

$$d_n d_{n-1} \ldots d_2 d_1 d_0$$

where the d's are digits, then, for each i between 0 and n, d_i represents the value of the digit d_i multiplied by the radix raised to the ith power. Thus, in decimal, we call the rightmost position the ones (10^0) place, the next (from the right) position the tens (10^1) place, the next the hundreds (10^2) place, and so on. For an arbitrary radix r, the rightmost place is the ones (r^0) place, the next is the r's place, the next the r^2's place, etc. Using the radix r, the number written above would have the decimal value

$$(\bar{d}_n \times r^n) + (\bar{d}_{n-1} \times r^{n-1}) + \cdots + (\bar{d}_2 \times r^2) + (\bar{d}_1 \times r^1) + \bar{d}_0 \qquad (3.1)$$

where $\bar{d}_i$ is the decimal value of the radix r digit d_i, for i between 0 and n. We will return to this formula and do some examples later.

The hexadecimal number system is the positional representation number system with radix 16. The first few positions (from the right) in a hexadecimal number are the ones place, the 16's place, the 256's place, and the 4096's place. (It is often useful to know these first few powers of 16.)

If r is the radix being used, then we need digits, or distinct symbols, to explicitly represent the numbers 0 through $r - 1$, since we can represent r by putting a 1 in the r's place and a 0 in the ones place, and we can represent higher numbers similarly by putting digits in the various positions. For radices no larger than ten, we can use the usual digits 0 through $r - 1$, but for larger radices, e.g., 16, we have to invent new digits. By convention, the digits for the hexadecimal system are 0, 1, 2, . . . , 8, 9, A, B, C, D, E, and F, where A through F represent ten through fifteen, respectively.

Converting between Hex and Binary

In binary, using four bits, we can represent the numbers zero through fifteen. The correspondence between the bit patterns and the decimal and hexadecimal representations is shown in Table 3.1. Each four-bit binary number corresponds to one hexadecimal digit and vice versa. Thus we may think of hexadecimal as a shorthand for binary. To convert a hex number to binary we simply replace each hex digit in the number by its binary equivalent. For example, we convert 2B70F3 as follows:

2   B   7   0   F   3

001010110111000011110011

We can omit the first two zeros without changing the value of the number, but the hex zero must be encoded as four binary zeros, and in general leading zeros in the

TABLE 3.1 *Binary and Decimal*
Values of Hexadecimal Digits

Binary	Decimal	Hexadecimal
0000	0	0
0001	1	1
0010	2	2
0011	3	3
0100	4	4
0101	5	5
0110	6	6
0111	7	7
1000	8	8
1001	9	9
1010	10	A
1011	11	B
1100	12	C
1101	13	D
1110	14	E
1111	15	F

encoding of each hex digit, except the leftmost, must be included. They are needed as place savers.

To convert from binary to hex, we reverse the process we just used—i.e., replace each group of four bits by the hex digit with the same value. Since the number of bits may not be divisible by four, we must start grouping the bits from the right end of the string. If the last, or leftmost, group has fewer than four bits, we simply imagine extra zeros on the left. Consider the following example:

$$110100100011101010100110010$$
$$1 \quad A \quad 4 \quad 7 \quad 5 \quad 3 \quad 2$$

We have not justified the validity of the conversion methods, but rather than do a formal proof (which we leave to the mathematically inclined reader), we will use the example to indicate how the argument would go. Consider the digit 5 in 1A47532. Since it is in the third place from the right, it represents 5×16^2. The corresponding bits in the binary string, 0101, are in the 2^8 through 2^{11} places, so we can compute the value they represent as follows:

$$(0 \times 2^{11}) + (1 \times 2^{10}) + (0 \times 2^9) + (1 \times 2^8)$$
$$= [(0 \times 2^3) + (1 \times 2^2) + (0 \times 2^1) + (1 \times 2^0)] \times 2^8$$
$$= (5) \times (2^4)^2$$
$$= 5 \times 16^2$$

the same value represented by the 5 in 1A47532.

Converting from Hex or Binary to Decimal

The evaluation formula (3.1) is used to convert numbers from a radix other than ten into decimal. It is fairly easy to use if you have a table of powers of the radix (or are willing to compute them) and can do addition and multiplication.

EXAMPLE 3.1

$$E2407_{16} = (14 \times 16^4) + (2 \times 16^3) + (4 \times 16^2) + (0 \times 16^1) + (7 \times 16^0)$$
$$= 917{,}504 + 8192 + 1024 + 7$$
$$= 926{,}727$$

$$10011101_2 = (1 \times 2^7) + (0 \times 2^6) + (0 \times 2^5) + (1 \times 2^4) + (1 \times 2^3)$$
$$+ (1 \times 2^2) + (0 \times 2^1) + (1 \times 2^0)$$
$$= 128 + 16 + 8 + 4 + 1$$
$$= 157$$

The multiplications can be eliminated, simplifying the conversion, by keeping larger tables that contain the values of $d \times r^p$ for each nonzero digit d and each power p up to some reasonable limit. Such a table for radix 16 appears in Appendix B. It contains columns for powers between 0 and 7; that is sufficient to convert the contents of a longword to decimal. The entries in the table are all decimal numbers. Suppose a longword contains $00014A2E_{16}$ and we want to convert it to decimal. (To emphasize that bits are never "empty"—they always have value 0 or 1—when specifying the contents of a register or a memory location, we will show leading zeros.) We use the table as follows to do the conversion.

Beginning at the right end of the number, we look in the rightmost column, the 16^0 column, and the row for the digit E, and we find the value 14. Write it down. Then, moving left one place in the longword and left one column in the table to the 16^1 column, we look in the row for the digit 2 and find 32. Write that down. Moving left in the longword and in the table again, we look in the row for the digit A and find 2560. For the digits 4 and 1 we find the values 16,384 and 65,536, respectively. Since zeros in any position have the value 0, we are finished looking up table entries, and we now add up the values found. The result is 84,526. The computation is summarized in Fig. 3.1.

We did not really have to look up all five nonzero digits in the table. After a bit of familiarization with hexadecimal numbers, the first three could be done directly. E is 14, a 2 in the 16's place is obviously 32, and multiplying by ten (A) is always easy; in this case one must only remember that 16^2 is 256. There are many times when it is more efficient to use one's head, with care, than to use tables or follow an algorithm slavishly.

Note that the first row in the table gives the powers of 16 and may be useful for purposes other than conversion. For example, if we want to determine how many numbers can be represented using four hexadecimal digits (a word of memory) we

The caret (^) points to the digit being evaluated in each line.

$$
\begin{array}{lr}
000\underset{\wedge}{1}4A2E & 14 \\
 & + \\
0001\underset{\wedge}{4}A2E & 32 \\
 & + \\
00014\underset{\wedge}{A}2E & 2560 \\
 & + \\
00014A\underset{\wedge}{2}E & 16384 \\
 & + \\
00\underset{\wedge}{0}14A2E & 65536 \\
\hline
 & 84526
\end{array}
$$

Figure 3.1   Converting from hexadecimal to decimal

Problem: Convert 110100010000001110 (binary) to decimal.

Method 1:   Add up the powers of 2 corresponding to the 1's in the number.

$$
\begin{array}{llr}
1101000100000011\underset{\wedge}{1}0 & 2^1 & 2 \\
 & & + \\
11010001000000\underset{\wedge}{1}110 & 2^2 & 4 \\
 & & + \\
1101000100000\underset{\wedge}{0}1110 & 2^3 & 8 \\
 & & + \\
110100\underset{\wedge}{0}10000001110 & 2^{10} & 1024 \\
 & & + \\
110\underset{\wedge}{1}00010000001110 & 2^{14} & 16384 \\
 & & + \\
1\underset{\wedge}{1}0100010000001110 & 2^{16} & 65536 \\
 & & + \\
\underset{\wedge}{1}10100010000001110 & 2^{17} & 131072 \\
\end{array}
$$
The result is: 214030

Method 2:   Convert to hex, then use the hex conversion table.
Convert to hex:

110100010000001110

3   4   4   0   E

Then, using the table:

$$
\begin{array}{lr}
344\underset{\wedge}{0}E & 14 \\
 & + \\
34\underset{\wedge}{4}0E & 1024 \\
 & + \\
3\underset{\wedge}{4}40E & 16384 \\
 & + \\
\underset{\wedge}{3}440E & 196608 \\
\hline
\end{array}
$$
214030 is the result again.

Figure 3.2   Converting from binary to decimal

can just look up 16^4, since each of the four digits may have any one of 16 values. This explains why the range of unsigned integers that can be represented in a word is 0 through 65,535.

Converting from binary to decimal can be done by the same method—i.e., essentially, using the evaluation formula (3.1)—but with binary there is no need for multiplications, since the only digits are 0 and 1. Thus the 1's simply tell us which powers of 2 to add up. A conversion table comparable to the hexadecimal conversion table in Appendix B would be much shorter but much wider; we need 2^0 through 2^{31} to evaluate a longword. A list of these powers of 2 is included in Appendix B. (Most of the information in the tables in Appendix B appears on the *VAX-11 Programming Card.*)

Another way to convert binary to decimal is to first convert to hexadecimal by the straightforward substitutions described above, then convert from hex to decimal. When the hex conversion table is available, this method probably will require less work because there will be fewer values to add up (at most eight rather than 32 for a longword). Figure 3.2 illustrates both methods.

Converting from Decimal to Hex

Converting from decimal to another radix involves division instead of multiplication. We will present two methods for decimal-to-hex conversion. The first is a general method for converting numbers from decimal to a different radix. The second method makes use of the hexadecimal conversion table (and could be generalized to other radices if we had the appropriate tables).

The first method uses the evaluation formula for an $(n + 1)$-digit number in radix r. Notice that in the formula

$$\text{value} = (\bar{d}_n \times r^n) + (\bar{d}_{n-1} \times r^{n-1}) + \cdots + (\bar{d}_2 \times r^2) + (\bar{d}_1 \times r^1) + \bar{d}_0$$

all the terms are clearly divisible by the radix except the last, d_0, the rightmost digit of the hex number. Since d_0 is in the range 0 to $r - 1$, it is the remainder when the number is divided by the radix. Thus, starting with a decimal number, we can find the rightmost digit of its hex representation by dividing the number by 16 and finding the remainder. The arithmetic is all done in decimal. The quotient from the division is

$$(\bar{d}_n \times r^{n-1}) + (\bar{d}_{n-1} \times r^{n-2}) + \cdots + (\bar{d}_2 \times r^1) + \bar{d}_1$$

Now every term is divisible by r except d_1, so d_1 is the remainder if we divide this new number by r. (If $d_1 = 0$, it is divisible by r, but then the remainder is 0 too.) The new quotient will be

$$(\bar{d}_n \times r^{n-2}) + (\bar{d}_{n-1} \times r^{n-3}) + \cdots + (\bar{d}_3 \times r^1) + \bar{d}_2$$

and clearly we can continue the procedure of dividing by the radix and finding the remainder to get all the digits of the radix-r representation of the original decimal

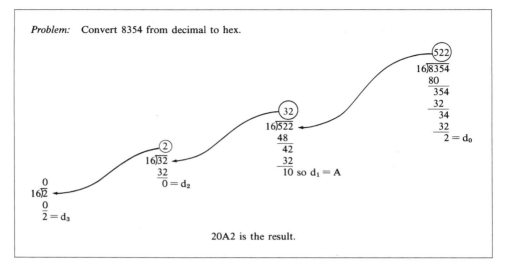

Problem: Convert 8354 from decimal to hex.

20A2 is the result.

Figure 3.3   Converting from decimal to hexadecimal

number. We quit when we get a zero quotient. The method is illustrated in Fig. 3.3.

The second method for converting from decimal to hexadecimal uses the hex conversion table in Appendix B. The first step determines how many hex digits there will be in the result and also determines the leftmost digit. Let k be the decimal number to be converted. Look in the table and find the largest entry that is not larger than k. The column in which this number is found indicates the number of digits in the hex representation of k: one more than the power of 16 at the top of the column. The hex digit in whose row we are looking is the leftmost digit of the result. At this point it is a good idea to mark a space for each digit and write down the leftmost. Subtract the number found in the table from k, and let k now be the difference. (All the arithmetic is done in decimal.) Move one column to the right in the table and again look for the largest value that is not larger than k. If all the values in this column are too large, then the next digit is 0, and we move right another column. Otherwise the next digit is the digit in whose row we found the largest number not larger than k. Once again, subtract this number from k, and let k now be the difference. Repeat this digit-finding procedure until all the digits are filled in. This method is illustrated in Fig. 3.4.

Converting from Decimal to Binary

A decimal number can be converted to binary by using either of the two methods just described for decimal-to-hex conversions. For the second method, the powers-

---

Problem: Convert 584,972 from decimal to hex.

Let $k = 584,972$.
The largest entry in the table no larger than k is 524,288. It appears in row 8 of the 16^4 column, so the hex result will have 5 digits and the first is 8. Thus we write down

$$\underline{8} \_ \_ \_ \_$$

$$
\begin{aligned}
\text{Subtract:} \quad k &= 584,972 \\
&\underline{-524,288} \\
\text{New } k &= 60,684
\end{aligned}
$$

In the 16^3 column we find 57,344 is the largest number that doesn't exceed k. It is in the E row, so we write E as the next digit.

$$\underline{8}\ \underline{E}\ \_ \_ \_$$

$$
\begin{aligned}
\text{Subtract:} \quad k &= 60,684 \\
&\underline{-57,344} \\
\text{New } k &= 3,340
\end{aligned}
$$

In the 16^2 column we find 3,328 in row D, so we now have

$$\underline{8}\ \underline{E}\ \underline{D}\ \_ \_$$

$$
\begin{aligned}
\text{Subtract:} \quad k &= 3,340 \\
&\underline{-3,328} \\
\text{New } k &= 12
\end{aligned}
$$

All the numbers in the 16's column are larger than 12, so the next digit is 0.

$$\underline{8}\ \underline{E}\ \underline{D}\ \underline{0}\ \_$$

Finally, in the 16^0 column (or from memory) we find that 12 is C, so the resulting hex number is

$$\underline{8}\ \underline{E}\ \underline{D}\ \underline{0}\ \underline{C}$$

Figure 3.4 Converting from decimal to hex using a conversion table

of-2 table would be used. A third method is to first convert the decimal number to hexadecimal, then substitute the four-bit binary representations of each hex digit.

Arithmetic in Hex

Sometimes we have to add or subtract (and occasionally multiply) hex numbers. Of course it is possible to convert the numbers to decimal, do ordinary decimal arithmetic, and convert the results back to hex, but this involves a lot of extra work and increased opportunity for making mistakes. Doing arithmetic in hex is not much different from doing arithmetic in decimal; the principle is the same; we just have to remember

Problem: Add 30E4 and 29A7.

$$\begin{array}{r} 30E4 \\ + 29A7 \\ \hline \end{array}$$

Working right to left: $4 + 7 = 11$, which is B in hex.

$$\begin{array}{r} 30E4 \\ + 29A7 \\ \hline B \end{array}$$

$E + A$ is $14 + 10 = 24$.
$24 = 16 + 8$, so write 8 and carry 1.

$$\begin{array}{r} {}^{1} \\ 30E4 \\ + 29A7 \\ \hline 8B \end{array}$$

$1 + 9 = 10$, which is A in hex.

$$\begin{array}{r} {}^{1} \\ 30E4 \\ + 29A7 \\ \hline A8B \end{array}$$

$3 + 2 = 5$.

$$\begin{array}{r} {}^{1} \\ 30E4 \\ + 29A7 \\ \hline 5A8B \end{array}$$

Figure 3.5   Addition in hex

Problem: Subtract 19B8 from 30E4.

$$\begin{array}{r} 30E4 \\ - 19B8 \\ \hline \end{array}$$

4 is less than 8, so we must borrow 16 from the next place,
leaving D there and giving us $16 + 4 = 20$ in the ones place.

$$\begin{array}{r} {}^{D20} \\ 30\not{E}4 \\ - 19B8 \\ \hline \end{array}$$

$20 - 8 = 12$, which is C.

$$\begin{array}{r} {}^{D20} \\ 30\not{E}4 \\ - 19B8 \\ \hline C \end{array}$$

$D - B = 2$.

$$\begin{array}{r} {}^{D} \\ 30\not{E}4 \\ - 19B8 \\ \hline 2C \end{array}$$

0 is less than 9, so borrow to get 16. $16 - 9 = 7$.

$$\begin{array}{r} {}^{216} \\ \not{3}0E4 \\ - 19B8 \\ \hline 72C \end{array}$$

Finally, $2 - 1 = 1$.

$$\begin{array}{r} {}^{2} \\ \not{3}0E4 \\ - 19B8 \\ \hline 172C \end{array}$$

Figure 3.6   Subtraction in hex

Problem: Multiply 4CA9 by 8.
$$\begin{array}{r} 4CA9 \\ \times\,8 \\ \end{array}$$

$8 \times 9 = 72$, but this result must be converted back to hex. $72 = 64 + 8$, and $64 = 4 \times 16$, so we write 8 and carry 4.
$$\begin{array}{r} {}^{4} \\ 4CA9 \\ \times\,8 \\ \hline 8 \\ \end{array}$$

Now $8 \times 10 + 4 = 84$ and $84 = 5 \times 16 + 4$, so we write down 4 and carry 5.
$$\begin{array}{r} {}^{5\ 4} \\ 4CA9 \\ \times\,8 \\ \hline 48 \\ \end{array}$$

$8 \times 12 + 5 = 101$ and $101 = 6 \times 16 + 5$, so we write 5 and carry 6.
$$\begin{array}{r} {}^{6\ 5\ 4} \\ 4CA9 \\ \times\,8 \\ \hline 548 \\ \end{array}$$

$8 \times 4 + 6 = 38$, which is 26 in hex, so finally:
$$\begin{array}{r} {}^{6\ 5\ 4} \\ 4CA9 \\ \times\,8 \\ \hline 26548 \\ \end{array}$$

Figure 3.7 Multiplication in hex

that we carry only when the sum of a column of digits exceeds 15, not 9, and when we "borrow" for a subtraction, we borrow 16, not 10. When adding or subtracting a column of digits, it may be easiest to translate the digits indicated by letters (A through F) to decimal in your head and do the digit sums and differences in decimal. Figures 3.5 and 3.6 show examples of addition and subtraction in hex.

Generally when we have to multiply hex numbers, one of the numbers has only one digit, often 2, 4, or 8. Again, you may find it easiest to do the digitwise multiplications in decimal, switching back and forth between hex and decimal in your head. See Fig. 3.7 for an example.

Why Hex?

We said at the beginning of this section that hex is a good shorthand notation for binary. We have since seen that each hex digit corresponds exactly to a group of four bits, making the conversion between hex and binary very easy. But it would be just as easy to convert between binary and octal (base 8) or between binary and base 32; if the radix is a power of 2, then one digit for the radix corresponds exactly to a group of bits. Some computer systems, in fact, use octal instead of hexadecimal. The choice depends on the architecture of the system. In the VAX there are 16 general registers, numbered 0 through 15. Thus a reference to a register in a machine instruction is encoded in four bits, or one hex digit. The standard instruction set for the VAX has slightly fewer than 256 machine instructions; thus most operation codes use eight bits, or two hex digits. The VAX uses eight bits to encode a character; thus character codes are given as two hex digits. The VAX has 16 different addressing modes (ways to specify where the operands of an instruction are to be found); thus each is encoded in one hex digit. Once we know the formats of the machine instructions (which will be covered in detail in Chapter 8), if we look at the encoding of an instruction in hex we can easily pick out the component parts. 5B53A0 is the encoding of a simple instruction. The operation code is at the right end, hence is A0, the code for an add instruction. The other two pairs of digits each include an addressing mode specifier and a register number. Thus both operands are addressed in mode 5, which means the operands are in registers, and the registers used are R11 and R3.

   Computers that have eight registers and 64 or fewer instructions, or perhaps close to 512 (8^3) instructions, and use six bits to encode characters, are more likely to use octal instead of hexadecimal, since the encoding of three bits by one octal digit would make the encodings easy to interpret. In some such computers, the number of bits in a word is a multiple of three.

3.2   INTEGER REPRESENTATION

Signed integers are used in computers in several ways. They may be data themselves or they may be a part of another type of data, e.g., the exponent in a floating-point number. They are also used as parts of instructions, to specify the location of operands. An obvious representation for nonnegative integers is the binary number system, and it is the representation used for most of these purposes.

   The interesting problem is how to represent negative integers. We will consider three possible solutions, including the two's complement representation used on the VAX and many other computers. All three methods have one common feature: one bit in the integer is reserved to represent its sign. By a convention standard throughout the computer industry, the leftmost bit is the sign bit, 0 indicates a positive (or nonnegative) number, and 1 indicates a negative number. The choice between the different representations depends partly on how quickly a computer can do commonly performed operations on data. For each representation scheme, we will consider how to negate a (positive or negative) integer and how to add two integers.

   For all our examples we will use 16 bits—i.e., a word. The largest integer we can accommodate is 0111111111111111, or 32,767. The representation schemes described can easily be generalized to any number of bits (greater than one).

Sign-Magnitude

The simplest way to handle negative integers is to represent the absolute value of the integer in binary and just use the leftmost bit to indicate the sign. This method is called *sign-magnitude* representation, because the sign and the magnitude (absolute value) are represented separately.

> **EXAMPLE 3.2: *Sign-Magnitude Representation of 92 and −92***
>
> 92   0000000001011100
>
> −92   1000000001011100

Negating a sign-magnitude integer is very easy; we simply complement—i.e., reverse—the sign bit. Addition is done in the usual way, but in binary. If both integers have the same sign, we add their magnitudes and put the same sign in the result. If the signs are different, then we determine which integer has the larger magnitude and subtract the other from it. The sign of the result is the sign of the operand with the larger magnitude. This doesn't seem very complicated, but it involves tests, decisions, and different potential courses of action. Sign-magnitude is a poor choice for an integer representation when we would like a computer to be able to do a million or more additions a second.

One's Complement

The next representation scheme is called *one's complement*. To represent a negative integer, we write out its absolute value in binary, then complement all the bits. Note that this will make the sign bit be 1, as it should be. In the examples for one's complement and two's complement, we will show the hex equivalent of the bit strings. The operations that we (humans) will sometimes have to do on integers (interpretation and addition, for example) can be done just as easily, if not more so, using the hex shorthand. Note that complementing a bit is the same as subtracting the bit from 1, so complementing the bits, given their hex representation, can be done by subtracting the hex digits from F (or 15_{10}).

> **EXAMPLE 3.3: *One's Complement Representation of 92 and −92***
>
> 92   0000000001011100   005C
>
> −92   1111111110100011   FFA3

To negate a positive or negative integer, we complement all the bits.

Addition can be done without regard to the signs of the operands. We add the two integers as if they were unsigned binary numbers—i.e., treat the sign bits just like the others. If we carry a 1 out of the leftmost bit position, it is added in at the right, or least significant, bit.

EXAMPLE 3.4: Adding 45 and −92 in One's Complement Notation

$$
\begin{array}{rll}
45 & 0000000000101101 & 002\text{D} \\
+ (-92) & + 1111111110100011 & + \text{FFA}3 \\
\hline
-47 & 1111111111010000 & \text{FFD}0 \\
& (0\text{ carry}) &
\end{array}
$$

EXAMPLE 3.5: Adding 1637 and −101 in One's Complement Notation

$$
\begin{array}{rll}
1637 & 0000011001100101 & 0665 \\
+ (-101) & + 1111111110011010 & + \text{ FF9A} \\
\hline
& 10000010111111111 & 105\text{FF} \\
& + 1 & + 1 \\
\hline
1536 & 0000011000000000 & 0600
\end{array}
$$

We leave it as an exercise for the reader to add two negative integers and verify that the same method works. Also, the theoretically inclined reader may wish to consider how to prove that the method always works.

Since there are no decisions to make and the steps followed are always the same (the carry bit is always added back in at the right, but is sometimes 0, as in the first example), addition of one's complement integers is relatively easy and fast on a computer. Unfortunately, though, adding in the carry bit may involve almost as much work as adding the two operands; in the second example the addition of the carried 1 caused ten bits of the result to change. One's complement notation has a peculiarity that, along with the extra work required for adding the carry bit, has made it an unpopular choice for integer representation. The number zero is represented by 0000000000000000. What happens if we negate it? We complement all the bits and get 1111111111111111. Thus −0 has a different representation from +0, but algebraically, −0 = +0. The different representations of zero cause problems when doing tests on results of arithmetic operations. Suppose we add two integers and test the result for zero. For example:

$$
\begin{array}{rll}
-8 & 1111111111110111 & \text{FFF}7 \\
+ 8 & + 0000000000001000 & + 0008 \\
\hline
0 & 1111111111111111 & \text{FFFF} \\
& = -0 & \\
& \text{not} = 0 &
\end{array}
$$

Some computers do use one's complement representation and regularly check the results of arithmetic, converting −0, when it occurs, to +0. Most computers now use a variation of one's complement, called two's complement, that eliminates the problem of the two zeros.

Two's Complement

To represent a negative integer in *two's complement,* we start with its absolute value in binary, then complement all the bits and add 1 to the result.

EXAMPLE 3.6: *Two's Complement Representation of* -92

92	0000000001011100	005C
Complement the bits	1111111110100011	FFA3
Add 1	$+1$	$+1$
-92	1111111110100100	FFA4

To negate a negative integer we must reverse this process. It is not obvious, but is nonetheless true, that we use the same steps. That is, given a negative integer in two's complement representation, to find its absolute value we complement all the bits and add 1.

EXAMPLE 3.7: *Negating* -92

-92	1111111110100100	FFA4
Complement the bits	0000000001011011	005B
Add 1	$+1$	$+1$
92	0000000001011100	005C

Thus, negating an integer (either positive or negative) is easy and doesn't depend on the sign of the integer being negated. But does this method always work? We will present a formal justification of it at the end of this section.

How do we add two's complement integers? We simply add the two bit strings as unsigned binary integers and ignore the carry out of the leftmost bit if there is one.

EXAMPLE 3.8: *Adding 92 and* -45 *in Two's Complement Notation*

92	0000000001011100	005C
$+(-45)$	$+$ 1111111111010011	$+$ FFD3
	10000000000101111	1002F
Drop the carry	0000000000101111	002F

The result is 47.

EXAMPLE 3.9: *Adding* -102 *and* -58 *in Two's Complement Notation*

-102	1111111110011010	FF9A
$+(-58)$	$+$ 1111111111000110	$+$ FFC6
-160	11111111101100000	1FF60
Drop the carry	1111111101100000	FF60

To check the result, we observe that it is negative because bit 15 is 1, and we determine its absolute value by complementing the bits and adding 1.

Result	1111111101100000	FF 6 0
Complement	0000000010011111	0 0 9 F
Add 1	$+1$	$+1$
	0000000010100000	00A0

| \|Result\| | $2^7 + 2^5 = 160$ | $10 \times 16 = 160$ |

It is just about as easy to negate and add two's complement integers as it is to do these operations on one's complement integers. What about the problem of the two representations of zero? Suppose we start with 0 and find its two's complement negation.

0	0000000000000000
Complement	1111111111111111
Add 1	$+1$
	10000000000000000
Drop the carry	0000000000000000

So $-0 = +0$, as it should.

In the VAX, two's complement representation is used for integer data, which may be stored in bytes, words, longwords, or quadwords, or in the rightmost byte or word of a general register, or in a full register. As we will see in Chapter 8, it is often necessary to store integers (negative or positive) in instructions to indicate the location of an operand of the instruction. Two's complement is used there too.

In our discussion of addition we assumed that the result of the addition would fit in a word. Of course that is not always the case. For example, if we add 29,676 and 3204, both of which are less than the maximum 16-bit integer, 32,767, we get 32,880, which is too big. What happens when we carry out the two's complement addition?

29,676	0111001111101100	7 3 E C
$+3,204$	$+0000110010000100$	$+0C8 4$
32,880	1000000001110000	8 0 7 0

Because the leftmost bit of the sum is a 1, the result would be incorrectly interpreted as a negative integer. Integer arithmetic instructions set an overflow condition code bit in the Processor Status Word when the result of an arithmetic operation will not fit in the designated space. It is the programmer's responsibility to check this bit if the data being used might cause an overflow. For the data in our example, there would have been no problem if we had been using longwords; then bit 31, not bit 15, would have been the sign bit.

Table 3.2 shows the interpretation of each three-bit pattern using each of the representation schemes we have discussed; bit 2 is the sign bit. Notice that -0 has a distinct representation from $+0$ in sign-magnitude as well as in one's complement. Since there is only one representation of 0 in two's complement, there is an extra bit pattern; using only three bits, as in the table, we find that we can represent -4 in two's complement but not in one's complement or sign-magnitude.

TABLE 3.2   *Integer Representation*

Bit pattern	Sign-mag.	One's comp.	Two's comp. [1]
000	0	0	0
001	1	1	1
010	2	2	2
011	3	3	3
100	−0	−3	−4
101	−1	−2	−3
110	−2	−1	−2
111	−3	−0	−1

[1] Note that in two's complement we can represent an "extra" negative number. This is true no matter how many bits are being used.

Why Two's Complement Works

To show that complementing the bits and adding 1 always negates a two's complement integer, and to show that the rules for addition of two's complement integers are correct, it is useful to use another characterization of negative two's complement integers. Let s be the number of bits in the representation (16 in all the examples in this section). Let n be a negative integer and let $|n|$ be its absolute value. Then the two's complement representation of n is the binary encoding of $2^s - |n|$. This is true because complementing the bits of $|n|$ is the same as subtracting $|n|$ from s 1's, and s 1's represents $2^s - 1$, so

$|n|$ with bits complemented	$2^s - 1 - |n|$
Add 1 to get n in two's complement	$2^s - 1 - |n| + 1 = 2^s - |n|$

Now, what happens when we start with a negative integer in two's complement and reverse the procedure? Again, suppose the number is n. Thus we start with $2^s - |n|$:

n (negative) in two's complement	$2^s - |n|$
Complement the bits	$(2^s - 1) - (2^s - |n|) = -1 + |n|$
Add 1. The result is $-n$, i.e., $|n|$	$-1 + |n| + 1 = |n|$

When s is a multiple of 4, as it is for the standard memory units, we can write the hex representation of a negative integer n in two's complement as $16^{s/4} - |n|$. An argument similar to the one above shows that the steps we described for negating and adding two's complement numbers written in hex are also correct.

Using the characterization of the two's complement representation of a negative integer n as $2^s - |n|$, it is not hard to prove that adding the bit strings and ignoring the carry always correctly adds two's complement integers (if the result fits in s bits). We leave the details as an exercise.

3.3   SUMMARY

The hexadecimal number system is used as a shorthand for bit strings. Hexadecimal is the positional number system with radix 16. Conversion between binary and hex is very easy: each four-bit pattern corresponds to one hex digit and vice versa. Conversion between hex or binary and decimal can be done by several methods, some of which use the tables in Appendix B.

Arithmetic in hex is similar to arithmetic in decimal, but one must take care to handle carries and borrows correctly.

Hex is particularly well suited to the VAX because the various components of machine instructions take up four, eight, sixteen, or thirty-two bits and can therefore be encoded separately by one, two, four, or eight hex digits. Also, character codes use eight bits, or two hex digits.

There are several schemes for representing signed integers in a computer. Three of these are sign-magnitude, one's complement, and two's complement. For all three, positive integers are represented in binary, and the leftmost bit is used to represent the integer's sign, with 0 indicating "plus" and 1 indicating "minus."

The two's complement notation is used in the VAX. To represent a negative integer in two's complement, we first write out its absolute value in binary, then complement all the bits, then add 1. Alternatively we can write its absolute value in hex, then subtract each digit from F (15, decimal), and then add 1.

Two's complement is used because it does not have two distinct representations for +0 and −0, as one's complement does, and because addition and subtraction of two's complement integers are very straightforward and independent of the signs of the operands. Two signed two's complement integers are added as if they were unsigned binary numbers. If there is a carry out of the leftmost bit, it is ignored. Arithmetic can be done on the hex representations instead of long bit strings.

Another way to look at the two's complement representation of a negative integer n is that it is $2^s - |n|$ in binary, or $16^{s/4} - |n|$ in hex, where s is the number of bits used in the representation.

If the result of an arithmetic operation does not fit in the designated space, the overflow condition code bit in the PSW is set.

3.4   EXERCISES

    1. Convert the following numbers from hexadecimal to binary.
       (a) 2047   **(c)** FAD
       (b) D104F   **(d)** 3A01

    2. Convert the following numbers from binary to hex.
       (a) 110100011011111001011   **(c)** 100000000
       (b) 111000110001   **(d)** 11111100000

3. Convert the following numbers from hex to decimal.
   (a) 86E   (c) F0
   (b) 209AB5 (d) 1000

4. Convert the following numbers from decimal to hex.
   (a) 80   (c) 3075 (Use both methods.)
   (b) 125 (d) 11,625,042

5. Convert the following numbers from binary to decimal.
   (a) 110011110   (b) 1111111011
                   (None of the methods given in the text is the quickest way to do
                   this one. Use some ingenuity.)

6. Convert the following numbers from decimal to binary.
   (a) 147   (b) 515

7. Do the following addition problems. All numbers shown are in hex.
   (a)   804E   (b)   1FF
       + BFD7   + 7305

8. Do the following subtraction problems. All numbers are in hex.
   (a)   7E043   (b)   4028
       − 48A7   − 1259

9. Do the following multiplication problems. All numbers are in hex.
   (a) 20C4   (b)   64
        × 8   × 4

10. Prove that the hex-to-binary conversion method given in the text is correct; i.e., if each hex digit is replaced by its four-bit binary equivalent, then the resulting binary number has the same value as the original hex number.

11. Write the 16-bit representation of −156 in sign-magnitude, one's complement, and two's complement. Show the two's complement representation in hex also.

12. What decimal number is represented by FF79 in two's complement notation? What data type is this number—byte, word, longword, or quadword?

13. Find the decimal equivalent of each of the following two's complement integers.
    (a) FFFF   (c) E021
    (b) FE00   (d) FFFF2A72

14. Represent each of the following decimal integers in two's complement form, using the smallest unit of memory among bytes, words, and longwords that is large enough for each datum. Do the conversion and show your results in hex.
    (a) −542   (c) 256
    (b) −25   (d) −40,800

15. There is an integer that can be represented in two's complement form using eight bits but whose negative can not. What is this integer?

16. What are the largest and smallest two's complement integers that can be represented in a byte? In a word? In a longword?

17. Prove that adding signed two's complement integers as if they were unsigned binary numbers and dropping the carry, if any, from the leftmost place always gives the correct two's complement sum (if the sum does not overflow).

18. Suppose 37,412 and −33,316 are represented as longword two's complement integers. Show their representations (use hex) and add them.

19. Describe an efficient method the computer could use to subtract one two's complement integer from another. Your method should be independent of the signs of the operands.

20. Figure out a rule or rules that the computer might use to determine if overflow occurred when it added two two's complement integers.

Chapter 4

Introduction to Assembly Language

Most assembly language source statements contain some or all of the following four fields: a label field, an operator field, an operand field, and a comment field. In this chapter we begin to examine the components of the fields, describe some frequently used assembler directives, and show how to put together a complete program. Since one of our aims is to provide enough information so that the reader can begin to write complete simple programs relatively soon, we do not give a thorough presentation of all the details and options for the topics covered in this chapter. More information may be found in later chapters and in DEC manuals. Also, we will use some machine instructions in examples without formal explanations. Their general functions should be clear; they will be explained in more detail in later chapters.

Note that unless the programmer indicates otherwise, the assembler will interpret all numbers that appear in instructions as decimal numbers.

4.1 SYMBOLS AND LABELS

Symbols are names of things. They name variables, arrays, and other data areas, and they label instructions. The names of general registers (R0, . . . , R12, AP, FP, SP, and PC), and instructions are permanent symbols. Those used to label instructions and data, and other symbols given values by the programmer, are called *user-defined symbols.*

A symbol may consist of up to 31 characters from among letters, digits, and the underline (_). The first character may not be a digit. (Dollar signs and periods are acceptable too, but should be avoided; they are used in system-defined symbols.)

Assemblers have a counter, called the *location counter,* for keeping track of the number of bytes used in the translation of a program section. The assembler sets it to zero at the beginning of the assembly of each program section and increments it by the number of bytes required for each machine instruction translated and each data area reserved. Thus, the value of the location counter is always the address of the next available byte (relative to the beginning of the program section).

User-defined symbols are most often defined—i.e., given a value—by being used in the label field of an instruction. [The symbol must be followed by a colon (:).] The value assigned to the symbol is the value of the location counter at that point; hence it is the location of the instruction or datum the symbol names. The assembler stores the symbol and its value in a symbol table so that when other instructions use the symbol the assembler can look it up, find its value, and properly encode the address in the translation of the other instructions. It is very important to understand that to the assembler, the value of a variable name is the location of the variable, not the contents of the location—what we usually think of as the value of the variable. To emphasize the distinction, we will work through an example.

Suppose a program contains the following statements, which direct the assembler to initialize longwords in memory with the specified values.

```
ALPHA:   .LONG   1186
BETA:    .LONG   -28
GAMMA:   .LONG   35
```

For the picture of memory below, we assume that the value of the location counter was 108 (locations are always given in hex) when the first .LONG directive was assembled. Since the lowest-numbered byte of a longword is the byte at the right end, we show the addresses and labels on the right. Remember that a longword consists of four bytes, so the address shown for each longword is four larger than the preceding one. The data in memory are shown in hex.

Memory contents	*Location*	*Symbol*
000004A2	00000108	ALPHA
FFFFFFE4	0000010C	BETA
00000023	00000110	GAMMA

The values of the symbols ALPHA, BETA, and GAMMA are 108, 10C, and 110, respectively. We may write, simply, ALPHA = 108, BETA = 10C, and GAMMA = 110. It is *not* correct, as it would be in a high-level language, to say ALPHA = $4A2_{16}$ or ALPHA = 1186_{10}. A commonly used notation for the contents of a memory location or register consists of the name (or address) of the location or register enclosed in parentheses. So, (ALPHA) means "the contents of ALPHA." In this example, (ALPHA) = $000004A2_{16}$, (BETA) = $FFFFFFE4_{16}$, and $(GAMMA) = 00000023_{16}$. Note that (ALPHA) may change often during execution of the program, whereas ALPHA never changes (unless the program is changed).

Now, suppose the program contains the following instruction, which moves a longword of data from the location specified by the first operand to the location specified by the second one.

```
MOVL    ALPHA+4,GAMMA
```

What gets moved into the longword at GAMMA? Not 000004A6, for that would be (ALPHA)+4. ALPHA+4 = $10C_{16}$, the address of the second longword shown. Thus the instruction moves FFFFFFE4 into GAMMA. (In fact, ALPHA+4 = BETA.)

Aside from emphasizing that the value of a symbol is an address, this example illustrates that a symbol may be combined with other terms to make up an expression that designates the location of an operand. We will cover the rules for forming expressions later; for now, if you remember that a symbol represents an address, not the contents of an address, it is safe to assume that any reasonably simple expression is valid.

User-defined symbols may be defined by explicitly equating them to the desired value in what is called a direct assignment statement. The format for such a statement is

$$\text{symbol} = \text{expression}$$

If any symbols appear in the expression, they must have been defined previously in the program. Direct assignment statements have many uses, one of which is to make it easier to read and modify a program by naming constants used by the assembler. (Remember that symbols no longer exist at execution time; constants to be used by a program then must be put in memory or a register.) A symbol that is defined in a direct assignment statement may be redefined—i.e., assigned another value later in the program—any number of times. We will see examples of the use of direct assignment statements in subsequent sections.

4.2 OPERATORS

The operator field specifies the operation or action to be performed by the statement. There are three categories of operators: machine instructions, assembler directives, and macros. *Machine instructions* are those that are translated by the assembler to machine code and perform execution-time operations such as arithmetic, data movement, and branching. *Assembler directives* are instructions to the assembler to perform ment, and branching. *Assembler directives* are instructions to the assembler to perform various bookkeeping tasks, storage reservation, and other control functions. A *macro instruction* is a pseudoinstruction invented by a programmer (or provided in a system library) to denote a certain sequence of machine instructions, assembler directives, and/or other macros. To be consistent with DEC's terminology, we will use the term "argument" for assembler directive and macro operands.

To perform a machine instruction, the computer needs several pieces of information: the operation to be performed, the number, locations, and types of the operands, and the type and location for the result. Some of this information is provided in the instruction name (some implicitly), the rest in the operand specifiers. In almost all machine instruction names, the first three or four letters indicate the operation to be performed. For many instructions the next letter (or in a few cases, the next two letters) specify the data type(s) of the operands and the result. (Usually the operands and the result are the same type.) The letters used for the types are

Letter	*Data Type*
B	Byte
W	Word
L	Longword
Q	Quadword
P	Packed decimal
F	Floating point (single-precision)
D	Double-precision floating-point
G	G_floating
H	H_floating
C	Character
V	Variable-length bit field

The number of operands is implicit for some instructions; for others it is specified by a digit at the end of the instruction name. Thus it is easy to figure out what many of the instructions do. Consider these examples:

MULW3	MULtiply Word integers, 3 operands.
CVTLF	ConVerT Longword to Floating-point.
SUBB2	SUBtract Byte integers, 2 operands. (The first operand is subtracted from the second.)
CMPF	CoMPare Floating-point operands.
CLRL	CLeaR Longword (i.e., set it to zero).
INCW	INCrement a Word integer by 1.
MOVC3	MOVe Characters, 3 operands.
BEQL	Branch if EQuaL (used after a comparison).

For ease of distinguishing them from machine instructions, assembler directive names begin with a period. A directive name is usually a word or an abbreviation for a word that indicates what the directive does. Some frequently used directives are presented in Section 4.4.

Macros can be very complex; we will present and use some in Chapter 5, but we defer most of our discussion of them to Chapter 11.

4.3 OPERAND ADDRESSING

The VAX has an unusually large variety of operand addressing modes, i.e., ways of specifying the locations of operands. With some exceptions, any addressing mode may be used with any machine instruction. This is different from many other computers where each instruction requires a specific operand format.

In instructions that have more than one operand, the order in which they are written determines which operands play which roles. For example, we indicated that in a subtract instruction, the first operand is subtracted from the second. Usually, the destination operand, i.e., the place where the result of an operation goes, is the last operand. Almost all of the addressing modes may be used to specify both the locations of data to be operated on and locations for results. The exceptions are fairly obvious; for example, an addressing mode that specifies a constant would not be used for the result of an operation.

An operand may be in a general register, in memory, or in the instruction itself. We will describe some simple addressing modes for specifying operands in each of these categories. All of the additional, more complex, addressing modes are for specifying operands in memory. We will describe a few in this section and leave some for later.

Register Mode: R*n*

Register mode is used to indicate that the operand is in a general register. The operand specifier is simply the name of the register. It may be any of R0, . . . , R12, or AP, FP, or SP.

For data types such as B and W that use fewer than 32 bits, the rightmost byte or word of the register is used. The leftmost portion of the register is ignored; it is not changed by a B or W instruction. For data types such as quadwords and double-precision floating-point numbers that take up 64 bits, or two general registers, the operand is in R*n* and R*n*+1. (For data types that have more than 64 bits, the appropriate number of registers is used beginning with R*n*.)

General registers should be used for intermediate results and data that are used often because it takes less time to access registers than memory.

EXAMPLE 4.1: Register Mode

Suppose R6 contains 00280E45 and R9 contains FFFFF3A6. After the MOVe, or copy, instruction

       MOVL   R6,R9

is executed, both R6 and R9 will contain 00280E45. However, if the instruction had been

```
MOVW    R6,R9
```

then R9 would contain FFFF0E45.

Relative Mode: *address*

Relative mode may be used for operands in memory. The operand specifier is an expression, usually just a symbol, whose value is the address of the datum to be used (or the address of the location where the result of the operation is to be stored). The reason why this is called relative mode will be explained when we consider its machine language encoding.

EXAMPLE 4.2: *Relative Mode*

```
MOVC3   #32,TITLE,LINE+12        ; Move title to output line
```

This instruction moves a string of characters from TITLE to LINE+12. The second and third operands use relative mode. The first operand is a literal, the addressing mode that is explained next.

Literal and Immediate Modes: *#number* or *#expression*

In a literal or immediate mode operand the actual datum to be used by the operation is specified in the instruction. Normally, the location of the datum is specified. Literal and immediate mode operands may be integer or floating point constants. The constant may be described by a number or an expression (usually just a symbol). The restrictions on the kinds of expressions that may be used will be described later. The constant is preceded by a # to indicate that it is a literal rather than an address.

In assembly language literal and immediate mode operand specifiers look the same, but in machine code they are different. (The assembler chooses between them depending on how much space is needed to assemble the constant. A literal is six bits long; an immediate datum may be longer. The machine code will be examined in detail in Chapter 8.)

EXAMPLE 4.3: *Literal Mode*

The instruction

```
MOVW    #25,R11                  ; Put max size in R11
```

puts the (decimal) integer constant 25 in the rightmost word of R11. For example:

R11

Before execution   `EFFE0972`

After execution   `EFFE0019`

An alternate way of doing the same thing is

```
MAX_SIZE = 25
        .
        .
        .
        MOVW    #MAX_SIZE,R11        ; Put max size in R11
```

The use of the symbol MAX_SIZE makes the program clearer, and if the max size is ever changed, only the direct assignment statement need be modified; the programmer would not have to search through the program for all uses of the number 25.

It is a common mistake for beginners to forget the # in a literal or immediate operand. If we had written

```
        MOVW    25,R11        ; Put max size in R11
```

the assembler would encode the 25 as an address and the CPU would try to copy the memory word whose address is 25 into R11. Most likely this would cause an execution-time error called an *access violation,* because memory location 25 is not in the section of memory available to the program. The error would also occur if MAX_SIZE were used without the #, because MAX_SIZE is not a label; it is equal to the constant 25.

It is sometimes very useful to specify a literal as a character; the value of the literal is the ASCII code for the character. The format for such literals is

$$\#^A/\text{char}/$$

For example, the instruction

```
        MOVB    #^A/*/,LINE
```

will put the ASCII code for the asterisk into the byte labeled LINE.

Branch Mode: *destination*

The branch destination may be specified by an expression; usually it is a symbol used as a label on an instruction. Branch mode is used to specify a location to which the program should branch if certain conditions are met. If the operator is an unconditional branch or if it is a conditional branch and the condition is satisfied, the destination address is loaded into the PC (program counter) register, so the next instruction executed is the one at the address. There are limits on how far from the current instruction the branch address may be. These will be discussed when we cover the machine code for the branch instructions.

Branch mode may look just like relative mode in assembly language, but they are encoded differently in machine language.

EXAMPLE 4.4: Branch Mode

The unconditional branch instruction

```
        BRB        NEXT
```

causes a branch to the instruction labeled NEXT.

The next three addressing modes specify operands in memory. The reader who wishes to begin writing some short programs as soon as possible may skim or skip these for now and return to them after reading Chapter 5.

The notation Rn used for describing the addressing modes denotes any of the registers R0 through R12 or AP, FP, or SP.

Register Deferred Mode: (Rn)

In register deferred mode the address of the operand, not the operand itself, is in a general register. Recall the notational convention that an address or register name enclosed in parentheses means the contents of the address or register. Thus in register deferred mode, the *location* of the operand is (Rn), the contents of Rn.

EXAMPLE 4.5: Register Deferred Mode

The instruction

```
        ADDW2     R5,(R8)                          ; Add  food  cost  to  budget
```

adds the word in (the right end of) R5 to the word whose address is in R8.

Suppose that before the instruction in the preceding example is executed, the data are as follows:

	Memory	*Address*
R5	F543	00000840
EFFE002E	FFFF	00000842
R8	FFB9	00000844
00000846	001C	00000846
	074D	00000848
	12C0	0000084A

The only locations changed by the instruction are bytes 846 and 847. Since 002E + 001C = 004A, the result is

Memory	Address
.	.
.	.
.	.
004A	00000846
.	.
.	.
.	.

Note that the left half of R5 is ignored, but since addresses are always 32 bits long, all of R8 is used. We have diagramed memory as a list of words because the instruction being considered acts on words. In general, in diagrams, we break up memory into units of a size appropriate to the example being considered. It is important not to be misled by the pictures. We could have drawn memory as a list of longwords like this (before execution of the instruction):

Memory	Address
FFFFF543	00000840
001CFFB9	00000844
12C0074D	00000848

The instruction would have the same effect; the affected area would be shown as

004AFFB9	00000844

Autoincrement Mode: (R*n*)+

Autoincrement is one of several addressing modes that are especially useful for processing data in arrays. The address of the operand is in a general register. After the operand location is determined, the register is automatically incremented so that it contains the address of the next array entry. The amount by which R*n* is incremented is the amount appropriate for the data type of the operand: 1 for a byte, 2 for a word, 4 for a longword or floating-point number, 8 for a quadword or eight-byte floating point number, and 16 for octawords and 16-byte floating point numbers. (For other data types such as character strings, R*n* is incremented by 1, so autoincrement mode is not useful for them.)

EXAMPLE 4.6: Adding Array Entries with Autoincrement Mode

A loop that adds up all the entries in an array would need only two instructions, one that does the addition and one that handles the loop control. Suppose the address of the beginning of a longword array AMNTS has been put in R10, and R7 has been cleared for the sum.

```
ADD:    ADDL2  (R10) + ,R7          ; Add next entry
```
(loop control instruction that causes a branch to ADD if not done yet)

Assume the ADDL2 instruction has been executed several times and the contents of registers and memory before the next execution of it are as follows:

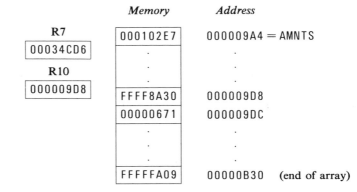

	Memory	*Address*
R7	000102E7	000009A4 = AMNTS
00034CD6		
R10		
000009D8	FFFF8A30	000009D8
	00000671	000009DC
	FFFFFA09	00000B30 (end of array)

After the next execution of the ADDL2 instruction we have:

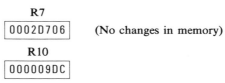

R7

0002D706   (No changes in memory)

R10

000009DC

Note that when the loop finishes, R10 will contain 00000B34, the address of the first byte following the end of the array.

Since R*n* is incremented after the operand address is determined, rather than after the operation is performed, if R*n* is used in autoincrement mode to specify two operands in the same instruction, the operands are in different locations and R*n* is incremented twice. For example, suppose R8 contains 000102C7. The instruction

```
MOVB   (R8) + ,(R8) +           ; Copy flag byte
```

will determine that the first operand's address is 102C7, increment R8 by 1 (since the operand is a byte), determine that the second operand's address is 102C8, increment R8 by 1, and finally copy the byte at 102C7 into 102C8. R8 will contain 000102C9.

Autodecrement Mode: −(R*n*)

The operand size (1, 2, 4, 8, or 16, as for autoincrement) is subtracted from R*n*; then the new contents of R*n* is used as the operand address.

The autodecrement mode may be used to process an array backward—i.e., starting with the higher-addressed entries and moving toward the lower ones. It is particularly useful for adding items to a data structure called a stack (described in Chapter 9) and, in conjunction with autoincrement, for searching arrays or strings.

> **EXAMPLE 4.7: *Autodecrement Mode***
>
> The instruction
>
> ```
> CLRW    −(R5)
> ```
>
> affects R5 and a word in memory as follows:
> Before execution:

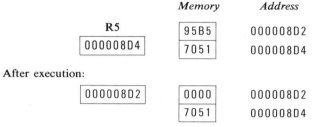

Note that there are two differences between autoincrement mode and autodecrement mode. Autoincrement mode *increments* the register *after* using the address it contained to locate the operand, while autodecrement mode *decrements* the register *before* using its contents to locate the operand.

4.4 RESERVING AND INITIALIZING DATA AREAS

In this section we cover two types of assembler directives: those that reserve blocks of storage (initializing the contents to zero) and those that reserve storage and initialize the contents to values specified by the programmer.

Recall that the assembler assumes any numbers used in source statements to be decimal numbers, unless the programmer indicates otherwise.

Reserving Space

The .BLK*x* directives tell the assembler to reserve storage for various types of data; the *x* indicates the type. The .BLK*x* directives are

.BLKB	for bytes
.BLKW	for words
.BLKL	for longwords
.BLKQ	for quadwords
.BLKO	for octawords
.BLKA	for addresses (longwords)
.BLKF	for floating-point numbers (longwords)
.BLKD	for double floating-point numbers (quadwords)
.BLKG	⌠for the optional extra
.BLKH	⌡floating point types

The format for these directives is

$$.\text{BLK}x \quad \text{expression}$$

The expression specifies the number of units of storage to allocate. It is usually just a constant or a simple expression. Any symbols used must be defined before the .BLKx statement appears. (There are other restrictions on expressions used in this and other assembler directives, but they need not concern us yet.) The assembler fills all the reserved space with zeros.

EXAMPLE 4.8: Storage Reservation Directives

```
NUM = 70                          ; NUM = max number of entries
AMNTS:   .BLKL   100
ACCNTS:  .BLKB   NUM*52
MPG:     .BLKF   40
```

The first statement reserves 100 longwords, or 400 bytes. For the second statement, we assume NUM is the maximum number of entries to be in the ACCNTS array, each of which contains 52 bytes. The third statement reserves space for a floating-point array called MPG with 40 elements.

What do we actually mean when we say that the assembler reserves space? Recall that the assembler updates its location counter (which is denoted by a period) as it processes source statements. Reserving space means increasing the location counter by the appropriate amount.

EXAMPLE 4.9: How the Assembler Processes the Directives

Suppose . = 9A4 when the assembler encounters the first statement in the previous example. The assembler records the symbol AMNTS in its symbol table and gives it the value 9A4. Then it determines that 400 bytes are to be allocated. Since $400_{10} = 190_{16}$, it updates . by setting . = . + 190 = B34. Then when it processes the next statement, ACCNTS will be assigned the value B34.

There is no .BLK*x* statement for explicitly reserving space for character strings or packed decimal data. The programmer decides how many bytes will be needed for such data and may use the .BLKB directive (or any of the others).

EXAMPLE 4.10

```
LINE:   .BLKB   80                    ; Output line
```

This statement reserves 80 bytes for a character string with up to 80 characters.

Initializing Integer Data

Directives for initializing data cause the assembler to store data in specified areas in memory. The directive name specifies the type of data to be stored and the argument(s) specify the values. (If a value specified is too large for the data type, an error message will be issued.) The argument formats differ slightly, depending on the type. The first group of data storage directives we consider are

.BYTE	argument_list
.WORD	argument_list
.LONG	argument_list

For each of these directives, the argument list may contain one or more arguments, separated by commas. Each argument has the form

datum[repetition_factor]

Both the datum and the repetition factor may be expressions. The assembler will store in the next available locations the number of copies of the datum specified by the repetition factor. The data are stored in two's complement form. The repetition factor is optional. If it is not used, a value of 1 is assumed. If it is used, it must be enclosed in square brackets as shown, and any symbols in the expression must be already defined.

EXAMPLE 4.11: Initializing Storage

Suppose . = 58A when the assembler encounters the following statements.

```
COORDS:   .WORD   2,27,-180,492
ALPHA:    .BYTE   5[3]
```

After these statements are processed, the affected area of memory will look like this:

Memory	Location
0002	0000058A
001B	0000058C
FF4C	0000058E
01EC	00000590
0505	00000592
05	00000594

Two symbols have been defined:

$$COORDS = 58A$$
$$ALPHA = 592$$

The final value of the location counter is 595.

EXAMPLE 4.12

Suppose that instead of just reserving space for the ACCNTS array used in an earlier example, we want to initialize all the bytes in the file to −1. Instead of using the .BLKB directive, we could use

```
ACCNTS:  .BYTE   −1[NUM*52]        ; Unopened accnts
```

For storing eight bytes of data, the .QUAD directive may be used. Its format is

$$.QUAD \quad constant$$

or

$$.QUAD \quad symbol$$

The .QUAD directive can have only one argument, which can not be a general expression, and it can not have a repetition factor. (The VAX does not support the quadword data type as fully as the other integer types; i.e., there are fewer instructions and less flexible assembler directives for quadwords than there are for the other types.)

Initializing Character Data

The VAX uses ASCII character codes to represent characters (letters, numerals, punctuation, special characters, and control characters). Each ASCII code has seven bits, so they are stored one per byte with the eighth, or leftmost, bit always 0. Appendix C contains a list of the codes. (They appear on the *VAX-11 Programming Card* too.) ASCII stands for American Standard Code for Information Interchange.

    A character string—a sequence of characters—is represented in memory in a contiguous sequence of bytes, one ASCII character code to a byte. The .ASCII directive (and a few variations of it) tell the assembler to store a character string. Headings and other messages to be printed by a program are set up using these directives. We will use the .ASCII and .ASCIZ directives. Their formats are

.ASCII   *character_string_specification*
.ASCIZ   *character_string_specification*

The .ASCII directive stores the string in the next available bytes; the first character in the string in the first (lowest numbered) byte, and so on. .ASCIZ stores the string in the same way, but it also adds an extra byte at the end of the string containing 0's. For some uses of character strings, it is handy to have the end of the string marked in this way. In Chapter 5 we will see some criteria for choosing between .ASCII and .ASCIZ.

The simplest way to specify a character string is to write it out preceded and followed by a delimiter character. The slash is most commonly used as a delimiter.

EXAMPLE 4.13: *Initializing a Character String*

    TITLE: .ASCII   /Daily Sales/

This directive stores the following data:

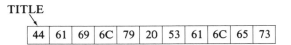

If a slash appears in the string, it can't be used as the delimiter. Any other character (except space, tab, equal sign, semicolon, or left angle bracket) that does not appear within the string may be used.

Control characters are ASCII codes that do not correspond to a printable symbol but rather indicate that some action, such as a carriage return, is to occur. If we want to include such a character in a string to be stored in memory, we can not simply type it; in the case of a carriage return, it would terminate the statement we were typing. In the .ASCII and .ASCIZ directives control characters must be represented by their ASCII code. The code must be enclosed in angle brackets *outside* the delimiters that delimit the rest of the string. (Noncontrol characters also may be specified this way, but it is clearer just to type them if possible.)

EXAMPLE 4.14: *A Character String Containing Control Characters*

The statements

    LF = 10   ; ASCII code for line feed
        .
        .
        .
    HDG: .ASCIZ <LF><LF>/THIRD LINE/

would cause the assembler to fill the next 13 bytes of memory as follows:

HDG

| 0A | 0A | 54 | 48 | 49 | 52 | 44 | 20 | 4C | 49 | 4E | 45 | 00 |

The assembler sets the value of the symbol HDG to be the location of the first byte of the character string. If this string were printed or displayed at the terminal, two lines would be skipped because of the "line feed" characters, and the string "THIRD LINE" would appear on the third line. Note that a blank, or space, is a character and has an ASCII code. Note also that the symbol LF is used in the directive for clarity.

EXAMPLE 4.15: *More Character Strings*

```
CR = 13                             ; ASCII carriage return
LF = 10                             ; ASCII line feed
     .
     .
     .
TITLE:  .ASCIZ  /DAILY TRANSACTIONS/
DEP:    .ASCII  /PAGE 1/<CR><LF>/DEPOSITS/
DATE:   .ASCII  '9/14/83'
```

The .ASCIZ directive defines a simple character string of length 18; it reserves 19 bytes altogether because of the extra byte of zeros added at the end. In the first .ASCII directive, the character string is broken up into several segments, each enclosed in delimiters. The complete string has length 16. If it were printed out on a terminal or line printer, "PAGE 1" would appear on one line and "DEPOSITS" at the beginning of the next line. In the last .ASCII statement, because slashes appear in the character string, apostrophes are used as the delimiters.

EXAMPLE 4.16: *Initializing a String of Blanks in Memory*

The directive

```
LINE:   .BYTE   32[80]                ; 80 blanks
```

initializes each of the next 80 bytes of memory to contain the byte integer 32, the character code for a blank. Note that even though we may think of the data in memory as character codes, we did not use an .ASCII directive here to fill the bytes.

4.5 BEGINNING AND ENDING A PROGRAM

Suppose we want to write a program to compute BETA = 3*ALPHA-20, where ALPHA and BETA are longword integers. (In describing the computation, we use the variable names ALPHA and BETA to mean the contents of the memory locations with those names, not their addresses; i.e., we use the names as we would in a higher-level language.) From the examples we have seen so far we know how to write the instructions to do the arithmetic and the directives to initialize ALPHA and reserve space for BETA. We may do as follows:

```
; DATA
;
ALPHA:  .LONG     224
BETA:   .BLKL     1
;
;
; PROGRAM TO COMPUTE  BETA = 3 * ALPHA - 20
;
; Register use:       R6 intermediate results
;
        MULL3     #3,ALPHA,R6      ; R6 = 3 * ALPHA
        SUBL3     #20,R6,BETA      ; BETA = R6 - 20
```

How does the computer know that the instructions begin at the third longword and that it should not try to execute the data? It doesn't, unless we tell it. How will the computer know that it is supposed to stop executing instructions after the SUBL3 instruction? Again, it doesn't. (One might argue that it should stop after the last instruction, but there is always *something* in the next memory location; the computer does not know what we intend to be the last instruction unless we tell it.) Several instructions and directives are needed to control assembly and execution of a program.

The statements described below are the standard statements for VAX assembly language programs. In Chapter 5 we will describe some macros that must be used in place of some of these if the I/O macros defined in this book are used. Readers who plan to use our I/O macros should not skip the discussion here, however.

The .ENTRY Directive

Part of the task of specifying where execution of a program section begins is accomplished by the .ENTRY directive, which establishes an *entry point*. An entry point is a place in a routine (a main program or a procedure) at which it can be entered, i.e., at which execution of that routine may begin. The format of the .ENTRY directive is

.ENTRY   *symbol,entry_mask*

The symbol is the name of the entry point. The assembler assigns to the symbol the current value of the location counter. We will consider the role of the entry mask when we study procedures. Until then, it is a good idea for beginning assembly language programmers to use $\wedge M\langle IV \rangle$. This entry mask sets the IV (Integer oVerflow) trap bit in the PSW so that a program interrupt will occur if the result of an integer arithmetic operation overflows the space alloted. (If the entry mask is 0, the IV trap bit will not be set.) The .ENTRY directive should be placed just before the first instruction to be executed.

The .END Directive

The .END directive is placed at the very end of the source file; it tells the assembler that it has reached the physical end of the module that it is translating. The format of the .END directive is

.END   *transfer_address*

The transfer address is a symbol that specifies where execution of the program is to begin. There is a distinction between the transfer address and an entry point. A main program and each procedure would have an entry point, the point where execution of that routine is to begin. The transfer address is where execution of the entire program begins, the entry point of the main program. It must be specified on the .END directive of a main program; it must be omitted from the .END directive in a procedure because execution of a program does not begin in a procedure.

The $EXIT_S Macro

$EXIT_S may be used to terminate execution of a program. $EXIT_S is a macro; that is, the assembler replaces it with a sequence of instructions that do the necessary work and transfer control back to the operating system.

A Complete Program

Here we have rewritten our sample program using these control instructions. The asterisks along the left margin indicate the statements that have been added; they are not part of the program.

```
        ; DATA
        ;
        ALPHA: .LONG   224
        BETA:  .BLKL   1
        ;
        ;
        ; PROGRAM TO COMPUTE BETA = 3 * ALPHA − 20
        ;
        ; Register use        R6       intermediate results
        ;
*              .ENTRY  COMPUTE,^M<IV>
               MULL3   #3,ALPHA,R6            ; R6 = 3 * ALPHA
               SUBL3   #20,R6,BETA            ; BETA = R6 − 20
*              $EXIT_S
*              .END    COMPUTE
```

We now have a correct program that can be assembled, linked, and executed.

Note that in our sample program we placed the data ahead of the machine instructions. If data and instructions are properly separated, the data may be placed before or after the executable portion of the program. However, for reasons that will be explained in Chapter 8, it is good practice to put the data first as we did here.

The symbols ALPHA and BETA are used in comments like variable names in high-level languages.

Note also the use of blank comment lines to visually separate parts of the program. The program contains a brief comment explaining what it does and what general registers it uses, and each machine instruction contains a brief comment. Every program should have at least this much documentation. Although the sample program is complete and will execute properly, it does not print any output. In the next chapter we describe instructions for doing input and output.

4.6 STATEMENT FORMATS

To increase the clarity of an assembly language program, the fields of each statement should begin in the columns specified below whenever possible.

Field	Column
Label	1
Operator	9
Operand	17
Comment	41

The operator field and operand field must be separated by at least one space or tab. The individual operands are separated by commas. The label field is terminated by a colon (:), and the comment field must begin with a semicolon (;).

A statement may be continued on more than one line by the use of a hyphen as the last nonblank character (before the comment, if any) on each line being continued. If the only field on the first line is the label field (and perhaps a comment), then the hyphen may be omitted. (If a label contains more than seven characters, DEC recommends putting the rest of the instruction on the next line so the operator can begin in column 9.) If a statement is continued over more than one line, it should be broken up at logical points, such as between fields or operands.

There are two exceptions to the general instruction format: direct assignment statements and statements that consist only of a comment. By convention, the symbol in a direct assignment statement begins in column 1; there may be a comment field. A comment statement begins with a semicolon in column 1.

4.7 SUMMARY

Most assembly language statements may have four fields: a label field (beginning in column 1), an operator field (beginning in column 9), an operand field (beginning in column 17), and a comment field (beginning in column 41).

Symbols are used to name data, instructions, and constants. User-defined symbols may be given a value by being used in the label field of a statement or by being explicitly assigned a value in a direct assignment statement. In the first case, the more common one, the value assigned to the symbol is the current value of the location counter. Thus the value of a symbol defined this way is an address, not the datum stored at the address.

There are three kinds of operators: machine instructions, assembler directives, and macros. The name of a machine instruction is a mnemonic for the operation it performs, the data type(s) it operates on, and (in some cases) the number of operands.

Machine instruction operands use a positional protocol; that is, the order in which the operands appear determines what role each one plays. The operands may be in registers, in memory, or in the instruction itself. The result of an operation, if any, usually goes in the last operand.

The VAX has an unusually large variety of operand addressing modes. Some of the more commonly used modes are summarized in Table 4.1.

TABLE 4.1   Some Addressing Modes

Mode name	Notation	Location of Operand	Other Features
Register	Rn	In register	Uses rightmost byte or word for B or W instruction; Rn and Rn+1 for Q, D, or G; Rn, . . . , Rn+3 for H
Relative	*address expression*	In memory	
Literal	#*expression*	In instruction	
Branch	*destination*	In memory	
Register deferred	(Rn)	In memory, address in Rn	
Autoincrement	(Rn)+	In memory, address in Rn	Rn incremented by data type size
Autodecrement	−(Rn)	In memory, address in Rn after decrementing	Rn decremented by data type size

The storage reservation and initialization directives described in this section are summarized in Table 4.2. The assembler reserves storage by incrementing the location counter by the required number of bytes. The assembler stores integer data in two's complement.

TABLE 4.2   Storage Reservation and Initialization Directives

Directive		Remarks
.BLK*x*	*expression*	The expression indicates the number of units to reserve; *x* indicates the type. (*x* = B, W, L, Q, O, A, F, D, G, or H.)
.BYTE	*list*	Store the listed values in successive bytes, words, or longwords, respectively. Repetition factors (enclosed in square brackets) may be used
.WORD	*list*	
.LONG	*list*	
.QUAD	*value*	Store the value in the next quadword.
.ASCII	*string*	Store the character string. .ASCIZ adds a byte of zeros at the end of the string.
.ASCIZ	*string*	

Character strings are represented in memory in ASCII code in a sequence of contiguous bytes, one character per byte. In the .ASCII and .ASCIZ directives, the string to be stored is written between matching delimiters. Some control characters must be specified by giving their character code enclosed in angle brackets.

The assembler interprets numbers that appear in machine instruction operands or assembler directive arguments as decimal numbers unless the programmer instructs otherwise.

The .ENTRY directive defines an entry point for a program module; i.e., it specifies where execution of that module may begin. The .END directive tells the assembler where the end of the source module is. The .END directive in a main program specifies the main program's entry point as its argument to indicate where execution of the whole program begins. The $EXIT_S macro may be used to terminate execution of a program.

Data must be separated from executable instructions in a program. Generally storage reservation and initialization directives are placed at the beginning of a module, ahead of the .ENTRY directive.

4.8   EXERCISES

1. Write an instruction that assigns the symbol MARGIN the value 10.

2. What are some of the differences between the location counter and the program counter (PC)?

3. Suppose . = 04A2 when the assembler encounters the following statements:

```
LENGTH: .WORD    27               ; Length of rectangle
WIDTH:  .WORD    5                ; Width of rectangle
```

What is the value of LENGTH? What is the value of WIDTH?

4. Suppose that along with the statements shown in Exercise 3, the program has

```
AREA:     .BLKW   1                ; Area of rectangle
```

Write an instruction that computes the area of a rectangle whose length and width are stored in LENGTH and WIDTH; the area should be stored in AREA.

5. Try to figure out what each of the following instructions does, and write a brief explanation for each.

(a) ADDD3   (d) BLEQ   (g) CLRF
(b) CMPB   (e) CVTBW (h) DECW
(c) DIVL3   (f) MOVQ   (i) MULP

6. Write an instruction to add the longword contents of R7 and R4 and put the sum in R9.

7. Suppose R6 contains the address of an array of quadwords. Write a formula for the address of the third entry in the array.

8. R7 contains the address of a word integer. Write an instruction to put the integer in R10. Write an instruction to put the address of the integer in R11.

9. Suppose registers and memory contain the data shown.

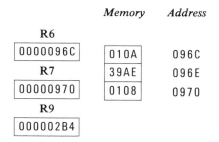

Show all changes that occur in memory and registers after the following instruction is executed.

```
ADDL3   R7,(R6),R9        ; Add Jan. and Feb. sales
```

10. The CVTLW instruction converts its first operand, a longword integer, to a word, its second operand. If 00183490 is in R5 and 001A38E4 is in R8 before the execution of the following instruction, what will be in R5 and R8 afterward?

```
CVTLW   (R5)+,(R8)         ; Truncate VOLUME to word
```

11. Write instructions to put the number 17 in the rightmost byte of R4 and in the byte of memory whose address is in R3.

12. Suppose each character of a character string called TEXT with length 30 is to be examined, starting from the end of the string, and that R7 will be used with the autodecrement addressing mode to address the characters. What number should be put in R7 to start?

13. Write instructions to allocate a block of 20 words called GRADES, a byte array called CODES with 13 entries, and space for a character string of length 11 called HEADING.

14. Write assembly language statements to reserve 120 contiguous bytes of memory and define symbols with the following values:

Symbol	Value
LINE	The location of the first byte
COL1	The location of the 11th byte
COL2	The location of the 26th byte
COL3	The location of the 41st byte

15. Suppose a program starts with the following directives.

```
ALPHA:  .WORD   250
BETA:   .LONG   5123,835
TITLE:  .ASCII  /Program 1/
```

(a) Give the values of ALPHA, BETA, and TITLE.
(b) How many bytes of memory will be used by these directives?

16. Suppose . = 828 when the assembler encounters the following statements. Show the contents of all affected areas of memory, list the values of all the symbols defined, and give the final value of the location counter.

```
DELTA:  .WORD   24,-18,3
IND:    .BLKB   2
LABEL:  .ASCII  /VAX-11/
TAG:    .BYTE   1
VOLUME: .BLKL   3
```

17. Write a directive to store each of the following character strings. Give each one an appropriate label.
(a) MPG = 3.785 * MILES /LITERS
(b) **** INVENTORY ****

18. Why is it preferable to initialize 80 bytes with the ASCII code for a blank by using

```
.BYTE   32[80]
```

rather than an .ASCII directive? (How would you do it with an .ASCII directive?)

19. Write a complete program to do the following task: There are three consecutive words of memory beginning at the location NUMBRS. Assuming that only the first number has been initialized, when the program terminates the second word should contain twice the number in the first word, and the third should contain twice the number in the second.

20. Write instructions to compute $3y^2 - 4y + 1$, where y is a longword in R6. Put the result in R8.

Chapter 5

Simple I/O Macros

5.1 THE MACROS

Input and output on a computer are complex processes. Many of the details are handled by the operating system, but even using the operating system procedures and macros requires more familiarity with I/O operations and the use of procedures than the reader may have at this point. In this chapter we present some fairly easy-to-use macro instructions that free the user from having to learn the intricacies of system I/O functions until later. Macros are pseudoinstructions; wherever they appear in a program, they will be replaced by the assembler by a sequence of other instructions that do the desired operations. The I/O macros presented here are *not* a VAX utility. A macro library containing the macro definitions in Appendix D must be created before these macros can be used, and the I/O module (also described in Appendix D) must be linked with the program.

There are four macros that do specific I/O operations: input a line from a terminal, input a record from a disk file, output a line (or several) to a terminal, and output (dump) hex data to the terminal. There are also two macros that do necessary initialization and termination chores related to I/O.

All the macros presented here may use registers R0 and R1 for their own work. Thus the user should not leave any important data in those registers. Some of the macros return useful information to the program in R0. (The conventions that we use here—that I/O macros may destroy the old contents of R0 and R1, and may use them to pass information back to the program—are conventions used by system I/O macros also.) The SP register should not be used to specify the arguments of the macros.

I/O Processing Macros

READLINE

The purpose of the READLINE macro is to input a line from the terminal. It displays two question marks and a space as a prompt, then reads in the line of text typed at the terminal. The format of the instruction is

READLINE whereto

The string of text read in will be stored, one character to a byte, in memory beginning at the byte addressed by the argument *whereto*.

The length of the input line is the number of characters typed (including spaces and tabs) before the carriage return. READLINE will read up to 80 characters. It will place the length of the line read in R0 for use by the program.

EXAMPLE 5.1: Reading Input from the Terminal

Suppose a program contains the directive

```
LINE:   .BLKB   30
```

and the instruction

```
READLINE LINE
```

Before the program is executed, the 30 bytes beginning at LINE contain zeros. Suppose that when READLINE is executed and the prompt appears, the person at the terminal types the line shown below and then hits the return key. (The portion of the line typed by the user is underlined to distinguish it from the prompt.)

```
?? 25     —18
```

The line will be read and the bytes in memory beginning at LINE will contain the data shown below.

LINE	LINE +1	LINE +2						LINE +8	LINE +9	. . .	LINE +29
32	35	20	20	20	20	2D	31	38	00	. . .	00

R0 will contain 00000009. Since the input line has only nine characters, the remaining 21 bytes reserved still contain zeros.

Note that the bytes in memory in Example 5.1 contain the ASCII codes for the characters in the input line; they do not contain the two's complement representation of the integers. Conversion of input data to its internal representation is not automatic in assembly language as it is in high-level languages. In Chapter 6 we will see how to convert between character code and two's complement.

READRCRD

The purpose of the READRCRD (READ ReCoRD) macro is to read a record from a sequential disk file called DATA.DAT. For now, records may be thought of simply as lines of text. A *sequential file* is a collection of records arranged in sequential order; i.e., there is a first record, a second record, and so on. When a program begins executing, a pointer is set to the first record in the file. Each time the macro READRCRD is executed, the record pointed to will be read in and the pointer will be moved ahead to the next record. This is done automatically by the VAX-11 Record Management Services.

If READRCRD is to be used in a program, the data file to be read must be given the name DATA.DAT. (The file on the disk is unchanged; a copy of the record read is stored in memory.)

The format of READRCRD is:

READRCRD *whereto*

As with READLINE, *whereto* is the address where the record read in is to be put in memory, READRCRD reads records of length up to 80, and it puts the length of the record read in R0. (If a record in the file is longer than 80 bytes, only the first 80 are read.)

If READRCRD is executed after all the records in the file have been read and the record pointer is at the end of the file, a branch is taken to the instruction labeled EOF. Any program module that uses READRCRD must have an instruction labeled EOF, even if the programmer does not expect to read past the end of the file.

EXAMPLE 5.2: Reading from a Disk File

If the first record in DATA.DAT is "25   −18," then READRCRD will affect memory and R0 the same way READLINE did in Example 5.1.

PRINTCHRS

PRINTCHRS displays (prints) a string of characters at the terminal. The address of the first byte of the string must be given as the first argument. The end of the string is indicated by a byte of zeros in memory following the last character, or by specification of the string length as a second argument. If a length is specified, it should be a word integer. Each control character, if any, counts as one character. If the string contains any bytes of all zeros, no further bytes will be printed even if a larger length was specified.

The formats for **PRINTCHRS** are:

PRINTCHRS *string*

and

PRINTCHRS *string,length*

The first version is most convenient for printing a message or heading initialized in memory using an .ASCIZ directive. It frees the user from the chore of counting the characters.

Any appropriate addressing modes may be used for the arguments.

PRINTCHRS will print strings of length up to 85 (thus allowing for one full line and several control characters such as line feeds). It always begins on a new line at the left margin.

Note that **PRINTCHRS** expects the memory locations specified for the string to contain ASCII code. It will not print two's complement data; such data must be converted to character code by the program before printing.

EXAMPLE 5.3: Printing a Heading

Headings may be set up and printed as follows:

```
HDG:    .ASCIZ   /OUTPUT FROM JUNE 12/
            .
            .
            .
        PRINTCHRS HDG
```

EXAMPLE 5.4: Printing Several Lines at Once

The ASCII codes for the control characters "carriage return" and "line feed" may be included in a string to accomplish the indicated control operations. Consider the following statements:

```
CR = 13                        ; ASCII carriage return
LF = 10                        ; ASCII line feed
    .
    .
    .
PAGE:  .ASCIZ  /PAGE 1/<CR><LF>/JUNE 12/<LF><LF>
            .
            .
            .
        PRINTCHRS PAGE
```

PRINTCHRS will print JUNE 12 on the line after PAGE 1, both beginning at the left margin, then skip down two lines.

EXAMPLE 5.5: Variations

To emphasize the independence between the initialization of the character string in memory and the printing of it, we show three variations on Example 5.4. It does not matter if one or several .ASCII and .ASCIZ directives are used to set up a string to be printed with one PRINTCHRS statement, or if several PRINTCHRSs are used, so long as the correct ASCII codes are in memory, the string is terminated by a byte of zeros or is of the correct length, and the PRINTCHRS statements specify correct starting addresses.

(a) Using the .ASCIZ directive in Example 5.4, we could have obtained the same result with

```
PRINTCHRS PAGE,#6
PRINTCHRS PAGE+8
```

because the character code for "J" is in the byte whose address is PAGE+8. PRINTCHRS always starts printing at the left end of a new line, so the first two control characters were not included in the strings to be printed. A length is needed on the first PRINTCHRS because there is no zero byte immediately after the bytes containing "PAGE 1."

(b)
```
      PAGE:   .ASCIZ  /PAGE 1/
      DATE:   .ASCIZ  /JUNE 12/<LF><LF>
                          .
                          .
                          .
              PRINTCHRS   PAGE
              PRINTCHRS   DATE
```

(c)
```
      PAGE:   .ASCII  /PAGE 1/<CR><LF>
      DATE:   .ASCIZ  /JUNE 12/<LF><LF>
                          .
                          .
                          .
              PRINTCHRS PAGE
```

Note that in (c) .ASCII is used in the first directive instead of .ASCIZ.

EXAMPLE 5.6: Printing a Record Read from the Disk File DATA.DAT

We must reserve space for a record to be read in; if we don't know its size, we can reserve 80 bytes, the maximum READRCRD will read. Since a record in general will not be terminated by a byte of zeros, we must know the actual length of the record to print it. READRCRD puts the length in R0, so we may use R0 as the length argument in PRINTCHRS.

```
      RECORD: .BLKB    80
                          .
                          .
                          .
              READRCRD    RECORD
              PRINTCHRS   RECORD,R0
```

Remember that PRINTCHRS may change the contents of R0, so we can no longer expect it to contain the length of the record.

DUMPLONG

     DUMPLONG prints the contents of longwords (in memory or registers) in hex. It can be used to examine the results of computation before one learns how to convert data from two's complement to character code. It can also be used to examine the internal representation of the various data types and machine instructions.

     DUMPLONG is a simple debugging tool, since it can easily be inserted at various points in a program to display intermediate results, addresses, etc.

     Its format is

DUMPLONG arglist

where the arglist may contain up to 12 arguments separated by commas and using any addressing modes. (Since DUMPLONG may change the contents of R0 and R1, if these registers are specified as arguments, the output shown for them may not be the original contents. To dump R0 and R1, their contents can be copied to other registers.)

     DUMPLONG always begins and ends its output with a line of three asterisks and prints the operand specifier for each longword it dumps. The output format is illustrated in the following example.

EXAMPLE 5.7: The DUMPLONG Format

The output generated by

```
DUMPLONG LINE,LINE+4,R10,ALPHA,R7,(R7)
```

would have the following form. (The data were somewhat arbitrarily chosen.)

```
***
LINE        20203532
LINE+4      312B2020
R10         FFFFFFE5
ALPHA       0034001A
R7          0000020B
(R7)        FFFFFFFC
***
```

Initialization and Termination Macros

The initialization and termination macros are BEGIN and EXIT. If any of the I/O processing macros are used in a program, then BEGIN and EXIT must be used instead of .ENTRY and $EXIT_S (described in Chapter 4), respectively, in the main program (even if the I/O is done in procedures).

     The format of the BEGIN macro is

BEGIN   entry_point_name

This statement will be replaced by an .ENTRY directive that specifies the entry‑point‑name and sets the integer overflow trap. Also, instructions to initialize the I/O files will be inserted in the program. The entry‑point‑name should appear as the argument of the program's .END directive.

The termination macro is

.EXIT

It has no arguments and is used as $EXIT_S would be.

EXAMPLE 5.8: Using DUMPLONG (A Complete Program)

```
; This program computes 6*ALPHA + BETA and stores the
; result in RESULT. ALPHA, BETA, and RESULT are longwords.
;
LF = 10                                        ; ASCII line feed
;
TITLE:   .ASCIZ      /Computation of 6*ALPHA + BETA/<LF>
ALPHA:   .LONG       -1
BETA:    .LONG       450
RESULT:  .BLKL       1
;
         BEGIN       EXAMPLE
;
; Register use:              R5        scratch
;
         PRINTCHRS   TITLE                     ; Print heading
         DUMPLONG    ALPHA,BETA                ; Show data
         MULL3       #6,ALPHA,R5               ; 6*ALPHA
         ADDL3       R5,BETA,RESULT            ; 6*ALPHA+BETA in RESULT
         DUMPLONG    RESULT                    ; Show result
         EXIT
         .END        EXAMPLE
```

The output from the program is

```
Computation of 6*ALPHA + BETA
* * *
ALPHA       FFFFFFFF
BETA        000001C2
* * *
* * *
RESULT      000001BC
* * *
```

The storage reservation and initialization directives in this and the other examples must be separated from the executable instructions. Generally they would appear before the BEGIN statement.

Copying Character Strings—The MOVC3 Instruction

Formatting data for output often requires moving character strings from one place in memory to another. The MOVC3 (MOVe Characters, 3 operands) instruction does this task. Its format is

MOVC3   *length,source,destination*

The length, a word integer, is the number of characters to be copied from the source to the destination. The last two operands specify the addresses of the first byte of the source and the destination, respectively. The source string will be unchanged (unless it overlaps the destination).

> *Warning: MOVC3 uses registers R0–R5 destroying the original contents of these registers.*

EXAMPLE 5.9: Formatting Characters for Output (A Complete Program)

Suppose the DATA.DAT file contains data for a telephone directory in which each record consists of a name and a phone number. To save space in the file, the phone number immediately follows the name. The (complete) program that follows prints out the whole directory in a format that is easy to read.

Recall that READRCRD causes a branch to the instruction labeled EOF if an attempt is made to read past the end of the file.

```
; PROBLEM STATEMENT
;
; This program reads a telephone directory from the file
; DATA.DAT and prints it at the terminal in an easy to
; read format.
;
; DATA FORMATS
;
; Each record in the file contains a 20 character name
; (which may be padded with blanks) followed by an 8
; character telephone number. The entries will be printed
; with 10 blanks separating the name and phone number.
;
; CONSTANTS
;
TAB = 9                                 ; ASCII tab
LF = 10                                 ; ASCII line feed
;
; STORAGE RESERVATION AND INITIALIZATION
;
HDG:    .ASCIZ  <TAB>/TELEPHONE DIRECTORY/<LF><LF>
LINEIN: .BLKB   28                      ; Input buffer
NAME:   .BLKB   20
        .BYTE   32[10]                  ; Blanks
```

```
PHONE:  .BLKB   8
;
        BEGIN   PRINT_DIR
;
        PRINTCHRS  HDG                    ; Print heading
READ:   READRCRD   LINEIN                 ; Read entry from file
        MOVC3      #20,LINEIN,NAME        ; Copy name
        MOVC3      #8,LINEIN+20,PHONE     ; Copy phone number
        PRINTCHRS  NAME,#38               ; Print entry
        BRB        READ                   ; Branch to READ
EOF:    EXIT                              ; Done
;
        .END    PRINT_DIR
```

Program Listings

Since the reader now has enough information to begin to write and run small programs, we will give a brief description of the format of the program listings produced by the VAX-11 MACRO assembler. Figure 5.1 shows the listing for the program in Example 5.9. The righthand half of the listing is a copy of the source program with line numbers just to the left of the statements. The column of four-digit numbers to the left of the line numbers shows the value of the assembler's location counter at each line. The leftmost section shows (in most cases) the machine-code translation or the data stored for the instruction on the same line. Note that the first (lowest-addressed) byte of each instruction is the one shown closest to the location counter value, so the machine code must be read right to left. The instructions that are substituted by the assembler for the I/O macros are not shown in the listing, but we can determine how many bytes they take up by observing the increase in the location counter value between a line containing a macro and the next line. See the notes on Fig. 5.1 for more detail about the listing.

5.2 SUMMARY AND COMMANDS FOR RUNNING PROGRAMS

General Notes on the I/O Macros

These I/O macros are not VAX system macros. To use them the macro library described in Appendix D must be created and the I/O module described in Appendix D must be linked with the program.

All of these macros may change the data in R0 and R1. The SP register should not be used to address arguments of the macros.

READLINE *whereto*

READLINE reads a line from the terminal and stores it in memory, beginning at the address specified by the argument *whereto*. READLINE prompts with "??". The maximum number of characters read is 80; the actual length is placed in R0.

```
0000            1   ; PROBLEM STATEMENT
0000            2   ;
0000            3   ; This program reads a telephone directory from the file
0000            4   ; DATA.DAT and prints it at the terminal in an easy to
0000            5   ; read format.
0000            6   ;
0000            7   ; DATA FORMATS
0000            8   ;
0000            9   ; Each record in the file contains a 20 character name
0000           10   ; (which may be padded with blanks) followed by an 8
0000           11   ; character telephone number. The entries will be printed
0000           12   ; with 10 blanks separating the name and phone number.
0000           13   ;
0000           14   ; CONSTANTS
0000           15   ;
0000  00000009 16   TAB = 9                          ; ASCII tab
0000  0000000A 17   LF = 10                          ; ASCII line feed
0000           18   ;
0000           19   ; STORAGE RESERVATION AND INITIALIZATION
0000           20   ;
000C           21   HDG:    .ASCIZ <TAB>/TELEPHONE DIRECTORY/<LF><LF>
0017           22   LINEIN: .BLKB   28               ; Input buffer
0033  00000033 23   NAME    .BLKB   20
0047  00000047 24           .BYTE   32[10]           ; Blanks
0051           25   PHONE:  .BLKB   8
0059  00000059 26   ;
0059           27           BEGIN   PRINT_DIR
0059           28   ;
00A9           29           PRINTCHRS HDG            ; Print heading
00B9           30   READ:   READRCRD  LINEIN         ; Read entry from
                                                       file
00C9           31           MOVC3   #20,LINEIN,NAME  ; Copy name
00D1           32           MOVC3   #8,LINEIN+20,PHONE ; Copy phone number
00D9           33           PRINTCHRS NAME,#38       ; Print entry
00E7           34           BRB     READ             ; Branch to READ
00E9           35   EOF:    EXIT                     ; Done
0119           36   ;
0119           37           .END    PRINT_DIR
```

Machine code / memory contents:

```
③  44 20 45 4E 4F 48 50 45 45 4C 54 54 09
   00 0A 0A 59 52 4F 54 43 45 52 49 00
   20'20'20'20'20'20'20'20'20'20

⑦  FF62 CF FF49 CF  14 28
   FF78 CF FF55 CF  08 28
            DO 11
```

①The location counter is not incremented for comments.
②The values of symbols defined in direct assignment statements are entered in the symbol table and shown on the listing, but they are not stored in memory; the location counter hasn't changed.
③ASCII code stored in memory.
④On storage reservation directives, the listing shows the location of the next available byte following the bytes reserved.
⑤The BEGIN macro takes up 80 bytes.
⑥The PRINTCHRS macro takes up 16 bytes.
⑦Machine code.

Figure 5.1 Part of a program listing

READRCRD *whereto*

READRCRD reads the next record from the sequential disk file called DATA.DAT. It stores the record in memory beginning at *whereto*. It reads at most 80 characters and puts the number of characters read in R0. If an attempt is made to read past the end of the file, a branch will be taken to the statement labeled EOF; there must be such a statement in the program.

PRINTCHRS *string,length*

PRINTCHRS prints at the terminal the ASCII string whose address is specified by the first argument. The length, a word, is optional and specifies the maximum number of characters to be printed. Fewer characters may be printed if the string is terminated with a byte of zeros.

DUMPLONG *arglist*

DUMPLONG dumps its arguments at the terminal in hex. It may have up to 12 arguments.

BEGIN *entry_point_name*

BEGIN must be used in place of .ENTRY to indicate the entry point of the main program in a program that uses any of the I/O macros described above. It does initialization needed by these macros.

EXIT

EXIT does termination operations for the I/O files and should be used instead of $EXIT_S to terminate a program that uses any of the I/O macros described above.

Commands for Running Programs

The commands described in the remainder of this section are in the VAX/VMS Command Language and are to be typed following the system prompt ($).

To assemble a program using the I/O macros:

MACRO *name* + [*directory*]IOMAC/LIB

where *name* is the name of the file containing the program and *directory* is the name of the directory that contains the macro definition file IOMAC described in Appendix D. The program file type should be MAR; it does not have to be specified here.

The /LIST option on the MACRO command will cause the assembler to create a listing file. The form of the command is

$$\text{MACRO/LIST} \quad name + [directory]\text{IOMAC/LIB}$$

The listing file will be given the name *name*.LIS.

To link:

$$\text{LINK} \quad name, [directory]\text{IOMOD}$$

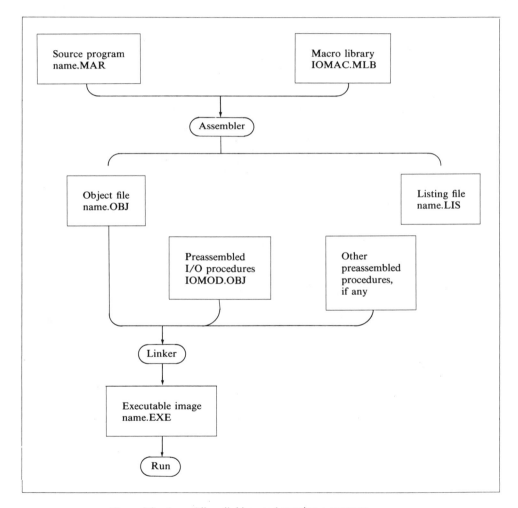

Figure 5.2 Assembling, linking, and running a program

If several modules are to be linked—e.g., if the program contains procedures—the format is

LINK *main,proc1, . . . ,procn,*[*directory*]IOMOD

To run the program:

RUN *name*

or

RUN *main*

Figure 5.2 illustrates the action of these commands. Note that program errors can show up at any of the three stages: assembly, linkage, or execution.

5.3 EXERCISES

1. Write instructions (including storage initialization) to print out your name at the terminal.

2. Write a complete program for Exercise 1 and run it.

3. Write instructions (including storage reservation and initialization) to print at the terminal the message "What is today's date?," read in the response, and print it out.

4. Write a complete program for Exercise 3 and run it.

5. Write instructions (including storage initialization) to print the words in the pattern shown below. "FIRST" should begin at the left margin.

FIRST
SECOND
THIRD

6. In Example 5.6 we reserved space for an input line by using a .BLKB directive that initialized the reserved bytes to zeros, but we specified a length argument on the PRINTCHRS macro that printed out the line read in. Why? That is, why is it not a good idea to rely on the zeros stored by the .BLKB directive to terminate the character string to be printed?

7. Set up a file called DATA.DAT that contains a list of names, each at most 24 letters long. Write and run a program to read the list and print it out at the terminal. The printed list should have an appropriate heading, separated from the names by a blank line.

8. Set up a file called DATA.DAT containing people's names in the following format: the family name appears first and is 12 characters long, and the given name appears next and is 10 characters long. (If the actual names are shorter, they are padded with blanks.) Then write and run a program that reads the names from the file and prints them out at the terminal with the given name first.

9. Suppose the DATA.DAT file contains data for a mailing list where each record has the following format:

Name	20 characters
Street address	20 characters

City   13 characters
State   2 characters
Zip code   5 characters

Write instructions to read a record and print out the name and address on three lines with at least one space between the city and state and between the state and zip code.

10. Write and run a program that uses DUMPLONG to dump the contents of registers R2 through R11. (The output emphasizes that the programmer can not assume the registers are cleared when a program begins execution.)

11. Write and run a program that initializes longwords ALPHA, BETA, and GAMMA to contain 25, −13, and 58, respectively, then computes the product of the three numbers and prints it using DUMPLONG.

Chapter 6

Integer Instructions

6.1 AN OVERVIEW

In this chapter we discuss instructions to do arithmetic on signed integers, integer data movement and conversion, arithmetic shifts, and several other operations. Almost all these operations can be performed by a single instruction for each of the three main integer data types: byte, word, and longword. Arithmetic on quadwords can not be done directly, but it can be programmed using other instructions.

All integer arithmetic instructions described in this chapter assume that the data are represented in two's complement form. There are other instructions that treat data as unsigned (i.e., nonnegative) binary integers. Table 6.1, in Section 6.6, shows the ranges of the integer data types.

All the instructions described in this chapter set condition code bits in the PSW to indicate the sign of the result of the operation and to indicate whether or not the result overflows the space alloted for it. We will consider how to use these bits in Chapter 7. (Also, if IV is included in the program module's entry mask, an overflow will cause a program interrupt.)

When a general register is specified as the location of a byte or word source operand—i.e., an operand to be used in the operation—the CPU always takes the operand from the rightmost byte (bits 7:0) or word (bits 15:0) of the register. The rest of the register is ignored. When a register is specified for a byte or word destination operand, the result of the operation is placed by the CPU in the rightmost byte or word. The remaining portion of the register is unchanged. (This differs from the practice on some other machines, where the sign bit of the result is extended through the high-order part of the register, so that the result always appears as a 32-bit two's complement integer.) All operands other than the destination operand remain unchanged by the instructions (unless the destination operand specifies the same location as a source operand).

6.2 ARITHMETIC

There is an instruction for each of the four arithmetic operations (addition, subtraction, multiplication, and division) for each of the data types (byte, word, and longword), with either two or three operands. Thus 24 instructions are formed by choosing from the options shown below.

Operation	Type	Number of operands
ADD	B	2
SUB	W	3
MUL	L	
DIV		

For all these instructions, the result goes in the last operand. If there are only two operands, the second is overwritten by the result. If the number of operands is omitted from the instruction name, the assembler will assume that "2" was intended.

ADD and MUL

Since addition and multiplication are commutative, there is no confusion about the roles of the operands. The action of the instructions is

ADDx2	$op1,op2$	$op1 + op2 \rightarrow op2$
ADDx3	$op1,op2,sum$	$op1 + op2 \rightarrow sum$
MULx2	$op1,op2$	$op1 * op2 \rightarrow op2$
MULx3	$op1,op2,prod$	$op1 * op2 \rightarrow prod$

where $x = $ B, W, or L. The number of significant bits in the product of two integers may be twice as many as in the operands, so the programmer should take care to use a large enough data size.

SUB

The first operand of a subtract instruction is subtracted from the second. This is probably easiest to remember by reading the instruction from left to right as: SUBtract op1 from op2. Schematically:

$$\begin{array}{lll} \text{SUB}x2 & op1,op2 & op2 - op1 \rightarrow op2 \\ \text{SUB}x3 & op1,op2,dif & op2 - op1 \rightarrow dif \end{array}$$

where $x = $ B, W, or L.

DIV

The first operand of a division instruction is the divisor; the second is the dividend. Thus:

$$\begin{array}{lll} \text{DIV}x2 & op1,op2 & op2/op1 \rightarrow op2 \\ \text{DIV}x3 & op1,op2,quo & op2/op1 \rightarrow quo \end{array}$$

where $x = $ B, W, or L. The quotient is truncated if necessary so that the result is an integer. Negative quotients are truncated toward zero. For example, the result of dividing -5 by 2 is -2. If the divisor is zero, an execution-time error occurs.

How Arithmetic is Done

In Chapter 3 we explained how addition of two's complement integers is done and gave some examples. The operands are added as if they were unsigned binary numbers, ignoring the carry, if any, out of the most significant bit position. Similarly, subtraction of two's complement integers can be done in a very simple way: one number is subtracted from the other as if the operands were unsigned binary integers. If a borrow is needed in the leftmost place, we borrow as if there were another bit to the left.

EXAMPLE 6.1: *Subtracting Two's Complement Numbers*

	Binary	Hex	Decimal
	Assumed extra 1		
	1000000001011110	1005E	94
	$-$ 0000000100000111	$-$ 0107	$-$ 263
	1111111101010111	FF57	$-$ 169

Multiplication and division are more complicated, of course, but the principles behind the operations are the same as for decimal integers. Let us consider multiplication. We describe here a basic, straightforward method. Actual implementations in the CPUs of different computers use various tricks to save time and space.

The two operands of a multiplication are called the *multiplier* and the *multiplicand*. A place for the product, twice as long as the operands, is cleared, i.e., set to zero. If the rightmost bit of the multiplier is a 1, the multiplicand is added to the product. The multiplicand is shifted one bit to the left (a 0 fills the vacated bit at the right), the multiplier is shifted one bit to the right, and again, the rightmost bit of the multiplier determines if the (shifted) multiplicand is added to the product. The process continues until each bit of the multiplier has been examined. Overflow occurs if any of the bits in the high-order half of the product are different from the sign bit in the low-order half. Figure 6.1 shows an example of multiplication.

EXAMPLE 6.2: Instruction Action

Suppose that before each of the instructions below, registers and memory contain the data shown. Examine carefully the results in the "Effect" column to be sure that each example is understood.

Registers	Memory	Address
R4		
FFED01A2	401A0010	00021044 = ALPHA
R6	FFFFF104	00021048 = BETA
123400D7	27480A3B	0002104C = GAMMA
R10		
00021044		

Instruction		Effect	
ADDB2	#25,ALPHA	**ALPHA:**	401A0029
ADDW2	R4,R10	**R10:**	000211E6
ADDL2	R4,R10	**R10:**	FFEF11E6
ADDL2	R4,(R10)	**ALPHA:**	400701B2
MULW2	ALPHA,R6	**R6:**	12340D70
DIVB3	BETA,R4,GAMMA	**GAMMA:**	27480AE9
SUBL3	BETA,ALPHA,R6	**R6:**	401A0F0C
SUBB	BETA+1,R10	**R10:**	00021053

EXAMPLE 6.3: Computation

Compute $3x^2 + 12x - 17$, where x is a longword stored in X, and put the result in the longword Y.

```
; This segment computes 3x^2 + 12x - 17, where x is the
; longword in X. The result is stored in Y.
;
; Register use:     R0, R1  scratch
;
        MULL3   X,X,R0          ; x^2 in R0
        MULL2   #3,R0           ; 3x^2 in R0
        MULL3   #12,X,R1        ; 12x in R1
        ADDL2   R1,R0           ; 3x^2+12x in R0
        SUBL3   #17,R0,Y        ; 3x^2+12x-17 in Y
```

Suppose the multiplier is 00001110 and the multiplicand is 00001011 (both shown in binary). We show the results of each step. (Note that the operands are sign-extended.)

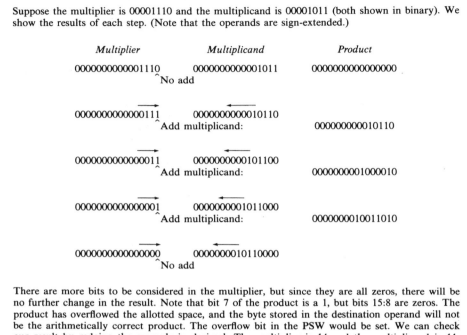

Multiplier	Multiplicand	Product
0000000000001110	0000000000001011	0000000000000000 .
^No add		
0000000000000111	0000000000010110	000000000010110
^Add multiplicand:		
0000000000000011	0000000000101100	000000000001000010
^Add multiplicand:		
0000000000000001	0000000001011000	0000000010011010
^Add multiplicand:		
0000000000000000	0000000010110000	
^No add		

There are more bits to be considered in the multiplier, but since they are all zeros, there will be no further change in the result. Note that bit 7 of the product is a 1, but bits 15:8 are zeros. The product has overflowed the allotted space, and the byte stored in the destination operand will not be the arithmetically correct product. The overflow bit in the PSW would be set. We can check our result by redoing the example in decimal. The multiplier is 14 and the multiplicand is 11. Their product, 154, is outside the range for signed byte integers.

Figure 6.1   Multiplying two's complement numbers

We have several remarks on Example 6.3. Note that R0 and R1 are used for intermediate results. By convention these registers are used for temporary data.

Instead of using R0, one might have written

```
MULL2   X,X
MULL2   #3,X
```

to compute $3x^2$ in X. The major reason why this is not good is that it destroys the original value of *x*. As a general rule, the input data used in a problem should not be modified by the program (unless modifying the data is inherent in the nature of the task to be performed—for example, rearranging a list to put the entries in order). That is because most programs that a programmer writes are only parts of much larger programs written by many people, and the data may be needed by other parts of the program.

It is faster to put intermediate results in registers than in memory. The location Y could have been used in place of R0 or R1, but that would have required more memory references. Also, as we shall see in Chapter 8, the instruction itself takes up less space if the operands are in registers.

EXAMPLE 6.4

Compute $R7 \leftarrow R4^4 + R3*R6$, where the registers contain word integers. [Note that to be technically correct, we should write $(R4)^4 + (R3)*(R6)$, but for brevity we omit the parentheses.]

```
MULW3   R4,R4,R7        ; R4^2 in R7
MULW2   R7,R7           ; R4^4 in R7
MULW3   R3,R6,R0        ; R3*R6 in R0
ADDW2   R0,R7           ; R4^4+R3*R6 in R7
```

EXAMPLE 6.5

In this example, as in many others from now on, we assume that the data operated on have been appropriately initialized.

```
; TOTAL is a longword containing the total cost of an order
; that qualifies for a 20% discount. The amount to be
; billed is computed and stored in the longword AMNT.
;
; Money is represented by integers by storing the amount
; in cents.
;
; Register use:      R7      amount of discount
;
    DIVL3   #5,TOTAL,R7     ; Compute discount
    SUBL3   R7,TOTAL,AMNT   ; Subtract discount
```

Some Special-Purpose Instructions

Some special cases of arithmetic operations are performed so often that it is reasonable to have specialized instructions that perform them faster and take up less space. An example of such a frequently performed operation is setting a register or memory location to zero. The VAX has special instructions to do this, and it has instructions to increment (add 1), decrement (subtract 1), and negate. These operations can be accomplished with the MOV, ADD, SUB, and MUL instructions, respectively, using the appropriate operands, but the special-purpose instructions, CLeaR, INCrement, DECrement, and Move NEGated, are more efficient and should be used instead. The MNEG instructions have two operands; the negation of the first, or source, operand is put in the second, or destination, operand. The formats of the instructions are:

CLR*x*	*destination*	$x = $ B, W, L, Q, or O
INC*x*	*operand*	$x = $ B, W, or L
DEC*x*	*operand*	$x = $ B, W, or L
MNEG*x*	*source,destination*	$x = $ B, W, or L

(Recall that CLRQ and CLRO with operand R*n* will clear R*n* and R*n*+1, or R*n*, R*n*+1, R*n*+2, and R*n*+3, respectively, and CLRO is not available on all VAXs.)

EXAMPLE 6.6: Instruction Action

Suppose that before *each* of the instructions below is executed, R8 contains 00009AFF.

Instruction		(R8) After Execution
CLRL	R8	00000000
CLRB	R8	00009A00
INCB	R8	00009A00
INCW	R8	00009B00
DECB	R8	00009AFE
DECL	R8	00009AFE
MNEGL	R8,R8	FFFF6501
MNEGW	R8,R8	00006501
MNEGB	R8,R8	00009A01

EXAMPLE 6.7: Computation

```
; Compute average of SCORE1, SCORE2, and SCORE3 (longwords);
; store rounded result in AVSCR.
;
        ADDL3   SCORE1,SCORE2,R0    ; Add first two scores
        ADDL2   SCORE3,R0           ; Add third score
        INCL    R0                  ; Add 1 to force rounding
        DIVL3   #3,R0,AVSCR         ; Divide; store average
```

6.3 A SIMPLE LOOP INSTRUCTION (SOBGTR) AND ARRAY ADDRESSING

The VAX has several specialized loop control instructions. We will cover these and other conditional branch instructions in Chapter 8, but we are introducing one simple loop instruction here so that the reader can begin to write and run nontrivial programs. The instruction is SOBGTR, which stands for Subtract One and Branch if GreaTeR than zero. Its format is

SOBGTR   *index,destination*

The index may be in a general register or in memory; it must be a longword. The instruction operates as follows:

index ← index − 1
if index > 0, then branch to destination
                    else continue with the next instruction

The following scheme describes the usual way SOBGTR is used.

$$\text{LOOP} \quad \begin{cases} \text{index} \leftarrow \text{number of times loop is to be executed} \\ \left\{ \text{instructions in loop} \right\} \\ \text{SOBGTR } index, \text{LOOP} \end{cases}$$

If the instruction is used this way, the index is always the number of times the loop is still to be executed; when the index = 0, control passes to the instruction following the loop.

EXAMPLE 6.8: Programming with an Array

Problem: Write a program segment to double each entry in a word array DATA. The number of array entries is stored in the longword NUM.

Discussion of Solution: The solution is very straightforward. We will use a register, say R6, to address each array entry in turn. A variable (or register) that contains an address is usually called a pointer, so we will call R6 our array pointer.

The autoincrement addressing mode is appropriate here; after doubling an entry, R6 will be automatically incremented to contain the address of the next entry.

The only problem we have is how to initialize the array pointer—i.e., how to get the address of the first array entry into R6 to start. We will use the MOVAW (MOVe Address of a Word) instruction. It puts the address of its first operand—not the contents of that address—into the second operand. The MOVe Address instructions will be described more fully in the next section.

Solution:

```
; PROBLEM STATEMENT
;
; This program segment doubles each entry in the word array
; DATA. The number of array entries is in the longword NUM.
;
; Register use:        R6      array pointer
;                      R9      loop index
;
; Initialization
;
        MOVAW   DATA,R6         ; Array pointer
        MOVL    NUM,R9          ; Loop index is # of entries
;
; The loop
;
DOUBLE: ADDW2   (R6),(R6)+      ; Double entry, increment ptr
        SOBGTR  R9,DOUBLE       ; Loop control
```

Remark: Note that the second operand address in the ADDW2 instruction is computed before R6 is incremented, and that that address is used for both the second summand and the location for the sum.

The program segment in the example above contains more lines of comments than of instructions. This is not unusual. Documentation is extremely important, even more so in assembly language programs than in higher-level language programs because assembly language is harder to read. The documentation block at the beginning of a program segment should contain a statement of the problem and of the data types used, a description of the method that points out any special or unusual things done, and a list of registers used and their roles. The program above does not describe the method used to solve the problem because it is straightforward.

Virtually every instruction in a program should have a brief comment on it that explains what the instruction does in terms of the problem. For example, consider the instruction

```
     MULL3    R7,R9,R10            ; pay = hours x wage
```

If the comment instead had been "put product of R7 and R9 in R10," it would have been just about worthless.

Note the use of blank comment lines to separate sections of the documentation and instructions. They make the program a little easier to read and are therefore very useful.

EXAMPLE 6.9: Programming with an Array

Problem: Write a program segment to store in each entry of a longword array LIST the entry's index number (starting with 1). The array size is stored in NUM, a longword.

Discussion of solution: The index used to control the loop in the SOBGTR instruction may also be used as the value to be stored in the array entries, but since SOBGTR counts down from the maximum index value to zero, we will fill the array backward. Therefore, the autodecrement addressing mode is the appropriate mode to use for addressing the array entries. Since this mode decrements an address before using it, we should initialize our array pointer just beyond the end of the array. Each entry takes up four bytes, so the address after the last entry is LIST + 4*(NUM). See Fig. 6.2 for an illustration.

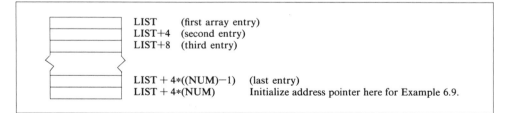

Figure 6.2 Addresses of array entries

Solution:

```
; PROBLEM STATEMENT
;
; This program stores in each entry of the longword array
; LIST the entry's index number. The array size is in NUM,
; a longword.
;
```

```
; METHOD
;
; The array is filled from the end to the beginning so that
; the loop index may be used as the array index value also.
;
; Register use:      R0        scratch
;                    R6        loop index
;                    R10       array pointer
;
; Initialization
;
        MOVL    NUM,R6          ; Loop index is # of entries
        MOVAL   LIST,R10        ; Initialize array pointer
        MULL3   #4,R6,R0        ;    4*(NUM) in R0
        ADDL2   R0,R10          ;    LIST+4*(NUM)
;
; The loop
;
STORE:  MOVL    R6,-(R10)       ; Store index, decrement ptr
        SOBGTR  R6,STORE        ; Loop control
```

This example illustrates or suggests several important points about loops, arrays, and some of the particular instructions used.

The index used to control the loop may be used in other instructions in the loop. One must be careful, though, to ensure that the loop index is not modified by any but the loop control instruction so that the instructions are executed the proper number of times.

What if (NUM) = 0? That is, what if the array were empty? A longword 0 would be stored at LIST. Usually it is necessary to test for the special case of the empty array. We will return to this point in Chapter 7 when we consider the general problem of loops that must, in some cases, be executed zero times.

The computation of the initial value for the array pointer required several instructions. Expressions are permitted for operands, so a novice might have thought of trying

```
        MOVAL   LIST+4*NUM,R10
```

This will not work because the value of NUM to the assembler is the address where the datum called NUM is stored. The datum (i.e., the contents of NUM) must be added at execution time with an ADDL instruction. The value of the datum is unknown at assembly time; it may be read in as input or computed by another part of the program.

If we wanted the program to compute the address of the last array entry, it could do so as follows:

```
        MOVAL   LIST-4,R10
        MULL3   #4,NUM,R0
        ADDL2   R0,R10
```

The expression LIST-4 can be computed by the assembler; a SUB instruction is not needed at execution time to subtract the 4.

Because of the variety of loop control instructions and addressing modes available on the VAX, this programming problem could have been solved several other ways. A few of them will be pointed out in exercises and in later sections.

EXAMPLE 6.10: Two-Dimensional Arrays

Problem: Compute the trace of a square n-by-n array of longwords. (The trace is the sum of the entries on the main diagonal.)

Discussion: Two-dimensional arrays are usually stored row by row. That is, the first entry of the second row is stored in memory immediately following last entry of the first row, and so on, as illustrated in Fig. 6.3. (Fortran compilers store two-dimensional array entries column by column, but that is not the usual scheme.) Thus the diagonal entries are $n + 1$ entries, or $4 * (n + 1)$ bytes, apart.

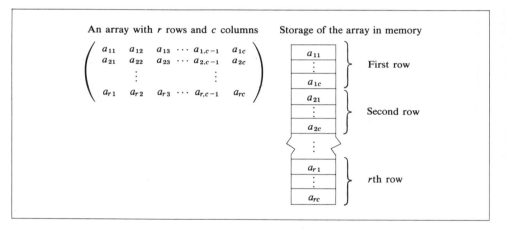

Figure 6.3   Storage of two-dimensional arrays

Solution: We assume the array is called MATRIX, N is a longword containing its dimension, and the trace is to be stored in the longword TRACE.

```
; Register use:        R6      address of a diagonal entry
;                      R7      loop index
;                      R8      trace
;                      R9      4*(n+1), the address increment
;
        MOVAL   MATRIX,R6       ; Set pointer to first entry
        MOVL    N,R7            ; Initialize loop index
        CLRL    R8              ; Clear for trace
        ADDL3   #1,R7,R9        ; n+1
        MULL2   #4,R9           ; 4*(n+1)
;
```

```
ADD:    ADDL2   (R6),R8        ; Add diagonal entry
        ADDL2   R9,R6          ; Increment pointer
        SOBGTR  R7,ADD         ; Loop control
        MOVL    R8,TRACE       ; Store trace
```

6.4 MOVING AND CONVERTING

Integer Move Instructions

The MOV (move) instructions copy the first operand into the second. The general format is

$$MOVx \qquad source, destination$$

where x = B, W, L, Q, or O. As we have indicated before (and will not repeat for instructions introduced later), only the rightmost byte or word of a register is copied or modified when the data type is B or W and register mode is used. Also, if Rn is specified as an operand of MOVQ or MOVO, the actual operand occupies two or four consecutive registers, respectively. The MOV instructions, like the arithmetic instructions, set condition code bits in the PSW to indicate the sign of the datum; they can be tested for conditional branching.

The source and destination operands for a MOV instruction must be of the same data type. Sometimes a programmer must extend or shorten the representation of an integer. The CVT (ConVerT) instructions convert between the various signed integer types. Conversion of a signed integer to one with more bits is done by sign extension—that is, by copying the sign bit into all the new bit positions at the high-order end of the destination operand. Converting from a longer representation to a shorter one is done by dropping the leftmost bits. Of course it is possible that the source operand may not fit in the smaller destination; in this case the overflow condition code is set (and a program interrupt will occur if IV was specified in the program's entry mask). Conversion from a long representation to a shorter one is successful if all the bits dropped are identical to the sign bit of the result.

The ConVerT instructions are as follows:

$$CVTxy \qquad source, destination \qquad \begin{array}{l} x = \text{B, W, or L} \\ y = \text{B, W, or L} \\ x \text{ not equal } y \end{array}$$

EXAMPLE 6.11: Integer Conversions

Suppose R5 contains FFE729A0 before each of the following instructions:

Instruction		*Effect on* R5
CVTBW	R5,R5	FFE7FFA0
CVTWL	R5,R5	000029A0
CVTBL	R5,R5	FFFFFFA0

EXAMPLE 6.12

Suppose R6 contains 000000B4. The instruction

       CVTLW   R6,(R8)

will put 00B4 in the word whose address is in R8. The instruction

       CVTWB   R6,(R8)

will put B4 in the byte whose address is in R8, but this is not a proper conversion because the word 00B4 is positive, but the byte B4 would be interpreted as a negative two's complement integer.

EXAMPLE 6.13

We wish to compute

$$10*\text{number} + \text{digit}$$

where "number" is a longword in R9 and "digit" is a byte in memory whose address is in R10. We want to replace the current value of number by the result and increment R10 so that it will contain the address of the next byte in memory. The following program segment does this.

```
MULL2    #10,R9         ; 10*number
CVTBL    (R10)+,R0      ; Convert digit to longword
ADDL2    R0,R9          ; Add digit
```

Why is the conversion in this example necessary? Suppose that the four bytes beginning at the address originally in R10 contain 04, 02, 01, and 07 (all in hex). We want to add 04 to R9, but if we had used an ADDL instruction to add the digit, the longword 07010204 would have been added.

Conversion instructions for unsigned integers are introduced in the exercises at the end of this chapter.

The Move Address Instructions

The MOVAL instruction was used in the examples in Section 6.3 to put the address of an array in a register. As in that example, it is often necessary to copy addresses. The MOVe Address instructions have the following format:

$$\text{MOVA}x \qquad source, destination$$

where $x =$ B, W, L, Q, or O. The first operand address is copied into the destination operand. The datum addressed by the first operand is not accessed or affected at all. Addresses are 32 bits, so the destination must be a longword or register.

EXAMPLE 6.14: Putting an Address in a Register

Suppose FLAG is the address of a one-byte flag in memory and that byte contains
08. Suppose R7 contains FFFFFE07. After

```
        MOVAB    FLAG,R7
```

is executed, the only change is to R7; it will contain the address of the flag, not the
flag itself.

Why is there a different **MOVA** instruction for each data type when they all
move a 32-bit address? The reason has to do with side effects of the instructions.
Recall that the autoincrement and autodecrement addressing modes increment or
decrement the register used to address the operand by the number of bytes in the
operand data type. An instruction of the form

$$\text{MOVA}x \quad (\text{R}n)+,\text{R}m$$

will increment Rn by 1, 2, 4, 8, or 16 if x is B, W, L, Q, or O, respectively.

EXAMPLE 6.15: Programming with CVTxy and MOVAx Instructions

Problem: Add up all the entries in the byte array BLOCKS, assuming that the sum
will be too large for a byte. The number of entries is in the byte NUM, and the sum
should be stored in the word TOTAL.

Discussion of solution: Each entry in the array will be converted to a word before being
added; the addition will be done with an **ADDW** instruction. The loop control instruction
SOBGTR requires a longword index, so the array size must be converted to a longword.
The sum will be accumulated in a register rather than in TOTAL because the addition
instruction may be executed many times in the loop, and register references are faster
than memory references.

Solution:

```
        ; PROBLEM STATEMENT
        ;
        ; This program segment adds the entries of the byte array
        ; BLOCKS. Since the sum may not fit in a byte, the entries
        ; are converted to words before being added. The number of
        ; entries is in the byte NUM, and the sum will be stored in
        ; the word TOTAL.
        ;
        ; Register use:     R6      array pointer
        ;                   R7      converted entry
        ;                   R8      loop index
        ;                   R9      sum
        ;
        ; Initialization
        ;
              MOVAB    BLOCKS,R6        ; Array address
              CVTBL    NUM,R8           ; Loop index
              CLRW     R9               ; Clear for sum
        ;
```

```
; Addition loop
;
NEXT:    CVTBW    (R6)+,R7          ; Fetch and convert entry
         ADDW2    R7,R9             ; Add entry
         SOBGTR   R8,NEXT           ; Loop control
         MOVW     R9,TOTAL          ; Store sum
```

EXAMPLE 6.16: Reading and Storing an Entire File

Problem: The disk file DATA.DAT contains a list of names, each with 20 characters (some of which may be blanks). Space in memory has been reserved for 50 names at NAMES. Read the list into memory, keeping a count of the number of names actually in the file, and print the list out at the terminal. The number of names read should be stored in the longword COUNT.

Discussion of solution: When the end of the file is reached, the READRCRD macro automatically causes a branch to the instruction labeled EOF. Thus there will be an exit from the loop when the end of the file is encountered. However, since the file may contain more than 50 records, we must explicitly ensure that no more than 50 records are read in; otherwise instructions and/or other data could be overwritten.

Solution:

```
;
; Register use:        R6      array pointer
;                      R7      loop counter
; Initialization
;
         MOVAB    NAMES,R6          ; Initialize array ptr
         MOVL     #50,R7            ; Read at most 50 records
;
READ:    READRCRD (R6)             ; Read next name
         PRINTCHRS (R6),#20         ; Print name
         ADDL2    #20,R6            ; Increment address
         SOBGTR   R7,READ           ; Loop control
EOF:     SUBL3    R7,#50,COUNT      ; Compute and store COUNT
```

Moving Character Strings

The MOVC3 (MOVe Characters, 3 operands) instruction was introduced in Section 5.1. We suggest that readers who skipped Chapter 5 go back now to read the description of this useful instruction.

6.5 CONVERSION BETWEEN CHARACTER CODE AND TWO'S COMPLEMENT

The Problem

When data are read in by an assembly language program, they are read as a sequence of characters and stored in memory in character code, one to a byte. If the data are integers and we want to do a lot of computation with them, or if we wish to store a large number of integer data, we convert the character code to two's complement representation. Two's complement is used because arithmetic is faster on numbers in this form, and because it takes less space to store an integer in two's complement than in character code. Many computers, including the VAX, have an intermediate data type called packed decimal. Packed decimal data are more compact than character code, but not as compact as two's complement. There are instructions that do arithmetic on packed decimal integers, but they are slower than two's complement arithmetic instructions. Packed decimal instructions will be covered in Chapter 13; in this section we will be interested in this format only as an intermediate step in the conversions between character code and two's complement.

Conversion between two data representations is not a trivial task. Without the powerful instructions available on some large modern computers, conversions require a lot of work—and a lot of thought about how to accomplish the task. In this section we will describe the VAX instructions that do the job. In Chapter 7, after we have more techniques available, we will consider the conversions in more depth to see how they might be done on a computer without special conversion instructions.

Leading Separate Numeric and Packed Decimal Data

The VAX has a data format called *leading separate numeric,* which is simply a signed integer in character code (with at most 31 digits). The sign may be $+$, $-$, or blank. The character codes occupy consecutive bytes of memory, with the sign in the lowest-addressed byte. We will draw diagrams of such data in memory with the lowest-addressed byte at the left so the characters may be read naturally, left to right. Figure 6.4(a) shows the format of a leading separate numeric string. The address of the string is the address of its sign byte—i.e., its lowest-addressed byte.

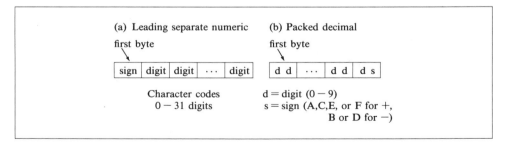

Figure 6.4 Leading separate numeric and packed decimal data formats

EXAMPLE 6.17: A Leading Separate Numeric String

For any character *c,* '*c*' denotes the hex character code. Note that the character codes for digits are in the range 30_{16}–39_{16}.

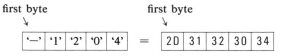

In *packed decimal* format, digits are "packed" two to a byte. This can be done because the value of each decimal digit can be represented in four bits in binary (0000–1001). The sign of the integer is in the rightmost half of the last byte; that is, the sign shares a byte with the integer's least significant digit. Since the bit patterns 0000–1001 are used for digits, the patterns 1010–1111 (the hex digits A–F) are available to represent signs. They are used as follows:

A, C, E, and F   represent +.
B and D   represent −.

C and D are the representations use by instructions that convert data to packed decimal form.

A packed decimal number may have at most 31 digits. Its address is the address of its lowest-numbered byte. As with leading separate numeric, the diagrams show the lowest-addressed byte at the left so that the datum can be read naturally, left to right. Figure 6.4(b) shows the format for packed decimal.

EXAMPLE 6.18: A Packed Decimal Datum

first byte

The datum is -1204_{10}.

Converting from Character Code to Two's Complement

The VAX has an instruction that converts from leading separate numeric to packed decimal, an instruction that converts from packed decimal to two's complement long-words, and two instructions that reverse these conversions. We will consider first the conversions that would be done on input—i.e., conversion from character code to two's complement.

The CVTSP instruction converts leading separate numeric to packed decimal. Its format is

CVTSP   *s_num_digits,lsn,p_num_digits,packed*

The first operand specifies the number of digits (*not* counting the sign) in the leading separate numeric string, and the second operand is the address of the string (i.e., the address of the byte containing the sign). The third operand specifies the number of digits (*not* the number of bytes) to be put in the packed decimal result, and the last operand is the address for the result. If the number of digits specified for the packed decimal result exceeds the number specified for the source, the leftmost digits will be filled with zeros. (If too few digits are specified, the result will be truncated, perhaps producing an incorrect value.)

> *Warning:* CVTSP *(and the other conversion instructions described in this section) use registers* R0–R3 *for scratch work, destroying the original contents of these registers.*

The CVT instructions must be used with care; there are many ways in which errors can occur. The source operand must be a leading separate numeric string; that is, the first byte must contain the character code for a +, −, or blank, and each of the other bytes must contain the character code for a digit. If the source contains a bad byte, or if the number of digits specified for either operand is outside the range 0–31, then a program exception, called a *reserved-operand fault* (an error condition usually causing program termination), will occur. If the source and destination operands overlap, the results of the instruction are unpredictable; in other words, a leading separate numeric string cannot be converted to packed decimal "in place."

> *EXAMPLE 6.19: Converting from Leading Separate Numeric to Packed Decimal*

Suppose the bytes beginning at DATUM are as follows:

DATUM

| 2D | 31 | 32 | 30 | 34 |

The instruction

```
CVTSP   #4,DATUM,#5,PKD
```

will cause the bytes beginning at PKD to be filled as follows:

PKD

| 01 | 20 | 4D |

Note that a packed decimal number always has an odd number of digits. If the programmer had specified #4 as the third operand of the CVTSP instruction in Example 6.19, three full bytes would have been filled (with five digits) anyway.

The CVTPL instruction converts from packed decimal format to a two's complement longword integer. Its format is

CVTPL   *p_num_digits,packed,long*

where the first two operands are the number of digits (not the number of bytes) in and the address of the packed decimal datum, and the third operand specifies the longword destination.

Many of the warnings mentioned above for the CVTSP instruction apply to CVTPL also: R0–R3 are used for scratch work (but they can be used as the destination operand because the result is stored last), the number of digits must be between 0 and 31, and the source operand must be in packed decimal format. Overflow can occur with CVTPL, since the largest two's complement longword integer has only ten digits. CVTPL will work properly if the operands overlap.

EXAMPLE 6.20: Converting Packed Decimal to Two's Complement

Using the data in the previous example, the instruction

```
CVTPL   #5,PKD,R7
```

puts the two's complement representation of −1204 in R7.

EXAMPLE 6.21: A Program to Read and Convert Data

```
; PROBLEM STATEMENT
;
; This program reads a line (from the terminal) that
; contains six 4-digit signed integers. The integers are
; converted to two's complement and are stored in the word
; array NUMBERS. The format of the integers in the line is
; assumed to be:
;
;       sddddbbbsddddbbbsddddbbbsddddbbbsddddbbbsdddd
;
; where              s = sign (+, −, or blank)
;                    d = digit (There may be leading zeros.)
;                    b = blank
;
;
;
NUMBERS: .BLKW    6
LINE:    .BLKB    100
PKD:     .BLKB    3
;
         BEGIN    CONVERT
;
; Register use:          R6       array pointer
;                        R7       pointer to leading separate
;                                 numeric string to be converted
;                        R8       loop index
;                        R9       scratch
;
         MOVAW    NUMBERS,R6          ; Initialize array ptr
         MOVAB    LINE,R7             ; Initialize string ptr
         MOVL     #6,R8               ; Initialize loop counter
         READLINE LINE                ; Read the line
;
CVT:     CVTSP    #4,(R7),#4,PKD      ; Convert to packed
         CVTPL    #4,PKD,R9           ; Convert to long
         CVTLW    R9,(R6)+            ; Convert to word and store
         ADDL2    #8,R7               ; Increment string ptr
         SOBGTR   R8,CVT              ; Loop control
;
```

⟨instructions to do some work on the data⟩
```
EXIT
.END    CONVERT
```

Remarks: The rigid format of the input makes the programmer's task of finding and converting the input data quite simple. However, it would be more convenient for the user of the program if the input could be typed in a less rigid format (for example, not requiring leading zeros on numbers with fewer than four digits). The test and loop instructions that will be presented in Chapter 7 can be used to process free-format input.

Converting from Two's Complement to Character Code

To print out integer data that are represented internally in two's complement, the process described above is reversed; that is, we convert first from two's complement to packed decimal, then to leading separate numeric. The instructions used are CVTLP and CVTPS.

CVTLP   long,p_num_digits,packed

converts a longword (the first operand) from two's complement to packed decimal. The second and third operands are the number of digits allowed for the packed result and the address where it is to be stored.

CVTPS   p_num_digits,packed,s_num_digits,lsn

converts from packed decimal to leading separate numeric. (The source and destination operands must not overlap.) CVTPS always puts a + or − character in the leading separate numeric result; i.e., it does not leave the sign blank for a positive number.

For both instructions, if the number of significant digits in the source operand is smaller than the number specified for the destination, leading zeros will be filled in. If the actual number of digits is larger than what is specified for the destination, then overflow occurs and the result stored is not the correct value.

EXAMPLE 6.22: Converting and Printing a Result

Suppose R4 contains a longword integer known to be no larger than 50,000, and we want to print the integer with an appropriate message. The following assembler directives set up the message and reserve storage space used for the conversions.

```
LINE:   .ASCII   /The answer is /
LSN:    .BLKB    7           ; 6 bytes for lsn, 1 for 0's
PKD:    .BLKB    3
```

Suppose R4 contains 000001E3. The conversion instructions and their effects are

```
CVTLP   R4,#5,PKD        ; Convert answer to packed
```

which produces

PKD
↘
| 00 | 48 | 3C |

and

CVTPS   #5,PKD,#5,LSN   ; Convert answer to lsn

which produces

LSN   **LSN**
↘   ↘
| 2B | 30 | 30 | 34 | 38 | 33 | = | '+' | '0' | '0' | '4' | '8' | '3' |

The message and the number may be printed out using

PRINTCHRS LINE   ; Print answer

which prints the line

The answer is +00483

Generally, we don't want the plus sign and the leading zeros to be printed. They can be eliminated, but not with instructions we have covered so far.

6.6   SUMMARY

There are signed integer arithmetic instructions to add, subtract, multiply, and divide bytes, words, and longwords. There are two-operand and three-operand versions of each kind of instruction. Integer division instructions truncate the quotient toward zero.

Byte and word instructions with register operands use only the rightmost byte or word, respectively, of the register.

There are special instructions to increment, decrement, clear (set to zero), and negate.

TABLE 6.1   Integer Ranges

Type	Bits	Range (signed)	Range (unsigned)
—	n	-2^{n-1} to $2^{n-1}-1$	0 to 2^n-1
Byte	8	-128 to 127	0 to 255
Word	16	$-32{,}768$ to 32,767	0 to 65,535
Longword	32	$-2{,}147{,}483{,}648$ to 2,147,483,647	0 to 4,294,967,295
Quadword	64	-2^{63} to $2^{63}-1$	0 to $2^{64}-1$

TABLE 6.2 Instructions

Arithmetic

ADDx2	*op1,op2*	x = B, W, or L	$op1 + op2 \to op2$
ADDx3	*op1,op2,sum*	"	$op1 + op2 \to sum$
SUBx2	*op1,op2*	"	$op2 - op1 \to op2$
SUBx3	*op1,op2,dif*	"	$op2 - op1 \to dif$
MULx2	*op1,op2*	"	$op1 * op2 \to op2$
MULx3	*op1,op2,prod*	"	$op1 * op2 \to prod$
DIVx2	*op1,op2*	"	$op2 / op1 \to op2$
DIVx3	*op1,op2,quo*	"	$op2 / op1 \to quo$
INCx	*op*	"	$op + 1 \to op$
DECx	*op*	"	$op - 1 \to op$
MNEGx	*source,dest*	"	$-source \to dest$
CLRx	*dest*	x = B, W, L, Q, or O	$0 \to dest$

Loop Instruction

SOBGTR	*index,dest*	*index* is longword	$index - 1 \to index$; if *index* $>$ 0, branch to *dest*

*Copy (**MOV**) Instructions*

MOVx	*source,dest*	x = B, W, L, Q, or O	$source \to dest$
MOVAx	*source,dest*	"	$source\ addr \to dest$
*MOVC3	*length,source,dest*		$source \to dest$ (*length* = number of bytes)

Data Conversion

CVTxy	*source,dest*	x and y = B, W, or L $x \neq y$	*source* (of type x) converted to type y $\to dest$
† CVTxy	*n1,src,n2,dest*	x = S and y = P, or x = P and y = S; *n1* and *n2* are words (0–31)	*src* (with *n1* digits) converted from type x to type y (with *n2* digits) $\to dest$
† CVTPL	*n,pkd,long*	*n* is a word	*pkd* (with *n* digits) converted from packed to 2's comp. $\to long$
† CVTLP	*long,n,pkd*	"	*long* converted from 2's comp. to packed (with *n* digits) $\to pkd$

---

* Uses R0–R5.
† Uses R0–R3.

Integer arithmetic instructions and virtually all other instructions described in this chapter set condition code bits in the PSW to indicate the sign of the result and to indicate if the result overflowed. Table 6.1 shows the ranges of integers that may be stored in the various memory units.

The SOBGTR instruction is a loop control instruction that may be used to execute instructions in a loop a specified number of times.

MOV instructions copy the datum addressed by the first operand into the location addressed by the second operand. MOVA instructions put the address of the first operand into the location specified by the second operand. The MOVC3 instruction copies character strings from one place in memory to another.

The CVT (ConVerT) instructions convert data from one data type to another.

Conversion between integer types is very straightforward: conversion to a longer integer is done by sign extension—i.e., by copying the sign bit into the left end of the result—and conversion to a shorter type is done by dropping bits at the left. (Overflow may occur in the latter case.)

Conversion between character code and two's complement is a more complex process and uses the data types *leading separate numeric* and *packed decimal* as intermediate data formats. The CVTSP, CVTPL, CVTLP, and CVTPS instructions do the conversions.

Table 6.2 lists all the instructions introduced in this chapter.

A register or variable used to address data is called a *pointer*.

Some general guidelines for good programming practices are

Document programs well. Include a statement of the problem, a description of the data used, an explanation of the method used to solve the problem, a list of the registers used and their roles, brief comments on the instructions, and blank comment lines to separate sections of a program.

Use registers rather than memory locations for intermediate results of a computation; references to memory take more time.

Don't destroy or modify input data if you don't need to. The data may be needed by another part of the program.

6.7 EXERCISES

1. Write an instruction to divide the word at EGGS by 12 and store the quotient in the word DOZENS.

2. Write an instruction to subtract the byte at USED from the byte at ONHAND, leaving the result in ONHAND.

3. Write instructions to compute $5x^4 - 27x^2 + 32$ and store the result in the word VALUE. Assume x is in the word DATUM and the numbers are small enough that overflow will not occur.

4. Using the characterization of negative two's complement numbers shown in Chapter 3 (i.e., that a negative number n is represented by $2^s - |n|$, where s is the number of bits in the representation), show that the method described in Section 6.2 for doing subtraction will always work no matter what the signs of the operands (assuming no overflow).

5. In Fig. 6.1 two positive integers are multiplied. Use the method shown there to multiply two negative byte integers. Does it work correctly?

6. For integer division, what is the relationship between the sign of the dividend and the sign of the remainder (when the remainder is not zero)? Are they always the same? Always opposite? Sometimes the same and sometimes opposite? Justify your answer with an argument or examples.

7. Write four different instructions that all have the effect of setting all the bits in R9 to zero.

8. Suppose the following statement appears in a high-level language program where all the variables are longword integers. (** is the exponentiation operator.) Write assembly language instructions to carry out the computation.

    K = (7*I+J / LL)**2

9. Write instructions to determine the profits made by an organization's fund-raising dinner using the following data. Advertising, speaker fees, and other fixed costs were $527, and the dinners cost $19 each (tax and tip included). The ticket price was $30 each, or $225 for a group of eight. Seventy-eight individual tickets and two group-of-eight tickets were sold. Use a data size you consider reasonable and include data-initialization directives for the variables in the problem.

10. Assume that the contents of registers and memory are as shown below before each of the instructions below is executed. For each instruction, show the new contents of all registers and memory locations that are changed by the instruction and indicate which, if any, will cause overflow.

Registers	*Memory*	*Address*
R6		
000184A0	00275041	184A0
R7	FFFFFE75	184A4
FFEAFF2C		
R8		
00002479	00000B42	148DE8
R9	00175CD3	148DEC
00148DE8		

(a)	ADDW2	(R9)+,(R6)	**(e)** CVTWB	R7,R7
(b)	DIVB2	#4,R7	**(f)** MNEGW	R6,R6
(c)	DIVB3	R7,R6,(R9)	**(g)** DECB	(R6)
(d)	CVTWL	R7,R8	**(h)** CLRW	(R6)

11. In Example 6.5 the following instructions were used to compute an amount to be billed, assuming a 20% discount:

```
DIVL3   #5,TOTAL,R7              ; Compute discount
SUBL3   R7,TOTAL,AMNT            ; Subtract discount
```

Suppose that these instructions were used instead:

```
MULL3   #4,TOTAL,R7              ; 4*total
DIVL3   #5,R7,AMNT               ; 80% of total
```

Will the result in AMNT be the same in both cases? Comment on any other differences you think there might be in speed or clarity between the two sequences of instructions.

12. Write instructions to compute the average of five ages stored in the word array AGES, and put the result in the word AVERAGE. Do not use a loop.

13. Suppose you want to divide the positive longword in ALPHA by the positive longword in BETA and to put the result in the longword GAMMA, but you want a rounded, rather than truncated, result. Write instructions to do this. (Three instructions suffice.) Will your method work if the divisor and/or dividend may be negative? If so, explain why. If not, show an example where it gives the wrong answer.

14. Suppose the VAX did not have the special-purpose instructions INCx, DECx, and MNEGx. For each of the following instructions, write one other instruction that would accomplish the same thing.

(a) `INCW    R8`   (c) `MNEGL   R5,R10`
(b) `DECL    (R6)+`

15. Quadword addition can be done using the ADDL2 and the ADWC (AdD With Carry) instructions. Like ADDL2, ADWC adds its first operand to its second operand, but it also adds the value of the C (Carry) condition code bit. The ADD instructions set the C bit to 1 if there is a carry out of the most significant bit. Write instructions to add the quadword at QUAD to the quadword in R8 and R9 (with the least significant part in R8).

16. Look up the SBWC, EMUL, and EDIV instructions in the *VAX-11 Architecture Handbook* and write sequences of instructions to subtract, multiply, and divide quadwords.

17. What will be in R6 and R9 at the end of the program segment in Example 6.8?

18. Write instructions to add up all the entries in the longword array LIST and put the sum in the longword SUM. Assume the longword KNT contains the number of array entries.

19. Write instructions to subtract 1 from every fourth entry in the word array COUNTS, beginning with the fourth entry. The number of entries is in the word NUM. You may assume there are at least four entries, but the number of entries may not be divisible by four.

20. Suppose we want to copy the entire word array A1 into the word array A2, and the longword NUM contains the number of entries. This could be done with a simple loop similar to those in examples in Section 6.3. However, it can also be done using only two instructions. Show how.

21. Suppose you are given a word array DATA and a longword N containing the number of array entries. Suppose we denote the entries $a_1, a_2, \ldots, a_n$, where $n = $ (N). For

each i between 1 and n, we define the ith partial sum to be $a_1 + a_2 + \ldots + a_i$—that is, the sum of the first i entries. Write a program segment to replace the entries by the partial sums; that is, when your program segment finishes executing, the ith partial sum should be in DATA[i]. [*Hint:* This can be done with a surprisingly short loop, only two instructions, using autoincrement mode appropriately. Look at Example 6.8.]

22. The MOVZxy (MOVe Zero-extended) instructions (for xy = BW, BL, and WL) extend the first operand by adding zeros at the left end, and put the result in the second operand. How do these instructions differ from the CVT instructions? Could a MOVZ instruction have been used in place of either of the CVT instructions in Example 6.15?

23. The entries in the byte array DELTA are to be subtracted from the corresponding entries in the longword array VALUES; the new values should replace the old ones in the VALUES array. The number of entries in each array is in the longword POINTS. Write instructions to do this.

24. Suppose R3 contains $00029A7C$, R4 contains $FFED5836$, and the two longwords in memory beginning at address 29A7C contain 00000028 and $003CE737$. Show what will be in R3 and R4 after each of the following instructions:

    (a) MOVL   R3,R4   **(c)** MOVB   R3,R4
    (b) MOVL   (R3),R4   **(d)** MOVB   (R3)+,R4

25. Assuming the same register and memory contents as in Exercise 24, show what will be in R3 and R4 after each of the following instructions is executed.

    (a) MOVAL   (R3)+,R4   **(b)** MOVAB   (R3)+,R4

26. Using the record format described in Exercise 9 of Chapter 5, write a program to read in all the records in the file and store them in memory in a character array called MAILING_ LIST, then go through the array and format and print the entries as described in that exercise with a blank line after each one. The program should reserve space for 20 entries and should make sure that no more than 20 are read and stored.

27. Suppose that a sequence of lines of varying lengths has been stored in memory beginning at TEXT, with the length of each line stored in one byte at the beginning of the line. For example:

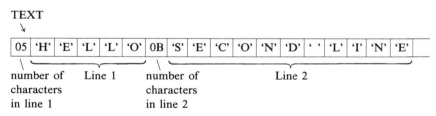

Suppose R8 contains the address of the length byte for one of the lines. Write instructions to print that line and reset R8 to contain the address of the length byte for the next line.

28. Suppose MATRIX is a two-dimensional longword array whose dimensions are stored in the longwords ROWS and COLMS. The row and column numbering begins at 1. Assuming I and J are longwords containing a row number and column number, write a formula for the address of the entry that would be denoted in a high-level language by MATRIX[I,J]. Do the same problem for an array where the row and column numbers start at 0.

29. Show the representation of the number −3105 in
   (a) Leading separate numeric format.
   (b) Packed decimal format.

30. Given the data shown, for each instruction below tell if it will cause a reserved-operand fault, and if not, show what it puts in the bytes beginning at PKD.

LINE
  ↘

20	20	2D	31	37	30	20	20	35	33	36	20	20

   (a) CVTSP   #3,LINE+2,#3,PKD
   (b) CVTSP   #2,LINE+7,#2,PKD
   (c) CVTSP   #3,LINE+8,#3,PKD

31. Write instructions to convert the word at ALPHA from two's complement to character code and print it preceded by a message saying "ALPHA = ".

32. Write instructions to convert and print out all of the longword integers in the array NUMBERS, assuming the longword NUM contains the number of entries and each entry has at most six digits. The numbers should be printed in a column with an appropriate heading.

33. Write a complete program that reads in I, J, and LL from the terminal, computes the expression in Exercise 8, and prints out K. The program documentation should describe the format in which the input data is expected.

34. Write a program to read in, convert to two's complement, and store data for a two-dimensional longword array. You may assume that all input numbers have five digits (including leading zeros) and are arranged in the input line in a standard format. The first line of input is to contain the array dimensions, number of rows first. The number of columns should be at most 12, so that each row fits on one line. After the line containing the dimensions, there should be one line for each row of the array.

35. Write instructions to print out a two-dimensional longword array. The entries have at most five significant digits, and ROWS and COLMS are longwords containing the number of rows and columns, respectively. You may assume that the number of columns—i.e., the number of entries in each row—is at most 10. If you have done Exercise 34, combine it with this one, and run the program to read, store, and then print the array.

Chapter 7

Branching and Looping

7.1 CONDITION CODES AND BRANCHING

Condition Codes and Branch Instructions

A branch instruction is an instruction that can load a new address into the program counter, so that the instruction executed next will be the one at that new address instead of the one that was physically next in memory. Most branch instructions are *conditional branches;* that is, they may or may not change the PC, depending on the condition of data just operated on. The VAX, and many other computers, use one-bit flags called *condition codes* to record properties of the operands of instructions. The conditional branch instructions test these flags to determine whether or not to change the PC.

On the VAX, the condition codes are the first (rightmost) four bits of the PSW. Their names are N, Z, V, and C, and they are located in the PSW as shown:

PSW | | N | Z | V | C |

The most frequent uses of the codes are as follows:

N—Negative   N = 1 if the result of an operation is negative; after a comparison, N = 1 if the first operand is less than the second.

Z—Zero   Z = 1 if the result of an operation is zero; after a comparison, Z = 1 if the operands compared are equal.

V—oVerflow   V = 1 if the result of an operation overflowed the space allotted for it.

C—Carry   C = 1 if an operation had a carry or borrow in the leftmost bit; after an integer comparison, C = 1 if the first operand is less than the second as unsigned integers.

Thus, conditional branching involves two steps. First the condition codes are set, either explicitly by a test or comparison instruction, or implicitly as a side effect of another operation. Almost all instructions affect the codes. All integer arithmetic, move, and convert instructions set N, Z, and V to indicate whether the result of the operation is negative, zero, or overflowed. (If a result overflows, N and Z indicate the condition of the true result, not the truncated part stored in the destination operand.) Integer arithmetic instructions set the C bit to indicate whether or not there was a carry or borrow at the leftmost bit. Arithmetic instructions for other data types (floating point and packed decimal) affect the N and Z bits similarly; the treatment of V and C depends on the particular instruction. From now on, whenever we introduce new instructions, we will indicate how they affect the condition codes. In general, the reader who wants more detail than we present in this book can consult the *VAX-11 Programming Card* or the *VAX Architecture Handbook*.

The second step in conditional branching includes testing the condition codes to determine whether the branch should be taken, and if so, loading the branch address into the PC. Usually the second step is performed by a conditional branch instruction, though some instructions perform both steps. SOBGTR, for example, does a subtraction on the loop index, setting the condition codes, then tests the codes and branches if the appropriate condition holds.

The VAX has a large set of conditional branch instructions. They may be divided into three groups: those used after operations on signed data (two's complement integers, floating point numbers, and packed decimal numbers), those used after operations on unsigned data (e.g., unsigned binary integers, addresses, character strings), and those that test for carry and overflow. The interpretation (by the programmer) of the branch instruction depends on the context in which the condition codes were set. After a test or an arithmetic operation, for example, they reflect the condition of one datum; after a comparison, they describe the relation between the two data compared. The CPU interprets the conditional branch instructions as indicating specific tests to be done on the condition codes. For example, BEQL will cause a branch if and only if the Z bit is 1; BGTR will cause a branch if both Z = 0 and N = 0. The conditional branch instructions themselves do not change the current settings of the condition codes. Table 7.1 lists the branch instructions and their interpretations. The two unconditional branch instructions, BRB and BRW, which cause a branch no matter what values the condition codes have, are included in the table.

The format of the branch instructions is

$$\text{B}xyz \qquad \textit{destination}$$

where *xyz* = one of the many branch conditions. The destination is specified by an address expression. For all the branch instructions in Table 7.1 there is a limit on how far away the branch destination may be. For all but BRW, the machine code for the instruction allows one byte to encode the distance to the branch destination, so it must be within approximately 127 bytes from the branch instruction. For BRW a word is used to encode the distance to the destination, so BRW can be used to branch to instructions that are quite far away.

TABLE 7.1 Branch Instructions

Instruction	Interpretation by Programmer		Branch If and Only If
	After a Test Branch If	*After a Comparison Branch If*	
For signed data			
BEQL	operand = 0	operands are equal	$Z = 1$
BNEQ	operand $\neq$ 0	operands not equal	$Z = 0$
BGTR	operand > 0	op1 > op2	$N = 0$ and $Z = 0$
BLEQ	operand $\leq$ 0	op1 $\leq$ op2	$N = 1$ or $Z = 1$
BGEQ	operand $\geq$ 0	op1 $\geq$ op2	$N = 0$
BLSS	operand < 0	op1 < op2	$N = 1$
For unsigned data			
B*xyz*U where *xyz* may be any of the six conditions above		Same as above	As above, but with C in place of N
For overflow and carry			
BVS		Branch if overflow	$V = 1$
BVC		Branch if no overflow	$V = 0$
BCS		Branch if carry	$C = 1$
BCC		Branch if no carry	$C = 0$
Unconditional branches			
BRB		Always branch	
BRW		Always branch	
Bit 0 tests			
BLBS *op,dest*		Branch if bit 0 is set	These do not use condition codes.
BLBC *op,dest*		Branch if bit 0 is clear	

Note that there are some pairs of conditional branches where both instructions branch on exactly the same condition code settings (for example, BEQL and BEQLU). They are really one machine instruction that has two names for the convenience of the programmer.

EXAMPLE 7.1: Conditional Branching

Problem: A person's bank balance is in the longword whose address is in R8, and R6 contains the amount of a check written on the account. There is a 20-cent check charge. All money amounts are stored as integers representing the number of cents. Compute and store the new balance if the check clears; branch to OVRDRN otherwise.

Discussion: The SUB instructions set the condition codes to indicate the sign of the result of the subtraction; thus a conditional branch instruction may be used immediately after subtracting the amount of the check and the check charge. The subtractions will be done in a register so that the old balance is not changed in the case where the account is overdrawn.

Solution:

```
; REGISTER USE          R6      amount of check
;                       R8      address of balance
;                       R10     computation
;
        SUBL3   R6,(R8),R10     ; Subtract check
        SUBL2   #20,R10         ; Subtract check charge
        BLSS    OVRDRN          ; Branch if overdrawn
        MOVL    R10,(R8)        ; Store new balance
```

We will examine how the condition codes are set using specific data. Suppose the balance was $150.00 and the check is written for $149.95. The result of the first subtraction is positive, but the result after subtracting the check charge is negative. The following table shows the values of the condition codes after each instruction.

Instruction	N Z V C
SUBL3 R6,(R8),R10	0 0 0 0
SUBL2 #20,R10	1 0 0 1
BLSS OVRDRN	unchanged

There is a branch to OVRDRN because $N = 1$.

The C bit is set by SUBL2 because subtraction of 20 from 5 requires a borrow in the leftmost place. Specifically:

$$
\begin{array}{rr}
1\ 00000005 & 5 \\
-\ 00000014 & -20 \\
\hline
\text{FFFFFFF1} & -15
\end{array}
$$

Test and Compare Instructions

Sometimes we want a conditional branch depending on the status of data that were not just used in another computation that affected the condition codes. We can set them explicitly with a test (TST) or compare (CMP) instruction. The formats of these instructions (for integer data) are:

$$\text{TST}x \qquad operand \qquad x = \text{B, W, or L}$$

$$\text{CMP}x \qquad op1, op2 \qquad x = \text{B, W, or L}$$

The main effect of these instructions is to set the condition codes; their operands are not modified at all. (Just like other instructions, they may alter the contents of registers used to address the operands if, for example, autoincrement mode is used.)

The TST instructions test two's complement integers. The N and Z bits indicate whether the operand is negative or zero; the C and V bits are cleared (set to 0).

The CMP instructions compare two operands as two's complement integers and also as unsigned integers. Z indicates whether or not the operands are equal, N indicates whether the first is less than the second as signed integers, and C indicates whether the first is less than the second as unsigned integers. V is cleared.

EXAMPLE 7.2: How a CMP Instruction Affects the Condition Codes

With the data

the instruction

```
CMPB    ALPHA,BETA
```

will set the condition codes as follows:

N = 0   because, as two's complement integers, (ALPHA) is positive and (BETA) is negative, so (ALPHA) is not less than (BETA).

Z = 0   because the operands are not equal.

V = 0   always after a CMP instruction.

C = 1   because, as unsigned binary numbers, 6A < 94.

Programming Considerations

Careful thought should be given to the organization of a program segment using conditional branches. The programmer should try to arrange instructions to satisfy the following two goals:

Use as few branches as possible.

Except for loops, branches should always go forward, not backward, in a program.

It is very helpful to write out conditional statements in a high-level language, then follow some straightforward guidelines to translate them into assembly language.

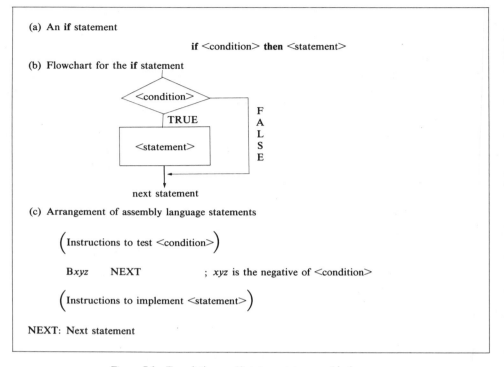

(a) An **if** statement

$$\text{\textbf{if} } <\!\text{condition}\!> \text{ \textbf{then} } <\!\text{statement}\!>$$

(b) Flowchart for the **if** statement

```
        <condition>              F
                                 A
          TRUE                   L
                                 S
       <statement>               E

       next statement
```

(c) Arrangement of assembly language statements

$$\Big(\text{Instructions to test } <\!\text{condition}\!>\Big)$$

B*xyz*   NEXT   ; *xyz* is the negative of <condition>

$$\Big(\text{Instructions to implement } <\!\text{statement}\!>\Big)$$

NEXT: Next statement

Figure 7.1   Translating an **if** statement to assembly language

Often a branch is used to distinguish between two cases where in one case some extra steps must be performed, while in the other case nothing special must be done. This situation is described by the high-level language **if** statement and flowchart segment in Fig. 7.1. As Fig. 7.1(c) indicates, the programmer should choose the conditional branch instruction to branch on the condition for which the extra instructions are *not* performed. Then the two guidelines above are likely to be met. Compilers translate **if** statements this way.

EXAMPLE 7.3: An **if-then** Statement

Problem: NAMES is an array of names, each 22 characters long. The word array SCORES contains word integers; each entry is associated with the name at the corresponding position in the NAMES array. The longword COUNT contains the number of entries in each array. The problem is to print the names associated with scores between 75 and 85, inclusive, or, in other words:

$$\text{\textbf{if} } 75 \leq \text{score} \leq 85 \text{ \textbf{then} print name}$$

Solution:

```
; PROBLEM STATEMENT
;
; This program segment scans the array SCORES and prints
; names from the array NAMES in positions that correspond
; to scores between LOW and HIGH, inclusive.
;
; DATA
;
;       SCORES    word array
;       NAMES     character array, LEN characters per entry
;       COUNT     the number of entries in the arrays (longword)
;       LEN       the name length
;
; CONSTANTS
;
LOW = 75
HIGH = 85
LEN = 22
;
; REGISTER USE    R6              SCORES pointer
;                 R7              NAMES pointer
;                 R8              loop counter
;
        MOVL    COUNT,R8          ; Initialize loop counter
        BEQL    DONE              ; Branch if arrays are empty
        MOVAW   SCORES,R6         ; Initialize SCORES pointer
        MOVAB   NAMES,R7          ; Initialize NAMES pointer
;
COMPR:  CMPW    (R6),#LOW         ; Compare score to LOW
        BLSS    NEXT              ; If score < LOW, don't print
        CMPW    (R6),#HIGH        ; Compare score to HIGH
        BGTR    NEXT              ; If score > HIGH, don't print
        PRINTCHRS (R7),#LEN       ; Print name
NEXT:   ADDL2   #2,R6             ; Increment SCORES pointer
        ADDL2   #LEN,R7           ; Increment NAMES pointer
        SOBGTR  R8,COMPR          ; Loop control
DONE:   ⟨next instruction⟩
```

Remarks: Note that the conditional branch instructions were chosen to branch on the negative of the condition in the **if** statement.

We have added a new feature to the documentation in this example: a list in tabular form of the data used and their types and roles. Putting it in tabular instead of paragraph form makes it especially easy to refer to. Such a table is extremely important and useful, even for moderate-sized programs, both to the programmer, to avoid getting confused and making errors, and to anyone else who has to read or modify the program.

Why was autoincrement mode not used for the SCORES pointer? If it were used in the first CMPW instruction, then R6 would not be pointing to the same score when the second CMPW was executed, thus potentially causing incorrect results. If autoincrement mode were used on the second CMPW, then after the branch back to COMPR we wouldn't know if R6 were pointing to the next score or still pointing to the previous one, because the second CMPW instruction is not executed every time through the loop. So R6 is incremented explicitly at NEXT every time.

The **if-then-else** statement describes the situation where there are two alternative sequences of operations to be performed depending on some condition. Figure 7.2 shows a flowchart and pattern of assembly language statements for this kind of situation.

EXAMPLE 7.4: *An* **if-then-else** *Statement*

In this program segment one of two output messages is constructed and printed depending on the value of a datum tested in the program. The task can be summarized by the statement:

if alpha $= 0$ **then** print "ALPHA IS ZERO"
    else print "ALPHA IS NOT ZERO"

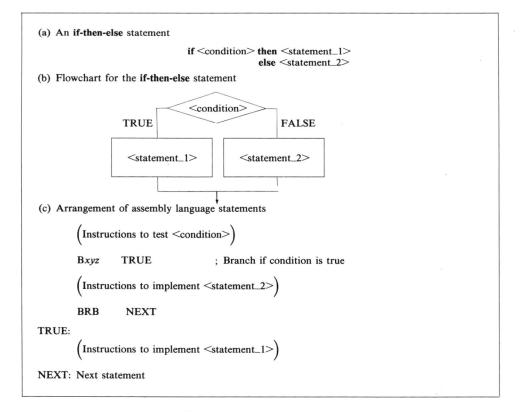

(a) An **if-then-else** statement

if <condition> **then** <statement_1>
      else <statement_2>

(b) Flowchart for the **if-then-else** statement

<condition>

TRUE   FALSE

<statement_1>   <statement_2>

(c) Arrangement of assembly language statements

(Instructions to test <condition>)

B*xyz*   TRUE   ; Branch if condition is true

(Instructions to implement <statement_2>)

BRB   NEXT

TRUE:

(Instructions to implement <statement_1>)

NEXT: Next statement

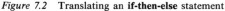

Figure 7.2 Translating an **if-then-else** statement

After considering the details of how this will be done in assembly language, we can write

Initialize message to "ALPHA IS "
if (ALPHA) = 0 **then** move "ZERO" into message
                          else move "NOT ZERO" into message
    Print message

The program segment follows. Note that we use .ASCIZ to store the string "ZERO" so that a byte of zeros will be added at the end. The extra byte is counted in the MOVC3 instructions.

```
MSG:      .ASCII   /ALPHA IS /
ANS:      .BLKB    9
NOT:      .ASCII   /NOT /
ZERO:     .ASCIZ   /ZERO/             ; End of msg marked by 0's
            .
            .
          TSTL     ALPHA              ; Test ALPHA
          BEQL     IS_0               ; Branch if ALPHA = 0
          MOVC3    #9,NOT,ANS         ; Move "NOT ZERO" into msg
          BRB      PRINT              ; Branch to print
IS_0:     MOVC3    #5,ZERO,ANS        ; Move "ZERO" into msg
PRINT:    PRINTCHRS MSG               ; Print message
```

Comparing Character Strings

There are two instructions intended for comparing character strings. The simpler one is

CMPC3   *length,string1,string2*

CMPC3 can compare long strings of bytes; the bytes may contain data other than character codes, though comparing character strings is what it is most commonly used for. Like the TST and integer CMP instructions, it doesn't modify its operands; its main effect is to set the condition codes.

The first operand gives the length of, or number of bytes in, each string. It must be a word integer and may be specified by a literal or any other addressing mode. The second and third operands specify the addresses of the first byte of each string. The strings must be in memory, not in registers or literals.

CMPC3 compares corresponding bytes in the two strings until it finds unequal bytes or reaches the ends of the strings (determined by the length operand). It sets the condition codes in the same ways as the integer CMP instructions; i.e., it does both signed and unsigned comparisons of the bytes.

The ASCII character codes for the letters of the alphabet are in numerical order; i.e., the character code for "A" is less than the code for "B," and so on. Thus the condition code settings after a CMPC3 instruction can be used to sort (alphabetize) character data. The reader should look over the ASCII codes in Appendix

C to see where various groups of characters are in the sequence of codes. For example, capital letters precede lower-case letters, and digits precede letters. The code for the blank is less than the codes for letters and digits, so, for example, the strings "Mill   " and Miller" could be put in the proper order without being treated as a special case.

If the strings compared do contain character codes, the N and C bits will have the same values, because all ASCII character codes are 0 in the leftmost bit and are interpreted as positive integers. Thus the signed or unsigned conditional branch instructions can be used with CMPC3 for searching and sorting character data.

Warning: The CMPC3 *instruction uses R0–R3, destroying the original contents of these registers.*

EXAMPLE 7.5: *Comparing Character Strings*

R7 contains the address of an eight-character name. Another eight-character name appears in memory immediately after the first. If the names are not in correct alphabetical order, they must be interchanged. In other words, the problem is to program the statement:

if first name $>$ second name **then** interchange names

We assume an eight-byte area called TEMP is available for temporary use.

```
        ADDL3   #8,R7,R8            ; Address of second name
        CMPC3   #8,(R7),(R8)        ; Compare names
        BLEQ    NEXT                ; Branch if in order
        MOVC3   #8,(R7),TEMP        ; Move first name to TEMP
        MOVC3   #8,(R8),(R7)        ; Move 2nd name to 1st place
        MOVC3   #8,TEMP,(R8)        ; Move 1st name to 2nd place
NEXT:   (next instruction)
```

(In Chapter 8 we will present another addressing mode, displacement mode, that would allow us to address the second name without needing another register.)

In many applications it is necessary to test a byte to see if it contains a particular character. For example, a program that monitors the characters coming in from a terminal might check each one to see if it is a carriage return. A test for one character can certainly be done with a CMPC3 instruction using a length of one, but it is better to use a CMPB instruction because the latter takes up less space in memory, requires less typing by the programmer, and can take a literal operand. The following instruction tests the byte at CHAR to see if it contains the character "+" (or more precisely, the ASCII code for a plus).

```
        CMPB    CHAR,#^A/+/
```

Bit Flags

Bit flags are used for a variety of purposes, particularly to indicate the status of tasks performed by various programs and I/O devices and to indicate properties of data. It is often useful for procedures, especially those that process input, to return flags that indicate whether or not their tasks were successfully completed. When a few flags are needed, a good choice of which positions within a register or memory location to use for them can make a program a little simpler and shorter. On many computers, the ideal position for a single flag is the sign bit because there are simple sign test instructions. For example, if a flag is stored in bit 7 of the byte STATUS, we can test and branch using the following instructions.

```
          TSTB    STATUS
          BLSS    STATUS_1      ; Branch if bit 7 = 1
STATUS_0:                       ; Bit 7 = 0
```

The VAX has two special instructions that make bit 0 an even better position for a flag. These are BLBS (Branch if Low Bit Set, i.e., is 1) and BLBC (Branch if Low Bit Clear, i.e., is 0). These instructions do both the indicated test and the conditional branch. They do not affect or test the condition codes. Their format is

$$\text{BLB}x \qquad operand, destination$$

where x = S or C. Although only bit 0 is examined, the first operand is assumed to be a longword. (This is relevant if an addressing mode such as autoincrement is used.) The branch destination must be within roughly 127 bytes from the BLB instruction.

The JMP Instruction

For the unconditional branch instructions BRB and BRW, the destination must be specified as an address expression. For most purposes, these instructions are quite adequate, but there are situations where the destination address can not be conveniently specified in branch mode. The JMP (JuMP) instruction may be used in such cases. Its format is

$$\textbf{JMP} \qquad destination$$

where the destination may be specified using almost any addressing mode. (Register and literal modes would be inappropriate.) To execute this instruction, the CPU computes the operand address in the usual way and then places it in the PC, so that the instruction at that address will be executed next. For example, if R9 contains 00028E47, the instruction

```
    JMP     (R9)
```

would cause 00028E47 to be put in the PC.

Many of the realistic applications of the JMP instruction involve the use of more complex addressing modes and programming techniques than we have covered so far, so we will not give programming examples at this time.

7.2   EXAMPLE: BINARY SEARCH

The Search Problem

There are many, many applications where an item must be looked up in a table. Each entry in the table may consist of several related data. For example, if we think of a dictionary as a table, each entry contains a word, its pronunciation and meaning, and perhaps its etymology and examples of its use. An entry in a telephone book contains a name, address, and telephone number. A symbol table entry contains a symbol, its value, and other information. In each case there is one datum in the entry that identifies that entry; in these examples the identifiers are the word, the name, and the symbol, respectively. The identifier for an entry in a table is often called a *key*. Usually when we must look up an item we know the key and want to find the other information associated with it, or sometimes we just want to know if a certain key is in the table at all. The general problem we are considering is called *searching*.

The most straightforward solution is to compare the key sought to the key in each entry in turn until it is found or the list is exhausted. This method is called *sequential search*. Programming a sequential search is not very difficult and is left for the exercises. The disadvantage of sequential search is that it can require a lot of work; at the worst, every entry in the list is examined, and on the average, at least half are. If the entries are sorted by key—i.e., if the keys are in numerical or alphabetical order—another method is much more efficient. It is called *binary search*.

How Binary Search Works

For the rest of this section we assume that the keys in the table to be searched are sorted in increasing order.

When describing an algorithm, it is natural to use variable names the way they are used in high-level languages—as names of data, not addresses. In the discussion of the binary search algorithm we will write variable names in italic.

Let *key* be the key sought. Suppose we compare *key* to an entry near the middle of the list and find that it is less than the key in that entry. Then, if *key* is in the list at all, it must be in the first half because all the keys in the second half are larger than the middle one, hence larger than *key*. (See Fig. 7.3 for illustration.) Thus, by doing one comparison we have reduced the problem of searching for *key* in the whole table to the problem of searching only half the table. The same "trick" is used again and again until *key* is found in the table or it is determined that it is

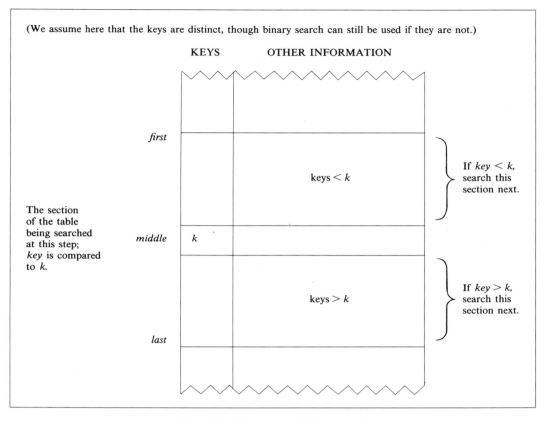

Figure 7.3 The strategy of binary search

not there: *key* is always compared to the middle entry in the section of the table being searched. If *key* is larger than the key there, the second half of this section will be searched. If *key* is smaller, the first half will be searched. Of course, if the key in the middle entry is *key,* the search terminates. The efficiency of binary search comes from the fact that when one entry in the list is examined, many other entries can be removed from consideration without ever being looked at.

As Fig. 7.3 indicates, we will use variables *first* and *last* to keep track of the beginning and end of the section of the table being searched. The index of the entry to be examined, *middle,* will be computed by averaging *first* and *last. Num* is the number of entries in the table.

We will assume that the desired output from the program is the index of the table entry containing *key,* or zero if *key* is not in the table. The algorithm is described in a (slightly hypothetical) high-level language below. Note the two tests in the **while** statement. The first, *index* = 0, determines that *key* has not yet been found; the second, *first* ≤ *last,* determines that the subsection to be searched is nonempty. If *first* > *last,* we can conclude that *key* is not in the table.

```
first : = 1;   last : = num;
index : = 0;
while (index = 0) and (first ≤ last) do
    begin
        middle : = (first + last)/2;
        case
            key = table(middle) : index : = middle;
            key < table(middle) : last : = middle−1;
            key > table(middle) : first : = middle+1
        endcase
    end
```

Figure 7.4 shows the subsections of the table that are searched and the comparisons done in an example.

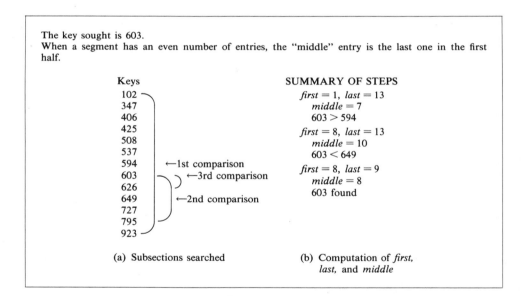

The key sought is 603.
When a segment has an even number of entries, the "middle" entry is the last one in the first half.

Keys		SUMMARY OF STEPS
102		*first* = 1, *last* = 13
347		*middle* = 7
406		603 > 594
425		*first* = 8, *last* = 13
508		*middle* = 10
537		603 < 649
594	←1st comparison	*first* = 8, *last* = 9
603	←3rd comparison	*middle* = 8
626		603 found
649	←2nd comparison	
727		
795		
923		

(a) Subsections searched   (b) Computation of *first,*
                                         last, and *middle*

Figure 7.4 An example of a binary search

Addressing Table Entries

Most of the statements in the algorithm can be easily programmed in assembly language. One point about which there may be some questions is: how do we find the key for the entry whose index is *middle?* We will derive a formula for the address of the key, assuming it to be the first field of its table entry. Now that we are again considering address computations in assembly language, we will be using the usual convention that a name written in capital letters is a symbol. Names of other data will be written in lower-case letters. The data used in the formula are

TABLE	the address of the table
index	the index of the desired entry
size	the number of bytes per entry

The address of the first entry, which is also the address of its key, is TABLE; the address of the second and third entries (and their keys) are TABLE + size and TABLE + 2*size, respectively. It should be easy to see that in general, for any index between 1 and *num:*

$$\text{address of index-th entry} = \text{TABLE} + (\text{index} - 1)*\text{size}.$$

The only datum in the formula that varies in the binary search loop is the index. The formula may be rewritten as

$$\text{address of index-th entry} = \text{TABLE}-\text{size} + \text{index}*\text{size}$$

where TABLE—size may be computed outside the loop, leaving only two operations, * and +, to be done in the loop each time an entry address is computed.

Programming the Binary Search

The reader should observe that most of the thinking about the program has already been done. Almost all we have to do now is follow the algorithm and write the assembly language instructions to implement each statement. It is almost always an excellent idea to either write an algorithm in a high-level language or draw a flowchart for it before writing the assembly language program. Then all the thought and planning about the problem and the algorithm for solving it can be done separately from the considerations of assembly language details. The high-level language program or flowchart can be used as a guide or outline for writing the assembly language statements. For the binary search program, we show a flowchart in Fig. 7.5 as an intermediate version between the high-level algorithm and the assembly language program. The first test in the **while** statement has been eliminated because we can branch out of the loop when *key* is found. In addition to doing the computation shown in the flowchart, the program must include the initialization and details for the computation of entry addresses, and we must make sure the data are the correct types for the instructions in which they are used. We also give some thought to choosing between two-operand and three-operand arithmetic instructions; two-operand instructions are shorter, hence preferred, but they cannot be used where the two operands are needed later and must not be destroyed.

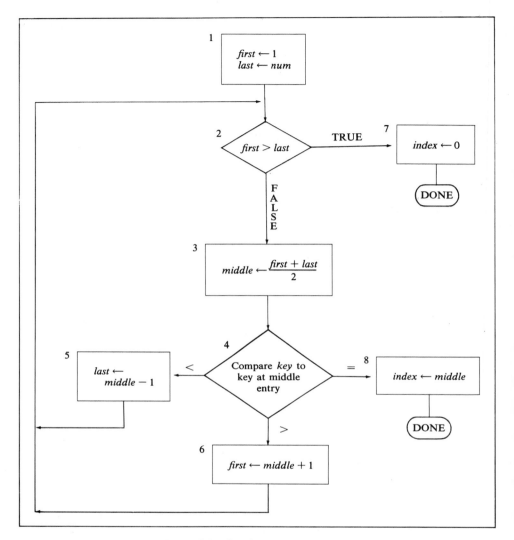

Figure 7.5 Flowchart for binary search

The program segment for the binary search appears in Fig. 7.6. Each section of instructions that corresponds to a box in the flowchart begins with a comment that indicates the correspondence. Note that well-chosen instruction labels help make the program easier to read. We have even put in the "label" RESET_LAST as a comment. *First, last, middle,* and *size* are longwords because they are used in address computations. Note that in the instructions to implement the **case** statement, one conditional branch instruction immediately follows another. Since conditional branch instructions do not change the condition code settings, both are testing the condition codes that result from the comparison of keys.

In writing the program for the binary search we have made a number of assumptions about various details; they are described in the documentation. Some of the exercises at the end of the chapter ask the reader to consider the effects of varying these assumptions.

```
; THE PROBLEM
;
; This program segment does a binary search in a table to find
; the index of the entry for a given key. If the key is not
; in the table, it sets the index to zero.
;
; DESCRIPTION OF TABLE
;
; The keys are word integers sorted in increasing order. The
; entry size is an input datum, not a constant.
;
; GIVEN DATA
;
;        TABLE              the table to be searched (address)
;        NUM                the number of entries (word)
;        KEY                the key sought (word)
;        SIZE               the number of bytes per entry (word)
;
;
; OUTPUT DATA
;
;        INDEX              the index of the entry containing
;                           the key sought; 0 if key is not in
;                           the table (word)
;
; VARIABLES USED IN THE PROGRAM
;
; First, last, and middle are used as in the flowchart.
;
; REGISTER USE           R5      entry size (number of bytes)
;                        R6      TABLE-size, for addressing
;                        R7      key
;                        R8      first (longword)
;                        R9      last (longword)
;                        R10     middle (longword)
;                        R11     address of entry to examine
;
; INITIALIZATION
;
       CVTWL    SIZE,R5          ; size, converted to longword
       MOVAB    TABLE,R6
       SUBL2    R5,R6            ; Table-size
       MOVW     KEY,R7           ; key (in register for fast access)
```

Figure 7.6 Binary search program

```
;
; FLOWCHART BOX 1
;
        MOVL    #1,R8               ; first <- 1
        CVTWL   NUM,R9              ; last <- (NUM)

; FLOWCHART BOX 2
;
SEARCH_LOOP:
        CMPL    R8,R9               ; compare first and last
        BGTR    NOTFOUND            ; if first > last, key not found

; FLOWCHART BOX 3
;
        ADDL3   R8,R9,R10           ; first + last
        DIVL2   #2,R10              ; middle <- (first+last)/2

; FLOWCHART BOX 4
;
        MULL3   R10,R5,R11          ; middle*size
        ADDL2   R6,R11              ; address of entry
        CMPW    R7,(R11)            ; compare keys
        BEQL    FOUND               ; if keys are =, exit loop
        BGTR    RESET_FIRST         ; if key >, search larger keys

; FLOWCHART BOX 5
;
; RESET_LAST:
        SUBL3   #1,R10,R9           ; last <- middle-1
        BRB     SEARCH_LOOP

; FLOWCHART BOX 6
;
RESET_FIRST:
        ADDL3   #1,R10,R8           ; first <- middle+1
        BRB     SEARCH_LOOP

; FLOWCHART BOXES 7 AND 8
;
NOTFOUND:
        CLRW    R10                 ; index <- 0
FOUND:  MOVW    R10,INDEX           ; store index (middle or 0)
```

Figure 7.6 (Concluded)

7.3 LOOP CONTROL INSTRUCTIONS

The VAX has a variety of loop control instructions. Generally speaking, they increment or decrement loop indexes (counters) and may branch to a destination specified in the instruction depending on the relation between the new value of the index and the loop limit.

   The VAX loop control instructions are designed to be placed at the end of the *body of the loop*—i.e., the instructions that are to be executed repeatedly. The branch destination is the first instruction of the loop body. Such a loop structure is illustrated in Fig. 7.7(a). Note, however, that since there is no test at the beginning of the loop, the instructions will always be executed at least once, even if the index is beyond the loop limit. This loop structure corresponds to a high-level language **repeat-until** statement shown in Fig. 7.7(a). This can sometimes produce incorrect results; an extra test before the loop body or a different loop structure is sometimes needed. An alternative that corresponds to a high-level language **while** statement is shown in Fig. 7.7(b).

The loop index may be used in computation in the loop body, but it should not be changed.

In Section 7.1 we pointed out that conditional branching requires two steps: setting the condition codes, then testing them to determine if a branch should be taken. Usually these steps are performed by two separate instructions. The loop instructions do both; the condition codes are set as a result of the incrementing or decrementing of the loop index.

For all the loop instructions there is a limit, depending on the particular instruction, on how far away the destination may be.

The loop instructions may be divided into three groups according to their flexibility. We begin with the simplest.

SOBGTR and SOBGEQ

The names of these instructions are mnemonics for "Subtract One and Branch if GreaTeR than zero" and "Subtract One and Branch if Greater or EQual to zero." Their formats are

$$\text{SOBG}xy \quad index,destination$$

The index must be a longword, and the destination must be within roughly 127 bytes of the loop instruction.

The action of the instructions may be described as follows:

SOBGTR	SOBGEQ
index ← index − 1	index ← index − 1
branch if index > 0	branch if index ≥ 0

AOBLEQ and AOBLSS

These differ from the previous group in two ways: the index is incremented by 1 instead of decremented by 1, and the loop limit is given by the programmer as an operand. The instruction names are mnemonics for "Add One and Branch if index is Less or EQual loop limit" and "Add One and Branch if index is LeSS than loop limit." The format is

$$\text{AOBL}xy \quad limit,index,destination$$

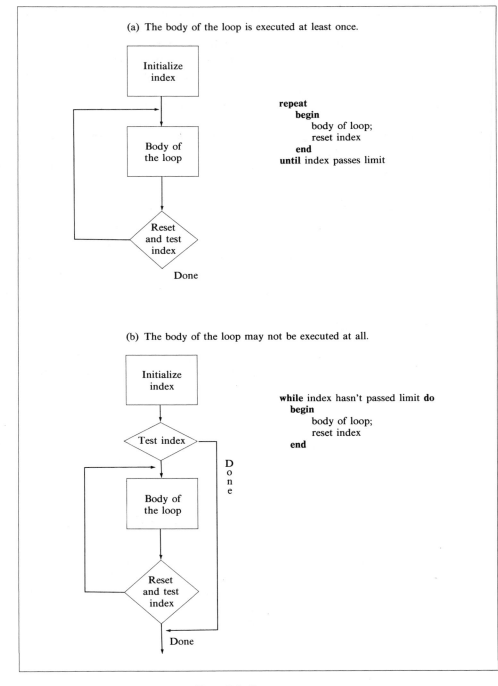

Figure 7.7 Loop structures

Both the limit and the index must be longwords, and the destination must be within roughly 127 bytes.

The action of the instructions may be described as follows:

AOBLEQ	AOBLSS
index ← index + 1	index ← index + 1
branch if index ≤ limit	branch if index < limit

The AOBLEQ instruction is most appropriate for implementing a Fortran DO statement or a Pascal **for** statement with an increment of 1. The DO loop has the following form:

$$DO\ n\ index = initial\_value, limit$$

⟨body of loop⟩

n   CONTINUE

It may be implemented in assembly language as follows:

```
; R7 is used for the loop index
;
        MOVL        initial_value,R7    ; index gets initial value
LOOP:
                    ⟨body of loop⟩
        AOBLEQ      limit,R7,LOOP       ; loop control
```

The statements in a standard Fortran DO loop are executed at least once, even if the initial value of the loop index exceeds the limit, so this assembly language segment corresponds to the DO loop without any additional tests. In some newer versions of Fortran (e.g., Fortran 77) and in languages that have a **for** statement, the body of the loop is not executed at all if the initial value exceeds the limit. The format of the Pascal **for** statement is

for ⟨index⟩ := ⟨initial_value⟩ **to** ⟨limit⟩ **do**

⟨body of loop⟩

To make the assembly language segment correspond exactly to the behavior of the **for** loop (as a compiler must do), an extra test can be inserted before the body of the loop that causes a branch to the statement that follows the entire loop if the initial value of the index is greater than the loop limit. A generalized implementation would be:

```
        CMPL        initial_value,limit
        BGTR        NEXT
        MOVL        initial_value,R7
```

```
LOOP:
        ⟨body of loop⟩

        AOBLEQ      limit,R7,LOOP
NEXT:
```

EXAMPLE 7.6: A Simple for Loop

Problem: Example 6.9 shows a program segment that stores the entry index number in each entry of a longword array LIST. The work to be done is described in the following **for** statement:

$$\text{for } i := 1 \text{ to number\_of\_entries do}$$
$$\text{list[i]} := i$$

SOBGTR was used to control the loop in the earlier version of this problem; here we use AOBLEQ. Note that since the initial value of the loop index is 1, we don't need an explicit comparison of the initial value and the limit.

Solution:

```
; PROBLEM STATEMENT
;
; This program segment stores the index number in each entry
; of the array LIST. If the array is empty, nothing will be
; stored. The indexes begin at 1.
;
; DATA
;
;       LIST            longword array
;       NUM             the number of entries (longword)
;
; REGISTER USE:         R6      loop index
;                       R7      loop limit
;                       R10     array pointer
;
; INITIALIZATION
;
        MOVL    NUM,R7          ; Get loop limit
        BEQL    DONE            ; If (NUM) = 0, done
        MOVL    #1,R6           ; Initialize loop index
        MOVAL   LIST,R10        ; Initialize array pointer
;
; THE LOOP
;
STORE:  MOVL    R6(R10)+        ; Store index, increment pointer
        AOBLEQ  R7,R6,STORE     ; Increment index, test & branch
DONE:   ⟨next statement⟩
```

ACB*x*

In the Fortran DO statement and in the **for** statements in some languages (PL/1 and ALGOL), the programmer may specify an increment for the loop index other than ±1. In some versions of Fortran and in other languages the increment may be positive or negative. The ACB instructions allow implementation of these more flexible loop control statements. They also allow for loop parameters that are not longwords; the loop limit, increment, and index may even be floating point numbers.

The instruction name is a mnemonic for Add, Compare, and Branch. The format is

$$\text{ACB}x \qquad \textit{limit,increment,index,destination}$$

where x = B, W, or L (or one of the floating point types F, D, G, or H). The limit, increment, and index must all be type x. The destination may be up to about 32,767 bytes away. The action of the instructions may be described by:

> index ← index + increment
> if increment ≥ 0 and index ≤ limit, then branch
> if increment ≤ 0 and index ≥ limit, then branch

EXAMPLE 7.7: Implementing a DO Loop with ACB

The loop

$$\text{DO } 10 \text{ I} = \text{J,N,INC}$$

⟨body of loop⟩

10   CONTINUE

where J, N, and INC are word integers, could be implemented as follows:

```
; R9 is used for the loop index
;
        MOVW    J,R9                ; Index ← (J)
LOOP:
        ⟨body of loop⟩

        ACBW    N,INC,R9,LOOP       ; Loop control
```

Suppose (J) = 5, (INC) = 3, and (N) = 28. Then the body of the loop will be executed for index = 5, 8, 11, 14, 17, 20, 23, and 26. On the last pass through the loop, when index = 26, the ACBW instruction will increment index to 29. Since 29 is not ≤ the limit (N), a branch will not be taken and the next instruction to be executed is the one that follows the ACBW.

Suppose (J) = 5, (INC) = −3, and (N) = −13. Then the body of the loop will be executed for index = 5, 2, −1, −4, −7, −10, and −13. Since the increment is negative, on each pass through the loop the branch is taken if the new value of index is ≥ the limit.

7.4   EXAMPLE: CONVERTING CHARACTER CODE INPUT—HORNER'S METHOD

The Problem

In this section we will consider how to convert integers from leading separate numeric format (or character code) to two's complement format without using the powerful VAX instructions CVTSP and CVTPL. We study this problem for a number of reasons. First, it is interesting to know how the VAX instructions might actually do the conversions. Second, many computers, particularly microprocessors, do not have such powerful instructions, and hence the assembly language programmer using those machines needs to know how to convert input data. Finally, the method we will use, Horner's method for evaluating polynomials, is a useful tool that has other applications.

Suppose that we have a decimal integer represented in character code. We know that the value of the number is given by the expression

$$\bar{d}_n \times 10^n + \bar{d}_{n-1} \times 10^{n-1} + \cdots + \bar{d}_2 \times 10^2 + \bar{d}_1 \times 10^1 + \bar{d}_0$$

where $\bar{d}_i$ is the value of the digit d_i, for $0 \le i \le n$. This expression is just a special case of a polynomial whose general form is

$$p(x) = c_n x^n + c_{n-1} x^{n-1} + \cdots + c_2 x^2 + c_1 x + c_0$$

where for $0 \le i \le n$, the c_i are the coefficients. In the representation of an integer, the coefficients are the values of the digits and x is the radix; in the present problem, $x = 10$. Thus we can solve the problem of converting character code to two's complement if we can convert the individual digits and efficiently evaluate a polynomial.

Evaluating a Polynomial

There are several algorithms for evaluating a polynomial; they vary quite a bit in efficiency. The following algorithm should seem very reasonable and natural. It computes and adds each term starting with the lower powers, and, to avoid unnecessary multiplication, it obtains the required power of x for each term from the previous one. The coefficients are assumed to be in the array c.

```
xpower := 1;
value := c[0];
for i := 1 to n do
        begin
                xpower := xpower*x;
                value := value + c[i]*x
        end
```

To compare the efficiency of this algorithm with that of others, we need some measure of how much work is done. We could program each algorithm in assembly language and count how many instructions would be executed, but that requires programming several algorithms that we will not use. We can make very useful comparisons of algorithms by counting the number of arithmetic operations done on the data. It is easy to see that the algorithm above does $2n$ multiplications and n additions (for a polynomial of degree n).

Horner's Method for Evaluating a Polynomial

Horner's method does significantly fewer multiplications than the algorithm presented above (and the same number of additions). The key to its efficiency is a particular factorization of a polynomial. The benefit of factoring an expression to be evaluated is illustrated even with a very simple example:

$$x*y + x*z = x*(y + z)$$

The first form of the expression implies that two multiplications and one addition would be used to evaluate it, but the second form shows that only one multiplication and one addition are sufficient.

Consider the polynomial

$$7x^4 + 3x^3 - 12x^2 + 6x - 9$$

Using our first method, evaluating this polynomial would require eight multiplications. However, x divides all the terms except the constant, so we can factor as follows:

$$(7x^3 + 3x^2 - 12x + 6)*x - 9$$

The polynomial within the parentheses can be evaluated by the first method using six multiplications; thus a total of seven would be done, and we have eliminated one multiplication. But we need not stop here; we can factor the polynomial within the parentheses. Repeated factoring eventually gives

$$((((7)*x + 3)*x - 12)*x + 6)*x - 9$$

Thus we see that the polynomial can be evaluated with only four multiplications.

The general form of the factorization for Horner's method is

$$(\cdots(c_n)*x + c_{n-1})*x + c_{n-2})*x + \cdots + c_2)*x + c_1)*x + c_0$$

Clearly, only n multiplications and n additions are done to evaluate a polynomial of degree n. The number of multiplications has been cut in half, but the algorithm is no more complicated than the first one. In fact, it is shorter and can be programmed with a very simple loop. Beginning with the innermost parentheses, each pass through the loop computes the value of the subexpression in the next set of parentheses.

```
value := c[n];
for i := n - 1 downto 0 do
    value := value*x + c[i]
```

Implementing Horner's Method to Convert Character Code

We now have an efficient polynomial evaluation algorithm. To convert a leading separate numeric integer we must convert the individual digits d_i from ASCII code to two's complement. This is very simple; the ASCII codes for digits are 48_{10} for "0" through 57_{10} for "9". Thus subtracting 48 from the ASCII code leaves the value of the digit. (The digit codes look more natural in hex; they are 30–39. The rightmost four bits are the binary representation of the digit's value.)

The following program segment does the conversion. Note that the algorithm used in the program has been modified slightly to simplify the initialization of *value*. The modification causes the program to do an extra multiplication and addition, so it is a matter of taste whether or not it is an improvement; we opted for simplicity.

```
MINUS = 45
LFTNBL = 48
;
; PROBLEM STATEMENT
;
; This program segment converts an integer from character code
; to a two's complement longword using Horner's polynomial
; evaluation method instead of the VAX conversion instructions.
;
; The evaluation algorithm is:
;
;        value := 0;
;        for i := n downto 0 do
;              value := value*10+d(i)
;
; where there are n+1 digits, d(n)d(n-1) . . . d(1)d(0).
;
; We assume that the leading separate numeric string begins at RECORD,
; and the two's complement longword is to be stored at NUMBER.
;
; REGISTER USE        R6      address of digit
;                     R7      two's complement value
;                     R8      number of digits (loop cntr)
;                     R10     conversion of digit
;
        CLRL    R7                      ; Value := 0
        CLRL    R10                     ; Clear for digit
        MOVAB   RECORD+1,R6             ; Addr of first digit
;
NEXT:   MULL2   #10,R7                  ; Value*10
        SUBB3   #LFTNBL,(R6)+,R10       ; Binary value of digit
        ADDL2   R10,R7                  ; Value*10 + digit
        SUBGTR  R8,NEXT
;
        CMPB    RECORD,#MINUS           ; Test for minus sign
        BNEQ    STORE                   ; If no -, done
        MNEGL   R7,R7                   ; Negate value
STORE:  MOVL    R7,NUMBER               ; Store value
```

Our algorithm accomplishes what is done by the two VAX instructions CVTSP and CVTPL. Consider the part of the tasks done by each of those instructions. CVTSP does a fairly mechanical operation: it extracts the rightmost nibble of each byte, the part that represents the digit in binary, and packs them two to a byte. No numerical computation is done. The CVTPL instruction starts with the packed decimal datum, essentially a string of digits in four-bit representation, and converts it to two's complement. Thus the work done by CVTPL is most closely comparable to the polynomial evaluation we have done with Horner's method.

7.5 SUMMARY

The condition codes are four one-bit flags in the PSW that are set by most instructions to indicate properties of one or more of their operands. The codes are N (negative or less than), Z (zero or equal), V (overflow), and C (carry or unsigned less than). Conditional branch instructions examine the condition codes to determine if the condition described in the branch instruction holds. If so, the PC is loaded with the branch destination address; otherwise, no branch is taken.

The branch destination in the conditional branch instructions must be within approximately 127 bytes from the instruction.

There are two unconditional branch instructions: BRB and BRW. The only difference between them is that the destination for the latter may be up to 32,767 bytes away.

TABLE 7.2 Loop Control Instructions

Instructions		Action	Data Type of Loop Parameters	Branch Displacement[1]
SOBGTR SOBGEQ	index,destination	Subtract one; branch if > 0, ≥ 0	L	B
AOBLEQ AOBLSS	limit,index,dest	Add one; branch if ≤ limit, < limit	L	B
ACBx	limit,incr,index,dest	Increment index; branch if not beyond limit	x = B, W, L, F, D, G, or H. The increment may be negative.	W

[1] The branch displacement is the distance in bytes to the branch destination. For instructions that encode the displacement in a byte, the distance must be between -128 and 127.

There are two instructions intended specifically for testing bit flags; they test bit 0 of a longword and branch depending on whether the bit is 0 or 1.

The branch instructions are listed in Table 7.1.

Test and compare instructions can be used to explicitly set the condition codes. Some of these instructions are: TST*x* and CMP*x* (where *x* = B, W, or L) and CMPC3, for character strings. (CMPC3 uses registers R0 through R3.)

Care should be taken when using branches to organize the instructions to use as few branches as possible and to keep the flow of control (the sequence in which instructions are executed) going in one direction, down the page, except for loops.

The JMP instruction, like the BRB and BRW, changes the sequential flow of control by loading the PC with the destination address, but almost any addressing mode can be used for the destination operand with JMP.

The VAX loop control instructions are summarized in Table 7.2. The instructions allow for varying amounts of flexibility, and some can be used very naturally to implement the common loop statements in high-level languages.

7.6 EXERCISES

1. Suppose R6 contains 001A8EF2 and R10 contains FFFE90F2. Show the condition code values after each of the following instructions.

(a) CMPL   R6,R10   (d) TSTB   R10
(b) CMPB   R6,R10   (e) TSTW   R6
(c) CMPW   R10,R6

2. Suppose R7 contains 50FA0049 and R8 contains FF0601F3. Show the condition code values after each of the following instructions.

(a) ADDL3   R7,R8,R9   (d) MOVW   R7,ALPHA
(b) SUBL2   R8,R7   (e) CVTWL   R8,BETA
(c) SUBL2   R7,R8

3. Suppose R6 contains FFEA609C and R7 contains FFFF4079 before the following instructions are executed. Where is the instruction that is executed next, at HERE or THERE?

```
          CMPL     R6,R7
          BGEQ     THERE
HERE:
```

4. Write instructions to branch to NOTYET if the longword at TIME is less than or equal to the longword in R8.

5. Write instructions to determine if the byte at CHAR contains the ASCII code for a digit. If not, there should be a branch to NOTDIGIT.

6. Write instructions to replace the word integer in R10 by its absolute value.

7. Even though there is no P condition code to indicate that a datum is positive, we can determine if a datum is positive from the values of the N and Z codes. Could all three of the properties "negative," "zero," and "positive" be determined if there were P and Z codes instead of N and Z? What if there were P and N instead of N and Z?

8. Suppose there is a byte array TAGS and a character string array NAMES in which each entry has 24 characters. Each entry in the TAGS array is associated with the name in the corresponding position in the NAMES array. COUNT, a longword, contains the number of entries in each array. Write instructions to print out all the names that have nonzero tags.

9. Write instructions to branch to SPECIAL if the byte in R8 is 7, 11, or 13. Otherwise, the next instruction should be executed.

10. Write instructions to branch to PASS if the longwords in ALPHA, BETA, and GAMMA are all greater than 1024; otherwise execute the next instruction.

11. Write instructions to branch to THERE if the word at WORD is between −100 and 100, and the byte at BYTE is 3 or 4.

12. Write an instruction (or instructions) to branch to ODD if the integer in the word COUNT is odd. (The integer is not necessarily positive.)

13. Suppose ALPHA and BETA are the addresses of two quadword integers. Write a sequence of instructions to branch to ABC if the quadword in ALPHA is larger than the one in BETA.

14. Using the information in Table 7.1, find a pair of conditional branch instructions (other than the one mentioned in the note at the bottom of the table) that branch on exactly the same conditions.

15. Write a program segment to find the largest entry in the word array DATA and store it in the word LARGEST. NUM, a longword, contains the number of entries in the array.

16. Suppose DATA is a longword array containing integers that range in size from very small to very large. BYTES, WORDS, and LONGS are three presently empty arrays, each of the type indicated by its name. Write instructions to distribute the integers in DATA into the other three arrays so that each integer uses the smallest memory unit it fits in. You may assume that the longword NUM contains the number of entries in DATA. You should store in the longwords NUM_BYTES, NUM_WORDS, and NUM_LONGS the number of integers put into each of those arrays.

17. Write instructions to read in a sequence of lines of varying lengths from the terminal and store them in memory beginning at TEXT in the format described in Exercise 27 of Chapter 6. You may assume that a line of length zero indicates the end of the input, and a byte 0 should be stored to mark the end of the text in memory.

18. Assuming the storage format described in Exercise 27 of Chapter 6 and Exercise 17 above, write instructions to print out all the lines of text.

19. Consider the following program segment. It does not do exactly what it claims. Find and correct the error.

```
; This program segment searches a character string for
; the first blank.
;
; DATA
;
;       CHARS       the character string
;       LENGTH      the length of the string (longword)
;       LOCBLANK    the address of the first blank
```

```
;
;  If there are no blanks in the string, a 0 is stored
;  in LOCBLANK.
;
;  Register use:      R6        pointer to current character
;                     R7        loop counter
;
         MOVL        LENGTH,R7       ; Initialize loop counter
         BEQL        NOTFND          ; Branch if length = 0
         MOVAB       CHARS,R6        ; Set pointer
;
TEST:    CMPB        #^A/ /,(R6)+    ; Test for blank, increment ptr
         BEQL        FOUND           ; Branch if blank
         SOBGTR      R7,TEST         ; Loop control
NOTFND:  CLRL        R6              ; No blank found
FOUND:   MOVL        R6,LOCBLANK     ; Store address of blank
```

20. Does the high-level language algorithm for the binary search work properly if the table is empty—i.e., if *num* = 0? Does the program in Fig. 7.6 work properly in this case?

21. Using data as described in the program in Fig. 7.6, except that the table may not be sorted, write a program segment that uses sequential search, instead of binary search, to find the index of the entry containing the key in **KEY**.

22. Show all the changes that must be made in the binary search program (Fig. 7.6) for an application where the keys are character strings of length six instead of words.

23. Show the changes that must be made in the binary search program to store the address, not the index, of the item sought. (As before, store 0 if the item is not in the table.)

24. The point of this problem is to modify the binary search program for the situation where there may be more than one entry in the table with the same key. Show what changes are needed to efficiently find all occurrences of the key sought. Store the index of the first entry containing the key in **INDEX**, a longword, and store the number of such entries in **NUM_COPIES**, a word. (If the key is not found, store zero in both **INDEX** and **NUM_COPIES**.)

25. Suppose that the binary search program is to be written for tables that have 32 bytes in each entry. Show the changes that should be made in the program for this special case.

26. For both sequential search and binary search (Exercise 21 and Fig. 7.6), the number of times the instructions in the search loop are executed depends on where in the table the item sought happens to be. Suppose the table has 127 entries. Tell how many times the instructions in the loop would be executed by each algorithm if the item sought were

    (a) In the 64th place.   **(d)** In the 96th place.
    (b) Not in the table.   **(e)** In the last place.
    (c) In the first place.

27. Suppose there were no **AOBLSS** instruction. Write an efficient sequence of instructions that could replace

```
AOBLSS   R10,R6,LOOP
```

28. Suppose there were no ACBW instruction. Write an efficient sequence of instructions that could replace

```
ACBW    CNT,#7,R9,CHECK
```

29. Suppose the instructions in a loop must be executed n times, where n is a longword in R9 and n may be zero. Write the initialization and loop control instructions to do this; use as few and as simple instructions as possible.

30. The general form of an ALGOL **for** statement is

> **for** ⟨index⟩ := ⟨initial_value⟩ **step** ⟨increment⟩ **until** ⟨limit⟩ **do**
>
> ⟨loop body⟩

If the loop increment specified after **step** is positive, the loop body is executed for each value of the loop index, beginning at ⟨initial_value⟩ and incremented by ⟨increment⟩, up to, but not including, the limit specified after **until.** If the increment is negative, the loop body is executed for values down to, but not including, the limit. Using appropriate VAX loop control instructions, write all the instructions needed to initialize and control loops described by the following ALGOL statements.

(a) for I := 2*(N+4) **step** 12 **until** LEVEL2 **do**

⟨loop body⟩

(b) for CNTR := START **step** SIZE **until** LIMIT **do**

⟨loop body⟩

(SIZE may be negative or positive.)

31. The sorting algorithm known as Bubble Sort puts a list in nondecreasing order as follows: Starting at the beginning of the list, compare each adjacent pair of entries (the first and second, then the second and third, the third and fourth, and so on) and interchange the entries in a pair if they are out of order. When the whole list has been processed once in this way, it may not be completely sorted, but the largest entry will be in the last position— where it belongs. The process of comparing adjacent pairs of entries and interchanging those out of order is repeated on all but the last entry to get the next largest entry into its proper place. The process is repeated, each time ignoring the last entry from the previous pass, until there are no more pairs out of order.

The algorithm can be improved by keeping track of the position where the last interchange occurred. If, for example, the last interchange during one pass through the list occurred at the ith position, then all the entries in the $(i + 1)$st to last positions must be in their proper places and do not have to be examined again.

In the following Pascal algorithm for Bubble Sort, *last* is the index of the last entry that may be out of order, *pairs* is the number of pairs to be compared, and *num* is the number of entries in the array *list*. Note that *last* is set to zero before each pass through the list to catch the case where no interchanges are done, indicating that the list is in order.

Using the Pascal algorithm as a guide, write an assembly language program segment for Bubble Sort.

```
        last := num;
        while last > 0 do
            begin
                    pairs := last − 1;
                    last := 0;
                    for j := 1 to pairs do
                        if list[ j] > list[ j+1] then begin
                                                    temp := list[ j];
                                                    list[ j] := list[ j+1];
                                                    list[ j+1] := temp;
                                                    last := j
                                            end
        end
```

32. Suppose R6 and R7 contain the addresses of the first and last byte, respectively, of a character string that contains integers in leading separate numeric format. The numbers are in *free format,* i.e., they may be anywhere in the string, but they are separated by at least one blank. (You may assume that the first character in the string is a blank or sign.) Write instructions to

    (i) find the first leading separate numeric integer in the string,

    (ii) convert it to a two's complement longword in R9,

    (iii) leave in R6 the address of the byte in the string that follows the number found, so R6 is pointing to the byte where the search for the next number should begin, and

    (iv) put a 1 in R0 if an integer was found and converted properly; put a 0 in R0 if no integer was found in the string.

33. When processing an input record, it is sometimes not reasonable to assume that the record is in exactly the form expected by the program. This is especially true of input typed by a person at a terminal, because it is of course possible that the person made a typing error or didn't know the correct format. Consider the problem in Exercise 32 and make a list of all the types of errors that could occur in the input record. For each type of error, indicate if it would be relatively easy or difficult for the program to check for the error and issue an appropriate message at the terminal.

34. Suppose an input record that is supposed to contain five integers in free format has just been read into memory beginning at RECORD. Assuming that you already have a program segment that meets the specifications of Exercise 32, write all the additional instructions that are needed to use that program segment in a loop to convert the five integers and store them in the longword array ARRAY. If there are fewer than five integers in the input record, an error message should be printed at the terminal.

Chapter 8

Machine Code Formats, Translation, and Execution

8.1 AN OVERVIEW

Machine Code Formats

In this chapter we examine how machine instructions are encoded in machine code and how the CPU interprets and executes the code. We also consider how the assembler translates operand specifiers from assembly language statements into machine code. We will begin with some of the simpler, very commonly used addressing modes described in Chapter 4, introducing more complex modes toward the end of the chapter.

For modern digital computers in general, instructions in machine code have two parts: the opcode, a pattern of bits specifying the operation to be performed, and an encoding of the operands. The details of the encodings vary with the different machine architectures and instruction sets, but we may divide the encoding schemes for various computers into two groups: those with fixed formats and those with flexible formats. The first group may have several different formats, but each instruction always is encoded with the same one. The IBM 360 and 370 are examples of this type. In the second group there is a variety of formats, called addressing modes, for encoding the individual operands, but, with few restrictions, any of the addressing modes may be combined with any opcodes to form an instruction. The VAX is in this group. In the VAX, and other computers that use the flexible scheme, the addressing modes vary a lot in the amount of space they require and how they access the operand. Thus choosing the appropriate mode can produce machine code that is efficient in terms of both time and space.

Note that the term *addressing mode* usually means the way an operand is specified in machine code. In Chapter 4 we used the same term when describing how operands are specified in assembly language source statements. In general the reader should be able to tell from the context when we are referring to source statement formats and when to machine code.

Figure 8.1 illustrates the general format for VAX instructions. The first, or lowest-addressed, byte is shown at the right, consistent with the way machine code appears on assembly language program listings. Instructions may begin on any byte boundary. The opcode comes first and is followed by a sequence of operand specifiers, the number of which depends on the instruction. (The maximum is six.) The order in which the operand specifiers appear in the machine code corresponds to the order in which they appear in the assembly language source statement. Opcodes for all instructions in the standard instruction set are one byte long. (There are optional floating point data types, in addition to the standard ones, whose instructions have two-byte opcodes. The instruction set may be expanded in the future to include more instructions with two-byte opcodes.) Each operand specifier (with the exception of branch mode) contains an addressing mode number and whatever additional information is needed for the particular addressing mode used. (Since branch mode *must* be used with branch instructions, it does not require a mode number.) For most

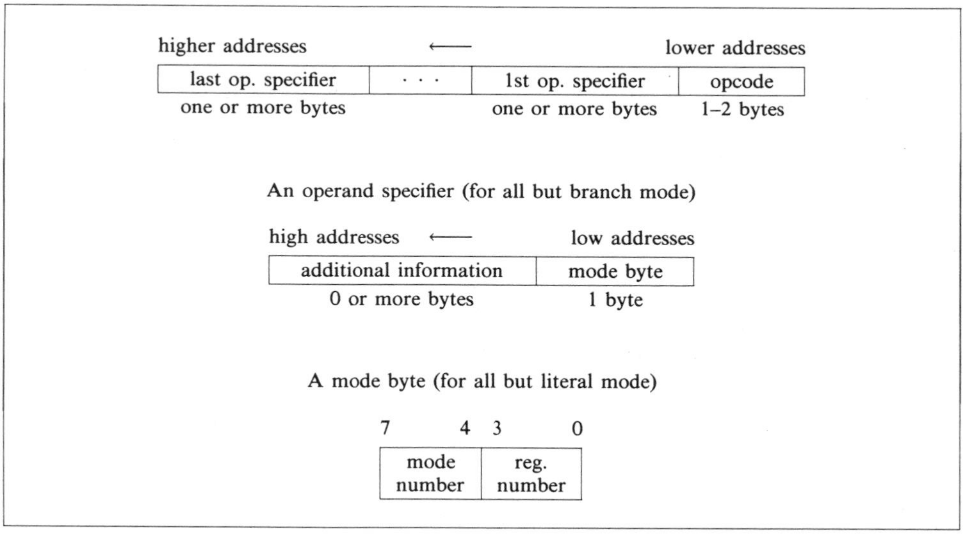

Figure 8.1   Machine code format

modes, the first byte of the operand specifier, the mode byte, contains the mode number in bits 7:4 and a register number in bits 3:0. The CPU can determine from the mode number how many additional bytes are part of the current operand. For example, if register mode is used, the operand specifier will contain the mode number, 5, and the register number. For mode 5 no additional bytes are needed.

Figure 8.2 shows the encoding of some instructions using some simple addressing modes. In these examples the operand specifiers consist only of a mode number and register number. Unless otherwise indicated, machine code will always be shown in hex. There will be some longer and more complex examples throughout this chapter.

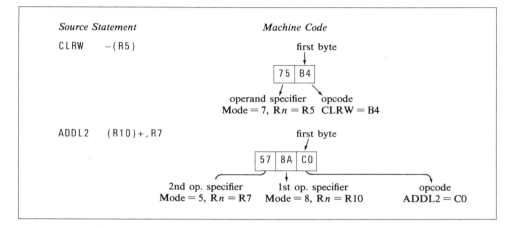

Figure 8.2   Examples of machine code

Instruction Execution

We will describe the execution process briefly here and give examples in the next few sections. The CPU uses the program counter, PC, to keep track of its place while executing instructions. When it is ready to start a new instruction, it fetches the byte whose address is in the PC and increments (PC) by 1. The CPU interprets the byte fetched as the opcode and determines from it what the instruction is and how many operands it has.[1] For each operand in turn (other than branch mode operands) the CPU first fetches[2] the byte addressed by the PC (the mode byte),

---

[1] The instructions for the optional G_floating and H_floating data types have two-byte opcodes. The first byte of a two-byte opcode is in the range FC to FF, so the CPU can determine if the next byte is part of the opcode. In this chapter, for simplicity, we consider only one-byte opcodes.

[2] The CPU does not actually fetch the instructions from memory byte by byte; to save time, it fetches several bytes at once and keeps them in an instruction buffer.

incrementing the PC by 1, and determines from the mode number how many bytes of additional information are needed. It then fetches the appropriate number of additional bytes beginning at the address in the PC and increments the PC by that number. When an entire operand specifier has been examined, the CPU computes the operand address, adjusting the contents of the register used if necessary (e.g., if the mode was autoincrement or autodecrement). After all operand specifiers have been evaluated, the operation is carried out. The PC will contain the address of the next instruction.

The Assembler's Task

It is the assembler's main task to translate assembly language source programs into machine code. We will give here a brief, somewhat simplified, description of some of the work done by the assembler so that we can understand how it translates some of the operand specifiers described in this chapter. (Some other aspects of the assembly process will be discussed in Chapter 10.)

The reader should take care to remember the distinction between assembly time and execution time. All the steps carried out by the CPU to fetch, interpret, and execute instructions occur at execution time after the assembler (and linker) have finished their tasks. Assembly—translation of the source program—is done first. In this chapter, however, we will often describe the execution process first, then consider how the assembler would have accomplished the translation. We present the discussion in this order because the machine code formats and the scheme for interpretation and execution of instructions by the CPU are fundamental to the computer (whatever computer we may be studying). The assembler is secondary; it is a program written to accomplish a particular task that is determined by the computer's architecture and instruction set.

There can be, and generally is, more than one assembler for a particular computer. Our discussion will be general enough to apply to many typical ones.

The assembler makes two passes through the module it is translating. The main purpose of the first pass is to find all the symbols used and determine their values (if possible). The assembler constructs a table, called the symbol table, containing the symbols, their values, and other information about them. Most symbols are labels on data areas and instructions. As we indicated in Chapter 4, the assembler has a location counter that it uses to keep track of the number of bytes used up so far by the data and instructions, so it can compute the address of a byte labeled by a symbol. Since the assembler doesn't know where in memory the program will actually be when it is executed, it initializes the location counter to zero. Thus the values in the symbol table are computed relative to the assembler's starting point. To correctly compute the symbol values, it is critical that the assembler be able to determine during its first pass how many bytes the encoding of each instruction will require.

During the second pass over the source program, the assembler generates the machine code. Translation of the mnemonic instruction names into opcodes is done by looking up the names in a table. Operand specifiers that don't use symbols can be encoded in a straightforward way. Where symbols are used in operand specifiers, the assembler looks up the symbols in the symbol table and encodes the operand specifiers appropriately.

8.2 SOME REGISTER MODES

In this section we will discuss the implementation of the register addressing modes presented in Chapter 4 and one new one: displacement mode.

The Simpler Register Modes

The first four modes may be considered in a group as their formats are very similar. They are:

		Assembly language format
Mode	*Mode number*	(Rn = R0, . . . , R12, AP, FP, or SP)
Register	5	Rn
Register deferred	6	(Rn)
Autodecrement	7	−(Rn)
Autoincrement	8	(Rn)+

For each of these modes, the operand specifier consists of only the mode byte; bits 7:4 contain the mode number and bits 3:0 the register number. (Recall that AP = R12, and FP and SP are encoded as 13 and 14, respectively.) For example,

$$\boxed{6\ \ 4}$$

is the operand specifier for (R4)—that is, register deferred mode using R4. The examples in Fig. 8.2 use these modes.

Since we described in Chapter 4 how these modes work, and they are fairly straightforward, we won't give execution examples here but instead will include them in other examples throughout this chapter.

Translating a source statement operand using one of these modes is very easy for the assembler to do; the mode and register number are clearly indicated by the assembly language format.

Displacement Mode

In displacement mode, the operand address is computed by adding a number, called a *displacement,* and the contents of a register. The simplest assembly language format for displacement mode is

$$dis(\mathrm{R}n)$$

where Rn is R0, . . . , R12, AP, FP, or SP. The CPU's formula for evaluating the operand specifier is

$$\text{operand address} = (\mathrm{R}n) + dis$$

The displacement may be an expression; often it is simply a decimal integer. It may be negative or positive, and it is stored in the instruction as a two's complement integer. There are actually three displacement modes; they differ according to how much space is used for the displacement—a byte, a word, or a longword. The operand specifier formats are shown in Fig. 8.3. The programmer may specify the particular mode to be used or may leave the decision to the assembler. To specify the mode, the displacement is preceded by the displacement type and a caret; i.e., the assembly language formats are as follows:

B$^\wedge dis(\mathrm{R}n)$	for mode A, byte displacement
W$^\wedge dis(\mathrm{R}n)$	for mode C, word displacement
L$^\wedge dis(\mathrm{R}n)$	for mode E, longword displacement

If the choice is left to the assembler, it will try to use as little space as possible. It must decide how many bytes to allow for the displacement during its first pass over the instruction so that its location counter can be incremented properly. In cases where the assembler does not have enough information to decide how many bytes are needed, it will allow two; i.e., it chooses mode C. (If it later turns out that more space was needed, the linker will give an error message.)

We will describe the kind of programming situation where displacement mode is particularly useful after the following example, which shows in detail how the CPU executes an instruction.

Mode	Mode Number (hex)	Format $(n = 0, \cdots, 15)$*
Byte displacement	A	dis A n
Word displacement	C	dis C n
Long displacement	E	dis E n

 * AP, FP, and SP are encoded as 12, 13, and 14 (C, D, and E in hex), respectively. If $n = 15$ (for the PC), the mode is called relative mode.

Figure 8.3 Displacement modes

EXECUTION EXAMPLE 8.1: Displacement Mode

Suppose the PC contains $24\mathrm{E}_{16}$, the CPU is about to begin execution of a new instruction, and the code shown below is in memory beginning at the byte whose address is 24E.

(The bytes are shown with the lowest address at the right, the way machine code appears on assembly program listings.) We will describe the steps carried out by the CPU and show where the PC is pointing each time the CPU uses it to fetch part of the instruction. The byte(s) being interpreted by the CPU at each step are underlined.

$$(PC) = 24E$$

. . . D6 87 01 2A C9 D0 . . .

Fetch the byte addressed by PC; increment (PC) by 1.

$$(PC) = 24F$$

D6 87 01 2A C9 D0

Interpret the byte fetched, D0, as an opcode.
D0 is a **MOVL** instruction. It requires two operands.
Fetch the byte addressed by the PC; increment (PC) by 1.

$$(PC) = 250$$

D6 87 01 2A C9 D0

Interpret the byte fetched, C9, as the mode byte for the first operand. The mode number is C so the mode is word displacement. The register used is R9. We will assume $(R9) = 408_{16}$.
Since a word displacement is used, fetch the word (two bytes) addressed by the PC and increment (PC) by 2.

$$(PC) = 252$$

D6 87 01 2A C9 D0

The displacement is 012A. Add this to the contents of R9 to get the address of the first operand. (R9) is not changed; the addition is done in a CPU scratch area.
The first operand address is 408 + 12A = 532.
The next byte will be interpreted as the mode byte for the second operand. Fetch it and increment (PC) by 1.

$$(PC) = 253$$

D6 87 01 2A C9 D0

The mode byte for the second operand is 87. Thus the mode is mode 8, autoincrement mode, and the register used is R7.
No additional bytes are needed for autoincrement mode.
The second operand address is the address now in R7.
Since the data type of the instruction, MOVL, is longword, the address in R7 is incremented by 4.
Carry out the operation; i.e., copy the longword that starts at byte 532 into the longword specified by the second operand address (the number in R7 before it was incremented).

The instruction we just decoded may originally have appeared in an assembly language program as

```
MOVL    298(R9),(R7)+
```

Note that the displacement is written in decimal; the assembler will convert it to two's complement form.

Now the CPU is ready to execute the next instruction. Note that the PC is pointing to the byte in memory that follows the current instruction. That byte will be interpreted as the opcode for the next instruction.

There are two details to remember about displacement mode: the address computation uses 32 bits, so the displacement is sign-extended if necessary, and the register contents will not be changed. For example, if the displacement is FF63 and the register contains 000045C2, the operand address is computed as

(R*n*):	000045C2
+ displacement:	FFFFFF63 (sign extended)
operand address:	00004525

The contents of the register will still be 000045C2.

Programming with Displacement Mode

Displacement mode is particularly useful for referring to individual data within a large block of related data organized in some standardized format. For example, suppose a block of memory contains information on computer jobs waiting to be run. The collection of information on each job, called a record, might be arranged as in Fig. 8.4. It is convenient, when processing each entry, or record, to use one register, say R10, as a pointer to the entry (i.e., to its first byte) and to use displacements from the contents of R10 to address the various subsections, called *fields*. The fields in the example in Fig. 8.4 would be addressed as follows:

job name	0(R10)	or	(R10)
user name	8(R10)		
time in	16(R10)		
priority	24(R10)		
blocks	25(R10)		
flags	26(R10)		

The main advantages of using displacement mode are that it provides a conceptually clear way to refer to the fields in the record, it saves steps, and it decreases the likelihood of programming mistakes. For example, suppose we want to make a list of all jobs of priority 6 or higher that require at least 100 blocks of disk space.

For this example we assume that the list of jobs to be run contains a block of information organized as shown below for each job. The BLOCKS field contains the number of disk blocks required by the job, and the RESOURCE FLAGS field contains flags indicating whether or not various system resources are needed. The roles of the other fields should be clear from their names.

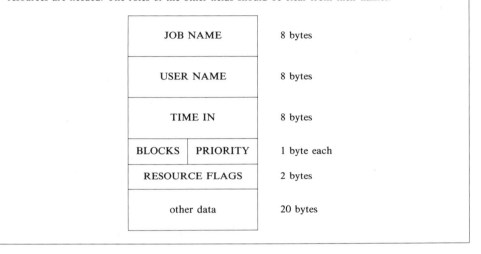

JOB NAME	8 bytes
USER NAME	8 bytes
TIME IN	8 bytes
BLOCKS / PRIORITY	1 byte each
RESOURCE FLAGS	2 bytes
other data	20 bytes

Figure 8.4 The format for a job description

Assuming R10 contains the address of a record, we would do the following steps, addressing the fields as shown.

	Examine priority.	24(R10)	
	If less than 6, go to NEXT.		
	Examine block requirement.	25(R10)	
	If less than 100, go to NEXT.		
	Print job name.	(R10)	
NEXT:	Set R10 to the address of the next record.	ADDL2	#48,R10

Using register deferred mode for each field would require more instructions, and it would require either that more registers be used or that the contents of R10 be modified, making it difficult to keep track of what is in R10 at any time because of the conditional branches. Clarity of a program, especially in assembly language, is very important for minimizing errors. It is best to use a register as a fixed reference point for each record and use displacement mode to refer to the fields in the record.

For increased readability of a program, the programmer can use names for the displacements. Direct assignment statements may be used to assign the displacement values to mnemonic symbols. For the job list problem described above, for example, we may define:

```
JOB_NAME = 0
USER_NAME = 8
TIME_IN = 16
PRIORITY = 24
BLOCKS = 25
RESOURCE_FLAGS = 26
```

and refer to the fields in the program by writing USER_NAME(R10), PRIORITY(R10), and so on. When the assembler translates these operands, it looks up the symbols in its symbol table, substitutes the values for the symbols, and translates just as though the programmer had written the numeric displacements in the instructions.

8.3 LITERAL MODE

Literal mode is used for encoding small nonnegative operands that are specified in the instruction itself, rather than being in a register or memory location. The assembly language format is

$$\# expression$$

Any mode number whose leftmost two bits are zeros (i.e., modes 0 through 3) is a literal mode number; the rightmost two bits of the mode number are actually part of the literal value. Thus the form of an operand specifier for a literal is

$$\boxed{00 \mid \textit{literal}}$$

Since six bits are used, an integer literal may have a value between 0 and 63. Figure 8.5 shows the encoding of an instruction with a literal operand. (Floating point literals will be described in Chapter 13.)

When the CPU encounters a literal operand while executing an instruction, it expands the six-bit datum to the data size required by the instruction. For example, the literal in Fig. 8.5 would be expanded (in a CPU scratch area) to 16 bits, by adding zeros at the left, because the instruction is MOVW.

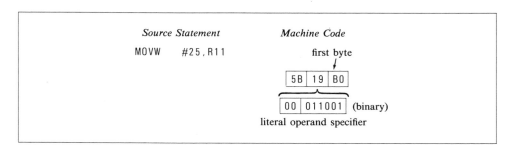

Figure 8.5 An example of literal mode

The Assembler's Task

The assembler must decide during its first pass whether to encode an operand beginning with a # in literal mode or immediate mode. If the operand is an integer between 0 and 63 (or a floating point number that fits in a six bits), the assembler will use literal mode. If it is not in the ranges required for literals, or if the assembler can not determine its value during the first pass over the instruction, it will encode the operand using immediate mode. We will give examples contrasting the two modes in Section 8.5, after immediate mode has been described.

The programmer can override the assembler's choice of mode and force it to use literal rather than immediate mode by preceding the operand with S^. The operand format is

$$S^\wedge \# \, expression$$

8.4 BRANCH MODE

Branch mode is used to encode the branch destination address in all branch instructions, including loop control instructions. Because it *must* be used for the branch destination in these instructions and can be used *only* for these operands, a mode byte is not needed in the operand specifier. A branch destination is always encoded as a displacement from the contents of the PC. Thus, if the branch is to be taken, the CPU computes the destination address as follows:

$$destination = (PC) + displacement$$

and puts it in the PC.

The displacement may be positive or negative and is stored as a two's complement integer in a byte or word, depending on the particular instruction. The unconditional branch instruction BRB (BRanch, Byte displacement), all the conditional branches, and some of the loop control instructions use byte displacements. The unconditional branch instruction BRW (BRanch, Word displacement) and some loop control instructions use a word displacement.

EXECUTION EXAMPLE 8.2: Branch Mode

Figure 8.6 shows the encoding of an SOBGTR instruction. To see how the CPU computes the branch address, we will go through the execution of this instruction. Suppose the instruction begins at byte 635.

$$(PC) = 635$$

```
. . .  B6 D2 58 F5  . . .
```

Fetch the opcode and increment (PC) by 1.

$$(PC) = 636$$

B6 D2 58 <u>F5</u>

F5 is the opcode for SOBGTR. There must be two operands—the loop index and the branch address.

Fetch the mode byte for the index and increment (PC) by 1.

$$(PC) = 637$$

B6 D2 <u>58</u> F5

The mode byte, 58, indicates that the mode number is 5, register mode, and the register number is 8, so the index is in R8.

The second operand is the branch address. Since the SOBGTR instruction always uses a byte displacement for the branch destination, fetch the next byte [incrementing (PC) by 1] and interpret it as the displacement.

$$(PC) = 638$$

B6 <u>D2</u> 58 F5

Now, to carry out the operation for this instruction, subtract 1 from the contents of R8 [(R8) *is* changed] and determine if the branch should be taken.

If the result in R8 is not greater than zero, then execution of this instruction is complete and the CPU will procede to interpret and execute the instruction beginning at 638.

If, on the other hand, (R8) is greater than zero, the branch is to be taken, so add the displacement, D2, to (PC).

Address computations are always done with 32 bits, so the computation looks like this:

current (PC):	00000638	
+ displacement:	FFFFFFD2	(sign extended)
new (PC):	0000060A	

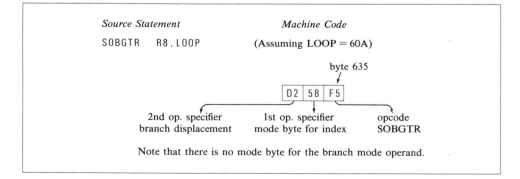

Figure 8.6   An example of branch mode

This completes execution of the instruction; the branch is effectively accomplished when the CPU begins processing the next instruction, because it uses (PC) to determine where the next instruction is.

Note that because the PC is incremented when the displacement is fetched, the branch address will be the sum of the displacement and the address of the instruction that follows the branch instruction. A byte integer is in the range from −128 to 127, so branch instructions with byte displacements may be used only to branch to other instructions within that range from the location of the next instruction.

Why Does Branch Mode Use a Displacement from (PC)?

In an assembly language statement, the branch destination is usually specified by a symbol that is the label on the target instruction (the one to be branched to). Why is that address encoded as a displacement from the contents of the PC rather than simply as the value of the symbol, or the address of the target instruction? Recall that the value of the symbol stored in the assembler's symbol table is the address of the instruction it labels *relative to the beginning of the module or program section* being translated. The module will be linked with others and may be loaded into memory at different places each time it is used. The true (virtual) branch destination address is not known to the assembler, but when the instruction is executed, the CPU must compute the true branch address. The *distance* between the branch destination address and the contents of the PC (the address of the instruction following the branch instruction) is constant; the number of bytes used to encode the instructions between the branch instruction and the target instruction is independent of the location of the program in memory. Thus several addressing modes allow the assembler to encode address expressions as displacements from the contents of the PC. By using displacements we are assured that the program will run correctly anywhere in memory without adjustments to the operand specifiers when the program is loaded. All modern computers use some variation of this displacement scheme to translate address expressions.

The Assembler's Task

Consider the statement in Fig. 8.6:

```
SOBGTR  R8,LOOP
```

Suppose that when the assembler encounters this statement during its first pass . = 235. (Recall that . is the notation used for the location counter.) At this time, the assembler determines that the machine code for this statement will require three bytes: one for the opcode, one for the first operand specifier because it uses register mode, and one for the second operand specifier because SOBGTR always uses branch mode with byte displacement. The assembler can increment . to .+3 and go on to the next instruction. When the assembler encounters this instruction during its second pass, it does the translation. It encodes SOBGTR as F5 and R8 as 58, incrementing . by 1 for each byte used. When it computes the displacement for the branch address, . = 237. To compute the displacement, the assembler looks up LOOP in the symbol table and finds, say, that LOOP = 20A. It knows that during execution the CPU will use the formula

$$\text{destination} = (\text{PC}) + \text{displacement}$$

So the assembler solves the following equation for the displacement:

$$\text{LOOP} = \text{location of next byte} + \text{displacement}$$

$$20A = 238 + \text{displacement}$$

$$\text{displacement} = 20A - 238 = FD2$$

Thus the third operand specifier is translated as D2. Note that in Fig. 8.6 we assumed that the instruction appeared in memory at byte 635, not 235, and that the instruction labeled LOOP is at byte 60A, not 20A. Figure 8.6 assumes that the module containing this instruction is loaded in memory beginning at byte 400. The assembler doesn't know that, but its computation of the displacement is correct regardless of where the program is put in memory.

   If the displacement computed by the assembler is too large for one byte (i.e., is outside the range −128 to 127), the assembler will issue an error message.

8.5 SOME PROGRAM COUNTER MODES: RELATIVE MODE AND IMMEDIATE MODE

As we have seen, the PC is used by the CPU to keep track of its place in the instruction stream. But the PC is a register. What happens if it is used in an operand specifier just as R0 through R12, AP, FP, and SP may be used? For addressing modes where use of the PC would have strange and undesirable effects, it is simply prohibited. For other modes, however, the PC can be used with very useful effects, but because the effects and uses of addressing modes with the PC are very different from their effects and uses with other registers, addressing modes using the PC are given special names and must be studied carefully. Relative mode and immediate mode, introduced in Chapter 4, are special cases of displacement mode and autoincrement mode, respectively, using the PC.

Relative Mode

An operand address specified in a source statement by a symbol, or more generally, an expression, is a relative mode operand. In machine code, a relative mode operand is encoded in displacement mode using PC as the register. Thus the formula used by the CPU to determine the operand address is

$$\text{operand address} = (PC) + \text{displacement}$$

A displacement from (PC) is used for address expressions for the same reason as it is used for branch mode—to make the code independent of where the program is loaded in memory.

Any one of the three displacement modes, A, C, or E, may be used, depending on how much space is needed for the displacement. Figure 8.3 shows their formats. When used for relative mode, the rightmost nibble of the mode byte contains F, or 15, the PC's register number.

When the assembler encounters a source instruction with a relative mode operand during its first pass, it can evaluate the address expression if the symbols in the expression are already in the symbol table. It can compute the appropriate displacement using its location counter, and it will choose the mode using the smallest number of bytes needed to represent the displacement in two's complement form. If any symbol in the expression is not yet in the symbol table, the assembler will allow for the maximum possible displacement size, a longword, and either it or the linker can compute and fill in the displacement later. This is why in Chapter 4 we recommended placing storage reservation and initialization directives at the beginning of a program section. When the labels on the data areas are used as operands later in the program, they will already be in the symbol table and the assembler will be able to economize on the space used for displacements.

EXECUTION EXAMPLE 8.3: *Relative Mode*

We will follow the steps carried out by the CPU to interpret and execute the instruction encoded below. We assume it starts at byte 13A6.

$$(PC) = 13A6$$

66 FE B9 CF 03 C5

Processing of the first two bytes is straightforward. The instruction is MULL3 and the first operand is the literal #3. We now have

$$(PC) = 13A8$$

66 FE B9 CF 03 C5

Fetch the mode byte for the second operand, incrementing (PC) by 1.

$$(PC) = 13A9$$

66 FE B9 CF 03 C5

The mode byte contains CF, so the mode number is C and the mode is displacement mode with word displacement. The register used is F, or 15—i.e., the PC.

Fetch the displacement and increment (PC) again, but by two this time because the displacement uses a word.

$$(PC) = 13AB$$

66 <u>FE B9</u> CF 03 C5

The displacement is FEB9. Compute the address of the second operand by adding the displacement and the current contents of the PC, 13AB, as follows:

(PC):	000013AB
+ displacement:	FFFFFEB9
operand address:	00001264

The longword beginning at byte 1264 will be used as the second operand for the MULL3. Fetch the mode byte for the third operand, incrementing (PC). The mode byte is 66, so the third operand uses register deferred mode with R6. Perform the multiplication and put the result in the longword whose address is in R6.

At this point (PC) = 13AC, the address of the next instruction. The instruction we just decoded may have originally appeared in an assembly language program as

MULL3 #3,SYMBOL,(R6)

where SYMBOL was defined earlier in the program section and the instruction appears 142_{16} bytes later. Note that the assembler had to use a word for the displacement for SYMBOL because it would not fit in a byte.

Two points to remember about relative mode were illustrated by this example. At the time the operand address is computed, the PC contains the address of the next operand specifier (or the next instruction). As with displacement mode in general, the computation of the operand address is done in a CPU scratch area; (PC) is unchanged.

Note that a relative mode operand requires from two to five bytes of storage while all the register modes we have described, with the exception of displacement mode, use only one byte. Thus the programmer can write more compact programs by using the register modes where possible instead of address expressions.

The Assembler's Task

We have already described some of the assembler's considerations in using relative mode, so we will begin here with an example. Let us consider the first example of assembly language and machine code we presented in Section 1.1. It is reproduced in Fig. 8.7. The instructions do floating point arithmetic, but the fact that we haven't studied those instructions yet should cause no problem here, since we are interested only in the fairly mechanical task of translating into machine code.

Since we already have the machine code, we will work backward from it and figure out what the assembler did. Let us assume that when the assembler encountered

FORTRAN	ASSEMBLY LANGUAGE		MACHINE CODE
	COST:	.BLKF 1	
	BASE:	.BLKF 1	
	VAR:	.BLKF 1	
	NUM:	.BLKL 1	
		.	
		.	
		.	
COST=BASE+NUM*VAR	CVTLF	NUM,R3	53DBAF4E
	MULF2	VAR,R3	53D3AF44
	ADDF3	BASE,R3,COST	C4AF53CBAF41

Figure 8.7 Example 1.1 revisited

the storage reservation instructions in the example, . = 20. (We could assume . = 0 or any other value.) Then, when the assembler encounters the machine instructions, it will have the following entries in its symbol table:

Symbol	Value
COST	20
BASE	24
VAR	28
NUM	2C

The machine code for the first instruction is

first byte
|
53 DB AF 4E

4E is the opcode for CVTLF, and AF is the mode byte for the first operand. Thus the assembler encoded NUM using relative mode with byte displacement. DB is the displacement. The assembler knew that when the displacement is added to (PC) during execution, PC will contain the address of the next operand specifier, following the displacement. Thus the assembler used the following equation to compute the displacement:

$$NUM = 2C = \text{location of next byte} + \text{displacement}$$

Since it used DB for the displacement, the location counter value for the next byte must have been $2C - DB = 51$. By counting back, we can determine that . = 4E at the beginning of the instruction, and we can write down the location counter value for each byte.

Location counter:	51	50	4F	4E
Machine code:	53	DB	AF	4E

Now let's consider the second instruction:

first byte

53 D3 AF 44

44 is the opcode for MULF2, and once again the mode byte for the first operand is AF. Thus the assembler encoded the symbol VAR using relative mode with byte displacement. It used the equation

$$\text{VAR} = 28 = \text{location of next byte} + \text{displacement}$$

and computed D3 for the displacement. So the location of the next byte (the one containing the next operand specifier, 53) must be $28 - \text{D3} = 55$. Thus the locations of the bytes of the second instruction are

Location counter:	55 54 53 52		
Machine code:	53	D3	AF	44

The second instruction should follow immediately after the first one, and we see from our computation that it does. We leave it to the reader to decode the third instruction and see how the assembler computed the displacements for BASE and COST.

In this example we already had the machine code, so we knew that the assembler used byte displacements. We will consider now how the assembler determines the displacement and the particular relative mode to use, not knowing in advance how large the displacement is. Suppose the operand being encoded is specified by a symbol. Because the PC will contain the address of the byte following the operand specifier when it and the displacement are added, the equation used by the assembler to determine the displacement is

symbol value = location of byte following the operand specifier + displacement

The problem here is that there are two "unknowns" in the equation: the displacement, of course, and the location of the byte following the operand specifier. The latter is unknown because it depends on how many bytes are used for the displacement. Suppose . = the location of the relative mode operand specifier we are working on. The assembler could first try to determine if the displacement will fit in a byte by solving for the displacement in

symbol value = .+2 + displacement

The location of the byte following the operand specifier will be .+2, because the mode byte and the displacement will each take up one byte. If the solution for the displacement is in the range -128_{10} to 127_{10}, then it fits in a byte and the assembler is done. Since the computation is done in hex, let us consider what an acceptable displacement looks like in hex, so we don't have to convert to decimal to check it. If the displacement can be described in two hex digits *in two's complement form,* it fits in a byte. Recall that the leftmost bit indicates the sign of the number, so, for example, if we compute a negative displacement of FF7A, it can not be stored in a byte because 7A will be interpreted as a positive number.

If the assembler's solution for the displacement in the above equation fits in a word but not a byte, it can not just go ahead and use that displacement. If the displacement takes up a word, then the location of the byte following it will not be .+2; it will be .+3, making the solution no longer valid. It should be clear that the displacement can be corrected by decreasing it by 1. We leave it to the reader to decide how to correct the computed displacement if it requires a longword.

Immediate Mode

Immediate mode is used for assembling literal operands that are too big for the six-bit literal addressing mode. In immediate mode (as in literal mode), the operand itself—i.e., the datum to be used by the instruction,— rather than the operand address is stored in the instruction. The term *immediate operand* is used with a similar meaning for most assembly languages, though the details of how the operand is stored differ for different computers.

Immediate mode is autoincrement mode, mode 8, using the PC. The mode byte contains 8F and the immediate datum is stored immediately after the mode byte. The instruction

        ADDL2   #75,R10

would be encoded as follows:

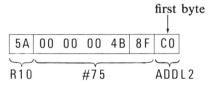

Let us consider what happens when this instruction is executed.

EXECUTION EXAMPLE 8.4: Immediate Mode

Suppose the instruction begins at byte 472. We start with

$$(PC) = 472$$

        5A 00 00 00 4B 8F C0

Fetch the opcode. The instruction is ADDL2.
Fetch the mode byte for the first operand. We now have

$$(PC) = 474$$

5A 00 00 00 4B 8F C0

The mode byte contains 8F; thus the mode is autoincrement and the register used is
the PC.

The operand address is the address now in the PC, 474.

As usual with autoincrement mode, increment the register by the number of bytes indicated by the data type of the instruction, in this case 4 for longword type. So
$(PC) = 474 + 4 = 478.$

$$(PC) = 478$$

5A 00 00 00 4B 8F C0

Note that this time the PC was incremented as a side effect of being used with autoincrement mode, not as a normal part of the instruction execution process.

Fetch the next byte and interpret it as the mode byte for the second operand. Increment
(PC) by 1 as usual; it now points to the first byte of the next instruction.

The second operand specifier is 5A, so the operand is R10.

Now, perform the operation: addition of longwords. The first operand address is 474,
so the datum in the longword beginning at that byte, 0000004B, is added to the
longword in R10. 0000004B is the longword two's complement representation of
the decimal integer 75, the first operand in the source statement.

The Assembler's Task

As we indicated in the discussion of literal mode, when the assembler encounters
an operand beginning with a #, it must decide whether to use literal mode or immediate mode. Suppose it has decided to use immediate mode. Then it must determine
the data type of the operand and encode the datum in the proper type.

Figure 8.8 shows several source statements and the machine code for each
one. Note that #75 is encoded as a longword in the first instruction, ADDL2, but

Source Statement		Machine Code	Mode of First Operand Specifier
ADDL2	#75,R10	5A 00 00 00 4B 8F C0	immediate, longword
ADDW2	#75,R10	5A 00 4B 8F A0	immediate, word
ADDL2	#55,R10	5A 37 C0	literal
MOVB	#^A/3/,(R8)	68 33 90	literal
MOVB	#^A/L/,(R8)	68 4C 8F 90	immediate, byte

Figure 8.8   Literal and immediate modes

as a word in the second instruction, ADDW2. Even though the third instruction operates on longword data, #55 is encoded as a literal using only one byte for the entire operand specifier. Recall that literal operands are expanded to the data type required for the instruction by the CPU at execution time.

The last two instructions in Fig. 8.8 each move a character code to a byte in memory. Note that although a byte is usually used for a character code, the assembler used a literal for the character '3' because its code is 33_{16}, or 51_{10}, which fits in six bits. The code for the character 'L' is 4C, or 76_{10}, which does not fit in six bits, so the assembler used immediate mode.

8.6 AN ASSEMBLY LISTING

We looked at the format of assembly language program listings in Section 5.1. There we saw, among other things, that the listing shows (reading from right to left) the assembly language source statements, the program line number, the value of the location counter at each line, the machine code and data the assembler puts in the object file, and miscellaneous other information. In this section we focus on the machine code.

Figure 8.9 shows the main part of a sample listing produced by the VAX-11 MACRO assembler. The program is a somewhat modified and expanded version of the program segment in Example 7.3. It is worth spending some time examining the listing carefully, as it illustrates many of the addressing modes described so far in this chapter.

Let us examine one instruction in detail. Line 73 contains

```
      Machine code              Loc     Line          Source statement

  FF29 CF   03   00000055 8F   F9   05D1      73          CVTLP   #HIGH,#3,PKD
  _____/   \/   _____/   \/
    PKD       #3     #HIGH    opcode
```

Notice that the assembler listing groups the bytes in the machine code according to their roles, making the code a little easier to interpret. F9 is the opcode for CVTLP. The first operand, #HIGH, is encoded in immediate mode because HIGH = 85, which is too large for a literal. The assembler allows a longword for HIGH because the first operand of CVTLP is of longword type. The second operand, #3, is small enough for a literal, so the operand specifier is 03. The third operand is given in relative mode. The assembler has used a word displacement. By observing that the instruction begins at the location 05D1 and counting bytes (or by looking at the location of the next instruction), we can determine that the location of the byte following the displacement is 05DB. Thus PKD should be equal to 05DB + FF29 = 0504. Looking back to line 36 where PKD is defined, we see that this is correct.

In the program in Fig. 8.9, there were no operand specifiers that the assembler

```
0000                          1 ; PROBLEM STATEMENT
0000                          2 ;
0000                          3 ; The point of this program is to scan an array containing
0000                          4 ; names and test scores and to print the names of people
0000                          5 ; whose scores are between LOW and HIGH, inclusive.
0000                          6 ; The data are read in from the DATA.DAT file.
0000                          7 ;
0000                          8 ; DATA
0000                          9 ;
0000                         10 ;   SCORES    array of names and scores. Each entry consists
0000                         11 ;             of a name in character code (NAME_LEN characters)
0000                         12 ;             followed by a word integer score.
0000                         13 ;   ENTRY_LEN the number of bytes per entry in the SCORES
0000                         14 ;             array (NAME_LEN+2)
0000                         15 ;   MAX       the maximum number of entries for which space
0000                         16 ;             has been reserved
0000                         17 ;   COUNT     the actual number of entries (longword)
0000                         18 ;   SCORE     the displacement of the score from the
0000                         19 ;             beginning of an entry
0000                         20 ;
0000                         21 ; Constants
0000                         22 ;
0000004B             0000    23 LOW = 75
00000055             0000    24 HIGH = 85
00000032             0000    25 MAX = 50
00000016             0000    26 NAME_LEN = 22
00000018             0000    27 ENTRY_LEN = NAME_LEN+2
00000016             0000    28 SCORE = NAME_LEN
0000000A             0000    29 LF = 10
                     0000    30 ;
                     0000    31 ; Storage reservation
                     0000    32 ;
000004B0             0000    33 SCORES: .BLKB   MAX*ENTRY_LEN
000004B4             04B0    34 COUNT:  .BLKL   1
00000504             04B4    35 BUFFER: .BLKB   80
00000506             0504    36 PKD:    .BLKB   2
                     0506    37 HDG:    .ASCII  /People with scores between /
20 68 74 69 77 20 65 6C 70 6F 65 50
65 77 74 65 62 20 73 65 72 6F 63 73
            20 6E 65 65
   20 64 6E 61 20 20  0521    38 LOWSCORE: .ASCII   / and /
      00 0A 00        052A    39 HISCORE:  .ASCIZ   /<LF>/             ; ASCII line feed
                      0530    40 ;
                      0530    41 ;         BEGIN   SCORELIST
                      0580    42 ;
                      0580    43 ; This section reads in the names and scores from DATA.DAT.
                      0580    44 ; Each record contains a name and a three digit score.
                      0580    45
```

```
                                        ; REGISTER USE:   R6    SCORES pointer
0580                                46  ;                 R8    loop counter
0580                                47  ;                 R9    scratch
0580                                48  ;                 R0-R5 used by MOVC3
0580                                49  ;
0580                                50  ;
0580   56   FA7C CF  9E             51          MOVAB    SCORES,R6              ; Initialize SCORES pointer
0585        58        32 DO         52          MOVL     #MAX,R8                ; Don't read more than MAX
0588                                53  READ:   READRCRD BUFFER                 ; Get record
0598  FF5D CF           66          54          MOVC3    #NAME_LEN,BUFFER,(R6)  ; Store name
059E  FF17 CF  16  28   03          55          CVTSP    #3,BUFFER+NAME_LEN,#3,PKD
05A7  FF27 CF  03  09   59          56          CVTPL    #3,PKD,R9
05AD  FF58 CF  03  36              57          CVTLW    R9,SCORE(R6)           ; Convert and store score
05B1       16 A6 59  F7            58          ADDL2    #ENTRY_LEN,R6          ; Increment SCORES pointer
05B4          56  18  CO           59          SOBGTR   R8,READ                ; Loop control
05B7                   D1          60  EOF:    SUBL3    R8,#MAX,COUNT          ; Compute number of entries
05BD  FEF3 CF  32  58              61  ;
05BD                               62  ; This section scans the array SCORES and prints the names
05BD                               63  ; of people with scores between LOW and HIGH, inclusive.
05BD                               64  ;
05BD                               65  ; REGISTER USE:   R6    SCORES pointer
05BD                               66  ;                 R8    loop counter
05BD                               67  ;
05BD                               68  ; Convert high and low scores for heading
05BD                               69  ;
05BD  FF3D CF  03   0000004B 8F F9 71          CVTLP    #LOW,#3,PKD
05C7  FF51 CF  03   FF38 CF  8F 08 72          CVTPS    #3,PKD,#3,LOWSCORE     ; Low score
05D0  FF2A CF  03   00000055 8F F9 73          CVTLP    #HIGH,#3,PKD
05DA  FF47 CF  03   FF25 CF     08 74          CVTPS    #3,PKD,#3,HISCORE      ; High score
05E3                               75          PRINTCHRS HDG,#41
05F3                               76  ;
05F3        58   FEB9 CF       DO  77          MOVL     COUNT,R8               ; Initialize loop counter
05F8             27            13  78          BEQL     DONE                   ; Branch if arrays are empty
05FA        56   FA02 CF       9E  79          MOVAB    SCORES,R6              ; Initialize SCORES pointer
05FF                               80  ;
05FF  004B 8F  16 A6  B1           81  COMPR:  CMPW     SCORE(R6),#LOW         ; Compare score to LOW
0605       0605      14  19        82          BLSS     NEXT                   ; If score<LOW, don't print
0607  0055 8F  16 A6  B1           83          CMPW     SCORE(R6),#HIGH        ; Compare score to HIGH
060D       060D      0C  14        84          BGTR     NEXT                   ; If score high, don't print
060F                               85          PRINTCHRS (R6),#NAME_LEN        ; Print name
061B       56    18            CO  86  NEXT:   ADDL2    #ENTRY_LEN,R6          ; Increment SCORES pointer
061E       DE    58            F5  87          SOBGTR   R8,COMPR               ; Loop control
0621                               88  ;
0621                               89  DONE:   EXIT
0650                               90          .END     SCORELIST
```

Figure 8.9 A program listing

153

could not handle. In general, if a relative mode operand uses a symbol that is defined after the instruction that uses it, or if the symbol is not defined in the module at all, the assembler inserts EF in the mode byte and leaves a longword for the displacement. The linker will fill in the displacement. On a listing the assembler flags such operand specifiers with an apostrophe; for example:

```
56  00000000'EF  D0        MOVL    SYMBOL,R6
```

8.7 MORE ADDRESSING MODES: DEFERRED AND INDEXED MODES

Deferred Addressing Modes

In all the addressing modes introduced so far for addressing operands in memory, the operand address is computed using the contents of a register (and, in some cases, a displacement). There are some programming situations where the address itself is stored in memory. To perform some operation on the operand, we could first move its address from its location in memory to a register, then use a register deferred mode operand specifier. Two separate instructions would be needed. The "deferred addressing" modes allow us to access an operand whose address is in memory in only one step. The form of a deferred mode operand specifier is

$$@ \, operand\_specifier$$

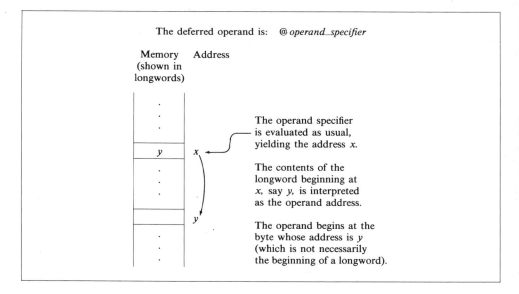

Figure 8.10   Accessing a deferred operand

where the operand specifier that follows the @ may be in displacement, relative, or autoincrement mode. This operand specifier is evaluated in the usual way, producing, say, the address *x*. The @ indicates that *x* is not the address of the operand but is *the address of the address* of the operand. Suppose the longword in memory beginning at the address *x* contains *y*. Then *y* will be used as the address of the operand for the instruction. Figure 8.10 illustrates deferred addressing.

EXAMPLE 8.5: Displacement Deferred Mode

Consider Fig. 8.11 and the instruction

      MOVW   @8(R7),R10

and suppose R7 contains 000002A4. When the displacement 8 is added, we get the address 2AC. The longword at 2AC contains 000000F2. Thus the first operand address for the MOVW instruction is 000000F2. The word beginning at that address is copied into R10.

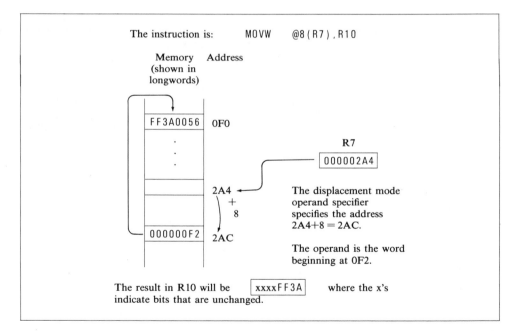

Figure 8.11 An instruction that uses displacement deferred mode

EXAMPLE 8.6: Relative Deferred Mode

Suppose LOC is a label on a longword. The operand specifier

               @LOC

is an example of relative deferred mode. It indicates that the longword at LOC contains the address of the operand. After searching a table and storing the address of the item sought in LOC, we might use this operand specifier to perform some operation on the item.

EXAMPLE 8.7: Autoincrement Deferred Mode

The operand specifier

$$@(R8)+$$

is an example of autoincrement deferred mode. The address in R8 is the address of the address of the operand. R8 is incremented by 4 regardless of the data type of the instruction, because R8 addresses an address, which is always a longword.

EXAMPLE 8.8: Using Deferred Addressing in a Program

Suppose we have a collection of student records, each containing the name, address, grades, and other information about a student. We would like to print out a list of the students in alphabetical order. Since the records are likely to be large, it would be very inefficient to move them around to rearrange them in order. Even if it were not very inefficient, rearranging the records may not be allowed for other reasons; for example, it may be required that they be maintained in some other order, say according to student ID number. To solve the problem, we can set up an array containing the addresses of the records of all the students. These addresses are called *pointers*. Initially the pointer array is in the same order as the records. The sorting algorithm will rearrange the pointers as it examines and compares student names, so that when it is done, the pointers will be in the order that corresponds to the alphabetical ordering of the student names. See Fig. 8.12 for illustration.

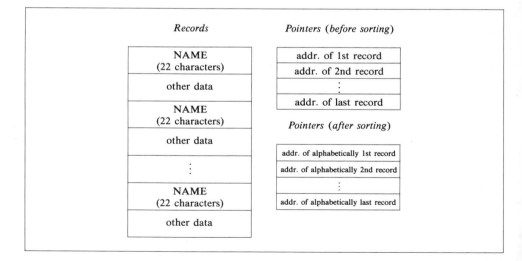

Figure 8.12   Sorting with an array of pointers

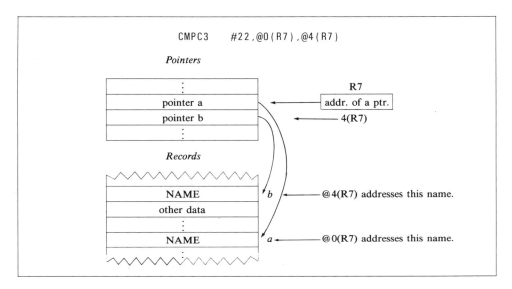

Figure 8.13   Using the pointers in Example 8.8

Suppose R7 contains the address of an entry in the pointers array (see Fig. 8.13) and, as part of the sorting procedure, we wish to compare the names pointed to by two adjacent pointers. The instruction to do this is

```
CMPC3    #22,@0(R7),@4(R7)
```

As we will see in the next chapter, one major application of displacement deferred mode is the accessing of procedure arguments.

Machine Code for Deferred Addressing Modes

Each of the deferred addressing modes has its own mode number. Recall that there are actually three displacement modes; they differ according to how much space is used to store the displacement (a byte, word, or longword). Also, recall that relative mode is just the special case of displacement mode where the register used is PC. The mode numbers and machine code formats are included in Table 8.1 (in the Summary, Section 8.9).

EXAMPLE 8.9: Machine Code for a Relative Deferred Operand

Suppose the value of the symbol ADDR is 22_{16} and the following instruction begins at byte 181:

```
MOVC3    #28,@ADDR,(R9)
```

The second operand specifier would be encoded as

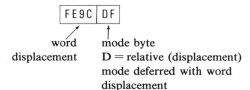

```
FE9C  DF
```
word   mode byte
displacement   D = relative (displacement)
                mode deferred with word
                displacement

The full instruction is

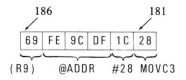

```
       186                    181
 69  FE  9C  DF  1C  28
 (R9)      @ADDR    #28 MOVC3
```

When the instruction is executed, the displacement, FE9C, will be added to 186 to get the second operand address: 0186 + FE9C = 0022 = ADDR. The displacement is determined by the assembler in the same way as it is determined for relative mode.

Indexed Modes

Recall that our general formula for the address of the *i*th entry in an array is

$$\text{address of } i\text{th entry} = \text{address of array} + (i - 1)*\text{entry\_size}$$
$$= \text{address of array} - \text{entry\_size} + i*\text{entry\_size}$$

(See Fig. 6.2.) This formula uses the assumption that the array indexes start at 1. If the array indexes begin at 0, as is common in some high-level languages, then the formula is

$$\text{address of } i\text{th entry} = \text{address of array} + i*\text{entry\_size}$$

In either case, some arithmetic operations must be done just to compute the entry address. Since array references are very common in high-level languages, the VAX provides addressing modes that compute array entry addresses. These are called *indexed modes*. The operand address is computed in two parts: a *base address* and an *index*. Any of several addressing modes already described may be used to specify the base address; the index is in a register. The general format for the operand specifiers is

$$base\_specifier[\text{R}x]$$

where R*x* is R0, . . . , R12, or AP, FP, or SP. The CPU determines the data type of the operand, hence the number of bytes it occupies, from the instruction's opcode. It computes the operand address as follows:

$$\text{operand address} = \text{base address} + (\text{R}x)*\text{size}$$

where *size* is the number of bytes in the operand. Thus the index register, Rx, should contain the index of the array entry to be accessed, and the base address should be the address of the first byte of the array (or the address of the array minus *size* if indexing begins at 1). The entire contents of Rx is used in the computation, so the index must be a longword.

Any addressing mode may be indexed; i.e., any mode may be used for the base address, except literal, immediate, register, branch, and index modes.

EXAMPLE 8.10: Relative Index Mode

Let LIST be a word array whose entries are indexed beginning at 0. Suppose R8 contains 00000005. In the instruction

```
TSTW    LIST[R8]
```

the operand specifier LIST[R8] addresses the fifth entry of the array. The computed operand address is

$$LIST + 5*2$$

If the entries in LIST are indexed beginning at 1, the fifth entry could be addressed by LIST-2[R8].

EXAMPLE 8.11: Implementing a Fortran "Computed GOTO" Statement

The Computed GOTO statement is a multiway conditional branch instruction. It has the following format:

$$\text{GOTO} \quad (s_1, s_2, \ldots, s_k), \; i$$

where i is an integer variable and $s_1, \ldots, s_k$ are statement labels. If the value of the variable i is between 1 and k, the GOTO causes a branch to the statement labeled s_i. It can be implemented in assembly language by a sequence of comparisons and conditional branches that test to see if $i = 1$, then 2, and so on, but this would be very inefficient. The compiler can set up a table in memory containing the branch destinations and use an indexed mode to select the proper one. Suppose the table is called GOTO_TABLE and the current value of i is in R5. The Computed GOTO is implemented as follows:

```
MOVL    I,R5                    ; Get i
BLEQ    BAD_INDEX               ; Branch if i <= 0
CMPL    R5,K                    ; See if i too large
BGTR    BAD_INDEX               ; Branch if i > k
MOVL    GOTO_TABLE-4[R5],R6     ; Get destination
JMP     (R6)                    ; Jump to destination
```

Machine Code for Indexed Addressing Modes

An indexed operand specifier is encoded with a mode byte for index mode (mode 4) followed by a complete operand specifier for the base address. Thus

$$\textit{base\_specifier}[\text{R}x]$$

is encoded as

first byte
(mode byte)

base address specifier | 4*x*

EXAMPLE 8.12: Some Indexed Operand Specifiers

In the machine code, as usual, the first byte of the operand specifier is shown at the right.

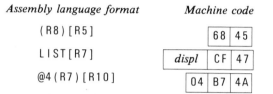

Assembly language format	*Machine code*
(R8)[R5]	68 | 45
LIST[R7]	*displ* | CF | 47
@4(R7)[R10]	04 | B7 | 4A

8.8 EXCEPTIONS, OR EXECUTION-TIME ERRORS

Exceptions

We have seen how the CPU uses the program counter to execute instructions, including branches, one after another in the proper sequence. This process may continue to run smoothly till the end of the program, or it may be interrupted by an error or an unusual condition. Whether or not the program is doing the correct computation and producing correct output is not our concern here. We are considering execution from the point of view of the CPU, which knows nothing of the programmer's intentions and simply carries out a mechanical process of decoding instructions and performing operations on data. In this section we will describe some of the things that can go wrong during this process and interrupt the normal flow of execution, usually preventing completion of the program. Such situations are called *exceptions*.

What can go wrong in the execution process? There are several potential problems. The byte that the CPU interprets as the opcode may not be a valid opcode or it may be privileged (not available to the ordinary user). The addressing mode used for an operand or the operand itself may be inappropriate for the instruction. There may be something wrong with the result of the operation; e.g., it may overflow.

For the beginning programmer such occurrences virtually always indicate errors in the program and should cause it to be terminated with an error message.

Our discussion up to this point is not specific to the VAX. *Exception* is a term commonly used for a problem in an instruction that causes an interruption in the normal flow of execution. The general types of exceptions that we mentioned, such as invalid opcodes or operands and improper results, can occur on other computers. As usual, there is variation in the details of exactly what events are exceptions and how the system responds to them.

On occasion a programmer does not want an exception to cause termination of a program. Many systems allow some flexibility in specifying the action to be taken when certain conditions occur. For some exceptions on the VAX, it is possible to specify that a special procedure, called a condition handler, be called to handle the problem that caused the exception and then continue execution of the program. The use of condition handlers is discussed in the *VAX-11 Architecture Handbook* and will not be covered in this book. We will describe exceptions from the point of view that they are caused by program errors and terminate execution.

For the VAX, exceptions are divided into three categories. *Faults* are exceptions that occur during an instruction and prevent its completion. *Traps* are exceptions that occur at the end of an instruction. The instruction executes successfully, but there is something wrong with the result. (It is possible for the programmer to enable or disable some traps—i.e., to indicate whether or not certain exceptions should occur. If a trap is disabled, the next instruction is executed in the usual way. We will indicate how traps may be enabled and disabled after describing the exceptions.) In the case of faults and traps, the program status is preserved; i.e., the contents of memory, registers, and the program's PSL are still available, so the location of the offending instruction can be determined, useful information can be provided by the system in an error message, and, if a condition handler was specified by the programmer, the program can be continued. *Aborts* are exceptions caused by more serious problems that leave the contents of registers or memory locations in an indeterminate state, so that it may not be possible to determine the cause of the problem or resume execution of the program.

For each of the exceptions that we describe below, we will give its name (assigned by DEC), its meaning, and the kind(s) of errors often made by beginning assembly language programmers that may have caused it.

OPCODE RESERVED TO DIGITAL FAULT

The opcode is invalid or privileged.

Possible cause: The program has branched into a data area or stored data in the middle of instructions.

ACCESS CONTROL VIOLATION FAULT

The program tried to reference a part of memory outside the area permitted to it.

Possible causes: An address was computed improperly. A loop that processes an array continues too long. The # was omitted from a literal.

RESERVED ADDRESSING MODE FAULT

An inappropriate addressing mode was used. For example, a literal may have been used as a destination operand.

Possible cause: Operands written in incorrect order. Misunderstanding of the instruction by the programmer.

RESERVED OPERAND EXCEPTION

The operand accessed is not the correct data type for the instruction. We have seen that any string of bits can be interpreted as a two's complement integer, but for some data types, such as leading separate numeric, floating point, and packed decimal, some bit patterns are not valid. A reserved operand exception may be a fault or an abort, depending on where it occurs.

Possible causes: Beginners often encounter reserved operand faults on the CVTSP instruction used to convert input data from character code. Usually either the data themselves are improperly formatted or the address used was computed incorrectly.

INTEGER OVERFLOW TRAP

The result of an integer arithmetic instruction requires more space than the destination operand has. (The low-order part of the result is stored in the destination operand.)

Possible causes: The programmer did not choose an appropriate data type. The wrong data were used because the operand address was computed incorrectly.

INTEGER DIVIDE-BY-ZERO TRAP

An integer division instruction had a zero divisor.

Possible causes: Either the wrong datum was used because of an address computation error or the programmer forgot to consider the special case of a potentially zero divisor.

FLOATING UNDERFLOW, OVERFLOW, AND DIVIDE-BY-ZERO EXCEPTIONS

Floating overflow and underflow occur when the result of a floating point arithmetic instruction has an exponent outside the range permitted for floating point data.

Possible causes: Similar to the corresponding integer exceptions. Of course it is possible that the data are simply outside the range that can be handled by the VAX instructions.

DECIMAL STRING OVERFLOW AND DIVIDE-BY-ZERO TRAPS

These are for instructions that operate on data of the packed decimal type.

Enabling and Disabling Traps

The PSW contains several trap-enable flags that are accessible by the programmer. They are for the Decimal oVerflow (DV), Floating Underflow (FU), and Integer oVerflow (IV) traps. The flags are located in the PSW as follows:

```
        15                    8  7  6  5  4  3  2  1  0
PSW     | 0 0 0 0 0 0 0 0 |DV|FU|IV| T| N| Z| V| C|
                           _____/  _____/
                           Trap-enable  Condition
                              flags       codes
```

When one of the conditions described occurs, it causes an exception if and only if the corresponding trap-enable bit is set to 1. The flags are all initially zero (disabled). The IV and DV traps may be enabled or disabled at the beginning of a main program or procedure, and all three of the trap bits can be set or cleared by the machine instructions BISPSW (BIt Set in PSW) and BICPSW (BIt Clear in PSW) at any point in a program. The BEGIN macro enables both traps, and we will see how to control IV and DV at the beginning of procedures in the next chapter. Thus, for example, if it is expected that integer overflow might occur in a procedure but can be handled by the program itself, the programmer can disable the IV trap for that procedure and include instructions to test the overflow condition code and handle the condition appropriately without an exception occurring.

The T bit (bit 4) in the PSW is the trace trap flag; it is used by the VAX-11 Symbolic Debugger.

Interpreting Execution-Time Error Messages

The error messages issued for execution-time errors tell the programmer the kind of fault that occurred and the location of the instruction that caused it. The location is described as the "relative PC" contents—that is, the actual PC contents minus the program section's starting address. This value corresponds to the location counter values shown on the program listing, so it helps the programmer find the error.

> **EXAMPLE 8.13: *Using the Error Message to Debug***
>
> Suppose we ran the program shown in Fig. 8.9, but with a slight difference. Figure 8.14(a) shows the error message displayed. The most useful parts are labeled. The error is an access violation, and it occurred at relative location 00000599. Figure 8.14(b) shows a segment of the listing. We can see that the error occurred in the MOVC3 instruction at line 54. Thus the address in R6 must be improper. If we check back to line 51, where R6 was initialized, we see that we incorrectly used a MOVB instruction where we need a MOVAB.

(a) The error message

```
%SYSTEM-F-ACCVIO, access violation, reason mask=05, virtual address=31000400, PC=00000BB3, PSL=0BC00024
%TRACE-F-TRACEBACK, symbolic stack dump follows

module name   routine name   line   relative PC   absolute PC
.MAIN.        .BLANK.                00000598      00000BB3
```

(b) Part of the listing of the incorrect program

```
                              0580   43 ;  This section reads in the names and scores from DATA.DAT.
                              0580   44 ;  Each record contains a name and a three digit score.
                              0580   45 ;
                              0580   46 ;  REGISTER USE   R6      SCORES pointer
                              0580   47 ;                 R8      loop counter
                              0580   48 ;                 R9      scratch
                              0580   49 ;                 R0-R5   used by MOVC3
                              0580   50 ;
FF5D CF   56   FA7C CF   90   0580   51       MOVB     SCORES,R6                 ; Initialize SCORES
                                                                                ;   pointer
          58   32        D0   0585   52       MOVL     #MAX,R8                   ; Don't read more
                                                                                ;   than MAX
                              0588   53 READ: READRCRD  BUFFER                   ; Get record
FF17 CF   66 03 16       28   0598   54       MOVC3    #NAME_LEN,BUFFER,(R6)     ; Store name
FF27 CF   03             09   059E   55       CVTSP    #3,BUFFER+NAME_LEN,#3,PKD
FF58 CF   59             36   05A7   56       CVTPL    #3,PKD,R9
          16   A6 59     F7   05AD   57       CVTLW    R9,SCORE(R6)              ; Convert and store
                                                                                ;   score
          56   18        C0   05B1   58       ADDL2    #ENTRY_LEN,R6             ; Increment SCORES
                                                                                ;   pointer
                    D1   F5   05B4   59       SOBGTR   R8,READ                   ; Loop control
FEF3 CF   32             C3   05B7   60 EOF:  SUBL3    R8,#MAX,COUNT             ; Compute number of
                                                                                ;   entries
```

Figure 8.14 An execution-time error

8.9 SUMMARY

The CPU uses the program counter, PC, as a pointer to the next byte to be processed in the instruction stream. It automatically increments (PC) as it fetches each part of an instruction.

Instructions are encoded in machine code with a one- or two-byte opcode followed by an operand specifier for each operand. The ways in which operands may be specified are called addressing modes. The VAX has a large variety of addressing modes. Each operand specifier (with the exception of branch mode operands) starts with a mode byte that contains the addressing mode number and a register number (or a literal). The CPU can determine from the mode number how many additional bytes (if any) are part of the operand specifier.

Most addressing modes use a general register in some way. For certain modes the PC may not be used. Other addressing modes, when used with the PC, are given special names and studied separately because using the PC has different effects.

In branch mode and the relative modes, the operand address is computed by adding a displacement and (PC). Thus address expressions are encoded by their position relative to (PC). This allows correct encoding of the address expression independent of where the program is loaded in memory.

Address computations are always done with 32 bits, so displacements are sign-extended if necessary.

The displacement modes are particularly useful for addressing fields within a data structure organized in a standardized format. The deferred modes allow the programmer to access an operand whose address is stored somewhere in memory without first loading the address into a register. The indexed modes are designed for addressing array entries.

Table 8.1 lists the addressing modes.

It is the assembler's job to translate assembly language source programs into machine code. Many assemblers accomplish this task by making two passes over the source program; they are called two-pass assemblers.

The main purpose of the first pass is to find all the symbols used in the module being assembled, determine their values (if possible), and build the symbol table containing the symbols and values. To determine the values of the symbols, the assembler uses a counter called a location counter which it initializes to zero. The location counter is incremented by the number of bytes that will be used for each statement (both directives that reserve space for data and machine instructions). When the assembler encounters a symbol in the label field of an instruction, it assigns to the symbol the current value of the location counter.

During the second pass, the assembler translates the machine instructions into machine code. For some operands, several addressing modes could be used to encode them. The assembler follows a specific set of rules that control the choices it makes. Some of these are described in the text; more detail is given in the *VAX-11 MACRO Language Reference Manual.* There may be some address references that the assembler can't handle; it leaves these for the linker to fill in later.

TABLE 8.1 Addressing Modes

Name	Number	Assembly format	Machine code
Register modes			
Register	5	R*n*	5 *n*
Register deferred	6	(R*n*)	6 *n*
Autodecrement	7	−(R*n*)	7 *n*
Autoincrement	8	(R*n*)+	8 *n*
Byte displacement	A	*dis*(R*n*) B^*dis*(R*n*)	*dis* | A *n*
Word displacement	C	*dis*(R*n*) W^*dis*(R*n*)	*dis* | C *n*
Longword displacement	E	*dis*(R*n*) L^*dis*(R*n*)	*dis* | E *n*
Literal	0–3	#*expression* S^#*expression*	00 | literal
Branch	none	*address expression*	*dis* *dis*
Program counter modes			
Immediate	8	#*expression* I^#*expression*	*datum* | 8 F
Byte relative	A	*address expr.*	*dis* | A F
Word relative	C	*address expr.*	*dis* | C F
Longword relative	E	*address expr.*	*dis* | E F
Deferred addressing modes			
Autoincrement deferred	9	@(R*n*)+	9 *n*
Byte displacement deferred	B	@*dis*(R*n*)	*dis* | B *n*

TABLE 8.1 (Continued)

Word displacement deferred	D	@ *dis*(R*n*)	*dis* | D*n*
Longword displacement deferred	F	@ *dis*(R*n*)	*dis* | F*n*
Byte relative deferred	B	@ *address expr.*	*dis* | BF
Word relative deferred	D	@ *address expr.*	*dis* | DF
Long relative deferred	F	@ *address expr.*	*dis* | FF
Index mode	4	*base_specifier*[R*x*]	. . . | *m n* | 4 *x*

where *m* is the mode number and *n* is the register used for the base operand specifier, which may be any mode except register, literal, immediate, branch, or index mode.

An *exception* is a problem that occurs during (or after) execution of an instruction that causes the operating system to intervene in the normal process of instruction execution. Exceptions may be caused by a bad opcode, addressing mode, address, or operand, or by some abnormal property of the result of a computation, such as overflow. Usually, especially for beginning programmers, an exception is caused by a programming error. The error messages displayed by the system for execution-time errors tell the programmer the type of fault that occurred and the location of the instruction that caused it.

8.10 EXERCISES

1. Translate each of the following instructions into machine code.

    (a) ADDL3   R8,R9,R4   (c) INCW   (R5)
    (b) MOVC3   #4,(R7),(R8)   (d) MOVB   (R10)+,-(SP)

2. Decode the following instructions and write them as assembly language source statements. Assume the lowest-addressed byte is at the right.

    (a)   59 67 C6
    (b) 6A 68 0A 28
    (c)   84 D5

3. Each of the instructions listed below has the effect of setting all the bits of R6 to 0, but they may differ in the amount of space they require in machine code and the amount of time it takes to execute them. For each instruction, tell how many bytes it takes up in machine code.

    (a) MOVL   #0,R6   (c) CLRL   R6
    (b) SUBL2   R6,R6   (d) MULL2   #0,R6

4. Give an example of a SOBGTR instruction that uses more than three bytes in machine code.

5. Suppose a person's medical record is made up of the following fields stored in memory in the order listed:

Medical record number	8 bytes
Name	20 bytes
Address	48 bytes
Date of birth	6 bytes
Blood type	1 byte
Allergy flags	2 bytes
Date of last physical	6 bytes
Other fields	95 bytes

(a) Suppose R7 contains the address of the record. Using displacement mode, write down operand specifiers (in assembly language source form) for the first seven fields.

(b) Suppose the next person's record is in memory immediately after this one and has the same format. Write an assembly language statement to put the address of the next record in R7.

6. Write a sequence of instructions for the problem in Example 7.5 using displacement mode.

7. Suppose that a collection of records is stored in memory, but they are not stored in sequential order. The third longword of each record contains the address of the one that is logically next. Suppose R7 contains the address of a record. Write an instruction to put in R7 the address of the next record.

8. Suppose that for each person who answered a questionnaire we have a block of information in the following format:

first byte

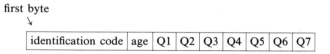

where the identification code is four characters, age is a byte integer, and Q1, . . . , Q7 are answers to questions, each represented by an ASCII code for a number between 1 and 5. Assuming that R8 contains the address of one such block, write instructions to increment a counter in R10 if the person is in the age group 20–29 and his or her answer to the fifth question is 3 or higher. Then, whether or not the counter is incremented, set R8 to contain the address of the block of data for the next person (assuming it immediately follows the current one in memory).

9. Encode the instruction

```
BRW     NEXT
```

assuming the instruction starts at 48E and NEXT = 4D5.

10. Show the machine code for the instruction

```
AOBLSS  #10,R3,LOOP
```

assuming that the instruction begins at 2D1 and LOOP = 2A9.

11. In each problem below decode the instruction starting at byte 25E assuming the lowest addressed byte is at the right. In cases where relative mode is used, show the operand address.

   (a) Addresses: . . . 265 264 263 262 261 260 25F 25E 25D . . .
       Memory: . . . AC 58 6A FF CF CF 15 29 87 . . .

   (b) Addresses: . . . 262 261 260 25F 25E 25D 25C . . .
       Memory: . . . 57 D5 F2 59 F5 56 20 . . .

12. Suppose the assembler's location counter = 14D when the instruction

```
SUBL3    ALPHA,R9,R10
```

is encountered. Show the encoding of the first operand specifier and the addresses of the bytes it is in for each of the following values of ALPHA.

   (a) ALPHA = 0B8   (c) ALPHA = 0D0
   (b) ALPHA = 03C   (d) ALPHA = 0CF

13. Suppose that for the program segment shown in Fig. 8.7, the symbol table contains the value 38 for COST. List the values for BASE, VAR, and NUM, and determine the locations at which each of the three machine instructions begin.

14. Show the machine code for

```
ADDL2    ALPHA,ALPHA
```

assuming ALPHA = 3C and the instruction begins at 12A. Will the two operand specifiers be identical? Why, or why not?

15. Suppose the following two instructions appear in a program.

```
ADDL2    BETA,R7
ADDL2    BETA,R7
```

The instructions are identical. Will the translations of them into machine code be identical? Why or why not?

16. Suppose you are writing the part of an assembler that encodes relative mode operands. The value of the symbol to be encoded is in R6, and the value of the location counter is in R10. Write instructions to compute the displacement, store it in DISPL, and increment R10 so it will contain the location of the byte following the operand specifier. Include comments to explain your computation.

17. Any symbols used in the repetition factor in a .BYTE, .WORD, or .LONG directive must be defined before the directive appears. Why?

18. Suppose BETA = 2A. Consider the instruction

```
INCB    BETA
```

   (a) At what location must this instruction appear so that the displacement used in the operand specifier is 80 (or -128_{10}), the largest negative byte displacement?

(b) At what location must the instruction appear so that the displacement is FF7E (or -130_{10})?

(c) Is there some location at which the instruction could appear where the displacement for BETA would be FF7F (-129_{10})? If so, what is it? If not, explain why.

19. Some computers do not have a special addressing mode for branch destinations. Branch addresses are encoded in the same way as other address expressions. Give one advantage and one disadvantage for the VAX's using branch mode instead of relative mode for branch addresses.

20. Which, if any, of the following instructions would cause an assembly-time error? (Indicate which part of the instruction is wrong.)

    (a) MNEGB   BETA,-5(R7)   where BETA $= 1$E and the instruction starts at 18A.

    (b) ADDL2   R7,#28

    (c) AOBLSS   R9,R4,LOOP   where LOOP $= 00$E2 and the instruction starts at 1C3.

    (d) CMPB   (R3),#100

21. Show the machine code for each of the following instructions.

    (a) SUBW2   #30,R8   **(b)** SUBW2   #70,R8

22. Show the machine code for each of the following instructions, assuming in each case that LOOP $= 00$E2 and the instruction begins at 14E.

    (a) ACBB   #10,#2,R8,LOOP   **(c)** AOBLSS   #10,R8,LOOP

    (b) ACBB   #80,#2,R8,LOOP   **(d)** AOBLSS   #80,R8,LOOP

23. Decode the instruction beginning at 6E7. If relative mode is used for any of the operands, invent a symbol and tell what address it refers to.

    Addresses: . . .   6E9   6E8   6E7

    Memory: 6A   FD   86   CF   01   2C   8F   29

24. The longest operand specifier we have used in any example has five bytes. Write an instruction with an operand specifier that has nine bytes.

25. List all the addressing modes used for operands in the program shown in Fig. 8.9.

26. Using the listing in Fig. 8.9, determine how many bytes are filled by the READRCRD and PRINTCHRS macros.

27. Show the machine code for the following operand specifiers.

    (a) @12(R5)   **(b)** @12(AP)

28. Consider the problem described in Example 8.8, where a collection of records is to be sorted without being physically rearranged. Using the strategy of the Bubble Sort algorithm described in Exercise 31 of Chapter 7, write a program segment to rearrange the array of pointers to reflect the ordering of the records.

29. Consider the data described in Example 8.8. Suppose that each record contains a field called UNITS that contains the number of course units the student has completed. The UNITS field is a word integer that occupies the 31st and 32nd bytes of each record. Suppose R7 contains the address of one of the pointers in the pointer array (as in Fig. 8.13, for example). Write an instruction (or instructions) to determine if the student whose record is pointed to by this pointer has completed 96 or more units. (Can a deferred addressing mode be used for this?)

30. Write a program segment that uses index mode to solve the problem described in Example 6.9.

31. Write a program segment that does a Bubble Sort (see Exercise 31 of Chapter 7) using index mode.

32. Consider the Binary Search program in Fig. 7.6. The instructions that compute the address of the table entry to be examined, and then compare the keys, are

```
; REGISTER USE        R5      entry size (number of bytes)
;                     R6      TABLE-size
;                     R7      key (word)
;                     R10     middle (longword)
;                     R11     address of entry to examine
                         .
                         .
                         .

          MULL3   R10,R5,R11          ; Middle*size
          ADDL2   R6,R11             ; Address of entry
          CMPW    R7,(R11)           ; Compare keys
```

Would it be correct to replace the three machine instructions with the following instruction using index mode? Why, or why not?

```
          CMPW    R7,(R6)[R10]       ; Compare key to middle entry
```

33. Suppose a program does arithmetic on quadwords (using the ADDL2 and ADWC instructions). Should that program have the IV trap enabled or disabled? Why?

Chapter 9

Procedures

9.1 ADVANTAGES OF PROCEDURES— AND IMPLEMENTATION PROBLEMS

The Advantages of Procedures

A *procedure,* or *subroutine,* is a section of code that performs a particular task and may be "called" from, or used by, other procedures or programs. A procedure acts on data given it by the routine that calls it, and when it completes its task, it returns control to the calling routine. A procedure may be assembled (or compiled, in high-level languages) independently; thus it may be developed and debugged separately from the programs that will eventually use it.

There are many reasons for using procedures. The most important is that their use makes large programs much easier to design, develop, understand, debug, and maintain. It is not that procedures have any magical properties; it is simply that they make it easy for a programmer to use a well-known technique for solving large and difficult problems: break the problem down to a set of subproblems and work on the subproblems one at a time.

It is good programming practice to code every logically separate task as a separate procedure. It is not easy to explain exactly what constitutes a "logically separate task," but examples and experience should help the beginning programmer to develop good judgment about how to break up a large program into procedures. A program that is made up of many procedures is said to be *modular.*

Since real-world programs tend to be very large (thousands of lines) and are written by several people over a long period of time, the independence of a procedure from the rest of the program is an important asset in program development. A programmer can be told what task the procedure is supposed to do, what kinds of data it will be given to work on, and what result, if any, it is to return. The programmer does not have to know anything about the rest of the program and may concentrate on one specific problem.

There are other advantages to using procedures. A procedure may be called from different places in a program, and from different procedures. The procedure is written only once and the code appears only once in memory, thus saving space and programming time.

Since procedures may be assembled or compiled separately, they may be written in different languages. The major part of a large program may be written in a high-level language, but tasks that can not be done conveniently in that language may be done in assembly language procedures.

Again, because procedures may be written and assembled separately, procedures for common problems can be kept in a program library and used by many programmers. Procedures that perform statistical computations, input/output operations, and a variety of other tasks are often available in such libraries. They save not only programming time but also the time required to learn the technical information required to solve the problem.

We can summarize the advantages of using procedures as follows:

1. Modular programs are easier to design, debug, understand, and maintain.
2. Procedures can be called from several places in a program, saving space and programming time.
3. Procedures written in different programming languages can be combined in one program.
4. Complex and frequently used procedures can be kept in procedure libraries for use by many programmers.

The Problems

Communication between procedures and the programs that call them (including other procedures) is a complex topic. We will consider some of the problems that must be solved so that procedures can be used smoothly.

Figure 9.1 illustrates the flow of control, or the order in which sections of instructions are executed, when a program calls a procedure. The sequence of instructions that make up a procedure are stored in memory separate from the programs that may call it. After the procedure completes its task, the next instruction to be executed is the one that follows the procedure call in the calling program. Thus the first problems are to devise a method to transfer control to the procedure (by appropriately changing the PC), and to transfer back to the correct place (by resetting the PC) afterward.

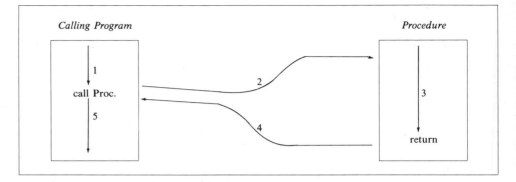

Figure 9.1   Executing a procedure

Normally, statement labels and other user-defined symbols have no meaning outside the procedure in which they are defined. They are *local* to the module where they are defined. Thus, one procedure can not refer by name to data or instruction labels in another procedure. This is a valuable restriction, because it allows procedures to be written without worry of conflicts with symbols used elsewhere in a large program. It also forces programmers to follow the specific, narrow rules for communication between procedures, and encourages clearer, easier-to-debug programs. However, we can see that an exception to the locality of symbol definition is needed so that a program can call a procedure by name.

Many of the advantages of the modularity that is achieved by using procedures depend on the procedure's performing its task without any side effects. Consider Fig. 9.1; if the calling program puts a datum in a general register in the section of code numbered 1, that datum should still be in the register in the section of code numbered 3. But the procedure may need to use some of the registers to do its work. Thus a scheme is needed to protect the original contents of the general registers while the procedure is executing.

Another problem is that of devising convenient and flexible ways to specify to a procedure exactly what data it is to use and what to do with its results. The data operated on and the results computed by the procedure are its *arguments*. The process of giving input arguments to a procedure and telling it where to put its results is called *passing arguments*.

We can summarize the procedure communication problems as

1. transferring control to the procedure,
2. saving the contents of registers,
3. passing arguments, and
4. returning to the next instruction in the calling program.

All these problems are made more difficult by the fact that procedure calls can be nested; i.e., one procedure may call another which calls another, and so on.

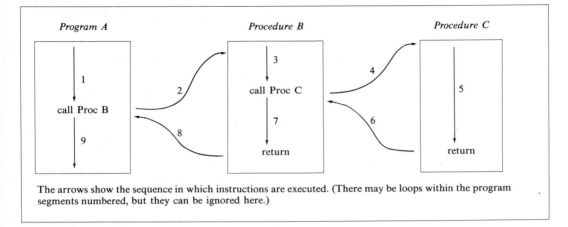

The arrows show the sequence in which instructions are executed. (There may be loops within the program segments numbered, but they can be ignored here.)

Figure 9.2   Nested procedure calls

Figure 9.2 illustrates the sequence of actions when a second procedure is called. The call to Procedure C requires space to save Procedure B's register contents, the return location, and information about Procedure C's arguments. Meanwhile, the same items of information concerning the call to Procedure B are still needed, since Procedure B hasn't completed its work yet. It is clear that we can not use one fixed location for passing this information between procedures.

The collection of conventions, methods, and instructions used to handle communication between procedures and calling programs is often called the *procedure linkage conventions*. DEC uses the term *procedure calling standard*. One may think of the linkage conventions as a big puzzle in which all the pieces must fit just right. There are many ways procedure linkage can be done, but if the details or methods used for one part of the whole problem are modified, then the details of another part have to be changed so that the pieces still "fit together" properly. The methods used on different computers vary in sophistication and capabilities as well as in details. For example, a simpler set of conventions may be used if recursive procedures (procedures that call themselves) are not allowed. Generally, the more flexibility allowed to the programmer, the more complex are the details. The VAX has powerful and flexible linkage conventions that make complex programming techniques such as recursive and reentrant procedures easy to use.

9.2   THE STACK

What Is a Stack?

A *stack* is a list of entries where all insertions and all deletions are made at one end, called the *top*. Since insertions and deletions are done at the top, the next item to be removed is always the item most recently inserted. Stacks are very useful and convenient for storing data that must be processed in this *last-in, first-out* order.

A stack can be set up by reserving a section of memory for it and establishing three pointers. A moving pointer is used to keep track of where the top is as items are inserted and deleted. Two fixed pointers may be used to prevent a program from removing an entry when the stack is empty and from putting into the stack more entries than there is room for. They point to the beginning, or *bottom,* of the stack, and to the other end of the reserved space, respectively.

To *push* means to insert an item into a stack, and to *pop* means to remove the top item. These terms come from the example of a stack of cafeteria trays in a spring-loaded container; when a tray is added to the stack, it pushes the others down, and when a tray is removed, the rest of the stack pops up. When a data stack is used in a computer, the entries do not actually move down and up when items are added and removed, but the terms push and pop have come to be widely used.

Figure 9.3 shows a stack as it might appear just after being set up and then again after being used for a while.

Stacks and Procedures

A stack is the natural data structure for storing much of the information that must be saved when procedures are called. This is essentially because procedures are returned

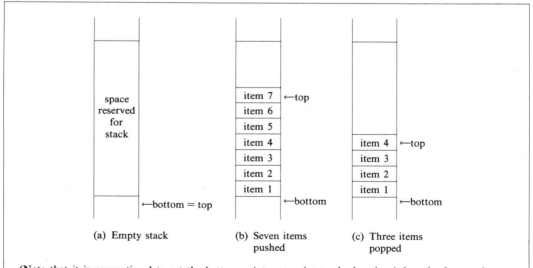

(a) Empty stack

(b) Seven items
pushed

(c) Three items
popped

(Note that it is conventional to set the bottom pointer to point to the location below the first stack location, so that the condition "bottom = top" means that the stack is empty.)

Figure 9.3   A stack at different stages of use

from in the order opposite to that in which they were called; i.e., they are "last-in, first-out." Consider, for example, the *return address*—the address of the next instruction in the calling program to be executed after the called procedure completes its task. When Program A calls Procedure B, the address of the instruction following the call is pushed on the stack. Then when Procedure B calls Procedure C, the address of the instruction following the call in Procedure B is pushed on the stack, on top of the return address in Program A. The return from Procedure C is executed before the return from Procedure B. Thus when Procedure C completes its work, the return address it should use is the one most recently put on the stack—the one on the top.

No matter how long the chain of procedure calls, the return address needed to properly return from a procedure is the one most recently pushed on the stack. The same reasoning shows that a stack is appropriate for storing register contents and other information that is saved when a procedure is called.

We have concluded that to properly return to the calling program, the return address should be put on a stack. But what exactly should we stack? In other words, how do we determine the return address? As we saw in so many examples in Chapter 8, when the operation specified by an instruction is carried out, PC contains the address of the next instruction. Thus when a procedure is called, PC contains the return address.

The User Stack on the VAX

Stacks are used on the VAX for many purposes. The operating system, for example, uses a stack for saving data needed while exceptions are being processed. The operating system also sets up a stack, called a user stack, for each program. The SP (Stack Pointer) register is intended to be used to keep track of the top of the stack; it should always contain the address of the most recently inserted item. The stack grows toward the lower-addressed end of memory; the first entry is in the highest-addressed location in the space reserved for the stack. As Fig. 9.4 illustrates, this lets us draw our diagram of the stack in a natural way, with the top of the stack toward the top of the diagram. [The operating system initializes SP to the address of the byte that follows the space reserved for the stack, where the *top* pointer is in Fig. 9–3(a).]

The user stack may be used for temporary storage for scratch work. It can be manipulated explicitly using PUSH and POP instructions and other instructions. Here we are primarily interested in its use for procedure linkage. The user stack is manipulated implicitly by the instructions that call and return from procedures. That is, the CALL and RETurn instructions push and pop data such as register contents and return addresses automatically.

A Slight Digression—Internal Subroutines

In addition to supporting linkage conventions for procedures, the VAX (like many other large computers) provides instructions for a similar, but much simpler, situation.

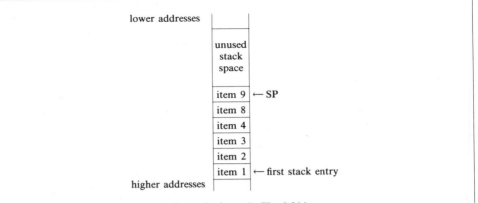

Two items have been pushed onto the stack shown in Fig. 9.3(c).

(Note that there is no bottom pointer. The VAX operating system puts the user stack between sections of memory that are inaccessible to the user's program, so pushing or popping too many items will result in a program exception.)

Figure 9.4   A user stack in the VAX

Since these instructions make use of one of the key ideas for solving the linkage problems of procedures—saving needed data on the stack—we will describe them here.

The simpler problem is to use, or "call," a sequence of instructions from more than one place *within one module*. DEC refers to a sequence of instructions used in this way as a *subroutine*. To emphasize the limitations of such subroutines, and to avoid confusion with the way the term *subroutine* is used in Fortran, we will call them *internal subroutines*. Internal subroutines do not have arguments in the usual sense (though they may operate on register contents that are different each time they are called). They are not assembled separately, and they may not be called from other programs. The advantage of internal subroutines is that they are much simpler to use and require very little overhead in time and space.

The only piece of information saved when an internal subroutine is called is the return address. It is saved, of course, on the stack. Thus if the contents of any registers are modified, their original contents are lost. Since there is no argument list, either the internal subroutine always works on the same data (e.g., printing out a specific array at various stages in some problem), or it uses data put in specific registers for it to work on.

The instructions that implement internal subroutines are:

BSBB	*destination* ⎫	Branch to SuBroutine
BSBW	*destination* ⎭	
RSB		Return from SuBroutine

In the BSB*x* instructions, the last letter indicates whether a byte or word is used to encode the branch displacement. The BSB*x* instructions push (PC)—the return address for the subroutine—onto the stack and then put into PC the branch destination address. The RSB instruction simply pops the top longword from the stack and puts it in the PC, thus causing a return from the subroutine. Of course, for RSB to accomplish its intended task, if any data are added to the stack in the subroutine, they must be popped before RSB is executed.

EXAMPLE 9.1: An Internal Subroutine

The following segment is part of a program that uses an internal subroutine to convert data from two's complement to character code. Note that the subroutine is placed after the EXIT statement so it is executed only when "called." Also, note that the stack is used for temporary scratch space. Since the datum put on the stack is popped (by the use of the autoincrement operand specifier in the CVTLP instruction), RSB will find the return address at the top of the stack when it looks for it.

```
                .
                .
        BSBW    CVTWS
                .
                .
        BSBW    CVTWS
                .
                .
                .
        EXIT
;
;
; CVTWS
;
; This subroutine converts the word whose address is in R8
; to character code and stores the resulting string at the
; address in R10. It assumes that R9 contains the number of
; digits desired in the result, and space has been reserved
; at PKD for the intermediate step.
;
CVTWS:  CVTWL   (R8),-(SP)
        CVTLP   (SP)+,R9,PKD
        CVTPS   R9,PKD,R9,(R10)
        RSB
; End of subroutine CVTWS
        .END    PROG
```

9.3 AN OVERVIEW OF THE VAX PROCEDURE-CALLING STANDARD

As we indicated in Section 9.1, many, many details are involved in setting up linkage conventions that will work properly. Some of the required tasks are done explicitly by the programmer; some are done by the CPU as part of the execution of certain instructions. Some of the work is done in the procedure and some in the program that calls it. All the pieces of the puzzle must fit together properly, and it may not be clear how this will happen until all the pieces have been described. To help guide the reader about what to expect, we will give a brief overview of the VAX calling standard here. The details are presented in the next three sections, along with examples. For the overview in this section we will describe the various steps, instructions, and techniques in more or less the order in which they are carried out at execution time.

The programmer must set up an argument list for a procedure in the program that calls the procedure. The argument list may be put on the stack or in some other part of memory, and some or all of it may be set up at assembly time. When the procedure is called, the VAX puts the address of the argument list in the AP (Argument Pointer) register.

Procedures are called using the CALLG or CALLS instruction. These instructions cause a lot of behind-the-scenes work to occur. They push register contents and other information onto the stack and put new data in certain registers (AP and PC, for example).

The procedure must contain an *entry mask* specified by the programmer to indicate which registers are used by the procedure. The CALL instructions use this information to determine which register contents must be saved on the stack.

The procedure uses AP to access its arguments. The addressing modes that are especially useful for this are displacement and displacement deferred.

The RET instruction is used in the procedure to return to the program that called it. RET pops the information that was put on the stack by the CALL instruction. It reloads the registers with the old contents that were saved on the stack.

The general organization of a procedure is shown in Fig. 9.5. The .PSECT directive is not required, but it assigns a name to the procedure that is used in execution-time error messages; thus it helps the programmer determine in what proce-

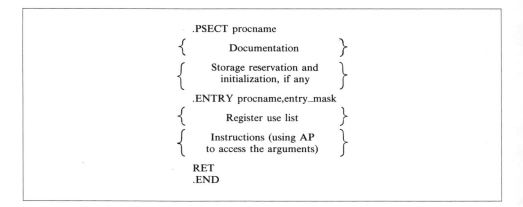

Figure 9.5   Procedure organization

dure the error occurred. (More features of .PSECT are described in Chapter 10.) The documentation for a procedure should include a list of the arguments with their roles and data types, and a description of the problem, the method used to solve it, and any special cases, details, and so on that are of interest. The .ENTRY directive is described in the next section. The .END directive should be the last statement in the procedure. It must not have an argument; the user transfer address should appear only on the .END directive in the main program.

9.4 THE .ENTRY DIRECTIVE

Strategies for Saving Registers

One of the problems to be solved in procedure linkage is protection of the contents of the registers used by the calling program. We can devise many possible solutions, depending on how we answer several strategic questions. We will briefly consider some of the alternatives.

The first question is: *where* should the old register contents be saved? For the VAX we have an obvious answer: on the stack. We should point out, though, that some machines do not have a "built-in" stack, so their standard procedure linkage conventions require that the calling program or the procedure reserve space for saving register contents.

The next question is: *which* registers should be saved? We could save them all to be safe, but that is inefficient in its use of time and space. The serious alternatives are: the registers being used in the calling program, because these registers *may* be used and modified by the procedure, or the registers that are used in the procedure, because they *may* have contained data needed by the calling program. (Note that, consistent with our emphasis on the independence of the procedure and a program that may call it, we assume that neither one actually knows which registers are used by the other.) The second alternative is the one that is generally chosen: the old contents of the registers used in the procedure are saved and put back in those registers when the procedure has completed its work. One reason for this choice is "esthetic"; it is more consistent with the view that the calling program be able to use a procedure easily without worry about side effects. The procedure has the responsibility to do its job without damaging the calling program's data. Another reason is that assigning the responsibility to the procedure is likely to use less space. A program may call several procedures and, using the first scheme, would have to provide information about which registers to save before each CALL. With the second scheme, information about what registers are used in the procedure need be represented just once in the procedure. Other reasons for giving the responsibility to the procedure are related to how well this fits with the other pieces of the linkage puzzle.

The next question is: *who* should actually store the register contents—the calling program or the procedure? The answer to the previous question seems to make it obvious that the procedure should store the old register contents; the calling program would not know which ones to save. This solution is used on some computers, but not the VAX. The VAX CALL instructions actually store the old register contents. The CALL instruction, of course, appears in the calling program, but it might be better to think of its work as occurring along the narrow numbered 2 in Fig. 9.1— i.e., as part of the transition from one routine to the other.

Our final question is specific to the VAX. Since the registers to be saved are those used in the procedure, but the actual storing of the old contents is done by the CALL instruction, how does the CALL know which ones to store? The .ENTRY directive provides the needed information.

The .ENTRY Directive

Although we can logically separate the problems involved in procedure linkage, we can't neatly separate the solutions. The .ENTRY directive does *some* of the work that helps solve *two* of the problems: saving registers and transferring control to the procedure. It defines an *entry point* for the procedure and sets up an *entry mask,* or *register save mask,* that indicates which registers are to be saved.

The form of the .ENTRY directive is

.ENTRY   *procname,regmask*

The procedure name, procname, is declared as an *entry point*—a point where execution of the procedure may begin. It will be flagged to the linker as a *global* symbol— one that is accessible from other modules. Its value will be the location of the .ENTRY directive, so the directive should appear at the beginning of the executable portion of the procedure.

The register save mask is a 16-bit pattern whose bits are to indicate which registers are used in the procedure and which traps are to be enabled in the procedure. Only registers in the range R2 through R11 should be specified. For each of these registers, bit n in the mask will be set to 1 if Rn is specified. R0 and R1 should not be saved because, by convention, these registers are used to return function values from function procedures. SP is *never* stacked, and AP, FP, and PC are *always* stacked by a CALL instruction so they don't have to be specified. Thus there are some bits in the mask that may be used for other purposes. Bits 14 and 15 are used to set the IV and DV (integer and decimal overflow) trap-enable flags in the PSW.

The programmer may specify the register save mask in the following form:

$\wedge$M<*register and trap list*>

The register and trap names in the list should be separated by commas. The assembler will construct the 16-bit mask from the registers and traps specified. The registers do not have to be listed in numerical order, but they should be. The mask will be placed at the location where the .ENTRY directive appears (the location assigned to the symbol *procname*).

EXAMPLE 9.2: A Register Save Mask

^M<R3,R7,R8,R9,IV>

The assembler will construct the mask shown below in binary. Recall that bits are numbered right to left, starting with 0.

0100001110001000

EXAMPLE 9.3: An .ENTRY Directive

.ENTRY OUTPUT,^M<R2,R3,R6,R7,R10>

This .ENTRY directive defines the symbol OUTPUT as an entry point for a procedure and indicates that the procedure uses registers R2, R3, R6, R7, and R10.

It is important that the programmer not tell a "lie" in the entry mask. The mask should include all registers (in the range R2 to R11) that may be changed in the procedure (including those changed as side effects of instructions like MOVC3). When the procedure is called, only the entry mask is examined to determine which registers will be saved. If a register is changed in the procedure and was not specified in the entry mask, the old contents will be lost, thus potentially causing errors after returning to the calling program.

How do the CALL instructions actually find the register mask so they can determine which registers to save? The procedure name (or more precisely, the entry point name) is an operand for the CALL instructions. Thus CALL is given the address of the register save mask and can easily examine it. Note that since the register mask takes up two bytes, the CALL will have to put the address *procname*+2 into the PC to accomplish the transfer of control to the procedure.

Although we called the first argument of the .ENTRY directive *procname*, the first argument is not always the procedure name. It is possible and sometimes useful for a procedure to have more than one entry point. In such cases the .ENTRY directive is used at each place where an entry point is to be established, and a different symbol is used to name each one.

9.5 ARGUMENT LISTS

What Is in an Argument List?

A procedure and the program that calls it communicate via an *argument list*. That is, the data the procedure is to work with are given to it as arguments, and any results that it is to return to the calling program are returned as arguments. (Function

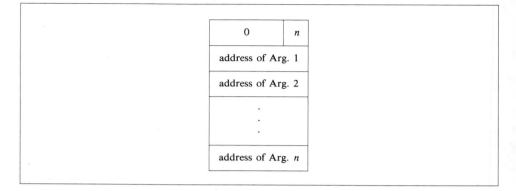

Figure 9.6   The format for an argument list

procedures return a value in R0 and perhaps R1.) Thus the next procedure linkage problems to consider are exactly what is in the argument list, what format it has, and where it is put.

Suppose a procedure has three arguments: two input arguments that it uses in its task and one output argument that it computes and sends back to the calling program. One's first thought may be to put the two data in memory somewhere, followed by an "empty" location for the procedure's result, and to tell the procedure, by putting the address of this list in the AP, where the arguments are. This scheme will work, but not for all situations. Suppose one of the arguments is an array. It would be extremely inefficient to copy the whole array into the argument list and later copy the possibly altered entries back to where the array belongs. Similarly, if one of the arguments is a long character string, or any datum that takes a lot of space, it is very inefficient to copy it into the argument list. Thus the most general mechanism for passing an argument is to put its *address* in the list, not the datum itself. This is known as *call by reference*. It is not that arguments *can't* be passed other ways, but using the argument addresses provides an extremely good and general standard. We will consider alternatives later.

The standard form for an argument list on the VAX (using call by reference) is shown in Fig. 9.6. Each row in the table is a longword. The number of arguments, n, is an unsigned byte integer, so $0 \leq n \leq 255$. The order in which the argument addresses are listed must be the same as the order in which the procedure expects them.

Creating an Argument List at Assembly Time: The .ADDRESS Directive

The .ADDRESS directive is a data initialization directive similar to the .BYTE, .WORD, and .LONG directives described in Chapter 4. Whereas the latter initialize storage to contain two's complement integers, .ADDRESS initializes storage to contain addresses. It is useful for creating argument lists at assembly time. Its format is

.ADDRESS *list_of_address_expressions*

The items in the list should be separated by commas. The assembler will put each of the addresses into memory, one after the other in the order specified, using a longword for each one. (Recall that the assembler computes the values of symbols relative to the beginning of the module or program section in which they are defined. When a procedure uses the argument list, it must have the actual addresses of the arguments. The linker makes the necessary adjustments to the values stored by the assembler.)

EXAMPLE 9.4: An Argument List

Suppose the procedure to be called has three arguments: two arrays and a longword datum that tells how many entries are in the arrays. If the procedure is to be called to work on the arrays NAMES and TAGS, and NUM contains the number of array entries, the argument list may be set up as follows:

```
ARGLST: .LONG    3              ; Number of arguments
        .ADDRESS NAMES,TAGS,NUM ; Argument addresses
```

The argument list set up by these directives is shown in Fig. 9.7. NAMES, TAGS, and NUM would of course have to be defined as usual somewhere in the program.

Often only part of an argument list can be created at assembly time, because some of the arguments are not known until execution time. For example, one procedure, say A, may call another and pass on to the second procedure some of the arguments provided by the program that called A. Also, a procedure may be called many times, perhaps in a loop, with different arguments each time. In such cases we can reserve space for the argument list and initialize those entries that will always be the same. Then, at execution time, we can move into the list those entries that will vary.

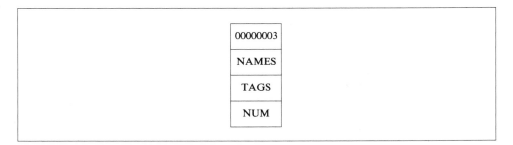

Figure 9.7 An example of an argument list

EXAMPLE 9.5: An Argument List

Suppose a procedure has four arguments: a table, its size, an item to be looked up, and a place for some information to be returned about the item looked up. The procedure will be called many times to look up different items. The argument list might be initialized as follows:

```
ARGLST:  .LONG     4              ; Number of arguments
         .ADDRESS  TABLE,SIZE     ; First two arguments
         .BLKA     1              ; Space for third argument
         .ADDRESS  INFO           ; Last argument
```

Suppose that at execution time the address of the item to be looked up is in R8. It can be inserted into the argument list as follows:

```
         MOVL      R8,ARGLST+12   ; Insert third arg. addr.
```

Creating Argument Lists on the Stack: The PUSH Instructions

An argument list set up in memory as in the examples above is permanent; i.e., the space it uses is reserved for it throughout execution of the program even if it is needed only for a short time. The user stack described in Section 9.2 is available for temporary storage and is particularly useful as a place for setting up argument lists. The list is popped from the stack upon return from the procedure, so the space can be reused. For recursive procedures (procedures that call themselves), a stack must be used for the argument lists, since each time the procedure calls itself it needs a new argument list and must not destroy the lists for the earlier calls from which it has not yet returned.

The format for an argument list on the stack is the same as the format for an argument list elsewhere in memory—i.e., the format shown in Fig. 9.6. The programmer must include instructions to explicitly push onto the stack the addresses of the arguments. The first longword of the argument list, the one containing the number of arguments, will be pushed as a side effect of the CALLS instruction.

The VAX has several instructions that simplify pushing argument addresses onto the stack. They are

$$\text{PUSHA}x \quad operand \qquad x = \text{B, W, L, or Q}$$
$$\text{PUSHL} \quad operand$$

The PUSHA instructions push the operand address onto the top of the stack; PUSHL pushes its longword operand. Since the stack pointer contains the address of the top item on the stack, SP is decremented by 4 before the datum is moved to the stack. Thus the PUSH instructions have the same effect as

$$\text{MOVA}x \quad operand, -(\text{SP})$$
$$\text{MOVL} \quad operand, -(\text{SP})$$

but are shorter, and perhaps clearer. The PUSHA instructions always push a 32-bit address onto the stack. As with the MOVA instructions, the type, *x*, in the instruction names is relevant if the addressing mode used to address the operand is one that increments or decrements a register. For example,

```
PUSHAW  (R7)+
```

would push the address in R7 on the stack and then increment R7 by 2.

Note that argument addresses must be pushed onto the stack in the order opposite to the order in which the procedure expects them, since the one pushed first will be the bottom, or last, one in the list.

EXAMPLE 9.6: Pushing an Argument List onto the Stack

To create the argument list of Example 9.5 on the stack, we could write

```
PUSHAB  INFO
PUSHL   R8
PUSHAL  SIZE
PUSHAB  TABLE
```

(Here we have arbitrarily chosen data types for the second and fourth arguments.)

Using the Arguments in a Procedure

When a procedure is called, the address of the argument list is put in AP, the Argument Pointer register. More specifically, AP will contain the address of the first byte of the list, the one containing the number of arguments. Displacement mode addressing with AP can be used to refer to the entries in the list. That is, 4(AP), 8(AP), and 12(AP) are the locations of the first, second, and third argument addresses, respectively. To address the arguments themselves—i.e., to get the actual data from memory—displacement deferred mode would be used. Recall that in displacement deferred mode, the address specified by the operand specifier is the address of the address of the operand. One of the most frequent uses of this addressing mode is for accessing procedure arguments. 4(AP), for example, is the address of the address of the first argument. Thus to refer to the actual datum, we use @4(AP).

The contents of AP and the argument list should be treated as read-only data by the procedure. That is, the procedure should not modify AP while accessing its arguments, and it should not modify the data in the argument list or store in it results to be returned to the calling program.

EXAMPLE 9.7: An Argument List and a Search Procedure

Figure 9.8 shows a search procedure that has four arguments. Figure 9.9 shows an argument list that might be used when calling this procedure. The arrows in Fig. 9.9 show the memory locations "pointed to" by the addresses. Note that the MOVL instruc-

```
                .PSECT  SEARCH
        ;
        ;  PROCEDURE  SEARCH  (ARRAY,NUM,ITEM,LOC)
        ;
        ;  This  procedure  searches  for  a  specified  item  in  an
        ;  array  of  words.  It  uses  sequential  search.
        ;
        ;  INPUT  ARGUMENTS
        ;
        ;               ARRAY   a  word  array
        (word)          NUM     the  number  of  entries  (word)
        ;               ITEM    the  item  sought
        ;
        ;  OUTPUT  ARGUMENT
        ;
        ;               LOC     the  address  of  the  item  sought  (will
        ;                       be  0  if  the  item  is  not  in  the  list)
        ;
        ;  Offsets  for  argument  list
        ARRAY = 4
        NUM = 8
        ITEM = 12
        LOC = 16
        ;
                .ENTRY  SEARCH,^M<R6,R7,R8>
        ;
        ;  REGISTER USE:       R6      ARRAY  pointer
        ;                      R7      loop  index
        ;                      R8      ITEM
        ;
                MOVL    ARRAY(AP),R6    ;  Get  address  of  ARRAY
                CVTWL   @NUM(AP),R7     ;  Get  NUM  as  longword
                BLEQ    NOTFND          ;  Branch  if  ARRAY  empty
                MOVW    @ITEM(AP),R8    ;  Get  ITEM
        ;
        COMPR:  CMPW    R8,(R6)+        ;  Compare,  increment  ptr
                BEQL    FOUND           ;  Branch  if  match  found
                SOBGTR  R7,COMPR        ;  Loop  control
        NOTFND: CLRL    @LOC(AP)        ;  Store  0,  ITEM  not  found
                RET                     ;  Return
        FOUND:  MOVAW   -(R6),@LOC(AP)  ;  Store  address  of  ITEM  in  LOC
                RET                     ;  Return
                .END
```

Figure 9.8   A search procedure

tion in Fig. 9.8 uses displacement mode to fetch the first argument address (the address of an array) from the argument list. The next two instructions each use displacement deferred mode; that is, the entry in the argument list is the operand address, and a second memory reference is made to that address to get the operand. For example, using the argument list in Fig. 9.9, the source operand specifier, @NUM(AP), in the CVTWL instruction addresses the datum 50_{10} in KNT. The operand specifier @ITEM(AP) in the next instruction addresses the datum -134_{10} in ALPHA. The MOVAW instruction toward the end of the procedure uses displacement deferred mode

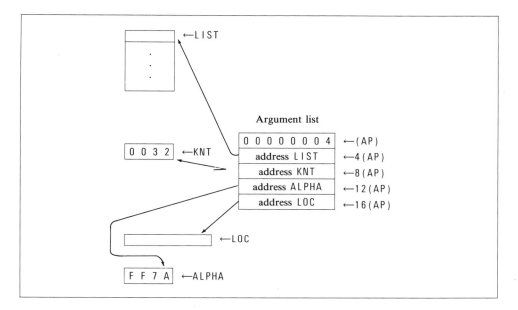

Figure 9.9   Argument list for the procedure in Fig. 9.8

to store its result in the memory location LOC addressed by the fourth argument, not in the argument list itself.

The search procedure in Fig. 9.8 contains a few very helpful documentation features. Since arguments are passed via the argument list, they can not be referred to using names, or symbols, in the procedure. In the search procedure we have introduced "dummy" names for the arguments and used them for two distinct purposes. First, it is often convenient to have names for the arguments to use in the procedure documentation, both in the general description of the procedure and in the comments on the instructions. Second, we can make the references to the argument list clearer by defining symbols whose values are the displacements from (AP) needed to reference each argument. Thus, for example, since we defined NUM = 8, we could write

```
CVTWL    @NUM(AP),R7
```

instead of

```
CVTWL    @8(AP),R7
```

Thus we can see exactly which argument is being referenced without having to remember or look up the format of the argument list.

Note also that the first comment line contains what looks like a high-level language procedure header statement. This line identifies the procedure and specifies to the reader the ordering of the arguments in the argument list.

EXAMPLE 9.8: Passing an Argument from One Procedure to Another

Suppose a main program calls Procedure A, which has three arguments, and A calls Procedure B, which has two arguments. We will consider how A can pass one of its own arguments, say the first one, to B as B's second argument. (See Fig. 9.10.) A will set up the argument list for B on the stack. It uses AP to find its own arguments. Thus it uses the instruction

```
PUSHL    4(AP)
```

to push B's second argument. Next A will push the address of B's first argument; then it will call B.

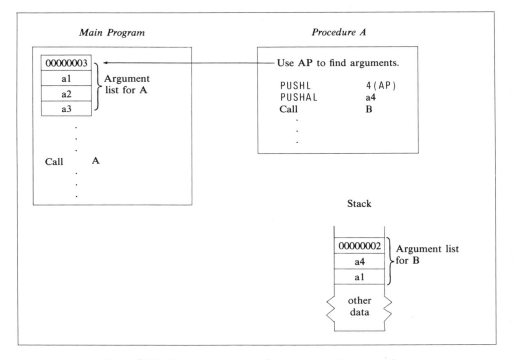

Figure 9.10   Passing an argument from one procedure to another

Variations

All the argument lists in this section pass arguments by reference; i.e., the argument list contains the addresses of the arguments. As we said earlier, this is a good general way to pass arguments, but other mechanisms are more suitable in some instances. One alternative is for the calling program to put the argument value itself in the argument list. DEC calls this the *immediate value mechanism*. A longword in the argument list is always used for each argument, whether it is passed by reference or by immediate value. This mechanism may be very convenient for constants and simple variables that are not to be changed by the procedure. It would not be used for an output argument from a procedure; the procedure never stores anything into the argument list.

Another argument passing mechanism used on the VAX is the *descriptor mechanism*. It is intended for strings (character, packed decimal, etc.) and other data types that require more than just an address to fully describe them. A character string, for example, is described by its address and length, a packed decimal datum by its address and number of digits. To pass an argument by descriptor, the calling program sets up an argument descriptor in memory and puts its address in the argument list. Figure 9.11 shows the standard descriptor format.

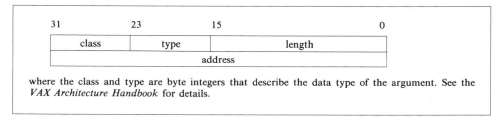

where the class and type are byte integers that describe the data type of the argument. See the *VAX Architecture Handbook* for details.

Figure 9.11   An argument descriptor

Instead of passing a string argument by descriptor, we could include both the address of the string and the address of its length in the argument list, using two arguments passed by reference just as machine instructions use two operands to describe such data types.

Of course, if different mechanisms are to be used to pass arguments, there must be an understanding between the calling program and the procedure about which mechanism is used for each argument. The procedure must use different addressing modes to access the argument, depending on how it is passed. For example, for the first argument, the following operand specifiers could be used:

4(AP)	If passed by immediate value
@4(AP)	If passed by reference
@4(R0)	After executing `MOVL  4(AP),R0` to get the descriptor address, if passed by descriptor

If the calling program and the procedure are being written by the same programmer, he or she may choose whatever mechanism is most convenient. If either program is in a program library or is produced by a high-level language compiler, the programmer must find out which mechanism it uses.

9.6 CALLING AND RETURNING FROM A PROCEDURE

The Call Frame

As we have indicated earlier, when a procedure is called, a lot of linkage information is pushed onto the user stack by the CALLS and CALLG instructions. This collection of data, in a standardized format, is called the *stack frame* or *call frame*. The data in the call frame must be found and removed from the stack when the return from the procedure is executed. Since the procedure may put other data on the stack (including possibly a call frame for another procedure that it calls), the stack pointer may be changed and can not be relied on to find the call frame. The FP (Frame Pointer) register is intended for this purpose. When a procedure is called, the address of the call frame is put in FP, and FP will be used upon return to retrieve the linkage information saved on the stack.

We have already observed that the return address [(PC) when a procedure is called] and the contents of the registers specified in the procedure's entry mask will be saved on the stack. We now consider some of the other data that should also be part of the call frame.

When a procedure is called, the addresses of the argument list and the call frame are put in AP and FP, respectively. If the procedure, say Procedure A, calls another procedure, say Procedure B, then the addresses of the argument list and call frame for Procedure B will be put in AP and FP. But Procedure A may still need to use its argument list, and its call frame will certainly be needed later. Thus it is clear that whenever a procedure is called, the current contents of AP and FP

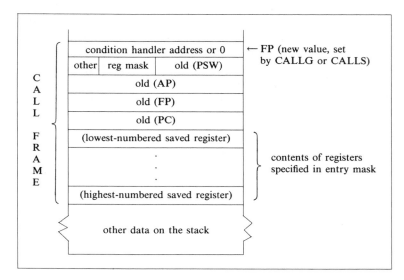

Figure 9.12 The format of the call frame

must be saved before they are changed; i.e., the contents of AP and FP will be part of the call frame.

The contents of the registers specified in the procedure's entry mask are saved on the stack and must be popped later and put back in the registers. How will the RET instruction know which registers were saved? The call frame will contain a copy of bits 11:0 of the register save mask.

Figure 9.12 shows the format of the call frame. (Some of the data included will be described later.)

Calling a Procedure

There are two procedure call instructions: CALLG and CALLS. They construct the call frame and transfer control to the procedure. CALLS is used when the argument addresses have been pushed on the stack; CALLG is used when the argument list is set up elsewhere in memory. The formats of the two instructions are

$$\text{CALLG} \quad \textit{arglist,procname}$$

$$\text{CALLS} \quad \textit{numargs,procname}$$

The first operand of CALLG is the argument list—i.e., an operand specifier that indicates the address of the argument list. The first operand of CALLS is the number of arguments, usually specified by a literal. CALLS assumes that the argument addresses are on the top of the stack. The second operand of both CALL instructions is the procedure name.

EXAMPLE 9.9: Calling Procedures

(a) Using CALLG

```
X:        .BLKL    1
Y:        .BLKL    1
Z:        .BLKL    1
ARGLST:   .LONG    3
          .ADDRESS X,Y,Z
             .
             .
             .
          CALLG    ARGLST,ADD
```

(b) Using CALLS

```
X:        .BLKL    1
Y:        .BLKL    1
Z:        .BLKL    1
             .
             .
             .
          PUSHAL   Z
          PUSHAL   Y
          PUSHAL   X
          CALLS    #3,ADD
```

CALLG and CALLS are very powerful instructions. On many computers, the programmer would have to explicitly do much of the work that these instructions do automatically. Most of the work done by the two instructions is the same. We will describe the steps carried out by CALLG in detail, then describe the few differences for CALLS.

CALLG

1. Align the SP to a longword boundary.

   The CALL instructions push several longwords onto the stack, and for efficiency they align the SP to a longword boundary first. This is done by setting the rightmost two bits of SP to zeros. See Fig. 9.13 for an illustration. The original values of the rightmost two bits will be saved (on the stack, in Step 5) so the SP can be restored to its original value by the RET instruction on return from the procedure.

2. Push contents of registers specified in the procedure's entry mask.

   The word at the address specified by *procname* is examined and interpreted as a register save mask. The registers to be saved are pushed onto the stack in decreasing order by register number (so that they appear on the stack in the natural order when read top to bottom).

3. Push contents of PC, FP, and AP.

4. Clear the condition codes in the PSW.

5. Push PSW, register mask, etc.

   A longword containing the following data is pushed onto the stack: the PSW (with the condition codes cleared), the part of the register mask that will be needed later (bits 11:0), a flag indicating that the procedure is being called with a CALLG instruction, and the rightmost two bits of the original address in SP. The format of this longword is shown in Fig. 9.14.

6. Push a longword full of zeros onto the stack.

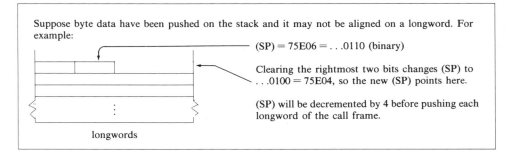

Suppose byte data have been pushed on the stack and it may not be aligned on a longword. For example:

$(SP) = 75E06 = \ldots 0110$ (binary)

Clearing the rightmost two bits changes (SP) to $\ldots 0100 = 75E04$, so the new (SP) points here.

(SP) will be decremented by 4 before pushing each longword of the call frame.

longwords

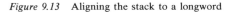

Figure 9.13   Aligning the stack to a longword

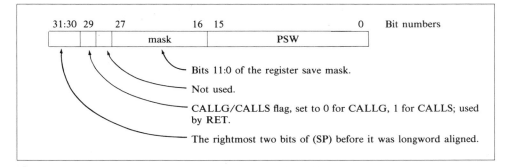

Figure 9.14 The second longword in the call frame

The procedure may store in this longword the address of a condition handling routine to be executed if an exception occurs during execution of the procedure.

7. Copy the current contents of the SP into the FP register.

The SP now contains the address of the last longword pushed onto the stack. This is the beginning of the call frame for this procedure call; its address is placed in FP.

8. Put the address of the argument list in AP.

The address of the argument list is the first operand address in the CALLG instruction.

9. Set the trap bits in the PSW.

The integer overflow and decimal overflow traps are turned on or off as indicated in the register save mask.

10. Put the address *procname*+2 into the PC.

Since the word at *procname* is the register save mask, the address where execution of the procedure is to begin is *procname*+2. Loading this address into the PC causes the transfer of control to the procedure. The CALLG instruction has now completed its work, and the CPU will fetch the next instruction to be executed as usual by using the address in the PC.

CALLS

Since the argument addresses are supposed to be at the top of the stack when CALLS is used, the first thing it does is push a longword containing the number of arguments (its first operand) onto the stack to complete the argument list. The updated value of the SP is saved in a temporary location for use in Step 8 described below.

The remaining steps carried out by the CALLS instruction are almost identical to the steps carried out by CALLG. The only differences are:

In Step 5: CALLS will set the CALLG/CALLS flag to 1 to indicate that CALLS is being used.

In Step 8: The address put in AP will be the value of the SP saved in a temporary location just after the number of arguments was pushed onto the stack.

Returning from a Procedure

The RET (RETurn) instruction is used to return from a procedure. (It has no operands.) The RET instruction must undo the work done by the CALLG or CALLS instruction; that is, it removes the call frame from the stack and restores the original contents of the registers that were saved. If the procedure was called with the CALLS instruction, RET also pops the argument list from the stack.

 At the time RET is executed, the SP may or may not be pointing to the beginning of the call frame. If data were added to the stack in the procedure and were not removed, the SP may be pointing to a higher position (lower-addressed position) on the stack. The FP, however, should always be pointing to the call frame. It is critical that the programmer not change the FP. RET will carry out the following steps:

1. Put (FP)+4 into SP.

   This pops anything that may have been added to the stack in the procedure, and it pops the first longword of the call frame, the one that may have contained a condition handler address.

2. Pop the next longword and save it in a temporary location.

   This longword contains the PSW, part of the register save mask, the CALLG/CALLS flag, and the rightmost two bits of the address that was in the SP before the procedure was called.

3. Pop the next three longwords and copy them into the AP, FP, and PC registers, respectively.

4. Pop and restore the contents of the saved registers.

   Bits 27:16 of the temporary location filled at Step 1 are examined to determine which registers were saved on the stack. The appropriate number of longwords are popped and the registers are reloaded in increasing order.

5. Reset (SP).

   At this point, the call frame has been popped from the stack and the SP points to the next longword on the stack. Bits 31:30 of the temporary location are added to SP to reset it to its original value before the procedure was called. This undoes the operation described in Fig. 9.13.

6. Load the PSW with bits 15:0 of the temporary location.

7. If CALLS was used to call the procedure, pop the argument list.

Bit 29 of the temporary is examined to determine which CALL instruction was used to call the procedure. If the bit is 1, CALLS was used and the argument list is at the top of the stack. The byte pointed to by SP contains the number of arguments, say n. SP is incremented by $4*(n + 1)$, thus effectively popping the longword with the number of arguments and all the argument addresses.

When the RET instruction completes the steps described above, the CPU will fetch and execute the next instruction as usual. Since the PC has been reloaded with the address it contained when the CALLG or CALLS was executed, the next instruction is the one that immediately follows the CALLG or CALLS in memory.

Returning Values and Flags from Procedures

The VAX convention for returning a function value from a procedure is that the procedure leaves the value in R0; if it is a quadword or double-precision floating point number, it is left in R0 and R1. Whether or not a procedure is a function, we may want it to return one or more flags. The flags might indicate whether or not the procedure successfully completed its task, whether or not certain special conditions occurred, and so on. In particular, it may be very useful for a procedure that does input (or processes input) to return flags, because there are many things that can go wrong in such a procedure. Our READRCRD macro, for example, calls a procedure that returns a flag to indicate if the end of the DATA.DAT file has been reached.

There are two convenient places for returning flags: R0 and the condition codes. (In a function procedure, R1 might be used for flags.) On the VAX it is especially easy to use R0 because the BLBS and BLBC (Branch if Low Bit is Set, or Clear) instructions can be used to test the flag upon return from the procedure. If we did not have these instructions (and many other computers do not have similar ones), an explicit test on R0 would be needed. In that case it would be preferable to use a condition code, because one conditional branch instruction could be used to test it. The VAX CALL instructions always clear the condition codes in the copy of the old PSW saved on the stack, so the programmer need only set one of the bits in the saved PSW if the condition to be indicated by the flag holds. Some of the procedures in the example in Section 9.8 return a flag by setting one of the condition codes.

9.7 LINKING WITH HIGH-LEVEL LANGUAGES AND LIBRARY ROUTINES

We mentioned in Section 9.1 as advantages of using procedures that a program may be made up of procedures written in different languages and that a program may use library procedures. So far, we have described the VAX linkage conventions from the point of view that both the calling program and the procedure are being written by the application programmer in assembly language. Here we will consider linking with high-level languages (Fortran, Pascal, and COBOL) and with procedures in the VAX-11 Run-Time Procedure Library.

The VAX procedure linkage conventions were designed with the goal of allowing linkage of programs written in different languages without a lot of extra overhead. Thus for the most part the VAX high-level language compilers translate procedures and procedure calls in a way consistent with the linkage conventions described in this chapter. A high-level language CALL statement is translated to a CALLS or CALLG instruction, so an assembly language procedure to be called by a high-level language program should establish its register mask in the usual way, use AP to find its arguments, and use RET to return control to the calling program. On the other hand, the high-level language compilers will provide register masks in the translation of high-level language procedures, translate argument references to operand specifiers using AP, and use RET to return, so such procedures can be called from assembly language programs. The only real problem to consider is which argument passing mechanisms are used.

The high-level language compilers and the procedures in the Run-Time Library use the standard argument list format described in Fig. 9.6 *except* that they do not always pass arguments or expect to receive their arguments by reference; i.e., the argument lists may not contain the addresses of the arguments. Depending on the language and the argument data type, immediate values and descriptors are sometimes used. Thus to communicate properly we must know what the particular compilers do. We will summarize the compiler standards here; for more detail and examples the reader may consult the User's Guides for the various languages.

The VAX-11 Fortran compiler normally uses call by reference for all arguments except character strings; for these it uses descriptors. Thus, for example, if the Fortran program contains the statement

```
CALL SUB1 (LIST, N, 25)
```

the compiler would set up the argument list using instructions similar to these:

```
ARGLST:  .LONG    3
         .ADDRESS LIST,N,CONST25
CONST25: .LONG    25
```

(The longword containing 25 is not part of the argument list.) To interface with an assembly language procedure that doesn't conform to the Fortran standard, the programmer can explicitly tell the Fortran compiler how the calling program should pass an argument. The VAX Fortran functions %VAL, %REF, and %DESCR cause the argument value, address, or descriptor address, respectively, to be put in the argument list. For example,

```
CALL SUB2 (%REF(STRING), LENGTH)
```

would have the compiler put the address of STRING, a character string, in the argument list instead of constructing a descriptor for STRING and putting *its* address in the argument list.

A Fortran subroutine expects its argument list to contain the addresses of its nonstring arguments and the address of a descriptor for a string argument.

The VAX Pascal compiler uses the reference mechanism for both value parameters and variable parameters. Since a variable passed as a value parameter must not be changed by the procedure, the procedure must copy its value to a temporary location and use that location, not the actual address of the parameter, in its computation. For Pascal procedures, the compiler takes care of this copying, but if the procedure is written in assembly language, the programmer must explicitly make the copy of the parameter.

If an assembly language procedure to be called from a Pascal program expects an argument to be passed by a mechanism other than by reference, an appropriate specifier must be used in the formal parameter list in the procedure declaration in the Pascal program. The specifiers are %IMMED for the immediate value mechanism, %DESCR for scaler and array descriptors, and %STDESCR for string descriptors. For example, consider the following procedure declaration.

```
procedure proc ( a  :  integer;
                 var result  :  integer;
                 %immed b  :  real;
                 %stdescr string  :  alfa ) ; extern;
```

The argument list will contain the addresses of the first two arguments, but the first argument should be copied by the assembly language procedure *proc*. The argument list will contain the current value of the third argument and the address of a descriptor (set up by the Pascal compiler) for the last argument. The *extern* statement is required to indicate that the procedure is external to the Pascal program.

An assembly language program that calls a Pascal procedure must put the argument addresses in the argument list as usual, except for a few data types that Pascal expects to be passed in other ways. (The exceptions are dynamic arrays and procedures and functions. The reader who wishes to use these may consult the manuals for more detail.)

The VAX-11 COBOL compilers use call by reference as the standard way to pass arguments. The programmer can override the standard by writing BY VALUE or BY DESCRIPTOR in front of an argument name in a COBOL CALL statement.

The VAX-11 Run-Time Procedure Library is a collection of assembly language utility procedures that can be called by assembly language and high-level language programs. Included are routines that do memory allocation, I/O, mathematical functions, data type conversion, error handling, and other functions. These procedures generally expect string arguments to be passed by descriptor, and some of them expect certain arguments to be passed by immediate value. Many of these procedures return status flags in R0. For the specific descriptions of the various procedures in the library and their argument formats, the reader should consult the *VAX-11 Run-Time Library Reference Manual.*

9.8 EXAMPLE: LINKED LIST MANIPULATION

In this section we present an example of a program that uses ten procedures. Many of them call others and must pass on some of their own arguments to the procedures they call. Thus the program illustrates a moderately complex program organization with procedure calls sometimes going four levels deep. The example is designed to illustrate some other points about program design too. Many of the procedures do fairly general operations and are written so that they could be used for applications with different data formats. All of the operations that depend on the specific data format are done in a few, very short, procedures. Thus all the data-dependent operations are isolated and easy to change. To make reading the procedures easier (and to make it easy to change them without errors), symbolic names are used for constants that depend on the data format and even for the displacements from (AP) used to refer to procedure arguments. The documentation for many of the procedures includes an algorithm written in a high-level language.

The program uses a linked list, a very useful data structure that we will describe next.

Linked Lists

In many of our examples and exercises we have had data stored in an array or table. The entries appear in consecutive locations in memory. Sometimes it is not convenient or efficient to maintain a list of items this way. If, for example, we want to keep the entries in numerical or alphabetical order, but we will often be adding or deleting items, it is inefficient to repeatedly rearrange the entries. Linked lists provide a way to separate the logical ordering of the entries from their physical arrangement in memory. In a linked list each entry has a pointer field that contains the address of the entry that is logically next, though it may be physically anywhere in memory. The term *node* is often used to refer to the group of bytes that constitute one entry in a linked list, including the pointer and all the data fields.

Since even the logically first node in a linked list may be located anywhere, we must keep track of its address. If we know where the first entry is, we can find the others by following the pointers. Thus with any linked list we would always have a pointer variable called, say *first*, pointing to the first node. The pointer field of the logically last node contains a special value called a *null pointer* (often represented by zero) to indicate that there is no next node. Figure 9.15 shows a diagram of a linked list; it assumes that the pointer field is the first field in each node.

Two of the operations we must often perform on a list are inserting new items

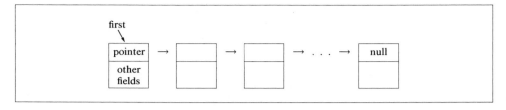

Figure 9.15   A linked list

and deleting existing items. In an array, these operations can require moving a lot of data. In a linked list, they require changing only one or two pointer values, as illustrated in Fig. 9.16. To standardize the steps used to insert or delete a node, it is helpful to have a fixed node at the beginning of the list that does not contain an actual entry and is never deleted (unless the entire list is no longer needed). Such a

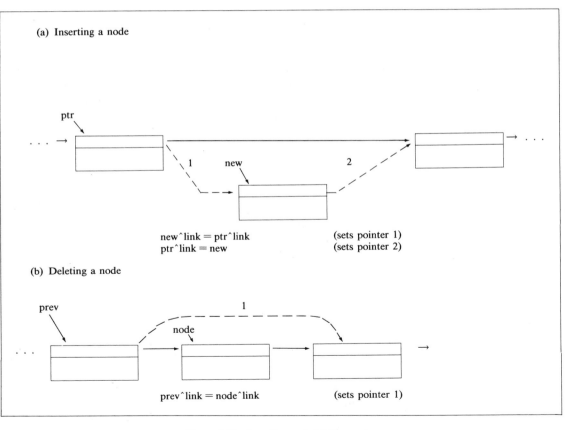

Figure 9.16   Inserting and deleting nodes

node is called a *header node.* Its use eliminates the special cases of changing *first* if a new entry is added at the beginning of the list or if the first entry is deleted. The header node may contain information about the list such as its name or the number of current entries.

In order to add a new item to a linked list, we must be able to find some space in memory that is not in use. Usually a large area of memory is reserved for linked list nodes (possibly for several different lists). This space is divided up into units of the size needed for a node, and these units, or empty nodes, are linked up in a linked list of available nodes. Whenever a program wants to construct a new node, it must get an empty one from the list of available nodes. When an item is deleted from a linked list, the space it occupied must be reclaimed; i.e., the node should be returned to the available node list so that it may be used again later if more items are inserted. Since the ordering of the empty nodes is irrelevant, nodes will be removed from and returned to the beginning of the available node list. The available node list does not need a header node.

Notation

To describe algorithms that operate on linked lists, we need some notation to refer to the various fields of arbitrary nodes in the lists. Each node in one list will have the same format, and we can give names to the fields. To refer to a particular field in a particular node, we will use the notation

$$ptr^\wedge field\_name$$

where *ptr* is a pointer to the desired node. Thus

$$first^\wedge link$$

would be the link (pointer) field of the node pointed to by *first.* The value of $first^\wedge link$ is the contents of that field: the address of the next node.

The Example

The sample program contains procedures to insert, delete, and find items, and to print all the items, in a linked list that is kept (logically) in numeric or alphabetical order. These procedures assume that the pointer field is the first field in the node, but they make no assumptions about the number, type, or size of the other fields. Thus they could be used for many different applications. They appear in Fig. 9.17.

The three data-dependent procedures are in Fig. 9.18. They compare, fill, and print the node key, or identifier, field. In this program the nodes contain only a pointer and key, which is an eight-byte character string. The field names are *link* and *key.*

```
        .PSECT  AVAIL
;
; PROCEDURE AVAIL
;
; This procedure manages the available node pool.
; It has three entry points:
;
;       INIT_AVAIL (NODES, BYTES, NODE_SIZE)
;           links up all the nodes in the node pool
;
;       GET_NODE (PTR)
;           removes a node from the available node list
;           and returns a pointer to it
;
;       RET_NODE (PTR)
;           adds a given node to the available node list
;
; AVAIL contains a pointer to the first node in the linked
; available node list. It is initialized by INIT_AVAIL and
; is used by GET_NODE and RET_NODE.
;
AVAIL:  .BLKL  1                     ; Ptr to first available node
;
; INIT_AVAIL (NODES, BYTES, NODE_SIZE)
;
; Input arguments
;       NODES           the node pool
;       BYTES           the number of bytes in the pool
;       NODE_SIZE       the number of bytes per node
;
;  Offsets for argument list
NODES = 4
BYTES = 8
NODE_SIZE = 12
;
        .ENTRY  INIT_AVAIL,^M<R6,R8,R9>
;
; Register use         R6      pointer to current node
;                      R8      node size
;                      R9      address of next-to-last node
;
; Use node size to determine address of next-to-last node.
;
        MOVL    NODES(AP),R6         ; Address of first node
        MOVL    @NODE_SIZE(AP),R8    ; Node size
        ADDL3   R6,@BYTES(AP),R9     ; Address+number of bytes
        SUBL2   R8,R9                ; Address of last node
        SUBL2   R8,R9                ; Addr of next-to-last node
;
; Set pointer to first available node.
;
        MOVL    R6,AVAIL             ; First node is first available
;
; Link up nodes. (Store pointer to next node in all but the
; last node; store null pointer in last node.)
;
LINK:   ADDL3   R6,R8,(R6)           ;Store ptr to next node
        ACBL    R9,R8,R6,LINK
        CLRL    (R6)                 ;Store null ptr in last node
        RET
```

Figure 9.17 Data-independent linked list procedures

```
;
;
; GET_NODE (PTR)
;
; Output argument
;        PTR                     pointer to an available node
;
         .ENTRY  GET_NODE,0
;
         MOVL     AVAIL,@4(AP)              ; Return ptr to a node
         BEQL     DONE                      ; Done if null
         MOVL     @AVAIL,AVAIL              ; Remove node from pool
DONE:    RET
;
;
; RET_NODE (PTR)
;
; Input argument
;        PTR                     pointer to node to be returned to pool
;
         .ENTRY  RET_NODE,0
;
         MOVL     AVAIL,@4(AP)              ; ptr^link = avail
         MOVL     4(AP),AVAIL               ; avail = ptr
         RET
         .END
```

```
         .PSECT   INSERT
;
; PROCEDURE INSERT (KEY, FIRST)
;
; This procedure inserts a new item into the linked list.
; The list is assumed to be sorted. A flag is returned
; in the Z condition code in the saved PSW to indicate
; whether or not there was room to add the new node.
;
; The algorithm is:
;
;      call get_node (new);
;      if new <> null then begin
;                        call fill_key (key, new);
;                        call find_place (key, first, ptr);
;                        new^link = ptr^link;
;                        ptr^link = new;
;                        set Z to indicate success
;                      end.
;
;
;
; Offsets for argument list
KEY = 4
FIRST = 8
;
NEW:     .BLKL    1                         ; For ptr to new node
PTR:     .BLKL    1                         ; For ptr returned by find_place
;
```

Figure 9.17 (Continued)

```
        .ENTRY  INSERT,0
;
; Construct node for new item.
;
        PUSHAL  NEW
        CALLS   #1,GET_NODE        ; Get node from pool
        TSTL    NEW                ; If new = null, return
        BEQL    RET
        PUSHL   NEW                ; Address of new node
        PUSHL   KEY(AP)            ; Address of KEY
        CALLS   #2,FILL_KEY        ; Fill key field
;
; Find position in list where new item belongs.
;
        PUSHAL  PTR
        PUSHL   FIRST(AP)          ; Address of first node
        PUSHL   KEY(AP)            ; Address of KEY
        CALLS   #3,FIND_PLACE
;
; Link in new node.
;
        MOVL    @PTR,@NEW          ; new^link = ptr^link
        MOVL    NEW,@PTR           ; ptr^link = new
        BISB2*  #^X04,4(FP)        ; Set Z to indicate insertion
;
RET:    RET
        .END
```

```
        .PSECT  DELETE
;
; PROCEDURE DELETE (KEY, FIRST)
;
; This procedure deletes the node with key KEY from the sorted
; linked list with header node pointed to by FIRST. It sets
; the Z bit in the saved PSW if KEY was found in the list and
; deleted. The deleted node is returned to the node pool.
;
; The algorithm is:
;
;     call find_place (KEY,FIRST,PTR);
;     node = ptr^link;
;     if node <> null then if node^key = KEY
;                          then begin
;                                  ptr^link = node^link;
;                                  call ret_node(node);
;                                  set Z
;                               end.
;
; Offsets for argument list
KEY = 4
FIRST = 8
;
PTR:    .BLKL   1                  ; For ptr returned by find_place
;
        .ENTRY  DELETE,^M<R6>
;
; Register use        R6      node pointer
;
```

Figure 9.17 (Continued)

```
; Find position in list where KEY may be.
;
        PUSHAL  PTR
        PUSHL   FIRST(AP)               ; Address of header node
        PUSHL   KEY(AP)                 ; Address of KEY
        CALLS   #3,FIND_PLACE
        MOVL    @PTR,R6                 ; node = ptr^link
        BEQL    RET                     ; Return if node = null
;
; Determine if KEY is really there.
;
        PUSHL   R6                      ; Address of node
        PUSHL   KEY(AP)                 ; Address of KEY
        CALLS   #2,COMPARE              ; See if KEY is in list
        BNEQ    RET                     ; Return if KEY not there
;
; Delete the node.
;
        MOVL    (R6),@PTR               ; ptr^link = node^link
;
; Return node to available list.
;
        PUSHL   R6                      ; Address of node
        CALLS   #1,RET_NODE
;
; Set flag.
;
        BISB2   #^X04,4(FP)             ; Set Z for deletion
RET:    RET
        .END
```

```
        .PSECT  FIND
;
; PROCEDURE FIND (KEY,FIRST,PTR)
;
; This procedure returns a pointer (in PTR) to the node
; containing the key KEY. FIRST is a pointer to the list
; header node. If KEY is not in the list, the returned
; pointer will be null.
;
; The algorithm is:
;
;     call find_place (KEY,FIRST,PREV);
;     ptr = prev^link;
;     if ptr = null then return null;
;     if ptr^key <> KEY then return null
;                       else return ptr.
;
; Offsets for argument list
KEY = 4
FIRST = 8
PTR = 12
;
PREV:   .BLKL   1                       ; For ptr returned by find_place
;
        .ENTRY  FIND,^M<R6>
```

Figure 9.17 (Continued)

```
;
; Register use        R6      ptr
;
; Find position where KEY may be.
;
          PUSHAL  PREV                ; For ptr returned by find_place
          PUSHL   FIRST(AP)           ; Address of header node
          PUSHL   KEY(AP)             ; Address of KEY
          CALLS   #3,FIND_PLACE
;
; Determine if KEY is really there.
;
          MOVL    @PREV,R6            ; ptr = prev^link
          BEQL    NODE                ; Return ptr if null
          PUSHL   R6                  ; Address of node
          PUSHL   KEY(AP)             ; Address of KEY
          CALLS   #2,COMPARE          ; Compare keys
          BEQL    NODE
          CLRL    R6                  ; Null
;
; Return ptr.
;
NODE:     MOVL    R6,@PTR(AP)         ; Return ptr or null
          RET
          .END
```

```
          .PSECT  FIND_PLACE
;
; PROCEDURE FIND_PLACE (KEY, FIRST, PTR)
;
; This procedure finds the place where a node with key
; KEY belongs in the sorted linked list pointed to by
; FIRST. It returns in PTR a pointer to the node that
; would precede the one containing KEY.
;
; The algorithm is:
;
;     ptr = first;
;     next = ptr^link;
;     while next <> null do
;        begin
;           if KEY <= next^key then exitloop;
;           ptr = next;
;           next = ptr^link
;        end;
;     return ptr.
;
;
; Offsets for argument list
KEY = 4
FIRST = 8
PTR = 12
;
          .ENTRY  FIND_PLACE,^M<R6,R7>
;
; Register use        R6      ptr
;                     R7      next
;
```

Figure 9.17 (Continued)

```
              MOVL     FIRST(AP),R6              ; ptr = first
NEXT:         MOVL     (R6),R7                   ; next = ptr^link
              BEQL     FOUND                     ; If next = null, done
              PUSHL    R7                        ; Address of node
              PUSHL    KEY(AP)                   ; Address of key
              CALLS    #2,COMPARE                ; Compare keys
              BLEQ     FOUND                     ; KEY <= node key
              MOVL     R7,R6                     ; ptr = next
              BRB      NEXT
;
FOUND:        MOVL     R6,@PTR(AP)               ; Return ptr
;
              RET
              .END
```

```
              .PSECT  PRINTLIST
;
; PROCEDURE PRINTLIST (TITLE, FIRST)
;
; This procedure prints out the entries in the linked list
; pointed to by FIRST. The list is assumed to have a header
; node. TITLE is a character string printed as a heading
; for the list.
;
; Offsets for argument list
TITLE = 4
FIRST = 8
;
              .ENTRY  PRINTLIST,^M<R6>
;
; Register use        R6      pointer to current node
;
              PRINTCHRS @TITLE(AP)              ; Print heading
              MOVL     FIRST(AP),R6              ; Get ptr to header node
NEXT:         MOVL     (R6),R6                   ; Get next ptr.
              BEQL     DONE
              PUSHL    R6                        ; Push pointer
              CALLS    #1,PRINTKEY
              BRB      NEXT
DONE:         RET
              .END
```

    * The BISB2 instruction is the only instruction used in these procedures that has not been described yet in the text. It sets a bit (to 1).

Figure 9.17 (Concluded)

Note that even though the data-dependent procedures are very short, it is very good programming style to use them; they clearly isolate the parts of the program that would have to be changed for an application with a different node format.

Figure 9.19 shows the main program and the procedure that processes input data to test the linked list procedures. Figure 9.20 shows the data file used for the tests and the output from the program.

```
            .PSECT  FILL_KEY
;
;  PROCEDURE FILL_KEY (KEY,NODE)
;
;  This procedure fills the key field of NODE with the
;  key KEY.
;
;  The number of bytes in the key, KEY_SIZE, and the
;  offset of the key field from the beginning of the node,
;  KEY_FIELD, are constants defined in this procedure.
;
KEY_SIZE = 8                            ; Number of bytes per key
KEY_FIELD = 4                           ; Offset for key field
;
;  Offsets for argument list
KEY = 4
NODE = 8
;
            .ENTRY  FILL_KEY,^M<R2,R3,R4,R5,R6>
;
;  Register use         R6      address of node
;                       R0-R5   used by MOVC3
;
        MOVL    NODE(AP),R6             ; Get address of node
        MOVC3   #KEY_SIZE,@KEY(AP),KEY_FIELD(R6)    ; Store KEY
        RET
        .END
```

```
            .PSECT  COMPARE
;
;  PROCEDURE COMPARE (KEY, PTR)
;
;  This procedure compares KEY with the key in the node pointed
;  to by PTR and sets the condition codes in the stacked PSW
;  to indicate the relation between the two keys.
;
;  The number of bytes in the key, KEY_SIZE, and the
;  offset of the key field from the beginning of the node,
;  KEY_FIELD, are constants defined in this procedure.
;
KEY_SIZE = 8                            ; Number of bytes per key
KEY_FIELD = 4                           ; Offset for key field
;
;  Offsets for argument list
KEY = 4
PTR = 8
;
            .ENTRY  COMPARE,^M<R2,R3,R6>
;
;  Register use         R6      ptr
;                       R0-R3   used by CMPC3
;
```

Figure 9.18 Data-dependent procedures

```
            MOVL    PTR(AP),R6                  ; Address of node
            CMPC3   #KEY_SIZE,@KEY(AP),KEY_FIELD(R6)
            BGTR    RET
            BLSS    SET_N
SET_Z:      BISB2   #^X04,4(FP)                 ; Set Z for equal keys
            BRB     RET
SET_N:      BISB2   #^X08,4(FP)                 ; Set N if KEY < ptr^key
RET:        RET
            .END
```

```
            .PSECT  PRINTKEY
;
; PROCEDURE PRINTKEY (PTR)
;
; This procedure prints the key in the node pointed to by
; the given pointer PTR.
;
; The number of bytes in the key, KEY_SIZE, and the
; offset of the key field from the beginning of a node,
; KEY_FIELD, are constants defined in this procedure.
;
KEY_SIZE = 8                                ; Number of bytes per key
KEY_FIELD = 4                               ; Offset for key field
;
; Offset for argument list
PTR = 4
;
TAB = 9
LINE:       .BYTE   TAB,0[KEY_SIZE]
;
            .ENTRY  PRINTKEY,^M<R2,R3,R4,R5,R6>
;
; Register use          R6      ptr
;                       R0-R5   used by MOVC3
;
            MOVL    PTR(AP),R6                  ; Get pointer
            MOVC3   #KEY_SIZE,KEY_FIELD(R6),LINE+1
            PRINTCHRS LINE,#KEY_SIZE+1  ; Print key
            RET
            .END
```

Figure 9.18 (Concluded)

```
; MAIN PROGRAM
;
; This program tests the linked list procedures. It calls
; INIT_AVAIL to link up all of the nodes, then calls TESTER
; to read and process the test data, and finally, calls
; PRINTLIST to print all the keys in the list.
;
;
POOL = 250                          ; Number of bytes in node pool
                                    ; Number of bytes per node
NODE_SIZE = 12
NODES:  .BLKB    POOL
BYTES:  .LONG    POOL
NODE_SZ: .LONG   NODE_SIZE
;
FIRST:  .BLKL    1                  ; Pointer to header node
ARGS1:  .LONG    3                  ; Argument list for INIT_AVAIL
        .ADDRESS NODES,BYTES,NODE_SZ
;
TAB = 9                             ; Tab
LF = 10                             ; Line feed
CR = 13                             ; Carriage return
TITLE1: .ASCIZ   /List is empty to start/
TITLE2: .ASCII   <LF><LF>/OUTPUT FROM PRINTLIST/
        .ASCIZ   <CR><LF><LF><TAB>/GOODIES/<LF>
;
;
        BEGIN    LINKED
;
        CALLG    ARGS1,INIT_AVAIL   ; Link all nodes
        PUSHAL   FIRST
        CALLS    #1,GET_NODE        ; Get a header node
        CLRL     @FIRST             ; Set ptr in header to null
;
        PUSHL    FIRST             ; Pointer to header node
        PUSHAB   TITLE1            ; Heading for empty list
        CALLS    #2,PRINTLIST      ; Print empty list (to be sure
;                                  ; PRINTLIST works properly)
;
        PUSHL    FIRST
        CALLS    #1,TESTER          ;Process test data
;
        PUSHL    FIRST
        PUSHAB   TITLE2
        CALLS    #2,PRINTLIST       ; Print list
;
        EXIT
        .END     LINKED
```

Figure 9.19 The main program and TESTER procedure

```
            .PSECT   TESTER
;
; PROCEDURE TESTER (FIRST)
;
; This procedure processes input data to test the linked list
; procedures. It reads records from DATA.DAT of the form
;
;        CODE KEY
;
; where CODE is a one-letter code telling what to do with the
; item and KEY is the item's key. (The number of bytes in
; the keys can be varied without changing TESTER.)
; TESTER prints out all of the records processed along with
; a brief message indicating the result of the action taken.
;
;
FIRST = 4                                  ; Offset for argument list
;
; Codes
INS = ^A/I/                                ; Insert
DEL = ^A/D/                                ; Delete
FND = ^A/F/                                ; Find
;
BUFFER:  .BLKB    80
BLANKS:  .BYTE    ^X20[80]
PTR:     .BLKL    1                         ; For pointer returned by FIND
;
LF = 10
TAB = 9
HDG:     .ASCIZ   <LF><LF>/TEST DATA/<LF>
INSMSG:  .ASCIZ   <TAB>/inserted/
NOROOM:  .ASCIZ   <TAB>/no more nodes available/
DELMSG:  .ASCIZ   <TAB>/deleted/
NOTIN:   .ASCIZ   <TAB>/not in the list/
ERRMSG:  .ASCIZ   <TAB>/Bad code!!/
;
;
         .ENTRY   TESTER,^M<R2,R3,R4,R5>
;
; Read and print test record.
;
         PRINTCHRS       HDG
READ:    MOVC3           #80,BLANKS,BUFFER
         READRCRD        BUFFER
         PRINTCHRS       BUFFER,R0
;
; Determine operation to be performed and call appropriate
; procedure.
;
         CMPB      BUFFER,#INS
         BNEQ      TRY_DEL
         PUSHL     FIRST(AP)              ; Call INSERT
         PUSHAB    BUFFER+2
         CALLS     #2,INSERT
         BEQL      IN
         PRINTCHRS NOROOM
         BRW       DONE
```

Figure 9.19 (Continued)

```
        IN:      PRINTCHRS INSMSG
                 BRW       DONE
        ;
        TRY_DEL: CMPB      BUFFER,#DEL
                 BNEQ      TRY_FND
                 PUSHL     FIRST(AP)          ; Call DELETE
                 PUSHAB    BUFFER+2
                 CALLS     #2,DELETE
                 BEQL      DELETED
                 PRINTCHRS NOTIN
                 BRW       DONE
        DELETED: PRINTCHRS DELMSG
                 BRW       DONE
        ;
        TRY_FND: CMPB      BUFFER,#FND
                 BNEQ      ERROR
                 PUSHAL    PTR                ; Call FIND
                 PUSHL     FIRST(AP)
                 PUSHAB    BUFFER+2
                 CALLS     #3,FIND
                 TSTL      PTR
                 BEQL      NOTFND
                 PUSHL     PTR
                 CALLS     #1,PRINTKEY
                 BRW       DONE
        NOTFND:  PRINTCHRS NOTIN
                 BRW       DONE
        ;
        ERROR:   PRINTCHRS ERRMSG
        DONE:    BRW       READ
        ;
        EOF:     RET
                 .END
```

Figure 9.19 (Concluded)

(a) The data file	(b) Output from the program (shown here in two columns)	

(a) The data file

```
I APPLES
I SPINACH
I CHOCOLATE
D PIZZA
I BROWNIES
I ICE CREAM
J COOKIES
D SPINACH
F SPINACH
I SPINACH
F SPINACH
F ICE CREAM
D APPLES
I EGGS
I MOO SHU PORK
D ALMONDS
I BANANAS
I CHEESECAKE
F COOKIES
F BROWNIES
I ALMONDS
D ZUCCHINI
I MILK
I COFFEE
I TURKEY
I YAMS
I SHRIMP
I BACON
I CHEESE
I PIZZA
I ABALONE
I DOUGHNUTS
F ALMONDS
F YAMS
I CROISSANTS
I PASTRY
D SPINACH
D COFFEE
I WINE
I CROISSANTS
I CANTALOUPE
I CASHEWS
```

(b) Output from the program (shown here in two columns)

```
List is empty to start


TEST DATA

I APPLES
          inserted
I SPINACH
          inserted
I CHOCOLATE
          inserted
D PIZZA
          not in the list
I BROWNIES
          inserted
I ICE CREAM
          inserted
J COOKIES
          Bad code!!
D SPINACH
          deleted
F SPINACH
          not in the list
I SPINACH
          inserted
F SPINACH
          SPINACH
F ICE CREAM
          ICE CREA
D APPLES
          deleted
I EGGS
          inserted
I MOO SHU PORK
          inserted
D ALMONDS
          not in the list
I BANANAS
          inserted
I CHEESECAKE
          inserted
F COOKIES
          not in the list
F BROWNIES
          BROWNIES
I ALMONDS
          inserted
D ZUCCHINI
          not in the list
I MILK
          inserted
I COFFEE
          inserted
I TURKEY
          inserted
I YAMS
          inserted
```

```
I SHRIMP
          inserted
I BACON
          inserted
I CHEESE
          inserted
I PIZZA
          inserted
I ABALONE
          inserted
I DOUGHNUTS
          inserted
F ALMONDS
          ALMONDS
F YAMS
          YAMS
I CROISSANTS
          no more nodes available
I PASTRY
          no more nodes available
D SPINACH
          deleted
D COFFEE
          deleted
I WINE
          inserted
I CROISSANTS
          inserted
I CANTALOUPE
          no more nodes available
I CASHEWS
          no more nodes available


OUTPUT FROM PRINTLIST

          GOODIES

          ABALONE
          ALMONDS
          BACON
          BANANAS
          BROWNIES
          CHEESE
          CHEESECA
          CHOCOLAT
          CROISSAN
          DOUGHNUT
          EGGS
          ICE CREA
          MILK
          MOO SHU
          PIZZA
          SHRIMP
          TURKEY
          WINE
          YAMS
```

Figure 9.20 The data file and program output

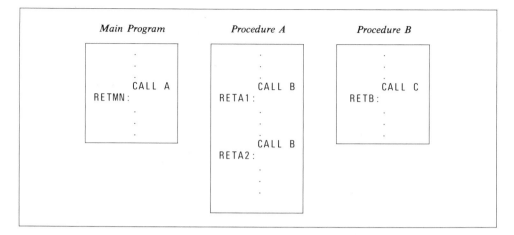

Figure 9.21 Procedures for Exercise 3

9.9 SUMMARY

A procedure is an independently written and assembled (or compiled) module that performs a particular task when it is called by another program. The use of procedures makes programs much easier to develop, debug, and modify.

The procedure linkage conventions are a set of instructions and conventions that transfer control to a procedure, pass arguments to it, protect data in registers used by the calling program, and return to the calling program. The VAX procedure linkage conventions make heavy use of the user stack supplied to a program by the operating system. The collection of information saved on the stack is called the *call frame.* Its format is shown in Fig. 9.12.

The procedure has the responsibility of specifying which registers it uses so that their original contents may be stacked and retrieved when control returns to the calling program. The .ENTRY directive in the procedure provides this information.

The standard argument list format is shown in Fig. 9.6. Argument lists may be set up on the stack or elsewhere in memory. Arguments are most often passed *by reference;* i.e., the argument list contains the addresses of the arguments, as in Fig. 9.6. The alternatives are to put the value of the argument or the address of an argument descriptor in the argument list. The address of the argument list is passed to the procedure in AP.

The address of the call frame is passed to the procedure in FP. It is used by the RET instruction to find the call frame and retrieve the stored data.

Table 9.1 summarizes the new instructions and assembler directives that were introduced in this chapter.

TABLE 9.1   Instructions and Directives Used With Procedures

For Transferring Control

.ENTRY	*procname,regmask*	Establish *procname* as a global symbol and as an entry point for the procedure; set up the register save mask.
CALLG	*arglist,procname*	Call the procedure *procname;* the argument list is not on the stack.
CALLS	*numargs,procname*	Call the procedure *procname;* the argument list is on the stack.
RET		Return from a procedure.

For Setting Up Argument Lists

.ADDRESS	*expressions*	Initialize longwords in memory to contain the values of the expressions.
PUSHA*x*	*operand*	Push the operand address onto the stack. (*x* = B, W, L, or Q.)
PUSHL	*operand*	Push the operand onto the stack.

For Internal Subroutines

BSBB	*destination*	Branch to subroutine (B for byte displacement, W for word displacement).
BSBW	*destination*	
RSB		Return from subroutine.

9.10 EXERCISES

(Unless otherwise stated, all arguments are passed by reference.)

1. Write a procedure to print out the entries in a character string array. The arguments should be the array and the number of entries (a longword). Assume the strings are each 12 characters long.

2. Rewrite the binary search routine in Fig. 7.6 as a procedure. The data TABLE, NUM, KEY, SIZE, and INDEX described in Fig. 7.6 should be the arguments.

3. Suppose a main program calls Procedure A, A calls B in two places, and B calls C. Suppose the labels on the return locations are RETMN, RETA1, RETA2, and RETB. (See Fig. 9.21 for an illustration.) Suppose C is now being executed, and it was called by B, which was called by the *second* call in A. Draw a diagram of the stack showing which return addresses are on it and in what order. (You may use the labels to denote the return addresses, and you may ignore any other data that would also be on the stack.)

4. Write instructions to set up an argument list for the binary search procedure described in Exercise 2. Include storage reservation and/or initialization directives for the arguments. Use any reasonable data.

5. This exercise considers possible alternative formats for the call frame. For each alternative

we will assume that the CALL instructions are modified to push the data in the order that would be required. The point is to determine if any information would be lost or if the RET instruction would have difficulties retrieving the stacked data later.

(a) Could the three longwords containing the old contents of the AP, FP, and PC be arranged in a different order?

(b) Could the old contents of AP, FP, and PC be pushed before the contents of the registers specified in the register save mask?

(c) Could the longword containing the register save mask and the PSW be pushed before the contents of the registers to be saved?

6. Why does the CALLS instruction save the address of the argument list in a temporary location instead of putting it into AP immediately?

7. Write an operand specifier that could be used to fetch

(a) The address of the fourth argument.

(b) The datum that is the third argument.

8. Consider the following argument list and memory contents.

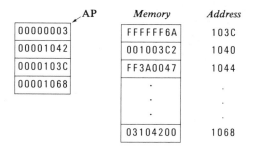

What will be in R8 after each of the following instructions? (You may assume R8 is cleared before each instruction.)

(a) MOVW   @8(AP),R8   **(b)** MOVL   12(AP),R8

9. Show the machine code for the following operand specifiers.

(a) 4(AP)   **(b)** @12(AP)

(c) @ALPHA (assuming ALPHA = 3A and the operand specifier begins at location 0E7).

10. Suppose a main program calls Procedure A, Procedure A calls Procedure B, Procedure B calls Procedure C, and Procedure C calls Procedure D. Write instructions to go in Procedure D that would

(a) Put the address of Procedure D's argument list in R10.

(b) Put the address of Procedure B's argument list in R10.

(c) Put the address of Procedure A's condition handler in R10.

11. Suppose you are writing an operating systems routine to process program exceptions. Write instructions to find the most recently stacked call frame that contains a nonzero condition handler address and put the handler address in R10. (You may assume there is a nonzero condition handler in one of the frames currently on the stack.)

12. The procedure PROC has four arguments, passed by reference, described as follows (and in the order listed):

TAG	a byte integer
STRING1	a character string
STRING2	another character string
MSGLOC	a longword for the result determined by PROC

If the byte tag is negative, PROC puts the address of STRING1 into MSGLOC. If the tag is nonnegative, it puts the address of STRING2 into MSGLOC. Write the procedure.

13. Write a function procedure to find the first blank character in a character string and return its address. If there are no blanks in the string, the function should return the address of the byte following the end of the string. The argument list contains the addresses of the first and last bytes of the string. (Recall that a function procedure returns its result in R0.)

14. Write the instructions needed to call the procedure PROC which has no arguments. Use CALLS, then CALLG. Which is preferable? Why?

15. Write a procedure for the Bubble Sort algorithm described in Exercise 31 of Chapter 7.

16. Suppose a true/false test with 20 questions has been given to 50 people. Each person's answers are encoded in the rightmost 20 bits of a longword, and all these longwords are in an array ANSWERS. The longword KEY contains the correct answers. There is a procedure SCORE that grades a test. Its arguments (in order) are: a person's answers, the key, and a byte in which SCORE returns the number of answers the person had correct. Assume space is reserved for a byte array GRADES. We want to put in each entry of GRADES the number of correct answers given by the person whose answers are in the corresponding position in ANSWERS. Write instructions to set up the argument list and call the procedure SCORE as many times as necessary to grade all the tests.

17. Write a procedure GETNUM with the following arguments:

Input arguments:

START	the first byte of a character string
END	the byte that follows the string

Output arguments:

NUMBER	the two's complement representation of the first leading separate numeric number found in the string (a longword)
NEWSTART	the address of the byte following the first leading separate numeric number found in the string

(The argument list, as usual, contains the addresses of the arguments described.) GETNUM should return a 1 in R0 if a leading separate numeric number is found in the character string and properly converted; it should return 0 in R0 otherwise (e.g., if no number is found or if the number found overflows a longword). In the latter cases, NUMBER and NEWSTART need not be stored.

18. Write instructions to set up an argument list using the same arguments in Example 9.5 except that the second and third arguments are to be passed by immediate value.

19. Using the data structure and general conventions of the example in Section 9.8, write a procedure FIND_ITH that has three arguments, FIRST, I, and PTR, where FIRST is a pointer to the header node of a linked list, I is an integer, and FIND_ITH returns in PTR a pointer to the *i*th node in the list (or a null pointer if there are fewer than *i* nodes).

20. (a) Suppose we have an array with *n* entries arranged in order. How many entries must be moved, in the worst case, to insert a new entry in the proper position? (Recall that with a linked list only two pointers need be changed and no entries are moved.)

(b) Suppose we are given a number *i* and we wish to find the *i*th entry in a list. Compare the amount of work that must be done if the list is kept in an array with the amount of work that must be done if the list is a linked list.

21. Suppose that the keys in the sample program in Section 9.8 were two's complement integers instead of character strings. Indicate which procedures would need changes and what the changes would be.

22. The INSERT procedure in Section 9.8 does not check whether the key to be inserted is already in the list. Modify INSERT to check for this condition and return a flag to the calling program to indicate if the item was not inserted because it was already in the list. Note that now INSERT must return a three-way flag: successful insertion, no insertion because no nodes are available, and no insertion because the item is a duplicate.

23. Rewrite the main program and the TESTER procedure for the example in Section 9.8 to work with two linked lists instead of one. The main program should initialize header nodes and pointers, LIST1 and LIST2, for the two lists. The data read by TESTER should have a list number, 1 or 2, in addition to the code for the operation and the key. TESTER should see that the operation is performed on the specified list.

Chapter 10

Some Assembler Features

10.1 PROGRAM SECTIONS

PSECTS and Their Attributes

An assembly language program may be divided into several program sections that can be named by the programmer and assigned various attributes. Two of the advantages of using program sections are that they allow for the protection of instructions and read-only data from accidental overwriting, and they can be used to permit different modules to access the same data.

The .PSECT (Program SECTion) directive tells the assembler to begin a new program section (or to continue an existing one). All the data and instructions that follow the directive and precede the next .PSECT directive (or the .END directive if there are no more .PSECTs) will be part of that program section. The format of the directive is

.PSECT   *psect_name,attributes*

The psect_name may be any name satisfying the rules for a symbol. We will describe a few, though not all, of the attributes that may be specified.

The WRT (WRiTe) and NOWRT (NO WRiTe) attributes indicate whether or not the contents of the program section may be modified at execution time. NOWRT may be specified for program sections containing read-only data or instructions. The default is WRT.

The EXE (EXEcute) and NOEXE (NO EXEcute) attributes indicate whether or not the contents of the program section may be executed as instructions. The default is EXE.[1]

The CON (CONcatenate) and OVR (OVeRlay) attributes indicate whether or not multiple .PSECT directives with the same name are to be considered as extensions to the program section or as overlays. The OVR attribute allows different modules to access the same data; we will consider examples later. The default is CON.

We have mentioned (in Chapter 2) that efficiency of instruction execution is improved if data are aligned on appropriate boundaries—i.e., if words begin at addresses divisible by 2, longwords by 4, and quadwords by 8. The alignment attribute of a program section specifies the maximum alignment that may be forced in the program section using the .ALIGN directive (described below). The program section itself is aligned to begin on a boundary indicated by its alignment attribute. The alignment may be specified by a keyword BYTE, WORD, LONG, QUAD, or PAGE. (A page boundary is an address divisible by 512.) The default is BYTE. Normally, when the assembler encounters a storage reservation or initialization directive, it reserves space or stores data beginning at the next available byte, the one whose location is given by the current value of the location counter. The .ALIGN directive tells the assembler to increase the location counter if necessary so that it will be on the next boundary of the requested type. The directive may be used as follows:

.ALIGN   *keyword*

where the keyword may be any of the keywords mentioned above for specifying the program section alignment. No .ALIGN directive may specify an alignment that exceeds the maximum for the program section.

Figure 10.1 illustrates a possible program organization for a program that contains some read-only data, some data to be used and modified by the program, and instructions. Note that one of the program section names is the same as the entry point name; this is permitted, but not required.

If, during execution, an attempt is made to write in a program section with the NOWRT attribute or to execute instructions in a program section with the NOEXE attribute, an error message will be displayed. Data will be protected, and some errors resulting from improper branch addresses or procedure calls may be detected quickly.

EXAMPLE 10.1: Aligning Data

When blocks of storage are being reserved for several variables and arrays, care can be taken to arrange the reservation and initialization directives to force and maintain alignment. In the first sequence of directives below, RANKS and SCORES would not be on word and longword boundaries, respectively, without the last two .ALIGN directives, but by rearranging the statements as in the second sequence, the .ALIGN's can

[1] At this time, the NOEXE attribute is not yet implemented.

```
                .PSECT  READ_ONLY_DATA,NOWRT,NOEXE,LONG

      {         data initialization directives for read-only data         }

      ;
      ;
                .PSECT  DATA,NOEXE,LONG

      {         storage reservation and initialization directives          }

                .ALIGN  LONG                    ; Force alignment to
                                                ; next longword boundary
      ARRAY:    .BLKL   50

      ;
      ;
                .PSECT  PROGRAM,NOWRT
                BEGIN   PROGRAM

      {         instructions                  }

                EXIT
                .END    PROGRAM
```

Figure 10.1   Program organization using program sections

be eliminated. Note that the statements in the second sequence are sorted in nonincreasing order by the size of the memory units being reserved.

```
                .PSECT  DATA,NOEXE,LONG
                          .
                          .
                          .
                .ALIGN  LONG
      SCALE:    .BLKF   2
      FLAGS:    .BYTE   7,0,1
                .ALIGN  WORD
      RANKS:    .BLKW   5
                .ALIGN  LONG
      SCORES:   .BLKL   10


                .PSECT  DATA,NOEXE,LONG
                          .
                          .
                          .
                .ALIGN  LONG
      SCALE:    .BLKF   2
      SCORES:   .BLKL   10
      RANKS:    .BLKW   5
      FLAGS:    .BYTE   7,0,1
```

Processing PSECT's

We will give a brief description here of how program sections are treated by the assembler and the linker. First, taking the assembler's point of view, we consider the processing of one source module independent of the program sections that may be in other modules.

The assembler keeps a table that contains the name, attributes, current size, and a number that it assigns for each program section in the module being assembled. It creates a default program section called ". BLANK ." for programs that do not contain a .PSECT directive. This psect has attributes WRT and EXE, so it may contain data and instructions. Its alignment is BYTE. Since we did not use .PSECT directives in our examples prior to Ch. 9, all our early sample programs would consist of the psect ". BLANK .".

The assembler sets the location counter to zero at the beginning of each program section. The symbol table entry for each symbol contains the number of the psect in which the symbol is defined (or the psect in which it is first referenced, if it is not defined in the module). Symbol values stored in the symbol table are locations relative to the beginning of the psect. The physical arrangement of the program sections in memory is determined by the linker, so the assembler can not completely assemble operand specifiers in an instruction in one psect that use symbols defined in another psect. It assembles a mode byte containing EF for relative mode with longword displacement, and it reserves a longword for the displacement. The linker will fill in the correct value. The program listing in Fig. 10.2 illustrates the resetting of the location counter to zero at the beginning of the second psect and the way the assembler handles relative mode operands.

Since the assembler saves the last value of the location counter for each program section (the size of the psect is the last location counter value), it can add more data or instructions to a psect later, after an intervening one. If it encounters a .PSECT directive for a psect name already in its table with the CON attribute, it will assemble the following statements (up to the next .PSECT or .END directive) as if they physically followed the last statement in the previous piece of the same psect. The linker will arrange the pieces of a program section so that they do appear consecutively in memory. (The attributes of any continuation of a psect must be the same as the attributes specified the first time, but they do not have to be listed again.)

When the linker links the various modules of a program, it collects all the pieces of each program section together so that one program section will form a contiguous segment in memory. There may be parts of one program section in several modules; the linker will concatenate them one after another (unless they have the OVR attribute) and make any necessary corrections to address references.

In Chapter 9 we studied how to use procedures and how to pass arguments back and forth between them. The use of procedures and procedure arguments is, for many purposes, the best way to allow different modules to work on the same

```
                0000         1  ; This program adds the five entries in the word array
                0000         2  ; ARRAY and stores the result in the word SUM.
                0000         3  ;
                0000         4  ; Register use:      R6    array pointer
                0000         5  ;                    R7    loop index
                0000         6  ;                    R8    sum
                0000         7  ;
               00000000      8          .PSECT DATA,NOEXE
FFD6 0007 005D FFDE 000A 0000 9  ARRAY: .WORD  10,-34,93,7,-42
                0000000C     10 SUM:   .BLKW  1
                000C         11 ;
                000C         12 ;
               00000000      13         .PSECT PROG,NOWRT
                0050         14         BEGIN  PROG
                0050         15 ;
56  00000000'EF  3E  0050    16         MOVAW  ARRAY,R6    ; Initialize pointer
            57  05  D0  0057 17         MOVL   #5,R7       ; Loop index
                58  B4  005A 18         CLRW   R8          ; Clear for sum
            58  66  A0  005C 19 ADD:   ADDW2  (R6),R8      ; Add entry
          FA  57  F5  005F   20         SOBGTR R7,ADD       ; Loop control
0000000A'EF  58  B0  0062    21         MOVW   R8,SUM       ; Store sum
                0069         22 ;
                0069         23         EXIT
                0094         24         .END   PROG
```

Figure 10.2 Multiple psects

```
                    .PSECT   COMMON_DATA,OVR,NOEXE,LONG
                    .ALIGN   LONG
        A:          .BLKL    1
        B:          .BLKL    1
        C:          .BLKL    1
        ;
        ;

                    .PSECT   PROG,NOWRT
                    BEGIN    PROG
        ;
        ; The main program stores data in A and B and calls the
        ; procedure PROC to add them and store the result in C.
        ;
                    MOVL     #1,A
                    MOVL     #-25,B
                    CALLS    #0,PROC
                    DUMPLONG A,B,C
        ;
                    EXIT
                    .END     PROG


                    .PSECT   COMMON_DATA,OVR,NOEXE,LONG
                    .ALIGN   LONG
        X:          .BLKL    1
        Y:          .BLKL    1
        Z:          .BLKL    1
        ;
        ;

                    .PSECT   PROC,NOWRT
        ;
        ; This procedure adds the first two longwords in the
        ; COMMON_DATA psect and stores the result in the third.
        ;
                    .ENTRY   PROC,0
                    ADDL3    X,Y,Z
                    RET
                    .END




        Output


        * * *
        A           00000001
        B           FFFFFFE7
        C           FFFFFFE8
        * * *
```

Figure 10.3 A program section with the OVR attribute

data, because this mechanism allows very tight control over what data are available to, and may be changed by, each procedure. Sometimes, though, the amount of data to be shared by a group of procedures is very large. A lot of time may be saved if long argument lists do not have to be constructed, and the programs may be clearer if they can refer to the data by name instead of indirectly via the AP register. Thus we can set up program sections that are comparable to the COMMON blocks in FORTRAN. Each module that has access to the data would contain a copy of the program section named, say, COMMON_DATA, that contains all the storage reservation directives for the shared data. The psect would have the OVR attribute, indicating to the linker that the storage reservation directives are to overlay the same space in memory rather than reserving additional space for each module. Figure 10.3 shows a simple illustration of the use of such a program section.

10.2 TERMS AND EXPRESSIONS

We have seen that operands on machine instructions and arguments for assembler directives may be specified using expressions. For example, we have used simple expressions such as

RECORD+1   LIST−4   NUM*SIZE

In fact, since an expression may consist of a single term; a symbol or number alone is an expression. Thus operand specifiers are, in general, described by one or more expressions along with special characters that denote the addressing mode being used (e.g., # for literals and parentheses for register deferred mode). In this section we will consider some of the general rules for forming expressions and how the assembler treats them.

Expressions are evaluated by the assembler, with help from the linker for those where not enough information is available to the assembler. They are not used like expressions in high-level languages; they do not do computations on execution-time data. Most often, expressions are used to describe addresses. They are also used to describe constants in forms convenient for the programmer.

Terms

Expressions are made up by combining terms. The three examples shown above use symbols and numbers, the most commonly used kinds of terms. The VAX-11 MACRO assembler allows four different categories of terms: numbers, symbols, the location counter, and certain kinds of text strings. A term preceded by a unary operator (for example, a minus sign or a radix operator) is also a term. Thus −25 and ^X20 are examples of terms.

A number may be specified in any of several radixes. The assembler assumes that the radix is decimal unless the number is preceded by a radix operator (or is part of an expression preceded by a radix operator). The radix operators are

Operator	Radix	
^B	2	(binary)
^D	10	(decimal)
^X	16	(hexadecimal)
^O	8	(octal)

Specifying ^XF011, for example, will have the same effect as specifying 61457; the assembler converts both to the bit string

$$0000000000000001111000000010001$$

Any symbol is a term, whether it be defined by the system (e.g., the register names) or by the user, whether a user-defined symbol be defined as a label or in a direct assignment statement. The value of a symbol defined as a label is, as always, an address, not the contents of the address; the latter is not accessible to the assembler. (The value of a symbol defined in a direct assignment statement may or may not be an address, depending on how it is defined.) We will consider the treatment of expressions containing symbols in more detail in the next section.

There are two types of textual terms: ASCII and register mask. Each is preceded by a unary operator, ^A or ^M, respectively, to indicate the type.

The format for an ASCII term is

$$^A/text/$$

The text may be from one to eight characters long, but no longer than is appropriate for the context where it is used. Often ASCII terms are used to specify literal or immediate operands. For example:

```
MOVL    #^A/NAME/,LINE
CMPB    (R8),#^A/-/
```

In the MOVL instruction the ASCII term could not contain more than four characters because the data type of the operand is longword. Similarly, the ASCII term in the CMPB instruction must have only one character. We have used the slash here as the delimiter for the ASCII string; as in .ASCII directives, another character may be used as a delimiter if a slash is part of the string.

We have already seen, in Chapter 9, how the ^M operator may be used to set up a register save mask for a procedure in its .ENTRY directive. The format for a register mask term is

$$^M\langle register\_list\rangle$$

Depending on where the term is used, there are some restrictions on what may be included in the register list. For example, we saw that a procedure's register save mask may not include R0, R1, AP, FP, SP, or PC. Our main interest here, however, is how the assembler evaluates the term. It evaluates it as a 16-bit string where a bit is on (set to 1) if the register (or trap enable designation) it corresponds to is included in the list. Thus, to the assembler, the value of the term

$$^M<R8,R5,R3,R9>$$

is equal to the value of the terms

$$^B0000001100101000$$

and

$$^X0328$$

The programmer should use whatever form is most convenient and clear.

The location counter, denoted by a period, may be used as a term in an expression. Consider the following statements.

```
TABLE:   .WORD   2,-17,45,29,-48,33,38,-21
TABLE_SIZE = . - TABLE
```

The value of . when the second statement is encountered is the location of the byte following the end of the table, so the value assigned to the symbol TABLE_SIZE will be the number of bytes in the table. (Note that defining TABLE_SIZE in this way helps to minimize work and possible errors if we later make additions or deletions in the table; only the .WORD directive setting up the table need be changed.)

The value of . when used in an operand specifier is the location of the first byte of that operand specifier. Consider the instruction

```
BRB        .+4
```

The value of . is the location of the byte containing the branch displacement. The next three bytes are at .+1, .+2, and .+3. Thus branching to .+4 means skipping over the three bytes that follow the instruction. Of course, for clarity and to minimize the likelihood of making errors, we would normally put a label on the instruction at the branch destination and use that label as the operand on the BRB instruction. The situations where the location counter is used in operand specifiers are somewhat esoteric.

Expressions

Terms are combined to form expressions by using binary operators. The arithmetic operators, particularly + and −, are used most often. In addition, the VAX-11 MACRO assembler has several operators that do logical operations on the binary representation of the values of the terms. We will not describe those here.

Terms in an expression may be grouped to form subexpressions. Since parentheses have another role in operand specifiers—they are used to denote certain addressing modes (e.g., register deferred, autoincrement)—subexpressions must be enclosed in angle brackets (< and >). Some examples are

$$SIZE*<NUM1+NUM2> \qquad ^\wedge X<3F-2B>$$
$$LIST+<3*INC> \qquad <80-LENGTH>/2$$

As the second example illustrates, a radix operator may be applied to an entire expression, not just a single term.

Some kinds of terms, such as register names, may not be combined with others in expressions. An expression such as R5+8 simply does not make sense because the value of the term R5 is *not* the contents of R5. The assembler will issue an error message if an improper expression is used.

When the assembler evaluates an expression, it does *not* use the usual operator priorities we expect in high-level languages and ordinary mathematical expressions. All binary operators have the same priority; operations are performed left to right. The only way to override this evaluation order is to use bracketed subexpressions, as these are evaluated first. Thus if the brackets were omitted from the third example above, the resulting value would be different.

It is not always necessary that a symbol be defined (i.e., already be entered in the symbol table and have a value assigned to it) before it is used in an expression. Expressions that contain undefined symbols will be evaluated by the linker.

In general, the assembler evaluates terms and expressions as 32-bit values. (There are a few exceptions.) The result will be truncated if the context in which the expression is used requires a smaller number of bits.

10.3 SYMBOL AND EXPRESSION TYPES

Relocatable, Absolute, and External Expressions

Every expression (hence also every term) in a module is of one of three types: relocatable, absolute, or external.

We have emphasized that the value assigned by the assembler to a symbol used as a label is the location of the byte it labels *relative* to the beginning of the module or program section it is in. The assembler can do no better; it doesn't know where in memory the program will be when it is executed. Such symbols are called relocatable. In general, an expression is *relocatable* if its value is fixed relative to the beginning of the program section in which it appears, but the actual location represented by the expression depends on where the program section is placed by the linker. Labels on data areas and labels on instructions are relocatable symbols. The location counter (for all the kinds of program sections we have considered) is a relocatable term.

An expression is *absolute* if its value is a constant, independent of where the program section containing it is placed in memory. All numbers and textual terms are absolute terms. The value of an ASCII term, for example, is the character code for the text; it is constant.

A symbol defined in a direct assignment statement may be absolute or relocatable, depending on the type of the expression that specifies the symbol value. All the symbols defined in the following statements are absolute.

```
MAX = 40
SIZE = 32
TOTAL_SPACE = MAX*SIZE
```

Suppose ARRAY is a label on an array containing 200 bytes. The symbol LAST defined by

```
LAST = ARRAY+199
```

is relocatable because its value is the location of the last byte of the array. The fact that the expression defining LAST includes the relocatable symbol ARRAY is not sufficient to determine that LAST is relocatable, however. Consider the following statements.

```
TABLE:  .WORD   2,-17,45,29,-48,33,38,-21
TABLE_SIZE = . - TABLE
```

TABLE and . are relocatable terms. Even though they are used in the expression that defines TABLE_SIZE, TABLE_SIZE is an absolute symbol. The number of bytes in the table—that is, the difference, or distance, between TABLE and the value of . in the second statement—is independent of where the program section is placed in memory. Similarly, an expression that is the difference between two relocatable symbols is an absolute expression.

Bearing in mind that the value of a relocatable symbol is an address, it should be clear that a sum (or product or quotient) of two relocatable symbols is not likely to be a useful expression. Many assemblers simply consider such expressions to be errors, but the VAX-11 MACRO assembler accepts them. The programmer who is forming complex expressions using relocatable symbols should take extra care to be sure that the expressions are meaningful.

A symbol is *external* if it is not defined in the module being assembled. An expression is *external* if it contains any external symbols. One common example of an external symbol is a procedure entry-point name used in a CALLS or CALLG instruction. The entry-point name is defined in the .ENTRY directive in the procedure module and is a relocatable symbol there. Another example is provided by the BEGIN macro presented in Chapter 5; it contains instructions that reference external symbols that are labels on data blocks used by the I/O macros.

The assembler, of course, can not complete the encoding of an operand specifier described by an external expression because it does not know the value of the expression. It stores a mode byte for relative mode, EF, and leaves room for a longword displacement. The linker will compute and fill in the correct displacement.

The VAX assembler assumes that any symbol not defined in the module is defined in some other module that will be linked with the present one before the program is run. Thus it classifies any undefined symbol as external. Many assemblers will not make this assumption; they expect an explicit declaration listing external symbols used in a module. If an undefined symbol is used and is not declared as external, many assemblers will issue an error message. This is helpful for catching errors such as misspellings and missing statements. Using the default assumption on the VAX, such errors are not detected until the program is linked (and possibly not even then if an undefined symbol happens to have the same name as, say, a procedure used by another module). Thus, requiring that all external symbols be declared is very helpful to the programmer, although it involves more work. The VAX programmer can use the directive

.DISABLE GLOBAL

to direct the assembler to treat any undefined symbols not declared external as errors. The directive

.EXTERNAL *list_of_symbols*

tells the assembler that the symbols listed are to be considered external.

Many assemblers put restrictions on the ways in which external symbols may be combined with other terms. VAX-11 MACRO does not, so the programmer has the responsibility of making sure that such expressions are used in meaningful ways.

The assembler records in the symbol table the type of each symbol it encounters. On program listings the type is indicated by an R (relocatable), X (external), or an equals sign preceding the symbol value (absolute).

Global Symbols

A symbol is *global* if it may be referenced from a module other than the one in which it is defined. Unless a symbol is made global by one of the means described below, it is local to the module where it is defined and may be accessed only in that module. This allows the same symbol name to be used in different modules without interference. When the linker is attempting to fill in an address reference to an external symbol, it considers only global symbols from other modules.

A symbol may be made global in one of several ways. A procedure or main program entry point, defined in an .ENTRY directive, is always global. A symbol used as a label is global if it is followed by a double colon (: :). (The labels on the data blocks used by the I/O macros are made global in this way.) A symbol defined in a direct assignment statement is global if it is followed by two equals signs instead of one.

Treatment of Relocatable Expressions

The distinctions between relocatable, absolute, and external expressions are important, both because the different types of expressions are treated differently by the assembler and the linker and because, as we have mentioned briefly, assemblers for many computers put restrictions on the way relocatable and global terms may be combined.

A major concern for an assembler and linker in any computer system is the translation to machine code of operand specifiers that contain relocatable expressions. When the program is executed, the machine code must specify the actual location of the data to be operated on. We have seen that on the VAX the use of relative mode addressing solves the problem in most cases. The operand specifier is encoded as a displacement from the contents of the PC. The displacement is often absolute and can be computed by the assembler, so the linker has no work to do. On computers that do not use this kind of displacement addressing, an assembler would encode the operand specifier by inserting in the instruction the value of the symbol or expression relative to the beginning of the program section—i.e., the value the assembler can compute using entries in its symbol table. The assembler would then tag the operand specifier in some way to indicate to the linker that a correction is needed. After the linker determines where each program section will be placed, it will add to each tagged operand the base address of its program section.

The use of displacement addressing has eliminated some of the work the linker might have had to do, but displacements are used in machine instruction operands, not in assembler directives. Thus there are still places where the linker must correct expression values computed by the assembler by adding the program section base address. Consider the following directives to set up a procedure argument list.

```
ARGS:   .LONG    3
        .ADDRESS LIST,COUNT,ITEM
```

The argument list will be used by a procedure at execution time. The procedure expects it to contain the actual 32-bit addresses of the arguments, not their locations relative to the beginning of the program section they are in. Thus when the assembler encounters an .ADDRESS directive, it computes the values of the expressions using symbol table entries and it tags these values for the linker to correct by adding the program section base address. The assembler can correctly assemble the .LONG directive because its argument, 3, is absolute; the linker makes no adjustments.

10.4 RESTRICTIONS ON EXPRESSIONS

Any expressions may be used in most machine instructions and assembler directives, but for some directives there are restrictions. The most common restrictions are that all symbols used in an expression must already be defined (in the same module) and that the expression must be absolute. In this section we will consider a few of the directives to which these restrictions apply, and we will see that they are necessitated by the way the assembler works and/or are reasonable in the context where the directive is used.

Recall from our discussion of the assembler in Chapter 8 that the main task performed in the first pass over the module being assembled is the construction of the symbol table. The assembler must be able to determine the values of the symbols defined in the module (relative to the beginning of the program section, of course). Thus it must be able to determine how many bytes will be allocated for each statement at the time the statement is first encountered.

Consider the following directives:

.BLK*x*	*number_of_units*
.BYTE	*arg_list*
.WORD	*arg_list*
.LONG	*arg_list*
.ADDRESS	*list_of_expressions*

where the *arg_list* on .BYTE, .WORD, and .LONG are lists of items of the form

value[*repetition_factor*]

The number of memory units to reserve, the values to be stored, the repetition factors and the addresses to be stored by .ADDRESS are all specified by expressions. Those that affect the amount of memory used, and hence the amount by which the location counter will be incremented, must be absolute and contain no undefined symbols. Specifically, *number_of_units* and *repetition_factor* must satisfy these restrictions. The expressions describing the values to be stored need not satisfy the restrictions because the linker can fill in the values later. The expressions listed in .ADDRESS need not satisfy the restrictions because the assembler always reserves a longword for each address.

In a direct assignment statement, the expression that describes the value to be assigned to the symbol must not contain any undefined symbols. If it did, the assembler could not determine the value of the symbol being defined during its first pass. (As we have seen in the previous section, the expression does not have to be absolute.)

The expression that describes the register save mask in an .ENTRY directive must be absolute and not contain any undefined symbols. Since the $\wedge$M operator is generally used for register masks, and the symbols denoting the names of the registers and the arithmetic traps are always defined, these restrictions are no inconvenience.

10.5 SUMMARY

A program may be divided into several program sections that may be given different attributes. Some of the attributes are described in Table 10.1. Breaking up a program into sections may improve the modularity of the program, allows for the protection of instructions and read-only data, and allows for several modules to directly access the same data.

Machine instruction operands and assembler directive arguments are specified using expressions that are evaluated by the assembler (or the linker). The terms that may be used to make up expressions are: numbers, symbols, the location counter, ASCII strings, and register masks. Numbers are assumed to be decimal unless they are preceded by a radix operator $^\wedge$B (binary), $^\wedge$X (hexadecimal), or $^\wedge$O (octal).

The assembler evaluates expressions containing symbols using the values in its symbol table. Expressions generally describe addresses or constants. They can not be used to do computation on data that will be in memory or registers at execution time.

Expressions are evaluated left to right; there are no operator priorities. Evaluation of subexpressions can be forced by enclosing the subexpressions in angle brackets.

Expressions are generally evaluated as 32-bit quantities and truncated to the size needed.

An expression is *relocatable* if its value is fixed relative to the beginning of the program section in which it appears, but the location represented by the expression depends on where the linker places the program section. An expression is *absolute* if its value is independent of where the program section is placed. An expression is *external* if it contains any symbols that are not defined in the current module. Numbers, ASCII strings, and register masks are absolute. Symbols may be relocatable, absolute, or external.

TABLE 10.1   Some Program Section Attributes

Default	Opposite	Meaning
WRT	NOWRT	Contents of the program section may (may not) be modified.
EXE	NOEXE*	Contents of the program section may (may not) be executed.
CON	OVR	Additional pieces of the same program section are to be concatenated (overlaid).
BYTE	WORD, LONG, QUAD, PAGE (and other values)	The keyword indicates the alignment of the program section and the maximum alignment that may be specified in an .ALIGN directive.

* At this time, NOEXE is not yet implemented.

A symbol is *global* if it may be referenced from a module other than the one in which it is defined. Procedure entry-point names are an example of global symbols.

The VAX solves the problem of encoding relocatable machine instruction operands by using the relative addressing mode. The operands are encoded as displacements from the contents of the PC; the displacements are usually constants independent of where the linker places the program. (If the assembler can not evaluate an expression when it first encounters it, the linker will do it later and compute the necessary displacement.) Many other computers use a similar scheme for handling relocatable operands. Others require that the linker add the program section base address to all such operands at the time the program is linked.

Restrictions are placed on the kinds of expressions that may be used in some assembler directives because the assembler must be able to determine how many bytes of memory each statement will require. For example, the expression in the .BLK*x* directives that indicates how many memory units to reserve must be absolute and contain no undefined symbols.

10.6 EXERCISES

1. Suppose . = 828 when the assembler encounters the following statements. List the values of all the symbols defined and give the final value of the location counter.

```
            .ALIGN  WORD
DELTA:      .WORD   24,-18,3
IND:        .BLKB   2
LABEL:      .ASCII  /VAX-11/
TAG:        .BYTE   1
            .ALIGN  LONG
VOLUME:     .BLKL   3
```

2. Reorganize the statements in the previous problem to minimize the number of wasted bytes.

3. Which of the following are valid terms?

   (a) 256
   (b) ^X123
   (c) ^B1001110111
   (d) ^X1001110111
   (e) -^X2A
   (f) ^A/ABCDE/
   (g) ^A*25/2*
   (h) ^M<R5,R10,IV,R11>

4. Which of the following are valid expressions? For those that are valid, tell if they are relocatable or absolute.

   (a) ALPHA+8   (ALPHA is relocatable.)
   (b) 4*BETA   (BETA is absolute.)
   (c) R7+1
   (d) ^X24+15*^B111
   (e) LINE+MARGIN   (Both symbols are absolute.)
   (f) LINE+MARGIN   (LINE is relocatable; MARGIN is absolute.)

(g) LINE+MARGIN   (LINE is absolute; MARGIN is relocatable.)
(h) LINE+MARGIN   (Both symbols are relocatable.)

5. What is the value of each of the following expressions? (Indicate whether you are showing the value in hex or decimal.)

(a) ^X36   **(d)** 11*^B11
(b) ^A/9/   **(e)** 15+3*2
(c) RECORD+12   where RECORD = 12A and the byte at 12A
                                      contains 38_{16}.

6. Suppose a program contains the following statements, and . = 1B4 when the assembler encounters them.

```
CODE = 36
ALPHA:   .BLKW   27
BETA:    .LONG   9
```

For each of the following expressions, tell if it is absolute or relocatable and give its value. If there is not enough information to determine the value, say so.

(a) BETA–ALPHA   **(c)** BETA–CODE   **(e)** ALPHA
(b) CODE   **(d)** BETA

7. **(a)** For each of the statements below, indicate whether the assembler can completely assemble the statement or the linker must do part of it.

```
MAX = 50
LIST:   .BLKB    MAX
ARGS:   .LONG    1
        .ADDRESS LIST
          .
          ..
        CALLG    ARGS,PROCEDURE
```

(b) Indicate for each of the four symbols used (MAX, LIST, ARGS, and PROCEDURE) whether it is absolute, relocatable, or external.

Chapter 11

Macros

11.1 INTRODUCTION

In Chapter 4 we described the three types of statements that can appear in an assembly language program: machine instructions, assembler directives, and macro instructions. *Macro instructions* are pseudoinstructions that are replaced by the assembler with a sequence of assembly language statements specified in a macro definition. Thus the use of macros allows us to give a name to a sequence of instructions used often and to use that name to refer to the whole sequence.

A macro facility, or macro processor, is the part of an assembler that processes macro definitions and macro instructions. Macro facilities are available in most assemblers for large computer systems. All the discussion in this section concerns general properties of macros and would be applicable to many other assembly languages. All of the specific directives and features described in later sections are for the standard VAX assembler, called VAX-11 MACRO.

A macro definition may be supplied by the programmer in the program that uses the macro, or it may be in a macro library available to one or more users. The I/O macros introduced in Chapter 5 and used in some of our programming examples are examples of macros whose definitions are in a library.

The process of replacing the macro instruction by the appropriate statements is called *macro expansion,* and the sequence of instructions substituted by the assembler for the macro instruction is called the *expanded macro,* or the *expansion of the macro.*

The instructions in a macro expansion need not be exactly the same each time the macro is used, or invoked. The most common way in which variations in instructions are generated is by using arguments in the macro instruction. When the macro is expanded, the assembler substitutes the actual arguments for formal arguments (sometimes called dummy arguments) that appear in the macro definition. There are several other ways, some fairly simple and some quite complex, to vary the instructions in a macro expansion. We will discuss many of these later in this chapter. This ability to vary the instructions themselves provides much of the power and flexibility of macros.

Macros are defined, used, and treated by the assembler quite differently from procedures. (We can not, for example, vary the instructions in a procedure each time it is used.) Nevertheless, the advantages of using macros are very similar to the advantages of using procedures. Specifically, macros

1. Make a program clearer by "hiding" a lot of perhaps obscure detail behind a macro name that describes the operation being done.
2. Help avoid errors by eliminating the need to write similar sequences of instructions many times.
3. Save the programmer's time (both programming time and, in some cases, time to learn how to do the task performed by a macro).

The I/O macros introduced in Chapter 5 illustrate these advantages. The reader may look at the I/O macro definitions and the procedures they call (in Appendix D) to see that the particular instructions used to, say, print a line, are rather obscure if one does not know more about the VAX/VMS I/O services. Certainly the instruction PRINTCHRS indicates much more clearly what is being done than the statements that will be in the expanded macro.

Macro facilities vary a lot in the amount of power and flexibility they provide. For example, some macro facilities allow recursive macro (macros that invoke themselves), and some don't. We will not cover all the features available in the VAX macro facility or all the techniques that may be used in macros, but we will describe and illustrate many features and techniques that are common to macro facilities. Additional details about macros on the VAX may be found in the *VAX-11 MACRO Language Reference Manual.*

Differences Between Macros and Procedures

Since a macro instruction is replaced in the source program, at assembly time, by its expansion, all evidence that a macro was used is gone when the object file is constructed. The macro instructions and assembler directives in the expanded macro are assembled just as if the programmer had written them all out in the source program without using the macro. Macros are not a feature of the VAX (or of any computer) itself, but of an assembler for the computer. A procedure, on the other hand, is a separate module, translated by the assembler into an object module and

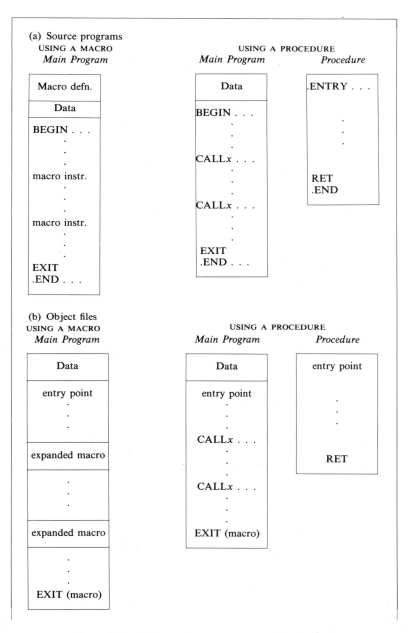

Figure 11.1 Differences between macros and procedures

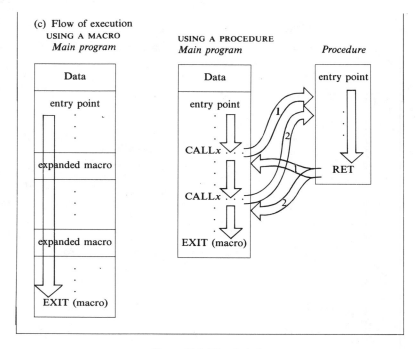

Figure 11.1 (Concluded)

executed when entered as the result of a CALL instruction. CALLS, CALLG, and RET are VAX machine instructions; hence they and the work they do in manipulating the procedure call frame are part of the VAX architecture.

To emphasize the differences between macros and procedures, we will compare the source program, object file, and execution of a program using a macro with one using a procedure. Figure 11.1(a) shows the general appearance of the source programs. Figure 11.1(b) shows the general format of the object files. Note that the macro definition does not appear at this stage. After the assembler has used it to expand the macros during the assembly phase, the macro definition is no longer needed. The expanded macro appears in the program at each point where the macro instruction was used. The procedure appears only once. When the program that used macros is executed [Fig. 11.1(c)], the expanded macro is executed in place. Each macro expansion is executed just once (unless the macro instruction is in a loop). In the program with the procedure, each CALL statement causes a branch to the procedure's entry point, and the RET causes a branch back to the calling program. There is only one copy of the procedure; the same code is executed more than once.

11.2 MACRO DEFINITIONS AND SOME EXAMPLES

The general format of a macro definition is

$$.\text{MACRO} \quad \textit{macro\_name} \qquad \textit{arguments}$$

$$\left\{ \textit{body of macro definition} \right\}$$

$$.\text{ENDM} \quad \textit{macro\_name}$$

The .MACRO directive marks the beginning of a macro definition and specifies the macro name and the formal argument names. Arguments are optional; most macros will have some, but the EXIT macro, for example, does not. The macro name and formal argument names may be any legal symbols.

The body of the macro definition may contain machine instructions, assembler directives, and other macro instructions that are to be inserted into the source program at the point where this macro instruction appears. In all the examples in this and the next few sections, there will be nothing else, but we shall see in Sections 11.6 and 11.7 that a macro body can be somewhat more complex.

The formal argument names may be used throughout the body of the macro. During macro expansion, the assembler will treat the actual arguments as character strings with no particular interpretation on them and will substitute them wherever the corresponding formal arguments appear. Then it will translate the constructed statement.

The .ENDM directive marks the end of the macro definition.

If a macro definition is not in a macro library, then it must be in any module that uses the macro, because the assembler must have access to the definition to expand the macro while assembling that module. We will always place macro definitions at the beginning of a module, just after the .PSECT directive.

When the assembler encounters a macro definition, it simply records the name of the macro in a table and saves the body of the macro for later reference. The macro definition is used only if and when the macro instruction appears in the program. When the assembler encounters the macro instruction, it looks up the macro definition to determine what statements to substitute for it in the program.

EXAMPLE 11.1 CVTSL Macro

As we saw in Chapter 6, converting a number from character code (leading separate numeric format) to two's complement requires two steps; the character code is converted to packed decimal format as an intermediate step. The following macro allows us to do the conversion using only one instruction.

```
.MACRO  CVTSL    NUM_DIGITS,LSN,LONG
CVTSP   NUM_DIGITS,LSN,NUM_DIGITS,PKD
CVTPL   NUM_DIGITS,PKD,LONG
.ENDM   CVTSL
```

Note that we used the VAX conventions for naming our macro and for the order in which the arguments are specified. NUM_DIGITS, LSN, and LONG are formal arguments; they are not symbols defined in the program.[1] When the macro is invoked, the actual arguments specified in the macro instruction will be substituted. Specifically, if the macro instruction

```
CVTSL   #5,RECORD+6,R8
```

appears in the program, the assembler will insert and assemble the following instructions:

```
CVTSP   #5,RECORD+6,#5,PKD
CVTPL   #5,PKD,R8
```

Note that **PKD** was not replaced because it is not a formal argument. If this macro is to be used properly, **PKD** must be defined somewhere in the program.

EXAMPLE 11.2

The program shown in Fig. 11.2 uses the macro **CVTSL** defined in **EXAMPLE 11.1** and illustrates the placement of the macro definition.

```
        .PSECT  TESTCVT
;
; PROBLEM STATEMENT
;
; This program reads and stores two lines of data from a
; terminal. The number on the first line tells how many
; numbers are on the second line.
;
; The number on the first line is stored as a longword
; integer in NUM; the data on the second line are stored in
; the longword array DATA.
;
; The data are assumed to be in fixed format as follows:
;
;       First line:     sdd
;       Second line:    sdddbbsdddbb . . . sddd
;
;   where       d = digit
;               s = sign
;               b = blank
;
; The program will read at most 12 numbers on the second line.
;
;
; MACRO DEFINITION
;
```

Figure 11.2   A program with a macro

[1] Formal argument names may be the same as symbols used elsewhere in the program; the assembler will not confuse them.

```
             .MACRO  CVTSL    NUM_DIGITS,LSN,LONG
             CVTSP   NUM_DIGITS,LSN,NUM_DIGITS,PKD
             CVTPL   NUM_DIGITS,PKD,LONG
             .ENDM   CVTSL
     ;
     ; STORAGE RESERVATION
     ;
NUM:         .BLKL   1
DATA:        .BLKL   12
PKD:         .BLKB   2
BUFFER:      .BLKB   80
     ;
     ;
             BEGIN   TESTCVT
     ;
     ; Register use        R6       _array pointer
     ;                     R7       loop counter
     ;                     R8       buffer pointer
     ;
             READLINE BUFFER              ; Read number of entries
             CVTSL   #2,BUFFER,R7         ; Convert number of entries
             CMPL    R7,#12               ; See if too many
             BLEQ    STORE
             MOVL    #12,R7               ; Set num to 12 if too big
STORE:       MOVL    R7,NUM               ; Store number of entries
     ;
             MOVAL   DATA,R6              ; Initialize array ptr
             MOVAB   BUFFER,R8            ; Initialize buffer ptr
             READLINE BUFFER              ; Read data line
CVT:         CVTSL   #3,(R8),(R6)+        ; Convert to 2's complement
             ADDL2   #6,R8                ; Increment buffer ptr
             SOBGTR  R7,CVT               ; Loop control
     ;
     ;       <other processing>
     ;
             EXIT
             .END    TESTCVT
```

Figure 11.2 (Concluded)

EXAMPLE 11.3: SUM Macro

The macro SUM adds three longwords.

```
        .MACRO  SUM      A,B,C,TOTAL
        ADDL3   A,B,TOTAL
        ADDL2   C,TOTAL
        .ENDM   SUM
```

Consider the following uses of this macro.

```
    SUM    4(R7),(R9)+,BETA,(R6)          SUM     #36,R5,BETA,(R9)+
```

The expansions are

```
ADDL3   4(R7),(R9)+,(R6)          ADDL3   #36,R5,(R9)+
ADDL2   BETA,(R6)                 ADDL2   BETA,(R9)+
```

The SUM macro is used correctly in the first instance but not in the second. The instructions generated are properly formed; that is, they would not cause any assembly-time errors, but the use of autoincrement mode for the argument TOTAL will have an unintended effect: R9 will be incremented by the first ADD instruction, so the destination addresses in the two ADD instructions will be different.

As Example 11.3 illustrates, several different addressing modes may be used for the actual arguments in a macro, but there are some restrictions. There are no fixed rules about which modes are permitted as macro arguments. Since the assembler simply substitutes the actual arguments for the formal arguments, whether or not a particular addressing mode is acceptable for a particular argument depends on how it is used in the body of the macro definition.

EXAMPLE 11.4: CALL Macro

The purpose of this macro is to call a procedure. It assumes the procedure has three arguments and sets up the procedure argument list on the stack.

```
.MACRO  CALL    PROC ARG1,ARG2,ARG3
PUSHAL  ARG3
PUSHAL  ARG2
PUSHAL  ARG1
CALLS   #3,PROC
.ENDM   CALL
```

Note that a space, not a comma, is used as a separator between the first two formal macro arguments, PROC and ARG1. Spaces and commas are both acceptable as separators. Note also that the PUSHAL instruction is used to push each argument address on the stack even though all the arguments may not be longwords. Will that cause any errors?

A general CALL macro is especially useful to have on a computer with a more primitive instruction set than the VAX has. If the programmer has to write out instructions to accomplish some of the tasks done automatically by the VAX CALLS and CALLG instructions, a macro could save a lot of bother. In Section 11.6 we will write a more flexible CALL macro that allows for a variable number of arguments.

Concatenation

Suppose we want to use a macro like the SUM macro in Example 11.3, but we sometimes want to add data of a type other than longword. Instead of writing different macro definitions for each type that may be used, we can include the type as an argument and write the definition of SUM so that the actual argument specified for the type will be substituted into the middle of the instruction names in the generated statements. To do this we will use an operation called *concatenation* of character strings. Concatenation means simply putting two character strings together to form a new string. In macros, arguments may be concatenated with other characters to form instruction names, operands, or any other strings that are useful. An apostrophe (') is used to indicate where concatenation is to be done.

EXAMPLE 11.5: SUM Macro Using Concatenation

```
.MACRO  SUM     A,B,C,TOTAL,TYPE
ADD'TYPE'3      A,B,TOTAL
ADD'TYPE'2      C,TOTAL
.ENDM   SUM
```

The expansion of the macro instruction

```
SUM     #36,R5,BETA,(R9),W
```

would be

```
ADDW3   #36,R5,(R9)
ADDW2   BETA,(R9)
```

The apostrophes in the macro definition in Example 11.5 are necessary to separate the formal argument name from the surrounding characters. In general, the assembler replaces the formal argument with the actual argument only if it finds the formal argument name set off from surrounding characters by a separator (comma, space, or tab) or some other special character such as the concatenation operator. If the first instruction in the macro definition had been written like this:

```
ADDTYPE3        A,B,TOTAL
```

the assembler would have considered **ADDTYPE3** to be one symbol and would have left it in the instruction without substituting anything for the letters **TYPE** (just as it did not substitute #36 for the A in ADDL3 in Example 11.3). The assembler would have generated the statement

```
ADDTYPE3        #36,R5,(R9)
```

and then would have issued an error message because there is no instruction called **ADDTYPE3**.

EXAMPLE 11.6: A Storage Reservation and Initialization Macro

To emphasize that the statements in the body of a macro definition need not be machine instructions, we include an example of a macro that reserves space for an array and for a variable that contains the number of entries reserved.

```
00000000            1              .PSECT  TESTCVT
     0000           2   ;
     0000           3   ; PROBLEM STATEMENT
     0000           4   ;
     0000           5   ; This program reads and stores two lines of data from a
     0000           6   ; terminal. The number on the first line tells how many
     0000           7   ; numbers are on the second line.
     0000           8   ;
     0000           9   ; The number on the first line is stored as a longword
     0000          10   ; integer in NUM; the data on the second line are stored in
     0000          11   ; the longword array DATA.
     0000          12   ;
     0000          13   ; The data are assumed to be in fixed format as follows:
     0000          14   ;
     0000          15   ;      First line:      sdd
     0000          16   ;      Second line:     sdddbbsdddbb . . . sddd
     0000          17   ;
     0000          18   ; where       d = digit
     0000          19   ;             s = sign
     0000          20   ;             b = blank
     0000          21   ;
     0000          22   ; The program will read at most 12 numbers on the second line.
     0000          23   ;
     0000          24   ;
     0000          25   ; MACRO DEFINITION
     0000          26   ;
     0000          27              .MACRO  CVTSL   NUM_DIGITS,LSN,LONG
     0000          28       CVTSP  NUM_DIGITS,LSN,NUM_DIGITS,PKD
     0000          29       CVTPL  NUM_DIGITS,PKD,LONG
     0000          30              .ENDM   CVTSL
     0000          31   ;
     0000          32   ; STORAGE RESERVATION
     0000          33   ;
00000004   0000    34   NUM:    .BLKL   1
00000034   0004    35   DATA:   .BLKL   12
00000036   0034    36   PKD:    .BLKB   2
00000086   0036    37   BUFFER:.BLKB    80
           0086    38   ;
           0086    39   ;
```

Figure 11.3 Listing showing macro expansions

```
                                          BEGIN  TESTCVT
                                        ;
                                        ; Register use R6            array pointer
                                        ;             R7             loop counter
                                        ;             R8             buffer pointer
                                        ;
0086                              40              READLINE BUFFER           ; Read number of entries
00D6                              41     ①        .SHOW    MEB
00D6                              42     ②        CVTSL    #2,BUFFER,R7     ; Convert number of entries
00D6                              43     ③        CVTSP    #2,BUFFER,#2,PKD
00D6                              44              CVTPL    #2,PKD,R7
00D6                              45
00D6                              46              CMPL     R7,#12           ; See if too many
00E1                              47              BLEQ     STORE
00E1                              48              MOVL     #12,R7           ; Set num to 12 if too big
00EA                                     STORE:   MOVL     R7,NUM           ; Store number of entries
00F0                              49     ;
00F3                              50              MOVAL    DATA,R6          ; Initialize array ptr
00F5                              51              MOVAB    BUFFER,R8        ; Initialize buffer ptr
00F8                              52     ⑤        .NOSHOW  MEB
00FD                                              READLINE BUFFER           ; Read data line
00FD                              53     ②        .SHOW    MEB
0102                              54     CVT:     CVTSL    #3,(R8),(R6)+    ; Convert to 2's complement
0107                              55     ③        CVTSP    #3,(R8),#3,PKD
0107                              56              CVTPL    #3,PKD,(R6)+
0112                              57
0112                              58              ADDL2    #6,R8            ; Increment buffer ptr
0112                              59              SOBGTR   R7,CVT           ; Loop control
0119                              60     ;
011F                              61     ;        <other processing>
0122                              62     ;
0125                              63              .NOSHOW  MEB
0125                              64              EXIT
0125                              65              .END     TESTCVT
0125                              66
0125                              67
0155

  ④ FF4A CF 02 FF50 CF 02 02 09
       57    FF45 CF 02 36
             0C 57 D1
                03 15
                57 0C D0
       FF03 CF 57 D0
       56 FF03 CF DE
       58 FF30 CF 9E

  ④ FF1B CF 03 68 03 09
       86    FF16 CF 03 36
             58 06 C0
       ED 57 F5
```

[1] The .SHOW directive.

[2] The macro instruction appears.

[3] The expansion of the macro. Note that there are no source program line numbers on the lines generated by the assembler.

[4] The object code for the expanded macros.

[5] The .NOSHOW directive suppresses listing of the macro expansions until another .SHOW directive is encountered. The expansion of the READLINE macro is not shown.

Figure 11.3 (Concluded)

247

```
                  .MACRO     RESERVE ARRAY,NUM,TYPE
ARRAY:            .BLK'TYPE NUM
ARRAY'SIZE: .LONG          NUM
                  .ENDM      RESERVE
```

This macro could be used in the storage reservation and initialization portion of a program as follows:

```
          RESERVE TAGS,50,B
```

The expansion would be

```
TAGS:       .BLKB   50
TAGSSIZE:  .LONG   50
```

Macro Expansions in Program Listings

Figure 11.2 is part of a program listing file. As that example indicates, VAX assembly language program listings normally show the source program as written by the programmer. Macro definitions, if they are in the source module rather than a macro library, will appear in the program listing. Macro instructions appear in the listing but their expansions do not. The .SHOW and .NOSHOW directives may be used to override the usual listing conventions. The directive

```
     .SHOW    MEB
```

will cause subsequent macro expansions (specifically, all lines that are assembled into the object file) to show in the listing. (MEB is one of several possible arguments for the .SHOW directive. It stands for Macro Expansion, Binary.) If the assembler encounters a

```
     .NOSHOW MEB
```

directive, it will not show the expansions of macros that follow. The use of these directives is illustrated in Fig. 11.3.

11.3 MORE ON MACRO ARGUMENTS

Positional and Keyword Arguments

As we have seen, the assembler replaces all occurrences of formal arguments in a macro definition with the actual arguments specified when the macro is invoked. We did not explain how the assembler determines which actual argument is to replace which formal argument, because the rule is natural and straightforward: the first actual argument is substituted for the first formal argument, the second actual argument is substituted for the second formal argument, and so on. That is, the role of each actual argument is determined by its position in the list of actual arguments. This positional scheme is, of course, similar to the way the roles of operands for machine instructions and arguments for procedures are determined. Some macros, however, may have a very large number of arguments, and it may be inconvenient to have to remember the exact order in which they must appear. We may write the actual arguments in any order if we include a keyword for each one to tell the assembler which argument is being specified. The keyword is the formal argument name. The format for specifying a keyword argument in a macro instruction is

$$formal\_arg\_name = actual\_arg$$

EXAMPLE 11.7: Using Keywords

A macro RANGE is to determine if a given integer datum (DATUM) is between two specified values (LOW and HIGH) and to cause a branch to a specified location (BAD) if not. RANGE is defined with the following .MACRO directive:

```
.MACRO  RANGE    LOW,HIGH,DATUM,TYPE,BAD
```

RANGE may be invoked using positional arguments in the usual way as follows:

```
RANGE   #0,#100,(R9),W,BADDATA
```

Alternatively, it may be invoked using keyword arguments like this:

```
RANGE   DATUM=(R9),LOW=#0,HIGH=#100,BAD=BADDATA,TYPE=W
```

Although the use of keyword arguments eliminates the problem of remembering the order in which the formal arguments are listed in the macro definition, it does require that the formal argument names be known to the user of the macro.

If keywords are used at all in a macro instruction, they should be used for each argument that is specified.

Default Values and Omitted Arguments

For some macros there may be one or more formal arguments for which a standard value (that is, a standard actual argument) is used most of the time. In the macro definition we may specify this value as the default value for that argument. Then, if the argument is omitted when the macro is invoked, the assembler will use the default value. If some other value for the argument is specified when the macro is invoked, the default is ignored and the assembler uses the specified value.

A default value is specified in the .MACRO directive of a macro definition by writing

$$formal\_arg\_name = default\_value$$

instead of just writing the formal argument name.

EXAMPLE 11.8: SUM Macro with a Default

Suppose the SUM macro defined in Example 11.5 is likely to be used most often to add longwords. We can specify that the default value of the formal argument TYPE is L as follows:

```
.MACRO  SUM     A,B,C,TOTAL,TYPE=L
```

Some sample macro expansions are

```
SUM     R5,R6,R7,XYZ                    SUM     R5,R6,R7,XYZ,B

ADDL3   R5,R6,XYZ                       ADDB3   R5,R6,XYZ
ADDL2   R7,XYZ                          ADDB2   R7,XYZ
```

EXAMPLE 11.9: A Default for PRINTCHRS

The PRINTCHRS macro has a default length of 85. Its .MACRO directive looks like this:

```
.MACRO  PRINTCHRS STRING,LENGTH=#85
```

Note that the default value includes the #, not just the number 85. The default value must appear exactly as it will be needed when substituted into instructions in the body of the macro. In the PRINTCHRS macro definition, LENGTH appears as an instruction operand.

An argument may be omitted from a macro instruction even if no default value is specified in the macro definition. In such cases, the assembler substitutes a null string for the associated formal argument when the macro is expanded. Thus we may think of a null string as being a default value for all arguments for which the macro definition does not specify some other default value. (We will see examples in Section 11.6, where it is useful to have null arguments.)

When positional arguments are being used in a macro instruction and any argument other than the last is omitted, the comma that would ordinarily follow the argument must be included as a place holder for that argument. If the comma is omitted, the assembler will substitute the next actual argument for the formal argument that the user wishes to be null. (If one particular argument is likely to be omitted, it should be placed last in the macro definition, as in Example 11.8; then the last comma may be omitted also.)

If keyword arguments are being used in a macro instruction, and some arguments are omitted, they are simply left out; commas are not needed as space holders because the order in which the arguments are specified is irrelevant. Thus keyword arguments are especially convenient for macros with a large number of arguments where many have default values that are used often. Many system I/O macros are in this category.

Keyword arguments and default values for arguments are very standard macro features. The details of how they are specified and used differ slightly in different systems.

Special Cases

If an actual argument for a macro contains a character that the assembler normally interprets as a separator (a comma, space, or tab), or a semicolon which normally indicates the beginning of a comment, the entire argument must be enclosed in delimiters to indicate that it is one argument. Angle brackets ($<>$) are the standard delimiters. For example, suppose we have a macro called **PRINTMSG** that displays its argument, a character string, at the terminal. We might use it like this:

```
PRINTMSG <TABLE OF TRANSACTIONS>
```

If the character string "TABLE OF TRANSACTIONS" were not delimited, the assembler would treat the spaces as separators and conclude that there were three actual arguments. If the macro definition had fewer than three formal arguments, the assembler would issue an error message.

The delimiters are not considered part of the actual argument; the assembler removes them before substituting the actual argument into the statements in the body of the macro definition.

If an angle bracket is one of the characters in an actual argument, some other character should be used as a delimiter. Any character will do, but the first delimiter must be preceded by a circumflex ($\wedge$). For example, in

```
PRINTMSG ^/ITEMS WITH COST > $100.00/
```

the delimiter is a slash. Since the circumflex plays a special role, an actual argument that contains one must be enclosed in delimiters. For example, $<\wedge XFF00>$ is the proper way to specify $\wedge XFF00$ as an actual argument.

11.4 LOCAL LABELS

The Need for Local Labels

Suppose we wish to write a macro that computes the absolute value of an integer. We could try to do it as in the following example.

EXAMPLE 11.10: A Macro that Uses a Label (unwisely, as we shall see)

```
        .MACRO  ABS    SOURCE,DEST,TYPE=L
        MOV'TYPE       SOURCE,DEST
        BGEQ           LABEL
        MNEG'TYPE      DEST,DEST
LABEL:  .ENDM   ABS
```

Some questions may occur to the reader. Is it legal to have a label on the .ENDM statement? If so, how is the label treated by the assembler? The label is legal and is treated in the usual way. As the assembler inserts each instruction from the macro definition into the program, it assembles it—i.e., translates it—incrementing its location counter as usual. When a label is encountered, the symbol is entered into the symbol table, and its value is set to the current value of the location counter. Since there is not a machine instruction or a storage reservation or initialization directive on the line with the label, the location counter will not be incremented. Thus the next statement in the program following the macro instruction will be assembled in the location addressed by LABEL.

Although the use of the label in the definition of ABS is technically correct, it will cause an error if the macro is used more than once in one program module. Since LABEL is not an argument for the macro, the assembler leaves it in the instructions just as it appears in the macro definition. Thus if ABS is used more than once, LABEL will appear on more than one instruction and cause a "multiple definition of label" error.

EXAMPLE 11.11: Expansion of ABS

Consider the program segment in Fig. 11.4(a); it invokes ABS twice. The expansions, with the error messages, are shown in Fig. 11.4(b).

The ABS macro illustrates a problem that occurs in any macro facility: we will often want to use labels in a macro definition, but ordinary labels can't be used if the macro might be invoked more than once in a module. Macro facilities include a mechanism for generating labels that will differ each time a macro is invoked. In the VAX assembler, the generated labels are called *created local labels*.

Local Labels

The format of a local label is

$$n\$$$

where n is a decimal integer in the range $1 \leq n \leq 65,535$. Local labels may be used outside of macros, though there are several restrictions on their use. We will discuss the use of local labels in macros only.

The incorrect macro definition used here is shown in Example 11.10.

(a) Statements in the program

```
                        ABS     R5,R5
                        ADDL2   R1,R5



                        ABS     (R4),ALPHA,W
                        CMPW    ALPHA,BETA
```

(b) Expansions with error messages

```
                                        005C    17      ABS.    R5,R5
              55      55      D0        005C            MOVL    R5,R5
                      11      18        005F            BGEQ            LABEL
              55      55      CE        0061            MNEGL   R5,R5
                                        0064        LABEL:
%MACRO-E-SYMOUTPHAS, Symbol out of phase
                                        0064
              55      51      C0        0064    18      ADDL2   R1,R5
                                        0067    19  ;       .
                                        0067    20  ;       .
                                        0067    21  ;       .
                                        0067    22      ABS     (R4),ALPHA,W
         95   AF      64      B0        0067            MOVW    (R4),ALPHA
                      F7      18        006B            BGEQ            LABEL
     8E  AF      90   AF      AE        006D            MNEGW   ALPHA,ALPHA
                                        0072        LABEL:
%MACRO-E-MULDEFLBL, Multiple definition of label               !
                                        0072
     8D  AF      8B   AF      B1        0072    23      CMPW    ALPHA,BETA
                                        0077    24  ;
                                        0077    25      .NOSHOW MEB
```

Figure 11.4 Incorrect use of a label in a macro

The assembler creates local labels beginning at 30000$. It keeps count of how many it has created so far, and whenever it creates a new one, it uses the next higher number. The programmer specifies that a local label is to be created for a macro by listing a formal argument name preceded by a question mark—e.g., ?LABEL—in the list of formal arguments on the .MACRO directive. Each time the macro is invoked, the assembler will create a new local label and substitute it for the formal name wherever it appears in the macro definition.

EXAMPLE 11.12 ABS Macro Using a Local Label

A correct macro definition for ABS is

```
            .MACRO  ABS     SOURCE,DEST,TYPE=L,?LABEL
            MOV'TYPE        SOURCE,DEST
            BGEQ            LABEL
            MNEG'TYPE       DEST,DEST
    LABEL:  .ENDM   ABS
```

Note that the question mark is not included in the formal label name when it appears in the body of the macro definition.

Assuming that the macro instructions in Figure 11.4(a) are the first ones that are expanded in the program, the expansions would be as shown in Fig. 11.5.

It is possible to use more than one local label in a macro. A different formal name must be specified for each one.

EXAMPLE 11.13: PRINTMSG Macro

The macro PRINTMSG prints a character string. It is similar to PRINTCHRS but simpler to use because the user does not have to put the string in memory. PRINTMSG could be used as follows:

```
    PRINTMSG <CLASS SCHEDULE>
```

(Recall that the brackets are used to delimit the character string so that the assembler will not interpret "CLASS" and "SCHEDULE" as two arguments.)

The macro definition for PRINTMSG is

```
            .MACRO  PRINTMSG MSG,?LBL,?LINE
            BRB     LBL
    LINE:   .ASCIZ  /MSG/
    LBL:    PRINTCHRS LINE
            .ENDM   PRINTMSG
```

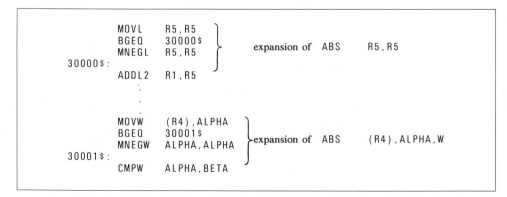

Figure 11.5 Expansions of ABS using local labels

We indicated in Section 11.1 that the body of a macro definition may contain a macro instruction (for another macro). Here, the PRINTMSG macro uses the PRINTCHRS macro.

   Note that a branch instruction is included to branch over the character string that will be stored in memory between machine instructions. Omitting the branch would, of course, be an error, for without it the CPU would try to execute the character data as if they were instructions.

When the assembler encounters a macro instruction, it sets up an argument substitution table to use while expanding the macro. Suppose that the assembler has already created three local labels in the current module when it expands the macro instruction

```
        PRINTMSG <CLASS SCHEDULE>
```

Its substitution table for this expansion would be

Formal Argument	Actual Value
MSG	CLASS SCHEDULE
LBL	30003$
LINE	30004$

The actual values are substituted just as they appear in the table, as character strings, for the formal argument names in the macro. Suppose PRINTMSG is used again to print another message immediately after the first, say as follows:

```
        PRINTMSG  <COURSE   DAYS   TIMES>
```

The substitution table for the expansion of this instruction would be

Formal Argument	Actual Value		
MSG	COURSE	DAYS	TIMES
LBL	30005$		
LINE	30006$		

EXAMPLE 11.14: *Expansions of PRINTMSG*

(a)
```
        PRINTMSG  <CLASS SCHEDULE>

        BRB       30003$
30004$: .ASCIZ    /CLASS SCHEDULE/
30003$: PRINTCHRS 30004$
```

(b)
```
        PRINTMSG  <COURSE  DAYS   TIMES>

        BRB       30005$
30006$: .ASCIZ    /COURSE  DAYS   TIMES/
30005$: PRINTCHRS 30006$
```

For clarity in the example, we have not shown the expansion of PRINTCHRS.

It might occur to the reader that it would be nice to have a macro like PRINTMSG that prints the character string centered in a line. Some of the techniques of Section 11.7 will be helpful for doing this.

11.5 USER-FRIENDLY MACROS

A macro is convenient to use if the user does not have to remember a lot of details, peculiarities, restrictions, and special requirements of the macro. A macro is safe to use if it is convenient (since convenience means there is less likelihood of its being used incorrectly), if it does not have unexpected side effects (e.g., destroying data in registers), and if when used incorrectly, the error is detected immediately rather than after destroying data or instructions or generating incorrect results that will be detected later when the cause is more difficult to track down. Macro definitions can be written so that they are very convenient and safe for the user, or so that they are less so. In this section we will consider some guidelines for writing user-friendly—i.e., convenient and safe—macros. These concerns are especially relevant when writing system macros, library macros that are to be used by many programmers, and even macros to be used by one programmer over a long period of time.

Some Guidelines for User-Friendly Macros

We have already seen several features of macros that increase convenience of use: default values for arguments, keyword arguments, and local labels. Thus we have the following guidelines:

Specify useful argument default values whenever possible.

Choose natural, easy-to-remember, formal argument names.

If labels are needed, use local labels.

The CVTSL macro defined in Example 11.1 is convenient to use because the macro definition adheres to the standard VAX conventions for naming instructions and for the order in which operands are specified. CVTSL illustrates the guideline:

Use standard conventions of the assembly language whenever appropriate— e.g., for naming instructions and operands, and for ordering the latter.

The required form of an actual argument depends on how it is used in the macro. Sometimes, because of the role of the argument, it is natural to have fairly stringent restrictions on its form. For example, the actual argument that replaces ARRAY in the RESERVE macro in Example 11.6 must be a symbol because it is used as a label. Sometimes, though, it is possible and desirable to allow for a variety of forms. The first three arguments of the SUM macro (Examples 11.3 and 11.5) may be specified using any operand addressing modes. Thus another guideline is

> Write a macro definition so that a reasonable variety of forms for the actual arguments will be valid.

We saw that autoincrement mode could not be used correctly for the fourth argument in the SUM macro. In Sections 11.6 and 11.7 we will learn techniques that can be used to modify the definition of SUM so that this mode is acceptable too.

Using Registers and Scratch Space in Macros

It is often necessary for a macro to use some registers or some scratch space in memory to accomplish its task. For example, consider the CVTSL macro (from Example 11.1):

```
.MACRO  CVTSL   NUM_DIGITS,LSN,LONG
CVTSP   NUM_DIGITS,LSN,NUM_DIGITS,PKD
CVTPL   NUM_DIGITS,PKD,LONG
.ENDM   CVTSL
```

PKD is scratch space needed for the packed decimal representation of the integer being converted from leading separate numeric to two's complement. This macro definition assumes that the user has defined PKD elsewhere in the program and has reserved enough space for it. If the user forgets to define PKD, the linker will issue an "undefined symbol" error message, so the error will be detected quickly. However, if the user defines PKD but does not reserve enough space, the CVTSP instruction will overwrite whatever data appear in memory immediately after the space reserved for PKD; this error will be much harder to detect. Thus the CVTSL macro would be both more convenient and safer to use if it reserved the scratch space needed for the packed datum. But where can the macro reserve scratch space? The answer is the user stack. To reserve temporary scratch space on the stack, we simply decrement the stack pointer by the number of bytes desired. (See Fig. 11.6.)

How many bytes should we reserve for the packed datum? Since the datum is to be stored in a longword, it should have at most ten digits. A ten-digit packed datum fits in six bytes. However, the leading separate numeric string being converted may have been incorrectly typed, or NUM_DIGITS may be specified incorrectly. In such cases, the string may have more than ten digits, and if only six bytes are reserved on the stack, other data on the stack would be overwritten, with perhaps very confusing effects. Since our aim here is to protect the user from bad side effects

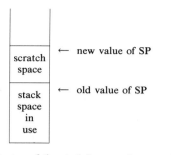

The SP must always point to the top of the stack because the operating system may, at any time, use the space above (SP). (SP) may be used to address the new scratch space reserved.

Figure 11.6 Using the stack for scratch space

of errors, we should reserve more space. But how much? What is a reasonable limit? The CVTSP instruction itself will cause a reserved operand fault if the number of digits specified for either the leading separate numeric or packed operand is outside the permitted range for these data types: 0 to 31. Thus a safe macro would allow for up to 31 digits. (If the integer being converted is too large for a longword, the overflow condition code will be set by CVTPL; we may leave to the user the responsibility for checking for that error.) The improved definition of CVTSL is:

EXAMPLE 11.15: A Macro that Uses the Stack for Scratch Space

```
.MACRO   CVTSL    NUM_DIGITS,LSN,LONG
SUBL2    #16,SP
CVTSP    NUM_DIGITS,LSN,NUM_DIGITS,(SP)
CVTPL    NUM_DIGITS,(SP),LONG
ADDL2    #16,SP
.ENDM    CVTSL
```

Note that the stack pointer must be reset by the macro, effectively popping the scratch data.

If a macro uses registers, it should save the original contents and reload them after finishing its work. Once again, the appropriate place for temporary storage is the user stack. There are two instructions that make it very easy to push and pop the contents of several registers: PUSHR and POPR. Their formats are

PUSHR   *register_mask*
POPR   *register_mask*

The register mask is similar (but not identical) to the register mask used in an .ENTRY directive to specify the registers to be saved when a procedure is called. It is a word in which bit n corresponds to Rn. Any register (except the PC) may be specified in a mask for a PUSHR or POPR instruction. The mask may be a literal using the $\wedge$M operator or it may be in memory. (The former is more commonly used.) Regardless of the order in which the registers are listed in the instruction, PUSHR will push the contents of all the specified registers onto the stack so that they appear in order by register number. POPR copies the first longword from the stack into the lowest-numbered register listed in its mask, the second into the second lowest register, and so on. Of course, for clarity, it is nice to list the registers in numerical order. Both PUSHR and POPR adjust the stack pointer as appropriate. They do not affect the condition codes.

Usually the same list of registers appears in the PUSHR and corresponding POPR instructions, but the two instructions are executed independently; whatever registers are specified will be used.

EXAMPLE 11.16: How PUSHR and POPR Work

```
PUSHR   #^M<R10,R5,R7,R0>
```

will cause the contents of the registers to be stacked as shown in Fig. 11.7(a).

```
POPR    #^M<R0,R8,R9,R5>
```

will cause the data on the stack to be put in the registers as shown in Fig. 11.7(b).

EXAMPLE 11.17: Saving Register Contents in a Macro

A macro that moves a character string as part of its task may contain lines like these:

```
PUSHR   #^M<R0,R1,R2,R3,R4,R5>
MOVC3   LEN,STR1,STR2
POPR    #^M<R0,R1,R2,R3,R4,R5>
```

The PUSHR and POPR instructions may, of course, be used outside of macros. One of the uses of PUSHR would be pushing procedure arguments onto the stack.

The CVTSL macro uses registers R0–R3, but they were not saved because the VAX instructions that convert between leading separate numeric, packed, and two's complement formats all use these registers. It is reasonable for the macro to adhere to the same conventions as similar VAX instructions.

Some system macros follow the convention that R0 and R1 may be used to return status flags just as procedures may do. Thus such macros generally would not save the old contents of these registers. As we indicated in Chapter 5, our I/O macros may change the contents of R0 and R1.

(a) Assume register contents as follows:

```
                              R0:    00000000
                              R5:    00000005
                              R7:    FFFFF3A2
                              R10:   0000000A
```

The instruction

```
              PUSHR    #^M<R10,R5,R7,R0>
```

will stack the register contents as follows:

```
          ┌──────────────┐
          │   00000000   │  ← SP
          ├──────────────┤
          │   00000005   │
          ├──────────────┤
          │   FFFFF3A2   │
          ├──────────────┤
          │   0000000A   │
          ├──────────────┤
          │    stack     │  ← old value of SP
          │    space     │
          │      in      │
          │     use      │
          └──────────────┘
```

(b) The instruction

```
              POPR     #^M<R0,R8,R9,R5>
```

will pop four longwords from the top of the stack, adjust the stack pointer, and put the data into the registers as follows:

```
                              R0:    00000000
                              R5:    00000005
                              R8:    FFFFF3A2
                              R9:    0000000A
```

Figure 11.7   The effects of the **PUSHR** and **POPR** instructions

The examples we have just discussed illustrate several more guidelines for user-friendly macros:

A macro should not rely on the user to reserve space for scratch work done by the macro.

If scratch space is needed in a macro, the stack should be used whenever possible. It is important that the stack pointer be properly set and reset to reserve and release the space.

When scratch space is used, the maximum amount of space that may be needed should be reserved (if practical) so that other data on the stack (or elsewhere) are not overwritten by mistake.

If registers are used in a macro, the original contents should be saved (on the stack) and reloaded when the macro finishes its task. R0 and R1 may, by convention, not be saved.

11.6 CONDITIONAL ASSEMBLY

What is Conditional Assembly?

One of the features of macro facilities that give them so much power is conditional assembly. A macro definition may specify different statements to be assembled depending on conditions that can be tested by the assembler. That is, the assembler may be told to do specified computations, test for certain conditions, and assemble certain statements depending on the results. We may think of the conditional assembly directives and some other directives used in macro definitions as making up a programming language that we use to give commands to the assembler.

Thus, in addition to machine instructions, ordinary assembler directives, and other macro instructions, the body of a macro definition may contain directives that control or affect the expansion of the macro. When the assembler encounters machine instructions or ordinary assembler directives (e.g., storage reservation and initialization directives), it inserts these in the program. When it encounters a macro instruction, it looks up the definition for that macro and expands it. When it encounters a directive related to conditional assembly or macro expansion, it carries out whatever steps are indicated by the particular directive.

To understand and use conditional assembly properly, we must remember that the assembler can test only conditions that exist at assembly time; it can compute only with data available at assembly time. For example, the assembler can test and do computation with the values of symbols but not the contents of memory locations or registers used in the program, because the latter simply do not exist at assembly time.

Many of the tests and computations done by the assembler are done on character strings—character strings that appear in the program itself, such as actual arguments for macros, not character strings in memory. Conditional assembly may be used, for example, to examine an actual argument for a macro to determine if it is of the proper form. We observed that the SUM macro (Examples 11.3 and 11.5) would not work correctly if the fourth argument were specified using autoincrement mode. With conditional assembly (and the tools of Section 11.7) we can modify the macro definition to test the actual argument and direct the assembler to assemble instructions that will work properly for this case. (See Exercise 21.) On the other hand, in the CVTSL macro (Example 11.15), it might be useful to know how many digits are in the leading separate numeric operand so that we don't reserve more scratch space than is needed. The number of digits can *not* be tested at assembly time, because the data are not read in and available until the program is executing.

If we are to "program" the assembler, we need some of the basic components of a programming language. We can not use the VAX instructions, because when the assembler encounters them in a macro definition it inserts them into the source program; it does not execute them. The three major components of the "programming language" for directing the assembler that we will describe and use are variables, a conditional directive (.IF), and loop directives (.IRP, .IRPC, and .REPEAT). We will also describe several other directives that are useful in macro definitions and are typical of macro facilities in general, but we will not cover all the details of their use or all of the VAX macro processor directives.

Variables

To the assembler, user-defined symbols are variables. Their values are stored in the symbol table and may be looked up, tested, and used by the assembler as needed. The values of symbols used as labels may not be changed in the course of a program module, but values of symbols defined in direct assignment statements may be changed in subsequent direct assignment statements. When such a symbol is redefined—i.e., when its value is changed—the assembler simply changes the entry in the symbol table.

To avoid conflict with symbols used in a program, symbols in a macro definition should be names not likely to be used by a programmer. Symbols for most purposes other than labels (i.e., symbols defined in direct assignment statements) can be generated during macro expansion by concatenating a created local label onto other characters. (There will be examples later.)

.IF—The Conditional Assembly Block Directive

The .IF directive is something like an IF statement in a high-level language. If the condition specified on the .IF directive is satisfied, the statements that follows are processed by the assembler; if the condition is not satisfied, they are skipped. The format for a conditional assembly block is

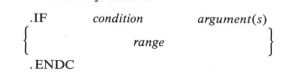

The conditions that may be specified are listed in Table 11.1. The arguments for .IF directives are the data to be tested for the specified condition; they may or may not be macro arguments.

The range of a conditional block may contain any statements that could appear in a macro definition including nested conditional blocks, looping directives, and other directives that control the expansion of the macro.

The .ENDC directive is needed to mark the end of the conditional block.

EXAMPLE 11.18: CVTSL Macro with Overflow Test

Suppose we wish to add an option to the CVTSL macro that allows the user to specify if an overflow test should be performed on the two's complement result of the conversion. If this option is selected, instructions will be assembled to test for overflow and clear the longword result if overflow occurred. The user would select this option by using a fourth argument; if the fourth argument is omitted, the macro will be expanded as before. The new macro definition is

```
        .MACRO  CVTSL   NUM_DIGITS,LSN,LONG,TESTOVFL,?LBL
        SUBL2   #16,SP
        CVTSP   NUM_DIGITS,LSN,NUM_DIGITS,(SP)
        CVTPL   NUM_DIGITS,(SP),LONG
        .IF     NOT_BLANK       TESTOVFL
        BVC     LBL
        CLRL    LONG
        .ENDC
LBL:    ADDL2   #16,SP
        .ENDM   CVTSL
```

Note that the actual argument specified for TESTOVFL is irrelevant; all that matters is whether or not it is null. Two expansions are shown below.

```
        CVTSL   #3,(R8),R6                      CVTSL   #3,(R8),R6,OVFL

        SUBL2   #16,SP                          SUBL2   #16,SP
        CVTSP   #3,(R8),#3,(SP)                 CVTSP   #3,(R8),#3,(SP)
        CVTPL   #3,(SP),R6                      CVTPL   #3,(SP),R6
30003$: ADDL2   #16,SP                          BVC     30003$
                                                CLRL    R6
                                        30003$: ADDL2   #16,SP
```

Note that the label 30003$ appears in the first expansion even though the condition tested was false and the BVC instruction is not included. This is because the statement containing the label is outside the range of the .IF block. (For these examples we have arbitrarily assumed that the next local label to be created was 30003$.)

Notice the difference between the two conditional tests, .IF and BVC, in Example 11.18. One is done at assembly time, and one *may* be done at execution time. The fourth actual argument is tested by the assembler, at assembly time, to determine whether or not it is null. The assembler does not test for overflow. If the fourth argument is not null, the assembler merely inserts the BVC and CLRL instructions in the program, and the CPU will perform the overflow test when the program is executed.

If the range of an .IF directive contains only one statement, a shorter form can be used. It is called the immediate conditional assembly directive and the format is

.IIF *condition   argument(s), statement*

The .ENDC directive is not used with .IIF, since it is not needed to mark the end of the conditional block. Example 11.19 illustrates the use of .IIF and the IDENTICAL and DIFFERENT conditions.

EXAMPLE 11.19: CVT2S Macro

This macro converts an integer from two's complement to leading separate numeric. The two's complement operand may be a byte, word, or longword. Temporary scratch space on the stack is used for both the packed decimal and longword forms of the integer. Note the use of displacement mode addressing to refer to the packed datum on the stack.

```
.MACRO  CVT2S  DATUM,NUM_DIGITS,LSN,TYPE=L
SUBL2   #20,SP              ; Scratch space
.IIF    IDN  TYPE,L,    MOVL        DATUM,(SP)
.IIF    DIF  TYPE,L,    CVT'TYPE'L  DATUM,(SP)
CVTLP   (SP),NUM_DIGITS,4(SP)
CVTPS   NUM_DIGITS,4(SP),NUM_DIGITS,LSN
ADDL2   #20,SP              ; Release scratch space
.ENDM   CVT2S
```

As Example 11.19 illustrates, often we want one sequence of statements assembled if a condition holds and another sequence if the opposite condition holds. The VAX assembler allows us to specify both alternatives by using the .IF_FALSE directive in a conditional block structured as follows:

.IF   *condition*   *argument(s)*

$\left\{ \textit{statements to be assembled if condition is true} \right\}$

.IF_FALSE

$\left\{ \textit{statements to be assembled if condition is false} \right\}$

.ENDC

The action of a conditional block using .IF_FALSE is similar to an if-then-else statement in a high-level language.

.IRP—The Indefinite Repeat Block Directive

The indefinite repeat block is the most useful of the conditional assembly looping directives. It causes the assembler to generate the same sequence of statements several times, with a parameter that varies each time the statements are generated. The format of an indefinite repeat block is

.IRP   *formal_repeat_arg,<actual_arguments>*

$\left\{ \qquad\qquad \textit{range} \qquad\qquad \right\}$

.ENDR

The formal repeat argument may be any symbol, though it shouldn't be one of the formal arguments of the macro. It may be used throughout the range. The actual arguments for the .IRP block are often formal arguments of the macro, though they may be other strings. The assembler will take each actual argument in turn and substitute it for the formal repeat argument throughout the range of the block. If the actual arguments for the .IRP are formal arguments of the macro, the assembler will be substituting the actual macro arguments for them, so the effect is to cause the range to be assembled for each of several actual macro arguments.

An indefinite repeat block is used below in Example 11.20, but before we examine the example, we will describe one of the new directives it uses, and extend our earlier explanation of the listing directives.

.NARG—The Number-of-Arguments Directive

In some macros, it is useful to have access to the number of actual arguments specified when the macro is invoked. The .NARG (Number of ARGuments) directive, whose format is

.NARG   *symbol*

sets the value of the symbol to the number of actual arguments.

.SHOW and .NOSHOW—Listing Control Directives

In Section 11.2 we indicated that the .SHOW and .NOSHOW directives with the argument MEB can be used to control whether or not the program listing will show statements in the macro expansion—specifically those that cause code to be inserted in the object file. It is often helpful, especially when debugging macro definitions, to see the conditional assembly and repeat block directives. If .SHOW is specified with the argument ME, then the entire macro expansion, not just the statements that generate code in the object file, will show in the listing. (For other options of .SHOW and .NOSHOW, consult the *VAX-11 MACRO Language Reference Manual.*)

EXAMPLE 11.20: CALL macro

This CALL macro can be used to call a procedure with up to ten arguments.

```
.MACRO  CALL    PROC ARG1,ARG2,ARG3,ARG4,ARG5,ARG6, -
                ARG7,ARG8,ARG9,ARG10,?LOCLBL
.IRP    ARG,<ARG10,ARG9,ARG8,ARG7,ARG6,ARG5,ARG4, -
        ARG3,ARG2,ARG1>
.IIF    NOT_BLANK  <ARG>,      PUSHAB  ARG
.ENDR
.NARG   N'LOCLBL
CALLS   #N'LOCLBL - 1,PROC
.ENDM   CALL
```

Note that the formal macro arguments used as arguments in the indefinite repeat block are listed in reverse order, so that the addresses of the (non-null) arguments will be stacked in the proper order. Note also how the indefinite repeat loop and the NOT_ BLANK conditional are used together, so that a PUSHAB instruction is generated for each (non-null) procedure argument. The same technique is used in the **DUMPLONG**

```
(a) Showing conditional directives

                            011C    23          .SHOW    ME
                            011C    24  ;
                            011C    25          CALL PROCESS LIST,DIM
                            011C               .IRP     ARG,<,,,,,,,-
                            011C                        ,DIM,LIST>
                            011C          ①    .IIF     NOT_BLANK  <ARG>,      PUSHAB  ARG
                            011C               .ENDR
                            011C               .IIF     NOT_BLANK  <>,  PUSHAB
                            011C
                            011C          ②    .IIF     NOT_BLANK  <>,  PUSHAB
                            011C
                            011C               .IIF     NOT_BLANK  <>,  PUSHAB
                            011C
                            011C          ③    .IIF     NOT_BLANK  <>,  PUSHAB
                            011C
                            011C               .IIF     NOT_BLANK  <>,  PUSHAB
                            011C
                            011C               .IIF     NOT_BLANK  <>,  PUSHAB
                            011C
                            011C               .IIF     NOT_BLANK  <>,  PUSHAB
                            011C
          ④  FEE0 CF   9F   011C               .IIF     NOT_BLANK  <DIM>,      PUSHAB  DIM
                            0120
              FEE0 CF   9F   0120               .IIF     NOT_BLANK  <LIST>,     PUSHAB  LIST
                            0124
          ⑤        00000003 0124               .NARG    N30000$
00000000'EF   02   FB   0124               CALLS    #N30000$ - 1,PROCESS

(b) Showing only lines that generate code

                            011C    23          .SHOW    MEB
                            011C    24  ;
                            011C    25          CALL PROCESS LIST,DIM
          FEE0 CF   9F   011C               .IIF     NOT_BLANK  <DIM>,       PUSHAB  DIM
          FEE0 CF   9F   0120               .IIF     NOT_BLANK  <LIST>,      PUSHAB  LIST
00000000'EF   02   FB   0124               CALLS    #N30000$ - 1,PROCESS
```

[1] The IRP loop is shown with the arguments to be substituted for the formal repeat argument.
[2] The expansion of the IRP loop.
[3] The condition is false, so no object code is generated here.
[4] Object code is generated.
[5] The value of N30000$ is 3.

Figure 11.8 Expansions of the CALL macro

macro (see Appendix D) to generate instructions to dump each of the arguments specified by the user.

Note that we concatenated a local label onto the letter "N" to generate a symbol for use in the .NARG and CALLS statements. The symbol appears as N30000$ in the expansions shown in Fig. 11.8.

The formal repeat argument ARG is enclosed in pointed brackets in the .IIF statement because, without the brackets, the assembler misinterprets the statement in cases when ARG is null.

.IRPC and .REPEAT—Other Loop Directives

The .IRPC (Indefinite RePeat block with Character parameter) directive is very similar to the .IRP directive. The actual arguments that get substituted for the formal repeat block argument throughout the range of the .IRPC are the individual characters of a specified string. The format of the .IRPC directive is

.IRPC   *formal_repeat_block_argument,<string>*

For relatively simple situations where the same sequence of instructions must be assembled some fixed number of times, the .REPEAT directive may be used. Its form is

.REPEAT *expression*

The expression indicates how many times the statements in the range should be processed by the assembler. It must be absolute and contain no undefined symbols.

Labels in Repeat Blocks

In Section 11.5 we considered a problem of using labels in macro definitions: the same label may not appear on more than one statement in a program module. Local labels created by the assembler solve the problem most of the time, since the assembler creates a new local label for each formal label name each time the macro is invoked. But if a label appears on a statement in the range of a repeat block, the same label may appear on many statements in the expansion. Consider the macro in Example 11.21; it attempts to compute the absolute values of up to four arguments. An expansion, with error messages, is shown in Fig. 11.9.

EXAMPLE 11.21: Using Local Labels Incorrectly

```
.MACRO  ABSVALS A1,A2,A3,A4,T=L,?LBL
.IRP    DATUM,<A1,A2,A3,A4>
.IF     NOT_BLANK    DATUM
TST'T   DATUM
BGEQ    LBL
MNEG'T  DATUM,DATUM
```

```
                              0065    18              .SHOW    ME
                              0065    19      ;
                              0065    20              ABSVALS R4,R5,R6
                              0065                    .IRP    DATUM,<R4,R5,R6,>
                              0065                    .IF NOT_BLANK DATUM
                              0065                    TSTL     DATUM
                              0065          .          BGEQ     30000$
                              0065                    MNEGL    DATUM,DATUM
                              0065        30000$:
                              0065                    .ENDC
                              0065                    .ENDR
                              0065                    .IF NOT_BLANK R4
                   54    D5   0065                    TSTL     R4
                   11    18   0067                    BGEQ     30000$
              54   54    CE   0069                    MNEGL    R4,R4
                              006C        30000$:
%MACRO-E-SYMOUTPHAS, Symbol out of phase
                              006C
                              006C                    .ENDC
                              006C
                              006C                    .IF NOT_BLANK R5
                   55    D5   006C                    TSTL     R5
                   FC    18   006E                    BGEQ     30000$
              55   55    CE   0070                    MNEGL    R5,R5
                              0073        30000$:
%MACRO-E-MULDEFLBL, Multiple definition of label    !
                              0073
%MACRO-E-SYMOUTPHAS, Symbol out of phase
                              0073
                              0073                    .ENDC
                              0073
                              0073                    .IF NOT_BLANK R6
                   56    D5   0073                    TSTL     R6
                   FC    18   0075                    BGEQ     30000$
              56   56    CE   0077                    MNEGL    R6,R6
                              007A        30000$:
%MACRO-E-MULDEFLBL, Multiple definition of label    !
                              007A
                              007A                    .ENDC
                              007A
                              007A
```

Figure 11.9   Expansion of incorrect ABSVALS

```
        LBL:
              .ENDC
              .ENDR
              .ENDM   ABSVALS
```

How can we solve this problem? How can we repeatedly generate a similar sequence of instructions that contains a label, but get a different label each time? One solution, at least for the task in the macro ABSVALS, is to require the user to use the ABS macro of Example 11.12 repeatedly. Each time ABS is invoked, a new local label is created. Let us suppose that this solution is unacceptable. Another solution, generally a better one, is to write another macro definition containing the range of the repeat block, and to modify the repeat block so that it contains only an instruction that invokes the second macro. The local label is now in the second macro, and each time it is invoked from within the repeat block of the first macro, a new label will be created. Example 11.22 incorporates this idea.

EXAMPLE 11.22: ABSVALS Using ABS

```
.MACRO   ABSVALS A1,A2,A3,A4,T = L
.IRP     DATUM,<A1,A2,A3,A4>
.IIF     NOT_BLANK  <DATUM>,     ABS   DATUM,DATUM,T
.ENDR
.ENDM    ABSVALS
```

Notice that the arguments for ABS are a formal repeat block argument and a formal macro argument for ABSVALS. They will be replaced by actual arguments for ABSVALS (or the default "L" for T). In the following listing segment we see an expansion of ABSVALS.

```
          .SHOW       ME
          ABSVALS     R4,R5,R6
          .IRP        DATUM,<R4,R5,R6>
          .IIF        NOT_BLANK  <DATUM>,ABS     DATUM,DATUM,L
          .ENDR
          .IIF        NOT_BLANK  <R4>,   ABS   R4,R4,L
          MOVL        R4,R4
          BGEQ        30002$
          MNEGL       R4,R4
30002$:
          .IIF        NOT_BLANK  <R5>,   ABS   R5,R5,L
          MOVL        R5,R5
          BGEQ        30003$
          MNEGL       R5,R5
30003$:
          .IIF        NOT_BLANK  <R6>,   ABS   R6,R6,L
          MOVL        R6,R6
          BGEQ        30004$
          MNEGL       R6,R6
30004$:
```

.ERROR—A Directive to Display Error Messages

The .ERROR directive directs the assembler to display an error message at the terminal and include it in the program listing. It is particularly useful in macro definitions where conditional assembly directives may be used to test actual macro arguments to see that they are of the required form. A simplified format of the directive is

> .ERROR   ; message to be displayed

Note that the error message is written as a comment. (This is a peculiarity of the VAX assembly language; it is not typical.)

.MEXIT—Macro Exit Directive

The .MEXIT directive may be used to terminate a macro expansion before reaching the .ENDM directive, or to terminate expansion of a repeat loop. If the assembler encounters .MEXIT inside a repeat loop, it will exit the loop and continue expanding the macro at the statement that follows the .ENDR. If it encounters .MEXIT outside a loop, it will exit the macro definition altogether.

EXAMPLE 11.23: Using .ERROR and .MEXIT

Suppose we want a macro definition to check that the type Q (quadword) is not specified as an actual argument in a macro that works only for B, W, and L. This could be done as follows:

```
.IF      IDENTICAL    TYPE,Q
.ERROR                ; Q IS AN INVALID TYPE
.MEXIT
.ENDC
```

If the condition is satisfied—i.e., if the type argument is Q—the error message will be displayed; the assembler will exit the macro definition and continue assembly at the statement that follows the macro instruction that was being expanded.

TABLE 11.1   *Conditions for the .IF directive*

Condition Long Form	Short Form	Meaning	Arguments
BLANK	B	String is null	Macro argument
NOT_BLANK	NB	String is not null	Macro argument

(Note that the names of the two conditions above are misleading; the assembler tests whether or not the argument is a null string—i.e., contains no characters—not whether it is the blank, or space, character.)

IDENTICAL	IDN	Arguments are identical	Macro args., strings
DIFFERENT	DIF	Arguments are different	Macro args., strings
EQUAL	EQ	Argument $= 0$	Expression
NOT_EQUAL	NE	Argument $\neq 0$	Expression
GREATER	GT	Argument > 0	Expression
LESS_EQUAL	LE	Argument ≤ 0	Expression
LESS_THAN	LT	Argument < 0	Expression
GREATER_EQUAL	GE	Argument ≥ 0	Expression
DEFINED	DF	Symbol is defined	Symbol
NOT_DEFINED	NDF	Symbol is not defined	Symbol

11.7 STRING FUNCTIONS

The VAX assembler has three string-processing functions that may be used to examine and manipulate character strings during macro expansion. Each function returns a number or a character string as its value. They may be used any place in a macro definition where the statement that results from substituting the function value would be a legal statement. Each function name begins with a percent sign to distinguish them from symbols.

The LENGTH Function

The format of the length function is

$$\%LENGTH(string)$$

Its value is the length of (number of characters in) the string. The string may be a macro argument or a delimited string. (It may be a formal repeat block argument that is replaced by a macro argument or other string.)

The value of the length function may be assigned to a symbol and tested using conditional assembly.

> **EXAMPLE 11.24: Using %LENGTH**
>
> Suppose the macro WORK must process a character string argument but can not handle strings with more than, say, eight characters. The following statements illustrate how a symbol can be set to the length to be used in subsequent statements.

```
.MACRO WORK    ARG,?LOCLBL
L'LOCLBL=%LENGTH(ARG)
.IIF    GREATER_THAN   L'LOCLBL – 8,    L'LOCLBL = 8
```

The EXTRACT Function

The purpose of the EXTRACT function is to extract a substring from a character string. Its format is

$$\%EXTRACT(start\_position, length, string)$$

The string argument is the string from which the substring is to be extracted. It may be a macro argument or a delimited string (or a formal repeat block argument that is replaced by either of the former). The start position and the length may be specified by decimal numbers or symbols. Positions in a character string are numbered left to right beginning with position 0. Thus, for example, the string "CLASS SCHEDULE" has C's in positions 0 and 7, S's in positions 3, 4, and 6, and a space in position 5.

EXAMPLES 11.25: %EXTRACT

The value of %EXTRACT(0,5,<CLASS SCHEDULE>) is the character string "CLASS".

The value of %EXTRACT(8,3,<CLASS SCHEDULE>) is the character string "HED".

If %EXTRACT(0,L'LOCLBL,ARG) appears in the macro definition begun in Example 11.24, its value is the actual argument substituted for ARG, or its first eight characters if its length is greater than eight.

The DUMPLONG macro prints only eight characters for the name of each of its arguments. It uses %EXTRACT to extract the first eight characters of the name (or the entire name if it has fewer characters). (See Appendix D for the macro definition.)

The LOCATE Function

The LOCATE function searches a string for a specified substring and returns its position if it is found. Its format is

$$\%\text{LOCATE}(target, string)$$

or

$$\%\text{LOCATE}(target, string, start\_position)$$

The target is the string to be searched for; the second argument is the string to be searched. These arguments may be macro arguments or delimited strings (or formal repeat block arguments). If the third argument, start_position, is omitted, the search begins at the beginning (position 0) of the string. If a start_position is specified, the search begins at that position in the string. Start_position may be a decimal number or a symbol. The value returned by LOCATE is the number of the position where the target begins in the string. If the target is not found, the value returned is the length of the string searched. (Since position numbers start at 0, the length is one position past the last character in the string.) For example, the value of

%LOCATE(<MA>,<GAMMA,SIGMA>)

is 3, but the value of

%LOCATE(<MA>,<GAMMA,SIGMA>,4)

is 9. The value of

%LOCATE(<MAA>,<GAMMA,SIGMA>)

is 11.

EXAMPLE 11.26: Using %LOCATE

To determine whether or not a target string has been found, the following conditional block may be used:

```
.IF    NE   %LOCATE(target,string)-%LENGTH(string)
```

$\left\{ \begin{array}{c} \text{statements to assemble if target was found} \end{array} \right\}$

```
.ENDC
```

For a specific example, suppose we wish to make sure that the actual argument specified for the formal argument TYPE is a B, W, or L. Example 11.23 showed how to determine if the argument was a Q, but not how to detect any other invalid character easily. The following conditional block illustrates a useful technique.

```
.IF    EQ   %LOCATE(TYPE,<BWL>)-3
.ERROR             ; BAD TYPE USED IN MACRO
.MEXIT
.ENDC
```

11.8 SUMMARY

The macro facility of an assembly language allows a programmer to use a single statement to refer to a sequence of assembly language statements. The use of arguments and conditional assembly allows the instructions to be varied each time the macro is used. Like procedures, macros can make a program clearer, more modular, and easier to write. Unlike procedures, the actual instructions to be assembled or executed by a macro are inserted directly into the program and appear in the object file each time the macro is used.

The actual macro arguments specified in a macro instruction and directly substituted for the corresponding formal argument names used throughout the macro definition. The actual arguments may be specified positionally or with keywords (the formal argument names). Default values may be specified in the macro definition and will be used if the programmer does not specify an actual argument value when using the macro.

Instructions in macros may be varied by concatenating arguments onto other strings in the macro definition.

Ordinary labels cannot always be used in macros because the same label may not appear on more than one statement within one module. Local labels are generated by the assembler for use in macros; each time a macro using a local label is expanded, the assembler generates a distinct label.

If scratch space is needed in a macro, the user stack may be used.

Macro definitions may include conditional assembly directives. These are directives that tell the assembler to test various conditions and assemble certain statements depending on the results. The assembler may be given other directions; for example, it may be told to repeat assembly of some statements, to terminate expansion of a macro if specified conditions hold, and so on. The VAX macro processor has three string functions, %LENGTH, %EXTRACT, and %LOCATE, that are particularly useful with conditional assembly.

11.9 EXERCISES

1. Write a macro that interchanges two longword data.

2. Write a macro that interchanges two data. Assume that the data are both of the same type (B, W, L, or Q) and let the type be an argument.

3. We pointed out that the last argument for the SUM macro (Example 11.3) could not be specified in autoincrement mode. Give two other addressing modes that would not be correct for that argument.

4. Write a macro definition for a macro called CVTLQ that converts its first argument from longword to quadword and puts the result in the second operand. It should leave the condition codes set to indicate the sign of the result. In other words, CVTLQ should act like the existing VAX instructions that convert between the various integer data types. Indicate what addressing modes may be used for the two macro arguments. (The list of valid modes for the second argument may be quite short.)

5. Suppose we want to use the CALL macro from Example 11.4 to call a procedure PROC whose arguments are located as follows: The address of the first argument is in R7, the second argument is in memory at the location labeled ALPHA, and the third argument is an array named ARRAY. Write the CALL macro instruction to call the procedure.

6. What addressing modes will cause errors if used in the actual arguments for the CALL macro in Example 11.4? Explain why.

7. Could the second argument in the RESERVE macro (Example 11.6) be a symbol? Why or why not?

8. Write a macro definition for a macro called PUSH that will push a byte, word, longword, or quadword onto the stack and correctly adjust the stack pointer (SP). Write a POP macro with similar specifications.

9. Consider the following macro definition

```
.MACRO   PRINTCHRS STRING,LENGTH=#85
CVTWL    LENGTH,-(SP)
PUSHAB   STRING
CALLS    #2,PTCHRS
.ENDM    PRINTCHRS
```

Show the macro expansion for

   (a) PRINTCHRS LINE+8,R4   (b) PRINTCHRS RECORD

10. The PRINTCHRS macro shown in Exercise 9 calls a procedure PTCHRS to actually print the line. Assuming PRINTCHRS has set up the arguments properly, describe the argument list expected by PTCHRS. (It is not in the standard argument list format.)

11. Referring back to the exercises in Chapter 6 and to the *VAX Architecture Handbook* for information on adding quadwords, write a macro definition for a macro called ADDQ2 that adds two quadwords. You may assume that the actual arguments will be specified by symbols.

12. Write a macro definition for the macro RANGE described in Example 11.7.

13. List several addressing modes that will work correctly as actual arguments for SOURCE and DEST in the ABS macro (Example 11.12). List several that would not be correct for DEST.

14. In the PRINTMSG macro defined in Example 11.13, why is the character string argument stored in memory with an .ASCIZ directive instead of on the stack?

15. What would happen if the PRINTMSG macro in Example 11.13 were used without an argument? Would it generate an assembly-time error, an execution-time error, or no error? If the latter, what would it print?

16. Write a macro definition for a macro SETREG that moves into each register Rn the longword n for $0 \le n \le 10$. The macro definition should be short; it should not have a separate statement for each register.

17. Why is it better for the I/O macros to call procedures to do their work rather than have the instructions in the macros themselves?

18. Write a macro definition for a PUSH macro that will push each of its arguments onto the stack. Assume that there may be any number of arguments up to ten. You may assume that all the arguments are longwords.

19. Write a macro definition for a macro called ARGLIST that sets up a procedure argument list in the standard form in memory for a procedure with at most ten arguments. Let the formal arguments for ARGLIST be LABEL, ARG1, ARG2, . . . , ARG10, where LABEL is to be the label on the procedure argument list and ARG1, . . . , ARG10 are the procedure arguments (all of which, you may assume, are address expressions). The number of arguments for the procedure is not an argument of ARGLIST.

20. Write a macro definition for a macro PRINTCTR that has a character string argument and prints the string centered on an 80-character line. A sample of the use of the macro instruction might be

```
PRINTCTR <OUTPUT FROM TEST RUN>
```

(The macro may use PRINTCHRS.)

21. The purpose of the SUM macro below is to add the first three arguments and put the result in the fourth argument. It is a modification of the SUM macro in Example 11.5.

```
.MACRO   SUM      A,B,C,TOTAL,T = L
LXXX = %LENGTH(TOTAL) - 1
.IF      IDN      +,%EXTRACT(LXXX,1,TOTAL)
ADD'T'3           A,B,%EXTRACT(0,LXXX,TOTAL)
.IF_FALSE
ADD'T'3           A,B,TOTAL
.ENDC
ADD'T'2           C,TOTAL
.ENDM    SUM
```

(a) Show the macro expansions for the following instructions. (Show just machine instructions generated, not the conditional assembly statements.)
   (1) SUM   #5,(R5) + ,R7,ALPHA
   (2) SUM   #5,R5,R7,(R10)+
   (3) SUM   R4,R5,R6,BETA + 8
   (4) SUM   #1,X,Y, - (R7)

(b) Explain the purpose of the conditional assembly statements in SUM; in particular, explain how they make this version of SUM better than the one in Example 11.5.

(c) What addressing modes would cause unintended results if used for TOTAL?

Chapter 12

Bit and Bit Field Operations

12.1 INTRODUCTION

For all the data types we have considered so far and the floating point data we will consider in the next chapter, a string of eight or more bits forms a pattern that represents one datum. Instructions operate on the bit string as a unit. In this chapter we will study instructions that treat their operands as strings of independent bits or small groups of bits. Bit instructions that are commonly available on large computers can shift bit strings, and test, set, clear, and complement individual bits or specified groups of bits within the operands. The bit strings may represent flags, sets, any of the usual data types, tables of small numbers packed together to save space, or anything else the programmer chooses to represent.

Many of the applications of bit instructions are in operating systems programming. Since we are not assuming that the reader is familiar with operating systems, we will mention only one or two such examples that are easy to explain and understand. The techniques illustrated in these and our other examples are useful in many applications.

We said in Chapter 1 that in some situations a programmer would use assembly language because the particular application or problem can not be handled easily, or at all, in a high-level language. The kinds of problems for which the instructions in this chapter would be used are in that category, because high-level languages rarely have operations that allow efficient manipulation of the individual bits within memory units. In addition to seeing how to do operations that are not done in high-level languages, we will also see how some unusual data types and operations, such as the set data type in Pascal, can be implemented.

In Sections 12.2 and 12.3 we will present the VAX bit instructions that do the kinds of operations that are commonly available on large computers (though, as we've said before, the VAX instructions are more numerous and more flexible than usual). In Section 12.4 we will consider an application: the implementation of sets and set operations.

The VAX has a data type—variable-length bit fields—and instructions to operate on them, that are not available on most computers, even fairly new systems with large instruction sets. The variable-length bit field instructions make some applications much easier than they would be using only the more commonly available bit operations. We will cover them in Section 12.5.

Certain terminology is used often with bit operations. A bit is *set*, or *on*, if its value is 1; a bit is *clear*, or *off*, if its value is 0. The *complement* of a bit is a bit with the opposite value. (That is, the complement of 0 is 1 and the complement of 1 is 0.) A *mask* is a pattern of bits in which the bits that are set indicate which bit positions (or data represented by them) are to be treated or operated on in some special way. For example, the bits that are set in a register mask indicate which registers are to be pushed on the stack. The masks used in this chapter indicate which bit positions in another operand are to be operated on by an instruction.

12.2 SIMPLE BIT OPERATIONS

In this section we will describe the VAX instructions to test, set, clear, and complement bits. For most of the instructions, one operand is a mask that specifies which bits in another operand are to be affected.

The BIT (BIt Test) instructions test specified bits in a bit string and set or clear the Z condition code to indicate whether or not all the bits tested are 0's. The instruction formats are

$$\text{BIT}x \qquad mask, bit\_string$$

where x = B, W, or L.

EXAMPLE 12.1: Testing a Group of Bits

Suppose we wish to determine if bits 14:7 in R9 are all zeros. The mask must contain 1's in positions 14:7 to indicate that those are the positions to be tested. We can construct the mask by marking these positions as shown in Fig. 12.1. The following instructions do the test and branch.

```
BITL    #^X00007F80,R9
BEQL    ALL_ZERO
```

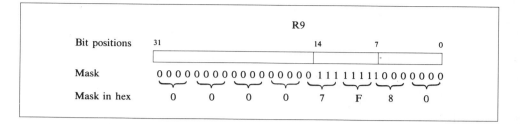

Figure 12.1   Constructing a mask

Since all the bits to be tested happen to be in the righthand word of the register, we can use the following slightly simpler instruction for the bit test:

```
BITW    #^X7F80,R9
```

For this example, and in many applications, it is most convenient to specify the mask as a literal or immediate operand. Any radix may be used, but hex is usually best because it is a simple matter to convert between the bit pattern and its hex representation.

The group of bits acted on by the bit instructions do not have to be contiguous. If we wanted to determine if, say, all the odd-numbered bit positions in the longword PAIRS contain zeros, we could use the instruction

```
BITL    #^XAAAAAAAA,PAIRS
```

followed by an appropriate conditional branch.

The instructions to set, clear, and complement bits all have the same operand formats, so we consider them as a group. The instructions are

$$\begin{Bmatrix} BIS \\ BIC \\ XOR \end{Bmatrix} x2 \quad mask, bit\_string \qquad\qquad \begin{Bmatrix} BIS \\ BIC \\ XOR \end{Bmatrix} x3 \quad mask, source, dest$$

where x = B, W, or L. The instruction names are mnemonics for BIt Set, BIt Clear, and eXclusive OR. For all the instructions, the mask indicates which bits in the second operand are to be operated on; the other bits of the operand are unchanged. In the two-operand formats, the second operand is replaced by the result. In the three-operand formats, the result of performing the operation on the source is stored in the destination; the source is unchanged (unless it overlaps the destination). For all these instructions, the Z and N condition codes are set as they are for integer instructions. V is cleared and C is unchanged.

EXAMPLE 12.2: Complementing Bits

Suppose R7 contains 083E8AC1. After the instruction

```
XORL2   #^X0F003060,R7
```

R7 will contain 073EBAA1. The bits in positions 27:24, 13:12, and 6:5 have been complemented.

EXAMPLES 12.3: Various Bit Operations

To turn off bit 15 in R4:

```
BICW2   #^X8000,R4
```

To turn off bit 15 in R4, but put the result in R8:

```
BICL3   #^X00008000,R4,R8
```

Note that the longword form of the instruction is needed here because BICW3 would copy only half the result to R8.

To set bits 22:18, complement bits 23 and 17 and clear the first and last byte in R10:

```
BISL2   #^X007C0000,R10   ; Set bits 22:18
XORL2   #^X00820000,R10   ; Complement 23 and 17
BICL2   #^XFF0000FF,R10   ; Clear end bytes
```

or, using only two instructions:

```
BISL2   #^XFF7C00FF,R10   ; Set bits 22:18 and
                          ;   first and last bytes
XORL2   #^XFF8200FF,R10   ; Complement 23 and 17
                          ;   and end bytes
```

EXAMPLE 12.4: Converting a Digit from ASCII to Binary

In Section 7.4, when we converted integers from their character code representation to two's complement, we used a subtraction to zero out the left nibble of the character code for each single digit. The result was the value of the digit in binary. The following instruction was used, where R6 contained the address of the character to be processed and R10 was cleared before the conversion loop began:

```
SUBB3   #48,(R6)+,R10     ; Get digit in binary
```

We can accomplish the same thing, perhaps avoiding any confusion about why a subtraction is done and what amount should be subtracted, by using the following instruction instead:

```
BICB3   #^XF0,(R6)+,R10   ; Get digit in binary
```

EXAMPLE 12.5: Returning a Condition Code Flag from a Procedure

In Chapter 9 we indicated that a procedure can return flags to a calling program by setting any of the condition codes in the saved PSW that is stored in the stack frame.

Suppose the procedure must set the Z bit. The saved PSW is in the first half of the second longword of the call frame, so Z can be set with the following instruction.

```
BISB2    #^B00000100,4(FP)         ; Set saved Z
```

Logical Operations: AND, OR, EXCLUSIVE OR, Negation

Bits may be thought of as representing logical variables: a value of 1 represents TRUE, and a value of 0 represents FALSE. Thus the standard binary logical operations AND, denoted by $\wedge$ or $\cdot$, OR, denoted by $\vee$ or $+$, and EXCLUSIVE OR, denoted by $\oplus$, and the unary operation negation, or complement, denoted by $\neg$, may be performed on bits or strings of bits. The logical operations are defined by the tables of their values shown in Fig. 12.2.

Some computers provide bit instructions called AND, OR, and XOR (or some slight variation of these names) that perform the logical operations on bit strings. (The operations, of course, are defined on individual pairs of bits; when the operands are strings of bits, the operation is performed independently on bit pairs in corresponding positions in the two operands.) Although we described the VAX instructions as setting, clearing, and complementing bits, two of the instructions, BIS and XOR, do exactly the logical operations OR and EXCLUSIVE OR. BIC is very close to a logical AND. To see these connections more clearly, we will look at the bit operations again.

The following table summarizes the Bit Set operation.

Bit Set

operand \ mask	0 (operand unchanged)	1 (operand set)
0	0	1
1	1	1

Now compare this table with the table in Fig. 12.2 that defines the OR operation. The two are exactly the same.

Similarly, let's look at the table for EXCLUSIVE OR in Fig. 12.2. Let the mask be the operand whose values are shown across the top of the table, and let the second operand be the one whose values are shown along the left side. Observe that in the column where the mask is 0, the results are identical to the values of the second operand; in the column where the mask is 1, the bits of the second operand have been complemented. (Both OR and EXCLUSIVE OR are commutative operations, so it actually doesn't matter which operand we consider to be the mask.)

AND	0 1		OR	0 1
0	0 0		0	0 1
1	0 1		1	1 1

$\oplus$	0 1		$\neg$	
0	0 1		0	1
1	1 0		1	0

Figure 12.2   Logical function tables

The table for the Bit Clear operation looks like this:

Bit Clear

mask / operand	0 (operand unchanged)	1 (operand cleared)
0	0	0
1	1	0

This is not the same as any of the logical operation tables shown in Fig. 12.2. However, the reader should easily verify that the Bit Clear operation is the same as a logical AND operation performed on the complement of the mask and the second operand.

The negation of a bit string is the same as its one's complement; the values of all the bits are reversed. The instructions to do this are

$$\text{MCOM}x \qquad source, dest$$

where $x =$ B, W, or L. The one's complement of the source is stored in the destination; the N and Z condition codes are affected in the same ways as by the other bit instructions described above. The effect of the MCOM instructions can be accomplished using XOR with a mask that consists entirely of 1's, so many large computers will not have a special instruction for complementing.

EXAMPLE 12.6: An AND Macro

In an application where a lot of logical operations must be done, it may be convenient to have one instruction for the logical AND. We can use an AND macro defined as follows:

```
.MACRO  AND3    OP1,OP2,DEST,TYPE=L
MCOM'TYPE       OP1,-(SP)
BIC'TYPE'3      (SP)+,OP2,DEST
.ENDM   AND3
```

12.3 ROTATE AND SHIFT INSTRUCTIONS

Shift instructions move the bits within a register or memory location. Several kinds of shift instructions commonly are found on large computers. *Logical shifts* treat all bit positions the same; none plays a special role. In *arithmetic shifts* the leftmost bit is considered as a sign bit and is treated differently than the others. In logical shifts the bits shifted out one end of the operand may be lost or they may be shifted into the other end; the latter are called *circular shifts*.

The VAX has a circular shift instruction, ROTL (ROTate Longword) and two arithmetic shift instructions, ASHL (Arithmetic SHift, Longword) and ASHQ (Arithmetic SHift, Quadword). The formats are

$$\left.\begin{matrix} \text{ROTL} \\ \text{ASHL} \\ \text{ASHQ} \end{matrix}\right\} \quad count, source, dest$$

The first operand, count, is a byte that specifies the number of bit positions to shift and the direction of the shift. The number of positions is the absolute value of the count. The shift is to the left if the count is positive and to the right if it is negative.

The Rotate Instruction

ROTL works as follows, assuming for the purposes of the diagram that the shift is to the left and the number of positions to shift is n. A rotation to the right works similarly.

ROTL sets or clears the Z and N condition codes to indicate whether the result is zero or negative. It clears V and leaves C unchanged.

EXAMPLE 12.7: ROTL

Suppose R7 contains 000013F5 and the longword at ALPHA contains 002BC801. Consider the following instruction:

```
ROTL    R7,ALPHA,BETA
```

In what direction is the rotation to be done? Remember that the count is a byte, so it is the rightmost byte of R7. Thus the count is F5, or -11 in decimal, and the shift is

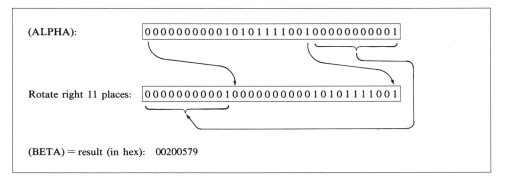

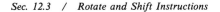

Figure 12.3 An example of rotation

to the right. To determine the result correctly, it helps to write out the source in binary. Figure 12.3 shows the bits before and after the rotation. The Z, N, and V condition codes will be 0.

EXAMPLE 12.8

To interchange the two words in R8:

```
ROTL    #16,R8,R8
```

EXAMPLE 12.9: Extracting Bit Fields

Suppose we must move bits 8:3 of R5 and bits 23:15 of R6 into the right end of R10, clearing the rest of R10. R5 and R6 should be unchanged. The result should be

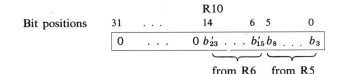

There are several different ways to accomplish this task. One solution, assuming R2 is available for scratch work, is

```
BICL3   #^XFFFFFE07,R5,R10    ; Extract bits 8:3 from R5
ROTL    #-3,R10,R10           ; Move them to right end
BICL3   #^XFF007FFF,R6,R2     ; Extract 23:15 from R6
ROTL    #-9,R2,R2             ; Move to positions 14:6
BISL2   R2,R10                ; Combine the two segments
```

EXAMPLE 12.10: Turning Off a Bit

See the procedure TURNOFF in Fig. 12.4. The techniques it uses would also be useful for many other applications, some of which are suggested in the exercises. We will see

```
            .PSECT  TURNOFF
;
; PROCEDURE TURNOFF (BIT_STRING, POSITION)
;
; The procedure TURNOFF finds and turns off the rightmost bit
; that is on in its first argument, a longword bit string.
; It returns the position number of the affected bit in the
; second argument, a byte. (If no bits are on, it returns
; 32.)
;
; METHOD
;
; A copy of the bit string is rotated so that, until a 1 is
; found, each bit is tested when it is in the low bit position.
; The loop counter keeps track of the original position being
; tested and is used to construct a mask to turn the bit off
; in the original bit string.
;
; Offsets for argument list
STRING = 4
POSN = 8
;
; REGISTER USE:      R6      bit string
;                    R7      loop counter
;                    R8      mask for turning off bit
;
            .ENTRY TURNOFF,^M<R6,R7,R8>
;
            MOVL    @STRING(AP),R6     ; Get bit string
            BEQL    ZERO               ; Branch if all bits off
            CLRL    R7                 ; Initialize loop counter
;
TEST:       BLBS    R6,FOUND           ; Test low bit
            ROTL    #-1,R6,R6          ; Get next bit
            AOBLEQ  #31,R7,TEST        ; Loop control
;
FOUND:      ROTL    R7,#1,R8           ; Move 1 to position
            BICL2   R8,@STRING(AP)     ; Turn off bit
            MOVB    R7,@POSN(AP)       ; Store position number
;
            RET                        ; Return
;
ZERO:       MOVB    #32,@POSN(AP)      ; Store position 32
            RET                        ; Return
            .END
```

Figure 12.4 **The procedure TURNOFF**

in Section 12.5 that the procedure can be made more efficient using variable-length bit field instructions.

Arithmetic Shifts

ASHL and ASHQ are called *arithmetic shifts* because they treat their source operands as two's complement integers, and the operations they do have the effects of multiplying and dividing by powers of 2. They affect the condition codes N, Z, and V as the other integer arithmetic instructions do. Of course these operations can be accomplished by using MUL and DIV instructions. On some computers the arithmetic shift instructions are more efficient, but a more important reason for having such instructions is that they are useful for general bit string manipulations. For this reason we include them here instead of in Chapter 6.

To see the connection between shifting and multiplication and division, consider ordinary decimal numbers. To multiply decimal integers by 10, or a power of 10, all we do is add zeros at the right end of the number. Division of a decimal integer by a power of 10 (with truncation) can be accomplished by erasing the appropriate number of digits from the right end of the number. Multiplying or dividing binary integers by powers of 2 is done similarly. Since an integer is located in a particular unit of memory or a register, we do not exactly add or erase digits at the right; we shift the number within its storage unit, dropping some bits off one end and filling the vacated bits at the other end. For multiplication, the shift is to the left and the vacated bits at the right are filled with zeros. For division, the shift is to the right and the vacated bits at the left are filled with copies of the sign bit. Thus, an ASHL instruction with a count of 3 has the effect of multiplying by 2^3, or 8; if the count operand is -6, the effect is to divide by 2^6, or 64.

The diagrams below illustrate the arithmetic shift operations.

Left arithmetic shift (multiplication by powers of 2):

dropped   fill with 0's

Note that if any of the bits dropped from the left end of the operand are not equal to the original sign bit, or if the sign bit of the shifted result is not the same as the original sign, then the result, considered as a two's complement integer, has overflowed the allotted space and the V condition code will be set.

Right arithmetic shift (division by powers of 2):

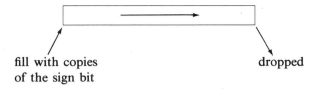

fill with copies   dropped
of the sign bit

EXAMPLE 12.11: Arithmetic Shift

Suppose the longword in memory at A1 contains FFFFF4A2 before the instruction

```
ASHL    #-6,A1,A2
```

is executed. The longword at A1 will be shifted six places right. Examining the bit pattern in A1, we determine the result:

FFFFF4A2 =	11 . . . 11010010100010
Shift right, dropping	
the rightmost six bits;	
fill in 1's at the left:	1 . . . 111 . . . 11010010xxxxxx
Convert to hex:	FFFFFFD2

Thus FFFFFFD2 will be stored in the longword at A2. We will check this result by doing a division. Shifting right six places should correspond to dividing by 2^6, or 64. The longword in A1, FFFFF4A2 is -2910_{10}. Dividing by 64 gives approximately -45.5. The integer division instructions truncate toward zero, so we might expect the result of the right shift to be -45. However, FFFFFFD2 is -46.

As Example 12.11 illustrates, an arithmetic right shift, interpreted as a division operation, will always truncate a negative result down, away from zero. Thus its effect is slightly different from the DIV instructions.

Sometimes masks for use in the bit instructions described in Section 12.2 must be constructed at execution time because the bit pattern needed is data dependent. We will see an example of such an application in Section 12.4. Example 12.12 shows how a fairly general form of a mask may be constructed.

EXAMPLE 12.12: Constructing Masks with ASHL

Suppose we want to construct a mask that has n 1's beginning at bit position p; i.e., bits $(p + n - 1):p$ should be 1's and all others 0. The following sequence of instructions takes advantage of the fact that if the sign bit is 1, a right arithmetic shift fills the vacated bit positions with 1's. We use ASHL to generate the correct number of 1's, then use ROTL to move them into the correct positions. We assume that R6 contains n, R7 contains p, the mask is to be constructed in R8, and R3 is available for scratch work.

```
SUBB3    R6,#1,R3              ; Shift count = -(n-1)
ASHL     R3,#^X80000000,R8     ; Get n 1's
ADDB3    R6,R7,R3              ; p + n
ROTL     R3,R8,R8             ; Rotate 1's to p+n-1:p
```

After Section 12.5, this problem can be solved with only two instructions, but the method used here can be used with slight modifications on other machines, whereas the instructions of Section 12.5 are not available on most machines.

12.4 EXAMPLE: SETS

Bit instructions are especially suited to doing set operations on sets represented as bit strings. We will assume that all the sets we operate on are subsets of a fixed universe set that has 32 elements. Each of the elements in the universe set is assigned an index between 0 and 31. Thus we can write

$$universe = \{x_0, x_1, x_2, \ldots, x_{29}, x_{30}, x_{31}\}$$

A set S is represented by a bit string in which each bit indicates whether or not the universe element with the same index is in S. In other words, S is represented by

$$b_{31}b_{30}b_{29} \ldots b_2b_1b_0$$

where

$$b_i = \begin{cases} 1 & \text{if } x_i \in S \\ 0 & \text{if } x_i \notin S \end{cases}$$

For example, if the bit string for S is

$$00010000010111000100000010000001$$

then $S = \{x_0, x_7, x_{14}, x_{18}, x_{19}, x_{20}, x_{22}, x_{28}\}$.

The SET data type in Pascal is implemented in this way. The limit on the size of a Pascal set is usually the computer's word size or a small multiple of it. (VAX-11 Pascal allows sets to have up to 256 elements and uses eight longwords for the representations.)

Suppose we have reserved space for several sets, say, S, T, and V, and we have initialized S and T in some way. We will assume the set names are the labels on the longwords that represent the sets. We would like to do the basic set operations: union, intersection, and complement, and various other useful operations.

An element is in the union of S and T if it is in either (or both) sets. Thus the union operation is a logical OR operation on the set representations and may be computed as follows:

```
BISL3   S,T,V                ; V = S union T
```

(Either S or T could play the role of the mask, since OR is a commutative operation.)

The intersection of two sets contains all the elements that are in both sets, so it can be computed using a logical AND on the representations. The VAX doesn't have a logical AND instruction, but we can use the AND3 macro defined in Example 12.6 as follows:

```
AND3    S,T,V            ; V = S intersect T
```

The complement of a set is computed using MCOML.

There are several tests that we may want to do. For example, we may want to determine if two sets are equal, if one is a subset of the other, if a particular element is a member of a set, or if a set is empty. We may want to know how many elements are in a set.

Testing for equality of two sets may be done easily with the CMPL and BEQL (or BNEQ) instructions.

How can we determine if $S \subset T$? Certainly we could write a loop that tests each bit of S in turn and checks whether each bit that is on in S is also on in T, but this would require several statements and as many as 32 passes through the loop. A much more efficient solution becomes obvious if we express the condition to be tested in another form:

$$S \subset T \qquad \text{if and only if} \qquad S \cup T = T$$

We leave it to the reader to write the instructions to test whether or not $S \cup T = T$.

Counting the elements of a set can be done using a loop similar to the one in the procedure in Fig. 12.4. It is left as an exercise, along with the other tests we mentioned above.

The task of initializing the bit string representation of a set is more complicated than the set operations. The procedure in Fig. 12.5 initializes a set assuming the

```
        .PSECT  SET_UP
;
; PROCEDURE SET_UP (SET)
;
; This procedure initializes the longword argument SET as a
; bit string representation of the set of integers that are
; input in one line from the terminal. The integers must
; be in the range 0 to 31. The representation is such that bit i is
; on if and only if i is in the set.
;
; SET_UP calls the procedure GETNUM to find each number in
; the input line and convert it to two's complement. GETNUM
; returns a flag in R0 that is 1 if a number was found and
; converted, and 0 otherwise. SET_UP assumes that if GETNUM
; returns a 0 flag, all set elements have been processed.
;
; SET_UP returns a success/failure flag in R0. If the set
; is initialized without problems, R0 will contain 1. If any
; of the numbers read in are outside the range 0-31, R0 will
; contain 0 and the longword argument will not be filled.
;
```

Figure 12.5 A procedure to initialize a set

```
LINE:       .BYTE       ^X20[81]            ; Space for input line
ARGS:       .LONG       4                   ; Argument list for GETNUM
            .BLKA       2                   ; For start and end addresses
            .ADDRESS    NUMBER,RESTART
NUMBER:     .BLKL       1                   ; Set element
RESTART:    .BLKA       1                   ; Where next search begins
;
;
; REGISTER USE:         R6      the set representation
;                       R7      mask
;
            .ENTRY      SET_UP,^M<R6,R7>
;
;
; Initialization
;
            CLRL        R6                  ; Set is empty to start
            READLINE    LINE+1              ; Read in set elements
            MOVAB       LINE,RESTART        ; Start addr. for first search
            ADDL3       #LINE+1,R0,ARGS+8   ; End address for input line
;
;
; Get next set element from input line.
;
NEXT:       MOVL        RESTART,ARGS+4      ; Where next search begins
            CALLG       ARGS,GETNUM         ; Get next number from input
            BLBC        R0,DONE             ; Branch if set is complete
;
; Check that the number is in the correct range, 0-31.
;
            TSTL        NUMBER              ; Test sign of element number
            BLSS        BAD                 ; Branch if negative, bad data
            CMPL        NUMBER,#31          ; Compare to upper limit
            BGTR        BAD                 ; Branch if > 31, bad data
;
; Enter element in set.
;
            ASHL        NUMBER,#1,R7        ; Construct mask
            BISL2       R7,R6               ; Turn on bit in set
;
            BRB         NEXT                ; Go back for another
;
;
; Store set representation and set success/failure flag.
;
DONE:       MOVL        R6,@4(AP)           ; Store the set representation
            MOVL        #1,R0               ; Set success flag
            RET                             ; Return
;
BAD:        CLRL        R0                  ; Set failure flag
            RET                             ; Return
            .END
```

Figure 12.5 (Continued)

universe set consists of the integers in the range 0 to 31, and the particular elements in the set being initialized are read in from the terminal in a free-format line. The procedure calls another procedure GETNUM to locate the input numbers within the line of characters and convert them to two's complement. GETNUM is described in Exercise 9.17.

12.5 VARIABLE-LENGTH BIT FIELDS

The Data Format

A *variable-length bit field* is a string of 0 to 32 contiguous bits that does not necessarily begin on a byte boundary. Thus it may occupy zero to five contiguous bytes. Variable-length bit fields are useful for packing together several small data to save space, for working with bit tables, for manipulating (e.g., converting) data representations, and for various other kinds of applications.

The operations performed by the VAX bit field instructions can be accomplished by using appropriate combinations of other instructions presented so far (particularly some from Sections 12.2 and 12.3), but, of course, the special-purpose instructions are more efficient than a sequence of several instructions. Also, the fact that these instructions can ignore byte, and even longword, boundaries is particularly handy for some applications.

Three operands are used to specify a variable-length bit field: a base address, an offset from that address, and a bit field size. The *base address* is the address of a byte in memory or is a register. The *offset,* or *position,* is the position of the first bit in the bit field relative to the first bit at the base address. That is, it is the number of bits (not bytes) separating the first bit of the bit field from the first bit of the byte at the base address. The offset is specified as a two's complement longword integer. Thus it can be positive or negative and can be quite large. The bit field *size* is the number of bits in the bit field. It is a byte operand.

Figure 12.6 illustrates how the three operands determine the bit field. Note that diagrams of bit fields show the lower-addressed bytes at the right, because VAX instructions treat memory as if the least significant bit, bit 0, were the first bit in a memory unit or register; thus bit 0 of the byte at address A (for any address A) follows immediately after the leftmost bit, bit 7, of the byte at $A - 1$. The first bit of a bit field is its rightmost bit.

If a register, say Rn, is specified as the base address for a bit field and the field extends beyond bit 31 of Rn, it continues at bit 0 of $Rn+1$. Thus, in diagrams, $Rn+1$ is shown to the left of Rn.

In variable-length bit field machine instructions the three operands describing a bit field are always given in the following order:

position, size, base_address

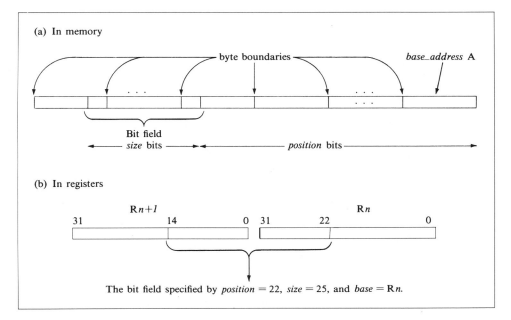

Figure 12.6   Specifying a variable-length bit field

Reserved operand faults will occur for bit field instructions if the size is not in the range 0–32, or if a register is specified as the base address, the position is greater than 31, and the size is nonzero (i.e., if a nonnull field does not begin in the specified register). If *size* = 0, the bit field is empty, or null. Most of the instructions have a fairly natural interpretation for this case.

The "Find First" Instructions

The FFS (Find First Set bit) and FFC (Find First Clear bit) instructions scan a bit field (from right to left) and locate the first bit that is set or clear, depending on the instruction. If such a bit is found, its position number is placed in the destination operand (a longword) and the Z condition code is cleared. The position is computed relative to the same base address that specifies the location of the bit field. If no bit in the desired state is found in the field, the position number of the bit following the end of (i.e., the bit to the left of) the bit field is put in the destination operand and Z is set. (As one should expect, if *size* = 0, Z is set and the destination is given the same value as position.)

The instruction formats are

FF*x* *posn,size,base,dest*

where x = S or C.

EXAMPLE 12.13. The Effects of FFS and FFC

Suppose memory contents are as shown:

											ALPHA ↙
F0	83	48	01	00	00	07	FE	24	44	00	89

	Instruction	Bit Field	Results: In R8	Results: Z Cond. Code
FFS	#56,#24,ALPHA,R8	480100_{16}	64	0
FFS	#39,#3,ALPHA+2,R8	000_2	42	1
FFC	#0,#32,ALPHA,R8	24440089_{16}	1	0
FFC	#35,#10,ALPHA,R8	0011111111_2	43	0

EXAMPLE 12.14: Improving the TURNOFF Procedure

In Section 12.3 we wrote a procedure TURNOFF (Fig. 12.4) that finds the rightmost bit in a longword that is on, turns off the bit, and returns its position as an argument. The procedure in Fig. 12.7 uses the FFS instruction to find the bit. The search loop and some of the initialization of the earlier procedure have been eliminated.

EXAMPLE 12.15: A Bit Table Disk Map

Problem: A bit table is often used by an operating system to keep track of whether or not each block on a disk is in use. Suppose BLOCKS is the number of blocks on the disk. The blocks are numbered from 0 to BLOCKS − 1. A disk map is a string of BLOCKS bits, where bit i is set if block i is in use and is clear if block i is free. The problem is to find the first clear bit, hence the number of the first disk block available for storing some data or programs.

Discussion: The size of a variable-length bit field can be at most 32, but the disk map may contain several hundred bits, so a loop is needed. It would seem that four operations must be done in the loop: scan for a clear bit (FFC), test to see if one was found, (if not) increment the position number by 32 to specify the next field to scan, and check that the scan does not go beyond the end of the table (in the case where no bits in the table are clear). It is desirable that operating systems programs run very quickly, so it is rather nice that the scan loop for this problem can be programmed with only two instructions. If the FFC instruction does not find a clear bit, it sets the destination operand to the position of the bit that follows the field scanned. That is the position where the next scan should start, so we use the same register for the position and destination operands. We need not test for the end of the table in the loop if we set up the table with a byte of zeros at the end to force an exit from the loop.

```
                .PSECT  TURNOFF_2
;
; PROCEDURE TURNOFF_2 (BIT_STRING, POSITION)
;
; This procedure finds and turns off the rightmost bit that
; is on in its first argument, a longword bit string. It
; returns the position number of the affected bit in the
; second argument, a byte. (If no bits are on, it returns
; 32.)
;
; METHOD
;
; The variable length bit field instruction, FFS, is used to
; find the first set bit. (Note that if no bits are set,
; FFS will return 32 as the position number.) A mask for
; turning off the bit is constructed by rotating a 1 into
; the proper position.
;
; Offsets for argument list
STRING = 4
POSITION = 8
;
; REGISTER USE:              R7        position of first set bit
;                            R8        mask for turning off bit
;
        .ENTRY  TURNOFF_2,^M<R7,R8>
;
        FFS     #0,#32,@STRING(AP),R7   ; Find first set bit
        BEQL    POSN                    ; Branch if none set
        ROTL    R7,#1,R8                ; Move 1 to position
        BICL2   R8,@STRING(AP)          ; Turn off bit
POSN:   MOVB    R7,@POSITION(AP)        ; Store position number
;
        RET                             ; Return
        .END
```

Figure 12.7 The procedure TURNOFF_2

Solution:

```
        BLOCKS  = the number of blocks on the disk
        DISK_MAP: .BLKB  BLOCKS/8+1            ; Disk map table
                      .
                      .
                      .
                CLRL    R6                      ; Initial posn = 0
        SCAN:   FFC     R6,#32,DISK_MAP,R6      ; Find clear bit
                BEQL    SCAN                    ; Repeat if none found
                CMPL    R6,#BLOCKS              ; See if disk is full
                BGEQ    DISK_FULL
        ; R6 now contains the number of an available disk block.
```

Inserting and Extracting Bit Fields

The INS (INSert) and EXT (EXTract) instructions can be used to construct and decompose long bit strings made up of many variable-length bit fields. The instruction formats are:

INSV	*source,posn,size,base*
EXTV	*posn,size,base,dest*
EXTZV	*posn,size,base,dest*

INSV inserts bits (*size* − 1):0 of its longword source operand into the bit field specified by the remaining operands. It does not affect the condition codes. EXTV extracts (copies) the specified bit field, extends the leftmost bit (the sign bit of the bit field), and puts the resulting longword into the destination operand; thus it treats the bit field as a two's complement integer. EXTZV (EXTract Zero-extended Variable-length bit field) performs a similar operation, but it fills the extra bits of the destination with zeros rather than copies of the leftmost bit of the bit field. Both EXT instructions treat a bit field of size = 0 as if it contained the integer 0. They affect the N and Z condition codes as usual, clear V, and leave C unchanged.

EXAMPLE 12.16: Extracting Bit Fields

In Example 12.9 we used bit instructions to extract bit strings from two registers and pack them together in a third. By using the EXT and INS instructions, we can eliminate the ROTL's used there. The effect of each of the instructions below is shown in Fig. 12.8.

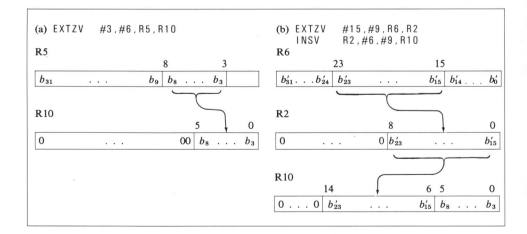

Figure 12.8   Instruction action in Example 12.6

```
EXTZV    #3,#6,R5,R10        ; Extract bits 8:3 from R5
EXTZV    #15,#9,R6,R2        ; Extract 23:15 from R6
INSV     R2,#6,#9,R10        ; Insert R6 bits in R10
```

EXAMPLE 12.17: Bit Matrix Graphics

For some graphics terminals the screen is represented in memory as a bit matrix. Each bit corresponds to one point, or pixel, on the screen; the bit is set if the corresponding pixel is on (lighted). To draw a picture on the screen we must set the appropriate bits in the matrix.

We will assume that the screen dimensions are 256 × 256 and the matrix occupies 256 × 8 longwords, as shown in Fig. 12.9. Note that the lowest-addressed longword is at the lower right corner. The right-to-left arrangement of the longwords should be quite familiar by now; here it ensures that adjacent bits in memory correspond to adjacent points on the screen. The lower-addressed longwords were put at the bottom of the screen so that addresses increase in the same direction as the usual vertical axis coordinates.

Clearly, where we wish to draw lines on the screen will have nothing to do with where the longword boundaries are. One of the main advantages of the variable-length bit field instructions for this application is that we can ignore the boundaries. Another is that by specifying the exact bit field to be affected, we don't have to worry about changing parts of the screen where something else may be drawn.

For this example we will set the bits that correspond to drawing a solid rectangle on the screen, as we might wish to do as part of a bar graph. (Several other possibilities are suggested in the exercises.) We assume that we are told the location and size of the rectangle by being given its bottom row number, its height in pixels, the offset of its right side from the right edge of the screen, and its width in pixels. We assume that the width is at most 32. (See Fig. 12.10.) Since each row on the screen is represented by a string of contiguous bits, we will "draw" the rectangle one row at a time, beginning at the bottom. The first byte of the screen matrix will be the base address for the bit field instructions. The following algorithm outlines the steps to be carried out.

bottom_posn := bottom_row*256+right_side
for posn := bottom_posn **step** 256 **to** bottom_posn+(height−1)*256 **do**
    Insert bit string

Figure 12.9 Bit matrix for graphics screen

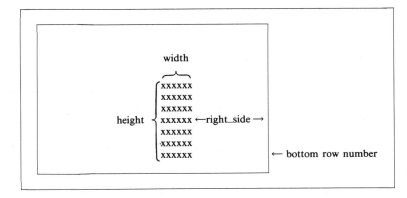

Figure 12.10 Specifications for a rectangle

The following program segment "draws" the rectangle.

```
SCREEN: .BLKL   8*256
        .
        .
        .
; REGISTER USE:        R6      row number of rectangle bottom
;                      R7      height of rectangle (in bits)
;                      R8      offset of right side (in bits,
;                              from right edge of screen)
;                      R9      width of rectangle (in bits)
;
; We are assuming that the above registers are already
; filled with the specified data.
;
;                      R10     posn (loop index)
;                      R11     loop limit
;
        MULL3   R6,#256,R10                 ; bottom*256
        ADDL2   R8,R10                      ; posn for bottom
        SUBL3   #1,R7,R11                   ; height-1
        ASHL    #8,R11,R11                  ; (height-1)*256
        ADDL2   R10,R11                     ; Loop limit
;
DRAW:   INSV    #^XFFFFFFFF,R10,R9,SCREEN   ; Insert bit string
        ACBL    R5,#256,R10,DRAW            ; Increment posn, branch
```

Comparing Bit Fields

The bit field comparison instructions treat bit fields as integers and compare them to longword integers. (A bit field with size = 0 is treated as the integer 0.) Their main role is to affect the condition codes. They are particularly useful when many small numbers using fewer than eight bits each are packed together to save space. The instructions are

$$\text{CMPV} \qquad posn, size, base, long$$
$$\text{CMPZV} \qquad posn, size, base, long$$

CMPV (CoMPare Variable-length bit field) extracts the bit field and extends its leftmost bit to make a longword; thus it treats the bit field as a signed two's complement integer. CMPZV (CoMPare Zero extended Variable-length bit field) extracts the field and fills in zeros at the left to make a longword; thus it treats the field as an unsigned integer. In both cases the extension is done in a CPU scratch register; the fields and the surrounding bits are not changed. The effects on the condition codes are the same as for the integer CMP instructions. N is set if and only if the first operand—i.e., the extended bit field—is less than the last operand, the longword. Z is set if and only if the operands are equal. V is cleared, and C is set if and only if the bit field operand is less than the longword when both are interpreted as unsigned integers.

EXAMPLE 12.18: Comparing Bit Fields

Suppose a questionnaire has ten questions that may be answered with numbers between 1 and 5, and each person's answers are stored in a longword with three bits used for each question. The format of the longword is

```
      29 27               . . .      5  3 2  0
    ┌────┬────┬────┬─────────┬────┬────┬────┐
    │ Q10│ Q9 │ Q8 │  . . .  │ Q3 │ Q2 │ Q1 │
    └────┴────┴────┴─────────┴────┴────┴────┘
```

Suppose the address of the longword containing a person's answers is in R8. The following instructions may be used to determine if the person answered 4 or 5 to question 7.

```
CMPV    #18,#3,(R8),#4
BGEQ    HIGH
```

12.6 SUMMARY

Bit instructions do logical operations on bit strings; that is, for the most part, they treat each bit in an operand as if it were independent of the other bits. Bit operations include testing, setting, clearing, complementing, and shifting bits. Many of the bit instructions have one operand that is a mask—i.e., a pattern of bits that indicates which bits in another operand are to be operated on. The bit instructions presented in this chapter are listed in Table 12.1.

One application of the bit instructions is performing set operations on sets represented as bit strings. Bit instructions are also useful for working with flags, converting data representations, packing small data together, manipulating bit tables, and other applications.

The VAX has a data type called *variable-length bit fields*. A variable-length bit field is a string of 0 to 32 contiguous bits that does not have to begin or end on

TABLE 12.1   Bit Instructions

Instruction		Remarks	Operation
BITx	mask,bit_string	x = B, W, or L	Set Z condition code to indicate if bits are all 0's.
BISx2	mask,bit_string	x = B, W, or L	Set indicated bits. (Logical OR of
BISx3	mask,source,dest	x = B, W, or L	*mask* and second operand)
BICx2	mask,bit_string	x = B, W, or L	Clear indicated bits. (Logical AND
BICx3	mask,source,dest	x = B, W, or L	of complemented *mask* and second operand)
XORx2	mask,bit_string	x = B, W, or L	Complement indicated bits. (Logical
XORx3	mask,source,dest	x = B, W, or L	EXCLUSIVE OR of *mask* and second operand)
MCOMx	source,dest	x = B, W, or L	One's complement of *source* $\rightarrow$ *dest*
ROTL	count,source,dest	*Count* is a byte;	Rotate *source* n places.
ASHL	count,source,dest	$n = \|count\|$.	Arithmetically shift n places.
ASHQ	count,source,dest	Shift left if *count* > 0, right if *count* < 0.	Arithmetically shift n places.

a byte or longword boundary. It is specified by a base address, the bit position number of the first bit in the field, and its size (in bits). Instructions that operate on such fields are not available on most computers; the operations performed by VAX bit field instructions can be implemented using some of the other bit instructions described in this chapter. The bit field instructions are listed in Table 12.2.

TABLE 12.2   Variable-Length Bit Field Instructions

Instruction		Operation
FFx x = S or C	posn,size,base,dest	Find first set (S) bit or first clear (C) bit. Z = 0 if found, 1 if not.
INSV	src,posn,size,base	Copy bits (*size* $-$ 1):0 of *src* to field.
EXTV	posn,size,base,dest	Copy field to *dest,* extend sign.
EXTZV	posn,size,base,dest	Copy field to *dest,* 0 extension.
CMPV	posn,size,base,long	Compare sign-extended field to *long.*
CMPZV	posn,size,base,long	Compare zero-extended field to *long.*

12.7 EXERCISES

1. Write instructions to set bits 5, 8, and 17 in R9 and clear all the others.

2. Write instructions to complement all the bits in the second byte (from the right) of R10 and put the result in R11.

3. Write instructions to clear the bits in even-numbered positions in R4, set bits 3, 19, and 31, complement bit 15, and leave the others unchanged.

4. Write instructions to copy the low-order byte of R8 into each of the other bytes in R8.

5. In Example 12.4 we saw two ways of converting a digit from character code to binary. Suppose the character string being converted has leading blanks instead of leading zeros. Will either method work properly? Explain why or why not for each.

6. The BIT, BIS, BIC, and XOR instructions test, set, clear, or complement the bits in their second operand specified by the mask (the first operand). The MCOM instructions do the same operation as XOR, but to *all* the bits in the source operand; no mask is needed. For each of the other types of bit instructions, BIT, BIS, and BIC, write instructions whose effect is to accomplish the same operation, but on all the bits, without a mask.

7. Write instructions that clear the rightmost bit that is on in R8 by using only two instructions, no loop, and no variable-length bit field instructions. (The procedure in Fig. 12.4 does much more work to solve this problem because it must determine the position number of the affected bit.)

8. Write instructions to do the following: If the rightmost bit in R7 is 0, turn on all the bits in the rightmost string of contiguous 0's; if the rightmost bit is 1, leave the string unchanged. For example, the string

$$00001010111010100001111011000000$$

would be changed to

$$00001010111010100001111011111111$$

(This can be done with only two instructions.)

9. What is the effect of the ROTL instruction with a count of 0? What is the effect of the ASHL instruction with a count of 0?

10. Write instructions to interchange the contents of the rightmost two bytes in R9. What happens to the other two bytes is irrelevant.

11. Show the machine code for the following instructions.
   (a) ROTL   #-1,R9,R3   (c) ASHL   R3,#^X80000000,R8
   (b) ROTL   #1,R9,R3   (d) ASHQ   #63,R7,R3

12. Consider the following program statement.

```
              MOVL    #32,R6       ; Initialize loop counter
     TEST:    ROTL    #1,R5,R5     ; Test bit
              BLSS    BIT_SET
                       .
                       .
     BIT_SET:          .
                       .
                       .
              SOBGTR  R6,TEST
```

Assuming that before the loop begins R5 contains

$$b_{31}b_{30}b_{29}\ldots b_2 b_1 b_0$$

which bit is tested first? Which bit is tested last? If the ROTL instruction were changed to

```
ROTL    #-1,R5,R5
```

which bit would be tested first, and which last?

13. Suppose three one-bit flags must be stored. What size memory unit would you use, and in which bit positions would you put the flags? Why? Answer the same questions for four flags.

14. In the procedure TURNOFF in Fig. 12.4 a copy of the bit string argument is rotated. Rewrite the procedure using a BIT instruction and a mask so that the mask is shifted and the bit string is not. Which procedure is better?

15. If the AOBLEQ instruction in the procedure TURNOFF (Fig. 12.4) were changed to AOBLSS (and no other changes were made), for what arguments, if any, would the procedure not work properly? Does this suggest an improvement?

16. Write instructions to count the bits in the longword S that are on.

17. Write a procedure to find the position of the leftmost bit in a longword that is set. The procedure should have two arguments, BIT_STRING and POSITION, as in the procedure TURNOFF (Fig. 12.4).

18. Write the procedure SCORE described in Exercise 16 of Chapter 9.

19. Assume that the datum in the byte at BYTE occupies bits 6:0, and write instructions to set or clear bit 7 so that the byte has even parity—that is, so that there is an even number of bits set in the byte. (This can be done in a rather long and tedious way, or in a shorter, slick way using an XORB instruction appropriately.)

20. Write a procedure REVERSE that reverses the ordering of the bits in its longword argument. In other words, if the argument is

$$b_{31}b_{30}b_{29}\ldots b_2 b_1 b_0$$

then REVERSE changes it to

$$b_0 b_1 b_2 \ldots b_{29}b_{30}b_{31}$$

21. Write a procedure that converts integers from character code (leading separate numeric format) to packed decimal without using the CVTSP instruction. The procedure should have three arguments:

     LSN   the leading separate numeric string (i.e., the address of the byte containing the sign is in the argument list)

     NUM   the number of digits in the string

     PKD   space for the procedure's output

The procedure should return a flag in R0 to indicate if the conversion was successful; 1 indicates success, 0 failure. (Some reasons for failure would be an invalid character in the leading separate numeric string or an improper number of digits.)

22. Suppose that when the instruction

```
ASHL    BITS,R7,R7
```

is executed, the byte at BITS contains an integer less than -32. If R7 had contained a positive longword integer, what would be in R7 afterward? Is the result consistent with the interpretation of an arithmetic shift to the right as division by a power of two? Answer the same questions for the case where R7 contained a negative longword integer.

23. Will the instructions in Example 12.12 achieve the intended result if $n = 0$? (Does the answer depend on whether or not the integer overflow trap is enabled?)

24. What will be in R8 after the instructions in Example 12.12 are executed if
(a) $n = 12$ and $p = 2$?   (c) $n = 12$ and $p = 25$?
(b) $n = 6$ and $p = 0$?   (d) $n = 1$ and $p = 17$?

25. Example 12.12 shows how to construct a mask consisting of a contiguous string of 1's somewhere in a register and 0's everywhere else. Suppose we want the opposite: a contiguous string of 0's with 1's everywhere else—for example,

$$1 \ldots 100000001 \ldots 1$$

What changes, if any, should be made in Example 12.12 to construct such masks? Consider both changes in the instructions themselves and changes in how the programmer should interpret n and p, and what should be put in R6 and R7.

26. Redo Exercise 11.4 (writing a CVTLQ macro) using an ASH instruction. (You may assume that the actual argument for QUAD will be a symbol.) Your macro definition should be shorter than the one you wrote before.

27. Suppose S and T are longwords that represent sets as described in Section 12.4. Write instructions to determine if $S \subset T$ and branch to SUBSET if so.

28. Suppose S is a longword that represents a subset of the universal set containing the integers 0 through 31. Write instructions to branch to IN_SET if the integer in R8 is an element of the set.

29. Suppose we wish to work with sets that may contain up to 256 elements. (This is the maximum size for sets in VAX-11 Pascal.) Each set is represented by a bit string in eight consecutive longwords in memory. Write macros called UNION, INTERSECTION, and COMPLEMENT that do the indicated set operations. You may assume that the actual macro arguments will be expressions.

30. Using the assumptions of Exercise 29, write macros called B_SUBSET, B_EQUAL, and B_EMPTY with arguments and operations described as follows:

		Branch to dest if
B_SUBSET	set1,set2,dest	set1 $\subset$ set2
B_EQUAL	set1,set2,dest	set1 $=$ set2
B_EMPTY	set,dest	set $= \phi$

31. The GETNUM procedure called by the SET_UP procedure in Fig. 12.5 returns a flag in R0 to indicate whether or not it successfully found and converted a number. Unfortunately, a failure setting may indicate that there was bad input or simply that there are no more numbers in the input line to be processed. Suppose GETNUM is modified to return two flags. As before, bit 0 of R0 will indicate whether or not a number was found and converted. If bit 0 is 0, bit 7 of R0 will indicate whether there are no more numbers in the line (bit 7 set) or there was an error of any kind (bit 7 clear). Rewrite the SET_UP procedure so that SET_UP returns a failure flag if GETNUM encounters any bad input.

32. The procedure SET_UP in Fig. 12.5 uses two instructions, ASHL and BISL2 to turn on the bit in a set representation that corresponds to the set element stored in the longword NUMBER. Write an INSV instruction that will do the same thing.

33. The problem described in Example 12.12 of constructing a mask given its starting position and length can be solved with only two instructions. Write the instructions. (Use an instruction from Section 12.5.)

34. The procedure TURNOFF_2 (Fig. 12.7) finds the first bit that is on in a longword, turns it off, and returns its position. Write a procedure TURNOFF_3 with three arguments, BIT_STRING, START_POSN, and POSITION, where BIT_STRING and POSITION are as before, but now the search for the first set bit should begin at the bit position specified in the byte argument START_POSN. The search must "wrap around"; that is, if there is no set bit in the range 31:START_POSN, then the procedure should scan bits START_POSN−1:0.

35. Using the description of the disk map problem in Example 12.15, write instructions to find an available disk block without using any of the bit field instructions.

36. In Example 12.15 we searched a disk map for a clear bit indicating an available disk block. Suppose that we need a contiguous group of n blocks, where $1 \leq n \leq 32$. Write instructions to find the block number of the first in a group of n available blocks or branch to NO_ROOM if no such group of blocks is available.

37. Write a sequence of instructions to determine if there is exactly one bit set in R10 and branch to ONE_BIT if so. (You might want to do this with and without using instructions from Section 12.5.)

38. Suppose R5 contains F F F F F F F F. What will be in R5 after executing the following instruction?

```
EXTV    #5,#0,#^XFFFFFFFF,R5
```

39. Consider the bit matrix graphics problem in Example 12.17. Write procedures to
   (a) Draw a horizontal line, given its row number, right endpoint (as a bit offset from the right side of the screen), and length (in bits).
   (b) Draw a vertical line, given its bottom row number, top row number, and distance from the right edge of the screen (in bits).
   (c) Draw the outline of a rectangle, rather than a solid rectangle, given the same specifications as in Example 12.17.
   (d) Draw a solid rectangle, given the specifications in Example 12.17, but allow for the width to be larger than 32.

40. Suppose there were no CMPV and CMPZV instructions. For each of these, write a sequence of other instructions that do the same operation.

41. In Example 12.18 we described a representation of questionnaire answers. Write instructions to pack a person's answers into a longword as described there, assuming that the answers are in the longword array ANSWERS.

42. Write a procedure to convert a string of character code for eight hex digits to a longword hex integer. In other words, if, for example, the first argument is the character string "FFC03008", the procedure returns in its second argument the longword containing FFC03008. (This procedure is useful for converting input for a program designed to test some of the examples of bit-manipulation instructions in this chapter!)

43. Suppose there were no CALLG and CALLS instructions, just a CALL instruction with one argument, the procedure entry point name, that causes a transfer of control to the procedure. Write instructions to do all the steps that are normally done by CALLG; i.e., construct the call frame on the stack and put the appropriate new values in AP and FP. (You may assume that the entry mask does not specify any trap enables. All of the instructions you need have been covered except

MOVPSL   *dest*

which copies the PSL to *dest*.)

Chapter 13

Floating Point and Packed Decimal

In this chapter we describe two data types found on many large computers (though generally not on small ones): floating point and packed decimal. The VAX supports both types with machine instructions that do arithmetic and miscellaneous other operations.

13.1 FLOATING POINT DATA REPRESENTATION

Scientific Notation

"Scientific notation" is commonly used for writing very large and very small real numbers. The format is

$$\pm m \times 10^p$$

where m (called the mantissa) is restricted to a small range, usually $1 \leq m < 10$, and p is an integer. Some examples are

$$1.48 \times 10^3 \qquad -3.0083 \times 10^{28} \qquad 4.87 \times 10^{-12}$$

The range of the mantissa is chosen so that any rational number can be written in this form.

The internal representation of floating point numbers in digital computers is similar to scientific notation. The representation contains a sign, a mantissa which is a fraction (i.e., is less than 1), and a (signed) power of a radix r (generally 2, 8, or 16, rather than 10). Thus we can write floating point numbers as

$$\pm f \times r^p \qquad \text{where } 0 \le f < 1.$$

On a computer the values of f and p are restricted by the number of bits used to store them, so not all rational numbers can be represented. For those that can be, this representation is not unique; i.e., there is more than one way to write a number in this format. For example,

$$.1101 \times 2^3 = .001101 \times 2^5$$

(where the fractions are shown in binary).

The Floating Point Data Types

The VAX has two standard floating point data types: single precision (type F_floating) and double precision (type D_floating). In addition, the G_floating and H_floating types are available as options; they allow for the representation of numbers with larger exponents and more significant digits. For all these types a floating point number is expressed as

$$\pm f \times 2^p \qquad \text{where } .5 \le f < 1$$

A single-precision floating point number occupies a longword, a D or G floating point number occupies a quadword, and H uses octawords. The types differ only in the number of bits used to store the exponent and fraction. The general format and the way of representing the three components (sign, fraction, and exponent) are the same.

To keep the discussion of the representations general enough to describe all the types at once, we will use t for the number of bits in the exponent and u for the number of bits in the fraction field.

A floating point number is said to be in *normalized* form if the first digit after the radix point is nonzero. VAX floating point numbers are always normalized; the first bit after the binary point will always be a 1, since $f \ge .5_{10}$. There are two advantages to using a normalized representation. Since the first bit is always a 1, it doesn't have to be included in the representation; it can be assumed. The fraction bits that actually appear in the representation do not include the first bit. Thus, a floating point representation with u fraction bits actually has $u + 1$ significant bits. The second advantage is that keeping numbers in normalized form increases the accuracy of floating point computation. Note that the normalized representation of a nonzero number in any one of the floating data types is unique.

The single precision (F_floating) format is

31	16	15	14	7	6	0
f_2		S	$b.\ exp.$		f_1	

where $S =$ the sign bit (0 is $+$, 1 is $-$, as usual),
                 $f = .1f_1f_2$, and
                 b. exp. = "biased exponent" = $p + 128_{10}$.

Several aspects of the representation need explanation. The location of the sign bit and the arrangement of the fraction segments are certainly peculiar. It would seem more natural for the two halves of the representation to be interchanged so that the sign would be in bit 31 and the fraction would appear as a contiguous string of bits. The VAX floating point representations were chosen for compatibility with the F and D floating point data types on DEC's PDP-11 computers, whose basic memory unit is a 16-bit word. The representations seem a bit more natural when viewed as a sequence of words, not longwords. All four types are shown this way in Fig. 13.1.

What is a "biased exponent," and why does the F_floating representation contain $p + 128$ rather than p? The VAX uses t bits ($t = 8$ for F and D, $t = 11$ for G, and $t = 15$ for H) for the exponent, so 2^t (256, for F and D) different values can be

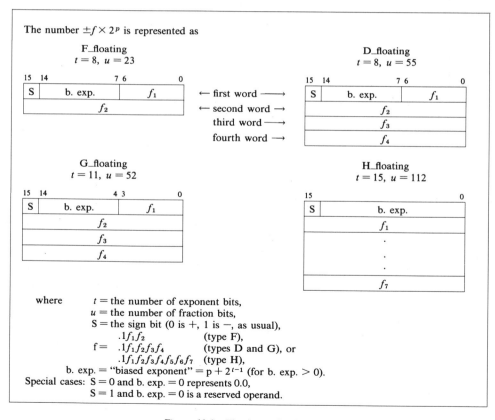

Figure 13.1   Floating point formats

represented. Since we want both negative and positive exponents, we could represent -2^{t-1} to $2^{t-1}-1$ in two's complement (-128 to 127 for F and D), but this is not done. The hardware that does floating point arithmetic can work more efficiently if the ordering of the actual exponents corresponds to the ordering of their representations interpreted as unsigned binary number. In two's complement, the sign bit makes negative integers "look" larger than positive integers. The representation used (by many computers) for the exponents simply assigns exponent values to the bit patterns in order. The assignment used by the VAX (with $t = 8$) is

Bit Pattern	Bit Pattern Value in Decimal	Exponent Represented
00000000	0	special case
00000001	1	-127
00000010	2	-126
.	.	.
.	.	.
.	.	.
01111111	127	-1
10000000	128	0
10000001	129	1
.	.	.
.	.	.
.	.	.
11111111	255	127

Thus what we call the biased exponent is simply the value of the bit pattern as an unsigned binary number. It is 2^{t-1} larger than the exponent, p, that it represents; that is, the "bias" is 2^{t-1}. A biased exponent of 0 does not represent the exponent -2^{t-1}; it is a special case. A floating point number with biased exponent 0 and sign (bit 15) 0 represents floating point zero—i.e., the number 0.0 (regardless of what is in the fraction bits). A biased exponent 0 and sign 1 is a reserved operand—i.e., an invalid number; if it is an operand in a floating point instruction, a reserved operand fault will occur.

The ranges of values and the accuracy of numbers that can be represented in floating point on the VAX are shown in Table 13.1.

TABLE 13.1 Ranges of Floating Point Numbers

Type	Exp. Bits	Frac. Bits	Magnitude Range (approx.)	Significant Digits (approx.)
F	8	23	$.29 \times 10^{-38}$ to 1.7×10^{38}	7
D	8	55	$.29 \times 10^{-38}$ to 1.7×10^{38}	16
G	11	52	$.56 \times 10^{-308}$ to $.9 \times 10^{308}$	15
H	15	112	$.84 \times 10^{-4932}$ to $.59 \times 10^{4932}$	33

There is nothing within a longword (or quadword or octaword) that represents a floating point number to indicate that it is, in fact, a floating point number rather than an integer. The CPU will interpret the bit pattern as being a datum of the type appropriate for the instruction that operates on it.

In all the examples in this chapter, when we refer to floating point numbers without specifying the type, we mean single precision, or F_floating.

EXAMPLE 13.1: *Interpreting a Floating Point Number*

The problem is to determine what floating point number is represented by $0000C150$. The bit pattern is

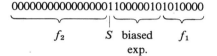

The number is negative because $S = 1$. The biased exponent, 10000010, is 130_{10}, so the actual exponent, p, is 2. The fraction is $.1f_1f_2$, so the number is

$$-.1101 \times 2^2 = -11.01_2 = -3.25_{10}$$

(Remember that the ith position to the right of the binary point represents 2^{-i}.)

Note that the leftmost bit of the biased exponent indicates the sign of the exponent becaue it is the 128's place (the 2^{t-1}'s place, in general) in the binary number. The biased exponent is ≥ 128 (2^{t-1}), and $p \geq 0$, if and only if bit 14 is set.

EXAMPLE 13.2: *Converting to Floating Point Representation*

The problem is to convert the decimal number 5031.1875 to its floating point representation.

$$5031.1875_{10} = 13A7.3_{16}$$
$$= 1001110100111.0011_2$$
$$= .1001110100111 0011 \times 2^{13}$$

$$f_1 \qquad f_2$$

So $p = 13$, and the biased exponent = 141, or 10001101. Thus the representation is

$$00111001100000000100011010011101$$

or

$$3980469D$$

EXAMPLE 13.3: *Double Precision*

To emphasize the arrangement of the fraction bits in a double precision floating point number we consider the following datum:

```
11111111111111110100000000000000    first longword
11111111111111110000000000000000    second longword
```

The number represented is

$.10000000111111111111111110000000000000000001111111111111111_2$

Initializing Storage

Floating point constants are written in decimal. They may be written with or without a sign, with or without an exponent (a power of 10), and, if the number is an integer, with or without a decimal point. If a decimal point is used, there should be at least one digit to the left of it.

EXAMPLE 13.4: Floating Point Constants

```
1.13     −27.00056E15     247     0.25     −5E−8
1.24E−3 = 0.124E−2 = 124E−5 = 0.00124 = 0.00000124E3
```

Storage may be initialized with the following directives:

.x_FLOATING   *list_of_floating_point_constants*

where $x = $ F, D, G, or H. The shorter directive names .FLOAT and .DOUBLE may be used for F_FLOATING and D_FLOATING, respectively. The assembler initializes the next available space in memory with the internal floating point representations of the constants listed.

Storage for floating point numbers may be reserved with the .BLKx directives described in Chapter 4 (where $x = $ F, D, G, or H).

EXAMPLE 13.5: Reserving and Initializing Storage

```
PI:      .FLOAT  3.14159
RADIUS:  .BLKF   1
AREA:    .BLKF   1
```

13.2 FLOATING POINT OPERATIONS

The VAX instruction set includes instructions for doing floating point arithmetic, tests and comparisons, a few other related operations, and conversion between the floating point data types and between floating point and integer. Machine instructions that convert between floating point and integer representations are uncommon, but not surprising for the VAX. The VAX also has a few very special, powerful instructions that perform complex operations on floating point data (the POLY and EMOD instructions) that we will not cover here.

The standard instruction set supports the F and D floating point types. The optional G and H type instruction set includes all of the same operations. (The opcodes for the G and H instructions are two bytes long.)

Floating point operands may be in memory, in registers, or in an instruction itself as literal or immediate operands. When a register, say Rn, is specified for an operand of a double precision instruction, Rn and R$n+1$ are used; Rn contains the first longword of the operand (with the sign, biased exponent, and most significant fraction bits), and R$n+1$ contains the additional fraction bits.

Arithmetic and Related Instructions

The basic arithmetic instructions are

$$\left\{\begin{array}{c}\text{ADD}\\\text{SUB}\\\text{MUL}\\\text{DIV}\end{array}\right\}\ \left\{\begin{array}{c}\text{F}\\\text{D}\\\text{G}\\\text{H}\end{array}\right\}\ \left\{\begin{array}{c}2\\3\end{array}\right.\quad\begin{array}{l}op1,op2\\op1,op2,dest\end{array}\left.\right\}$$

The roles of the operands follow the same conventions as in the integer arithmetic instructions. For example, in SUBF3 the first operand is subtracted from the second and the result goes in the third. All these instructions affect the condition codes as follows:

N = 1   if and only if the result is less than 0 (or is a reserved operand)

Z = 1   if and only if the result is 0.0

V = 1   if and only if the result overflows or the divisor in a DIV instruction is 0.0

C = 0

Program exceptions will occur for overflow (i.e., the result's exponent is greater than 127, for F and D, or greater than $2^{10} - 1$ or $2^{14} - 1$ for G and H), reserved operands, and division by zero. The programmer can choose whether or not underflow (resulting exponent less than -127, etc.) will cause an exception by setting or clearing bit 6 of the PSW, the floating underflow trap enable bit. When underflow results from an arithmetic operation, the floating point number 0.0 is stored in the destination operand.

Recall that 0.0 has many representations; any number with zeros in the sign and biased exponent fields is treated as zero regardless of what is in the fraction bits. However, if the result of a floating point operation is zero, the CPU always stores the representation with zeros in all the fraction bits.

After describing the other instructions, we will examine floating point arithmetic in more detail.

The special-purpose instructions available for floating point are

CLR*x*	*dest*
MOV*x*	*source,dest*
MOVA*x*	*source,dest*
MNEG*x*	*source,dest*

where $x = $ F, D, G, or H. The CLRx and MOVAx instructions, with $x = $ F or D, do exactly the same operations as CLRx and MOVAx, with $x = $ L or Q, respectively. In fact, they are just alternate names for the corresponding integer instructions; the opcodes are the same. The floating point MOV and integer MOV instructions are not identical because they do different tests to set the condition codes and determine if there is a fault. The MNEG instructions move a copy of the source operand with its sign bit complemented to the destination. (If the source $= 0$, the sign is not changed.) They affect the N and Z condition codes in the usual ways, and clear both V and C. There are no INC and DEC instructions for floating point.

The floating test and compare instructions are

TST*x*	*operand*
CMP*x*	*op1,op2*

where $x = $ F, D, G, or H. They follow the usual conventions.

The VAX has a complete assortment of CVT instructions for conversion between any pair of the integer and floating point data types, including two options for converting floating point to longwords: rounded or truncated conversion. The instructions are

CVT*xy*　　*source,destination*

where x and y may be F, D, G, H, B, W, or L, but $x \neq y$, $xy \neq $ DG, and $xy \neq $ GD, and

CVTR*x***L**　　*source,destination*

for ConVerT Rounded, where $x = $ F, D, G, or H. CVTxL truncates the floating point operand to an integer rather than rounding. As usual, if the converted result can not be represented properly in the destination, the V condition code is set.

EXAMPLE 13.6: Conversions

Suppose ALPHA is defined by

```
ALPHA:  .FLOAT  -15.9
```

The longword at ALPHA will contain 6666C27E. The table below shows the effects of several conversion instructions.

Instruction		*Result in R7*
CVTFW	ALPHA,R7	xxxxFFF1
CVTFL	ALPHA,R7	FFFFFFF1
CVTRFL	ALPHA,R7	FFFFFFF0
CVTFD	ALPHA,R7	6666C27E in **R7**
		00000000 in **R8**

(The x's indicate parts of R7 that are unchanged.)

Most of the CVT instructions do fairly complex operations that on other computers must be programmed with a sequence of instructions, including several bit operations. Therefore, it is worth giving some thought to how the conversions would be done if the CVT instructions were not available. In Section 13.5 we will write a procedure to convert from floating point to longword without using CVTFL. Some of the other conversions are considered in the exercises.

Conversion from floating point format to character code for output is an even more complex task, and not even the VAX has one or two powerful instructions to do the job. The VAX-11 Run-Time Procedure Library contains conversion procedures that are used by the high-level language compilers and may be called directly by the assembly language programmer.

One of the groups of loop control instructions presented in Chapter 7, the ACB instructions, allows floating point loop parameters. Recall that ACB is a mnemonic for Add, Compare, and Branch; the instruction format is

$$\text{ACB}x \qquad limit,incr,index,dest$$

where x may be F, D, G, or H (in addition to B, W, and L). These are the most flexible of the loop control instructions because they allow the programmer to specify the loop increment, which may be negative or positive, and the destination is encoded using a word, rather than byte, displacement.

EXAMPLE 13.7: Floating Point Loop Parameters

The Algol **for** loop

$$\textbf{for } x := 2.8 \textbf{ step } -.2 \textbf{ until } 1.0 \textbf{ do}$$

$$\langle loop\ body \rangle$$

could be implemented as follows:

```
; REGISTER USE      R6     loop index
;
        MOVF    #2.8,R6                  ; Initialize index
LOOP:

        ⟨loop body⟩

        ACBF    #1.0,#-0.2,R6,LOOP    ; Loop control
```

How Arithmetic Is Done

To gain some understanding of how floating point arithmetic is done we will consider addition and subtraction. Some of the points discussed here can readily be applied to multiplication and division.

Suppose we wish to add floating point numbers $f_1 \times 2^{p_1}$ and $f_2 \times 2^{p_2}$. We can not add the fractions as they are, unless the powers p_1 and p_2 are equal. The rules for addition may be summarized as:

1. Let $n = |p_1 - p_2|$.
2. Shift the fraction bits of the number with the smaller exponent to the right n places. (Now both exponents are equal to the larger of p_1 and p_2.)
3. Add the fractions.
4. Normalize the result if necessary by shifting the fraction bits and adjusting the exponent.

Before considering some additional details, we will show a simple example.

EXAMPLE 13.8: Addition

Problem: Determine what will be in R8 after executing the following instruction, assuming that R6 contains 6000580C and R7 contains 90005425.

```
ADDF3   R6,R7,R8
```

After decoding the representations, we have the following addition problem:

$$(R6) \qquad .8C6000 \times 2^{48}$$
$$(R7) \qquad +.A59000 \times 2^{40}$$

where the fractions have been left in hex for convenience. (The exponents are shown in decimal.) The second operand must be shifted right eight places (that is, eight binary places, or two hex places), yielding

$$.8C6000 \times 2^{48}$$
$$+.00A590 \times 2^{48}$$

Adding the fractions gives

$$.8D0590 \times 2^{48}$$

The sum is already in normalized form, since the first bit of 8 is a 1. The result in R8 will be 0590580D.

When one of the operands is shifted right to get equal exponents for addition or subtraction, some nonzero bits may be lost. For accuracy of results, some of those bits should be used in the computation. The way the VAX does computation is equivalent to keeping two extra bits, called *guard bits,* at the right end of the fractions. Also, it allows an extra bit to the left of the binary point for a carry out of the most significant fraction position. Recall that u is the actual number of fraction bits stored in the floating point representation; the first fraction bit is not stored. After normalization, the $(u + 1)$–bit fraction is rounded. That is, if the first guard bit is a 1, 1 is added to the fraction at the least significant place. The result is an exact result rounded to $u + 1$ bits; thus the error is at most one-half the value of the least significant bit of the fraction. (Though the error is quite small, we shall see below and in Section 13.4 that it can have significant impact.)

EXAMPLE 13.9: Addition with Rounding

Problem: Determine what will be in GAMMA after executing the following instruction, assuming (ALPHA) = 739E448D and (BETA) = 94704722.

        ADDF3   ALPHA,BETA,GAMMA

After decoding the representations we have the problem:

$$
\begin{aligned}
\text{(ALPHA)} \qquad &.100011010111001110011110 \times 2^9 \\
\text{(BETA)} \qquad + &.101000101001010001111101 \times 2^{14}
\end{aligned}
$$

The first operand is shifted right five places. Three bits are dropped from the right end; two are kept as guard bits.

$$
\begin{aligned}
&\hspace{7.5cm}\text{guard bits} \\
\text{(ALPHA) shifted} \qquad &.00000100011010111001110011 \times 2^{14} \\
\text{(BETA)} \qquad + &.101000101001010001111101 \times 2^{14}
\end{aligned}
$$

Adding fractions gives

$$0.10100111000000000001100111 \times 2^{14}$$

The sum is already normalized. Since the first guard bit is 1, the result is rounded up as follows:

$$
\begin{aligned}
&.101001110000000000011001 \times 2^{14} \\
+ &\hspace{4.6cm} 1 \\
\hline
0&.101001110000000000011010 \times 2^{14}
\end{aligned}
$$

GAMMA will contain 001A4727.

When is the second guard bit used? If the result of the operation requires a left shift by one place for normalization, the second guard bit is used for rounding. This is illustrated in the next example. Of course it is possible that normalization will require a left shift by more than one place (for subtraction of positive numbers of similar magnitudes, for example). Then both guard bits and additional zeros would be shifted into the right end of the fraction.

EXAMPLE 13.10: *Subtraction with Normalization*

Problem: Determine what will be in R7 after executing the following instruction, assuming R7 contains 00004000 (that is, $\frac{1}{2}$) and R9 contains $00013F00$ ($\frac{1}{8} + 2^{-26}$).

       SUBF2   R9,R7

The problem is

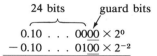

$$0.10 \ldots 0000 \times 2^0$$
$$-\ 0.10 \ldots 0100 \times 2^{-2}$$

First we put the operand to be subtracted in two's complement form. Note that we have explicitly shown the carry bit and the two guard bits here because they participate in the two's complementing of the second operand.

$$0.10 \ldots 0000 \times 2^0$$
$$+\ 1.01 \ldots 1100 \times 2^{-2}$$

Shifting the second operand (with the carry bit treated like a sign bit and extended), and adding gives

$$0.10 \ldots 0000 \times 2^0$$
$$+\ 1.1101 \ldots 1111 \times 2^0$$
$$\overline{0.0101 \ldots 1111 \times 2^0}$$

The sum is normalized by shifting left one place:

$$0.101 \ldots 11110 \times 2^{-1}$$

The first guard bit (which was the second guard bit in the sum) is added to the 24-bit fraction to round it, yielding

$$0.110 \ldots 00 \times 2^{-1}$$

which is $\frac{3}{8}$, the correct rounded result. It will appear in R7 as $00003FC0$.

Breaking Rules

The result of the subtraction in Example 13.10 was not exact. Because only a finite number of bits are used to represent the fraction of a floating point number, we can not always get exact results. For the same reason, floating point arithmetic on computers does not satisfy all the standard rules of arithmetic. Consider the following rule

$$\text{If}\quad a + b = b, \qquad \text{then } a = 0.$$

Suppose we add $\frac{1}{2}$ and 2^{24}, both of which can easily be put in floating point representation. The addition is done as follows:

$$.1 \times 2^0$$
$$+\,.1 \times 2^{25}$$

After shifting:

guard bits

$$.0000000000000000000000000\underline{01} \times 2^{25}$$
$$+\,.1000000000000000000000000\underline{00} \times 2^{25}$$
$$\overline{.1000000000000000000000000\underline{01} \times 2^{25}}$$

The first guard bit is 0, so those bits are dropped. The result is b, but $a = \tfrac{1}{2} \neq 0$. Clearly here the difficulty arises because the numbers being added are of very different magnitudes. This is a general problem with floating point arithmetic. To increase the accuracy of results, evaluation of long expressions should be arranged so that numbers of similar magnitudes are combined first. We will illustrate this principle with an extensive example in Section 13.4.

We leave it as an exercise for the reader to find an example to show that the associative law for addition

$$(a + b) + c = a + (b + c)$$

does not always hold for floating point arithmetic.

13.3 FLOATING POINT IMMEDIATE AND LITERAL OPERANDS

Floating point constants may be specified as literal or immediate operands in machine instructions. As with integers, the constant is preceded by a #. For example:

```
MULF3    #0.33333333,R6,AREA
MOVF     #40,R7
```

The first operand specifier in the MULF3 instruction will be assembled in immediate mode; the assembler will put the longword floating point representation of 0.33333333 into the instruction as follows:

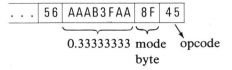

If the instruction type were D, the assembler would assemble the constant in a quadword as follows:

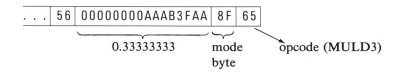

Note that the assembler fills the low-order fraction bits of an immediate operand in a double precision instruction with zeros. (It would have done so even if we had written out 16 digits in the constant.) To get significant double-precision fraction bits, the constant should be defined in a .DOUBLE directive.

We saw that literal mode operands are used for small integer constants to save space. The leftmost two bits of the mode byte are zeros to indicate that it is a literal, and the remaining six bits contain the constant. The assembler stores certain small floating point constants in literal mode instead of immediate mode, also to save space. The format of a floating point literal is shown in Fig. 13.2. Three of the six available bits are used for the exponent (a true, not biased, exponent) and three for the fraction. There is no sign bit; only positive numbers can be encoded in literal mode. As with the regular floating point representation, the most significant fraction bit is assumed to be 1 and is omitted.

Since the number 40 can be encoded as a floating point literal, the assembler will use literal mode in the MOVF instruction above. $40 = 101000_2 = .101 \times 2^6$, so the literal is 00110010. The machine code for the instruction is

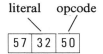

How does the CPU know, when executing an instruction, whether to interpret a literal as an integer or as a floating point number? There is nothing in the literal byte itself to distinguish between the two types. The CPU interprets the literal as being of the type appropriate to the instruction.

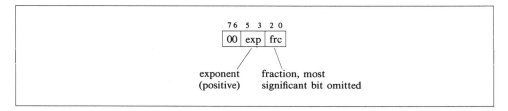

Figure 13.2 Floating point literal format

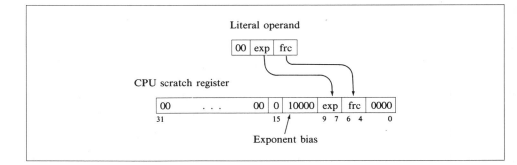

Figure 13.3 Expansion of a floating point literal

EXAMPLE 13.11: *Interpreting Literal Mode Operands*

Consider the machine code

$$\text{first byte} \qquad \qquad \text{first byte}$$
$$59 \ 03 \ C2 \qquad \text{and} \qquad 59 \ 03 \ 42$$

The first instruction is SUBL2; the second is SUBF2. The first operand for both instructions is the literal mode byte 03. For the SUBL2 instruction the CPU will interpret the literal as the integer #3; for the SUBF2 instruction it will interpret the literal as follows:

$$00000011 = .1011 \times 2^0 = \tfrac{1}{2} + \tfrac{1}{8} + \tfrac{1}{16} = .6875$$

In the first instruction the CPU will do an integer subtraction, subtracting 3 from the contents of R9, which will be interpreted as a two's complement integer. In the second instruction the CPU does a floating point subtraction, subtracting .6875 from the contents of R9, which will be interpreted as a floating point number.

When an instruction has a floating point literal operand, the CPU expands the literal to a full-length floating point format (depending on the instruction type) before performing the operation. Figure 13.3 shows how the expansion is done for type F. For types D, G, and H the additional longwords would contain all zeros.

13.4 EXAMPLE: COMPUTATIONAL ACCURACY IN COMPUTING VARIANCE

We showed in Section 13.2 that the results of floating point arithmetic operations are not always exact, and we suggested that in long expressions, numbers of similar magnitude should be combined first. In this section we will illustrate how the results may differ when the same quantity is computed using two different, but mathematically equivalent, formulas. A more thorough explanation of why the two formulas produce different results, and of how to estimate the accuracy of a computation, can be found in a numerical analysis course or textbook. Our example here is intended to alert the reader to the importance of such a course.

Suppose we have an array of n floating point numbers, $X(1), \ldots, X(n)$, which we call sample points. The mean, or average, is defined as

$$\text{mean} = \frac{1}{n} \sum_{i=1}^{n} X(i)$$

The standard deviation is a measure of how far the points are from the mean. The variance is the square of the standard deviation. For this example we will compute the variance of the set of sample points. The variance is defined by

$$\text{var} = \frac{1}{n} \sum_{i=1}^{n} [X(i) - \text{mean}]^2 \tag{13.1}$$

The formula is usually simplified to

$$\text{var} = \frac{1}{n} \sum_{i=1}^{n} X(i)^2 - \text{mean}^2 \tag{13.2}$$

Procedures to compute the variance using each of these formulas are shown in Figs. 13.4 and 13.5. Formula (13.1) implies the need of two loops, one to compute the mean first, then one to do the summation shown in (13.1). Using formula (13.2), one loop can be used to compute the sum of the sample points and the sum of their squares. Thus one might expect the procedure using formula (13.2) to be slightly simpler and run slightly faster. Unfortunately, it can yield poor results. Computing and summing the differences between each sample point and the mean, as in formula (13.1), will be more accurate than computing the sums separately and taking one difference at the end.

To illustrate the difference between the formulas, we ran both procedures with several sets of n sample points, where $n = 100$. For the first group of tests we generated points in normal distributions with an expected mean of .1234567 and expected standard deviations of .1, .01, .001, and .0001. For the second group of tests, half of the points are mean*$(1 + \text{epsilon})$ and half are mean*$(1 - \text{epsilon})$, where epsilon = .1, .01, .001, and .0001. From formula (13.1) it is clear that the correct value of the variance for this group is (mean*epsilon)^2. The third group of tests uses uniform distributions with gaps of 4*epsilon/n between points, for the same values of epsilon as above. For the second and third groups the mean is .1234567. Figure 13.6 shows the results of the tests. (The expected mean and variance are only estimates in the case of the normal distributions). We can see that the results from the two formulas are similar for the first three tests in each group, but when epsilon = .0001, formula (13.1) still gives accurate results, while formula (13.2) is worthless.

```
              .PSECT  VARIANCE_1
;
;  PROCEDURE VARNC1 (SAMPLE, N, MEAN, VAR)
;
;  This procedure computes the mean and variance of the numbers
;  in the floating point array SAMPLE. It uses the formula:
;
;              1/N * SUM [(SAMPLE(i) - MEAN)^2]
;
;  for the variance.
;
;  INPUT ARGUMENTS
;
;         SAMPLE          sample values (floating point array)
;         N               the number of sample points (longword).
;
;  OUTPUT ARGUMENTS
;
;         MEAN            the mean (average) of the sample points
;                         (floating point)
;         VAR             variance (floating point)
;
;
;  OFFSETS FOR ARGUMENT LIST
;
SAMPLE = 4
N = 8
MEAN = 12
VAR = 16
;
;  REGISTER USE         R5        array pointer
;                       R6        N, number of points
;                       R7        loop limit (addr of last sample pt)
;                       R8        scratch
;                       R9        sum of sample points & mean
;                       R10       variance
;
              .ENTRY   VARNC1,^M<R5,R6,R7,R8,R9,R10>
;
              MOVL     SAMPLE(AP),R5          ; Addr. of array
              MOVL     @N(AP),R6              ; N
              SUBL3    #1,R6,R8               ; N-1
              MULL2    #4,R8                  ; 4*(N-1)
              ADDL3    R5,R8,R7               ; Loop limit
;
              CVTLF    R6,R6                  ; N in floating point
;
              CLRF     R9                     ; Clear for sum of sample pts
;
ADD:          ADDF2    (R5),R9                ; Add sample value
              ACBL     R7,#4,R5,ADD           ; Loop control
;
              DIVF2    R6,R9                  ; Compute mean
```

Figure 13.4 Computing variance with formula (13.1)

```
            MOVF      R9,@MEAN(AP)              ; Store mean
;
            CLRF      R10                       ; Clear for summation
            MOVL      SAMPLE(AP),R5             ; Array addr
;
TERM:       SUBF3     R9,(R5),R8                ; SAMPLE(i)-mean
            MULF2     R8,R8                     ; (SAMPLE(i)-mean)^2
            ADDF2     R8,R10                    ; Add square
            ACBL      R7,#4,R5,TERM             ; Loop control
;
            DIVF3     R6,R10,@VAR(AP)           ; Variance
            RET                                 ; Return
            .END
```

Figure 13.4 (Continued)

```
        .PSECT   VARIANCE_2
;
; PROCEDURE VARNC2 (SAMPLE, N, MEAN, VAR)
;
; This procedure computes the mean and variance of the numbers
; in the floating point array SAMPLE. It uses the formula:
;
;           1/N * SUM[SAMPLE(i)^2] - MEAN^2
;
; for the variance.
;
; INPUT ARGUMENTS
;
;       SAMPLE        sample values (floating point array)
;       N             the number of sample points (longword)
;
; OUTPUT ARGUMENTS
;
;       MEAN          the mean (average) of the sample points
;                     (floating point)
;       VAR           variance (floating point)
;
; OFFSETS FOR ARGUMENT LIST
;
SAMPLE = 4
N = 8
MEAN = 12
VAR = 16
;
; REGISTER USE      R5      array pointer
;                   R6      N, number of points
;                   R7      loop limit (addr of last sample pt)
;                   R8      scratch
;                   R9      sum of sample points
;                   R10     sum of squares of sample pts
;
```

Figure 13.5 Computing variance with formula (13.2)

```
        .ENTRY    VARNC2,^M<R5,R6,R7,R8,R9,R10>
;
        MOVL      SAMPLE(AP),R5          ; Addr. of array
        MOVL      @N(AP),R6              ; N
        SUBL3     #1,R6,R8               ; N-1
        MULL2     #4,R8                  ; 4*(N-1)
        ADDL3     R5,R8,R7               ; Loop limit
;
        CLRF      R9                     ; Clear for sum
        CLRF      R10                    ; Clear for sum of squares
;
ADD:    ADDF2     (R5),R9                ; Add sample value
        MULF3     (R5),(R5),R8           ; (Sample point)^2
        ADDF2     R8,R10                 ; Add square
        ACBL      R7,#4,R5,ADD           ; Loop control
;
        CVTLF     R6,R6                  ; N in floating point
        DIVF2     R6,R9                  ; Compute mean
        MOVF      R9,@MEAN(AP)           ; Store mean
;
        DIVF2     R6,R10                 ; 1/N * sum of squares
        MULF2     R9,R9                  ; Mean^2
        SUBF3     R9,R10,@VAR(AP)        ; Variance
;
        RET                              ; Return
        .END
```

Figure 13.5 (Continued)

The output shown in Fig. 13.6 was produced by a main program written in Fortran. Since the VAX Fortran compiler uses the standard procedure linkage conventions described in Chapter 9, a Fortran main program can call assembly language procedures without any unusual requirements. The Fortran statements used to call the procedures shown in Figs. 13.4 and 13.5 are

```
CALL VARNC1 (SAMPLE,N,XMEAN,VAR1)
CALL VARNC2 (SAMPLE,N,XMEAN,VAR2)
```

One advantage of using Fortran for the main program is that we can use standard Fortran I/O statements for the complex task of converting floating point numbers from their internal representation to the character strings that appear in the output.

It should be clear that the points we have made here—that floating point computation is tricky and care is needed to obtain accurate results—are not relevant only to the assembly language programmer. The computation steps done are the same whether a procedure is written in assembly language or a high-level language.

```
                            NORMAL DISTRIBUTION

                                                              EXPECTED
      STD DEV           MEAN          VARIANCE 1      VARIANCE 2    VARIANCE

   0.1000000E+00    0.1329546E+00    0.8948188E-02   0.8948196E-02  0.1000000E-01
   0.1000000E-01    0.1244065E+00    0.8948187E-04   0.8948334E-04  0.1000000E-03
   0.1000000E-02    0.1235517E+00    0.8948180E-06   0.8912757E-06  0.1000000E-05
   0.1000000E-03    0.1234662E+00    0.8948234E-08   0.9313226E-09  0.9999999E-08


                                TWO  POINTS

                                                              EXPECTED
      STD DEV           MEAN          VARIANCE 1      VARIANCE 2    VARIANCE

   0.1000000E+00    0.1234565E+00    0.1524156E-03   0.1524547E-03  0.1524156E-03
   0.1000000E-01    0.1234566E+00    0.1524159E-05   0.1532957E-05  0.1524156E-05
   0.1000000E-02    0.1234566E+00    0.1524234E-07   0.4656613E-07  0.1524156E-07
   0.1000000E-03    0.1234568E+00    0.1524199E-09  -0.1210719E-07  0.1524156E-09


                            UNIFORM DISTRIBUTION

                                                              EXPECTED
      STD DEV           MEAN          VARIANCE 1      VARIANCE 2    VARIANCE

   0.1000000E+00    0.1234566E+00    0.1293599E-01   0.1293598E-01  0.1293600E-01
   0.1000000E-01    0.1234568E+00    0.1293617E-03   0.1293560E-03  0.1293600E-03
   0.1000000E-02    0.1234567E+00    0.1293722E-05   0.1295470E-05  0.1293600E-05
   0.1000000E-03    0.1234567E+00    0.1294222E-07   0.1583248E-07  0.1293600E-07
```

Figure 13.6   Output from variance calculations

13.5   EXAMPLE: CONVERTING BETWEEN FLOATING POINT AND INTEGER

In this section we examine in detail the conversion of a number, say x, from floating point representation (type F) to a two's complement longword integer, say n. We will write a function procedure that does the same operation as the CVTFL instruction. In addition to doing the conversion, the procedure sets the condition codes in the calling program's PSW saved in the stack frame. Thus on return from the procedure the condition codes will have the values they would have if the CVTFL instruction were used.

The steps that are followed in the procedure are summarized below and illustrated in Fig. 13.7. Recall that a function procedure returns its answer in R0.

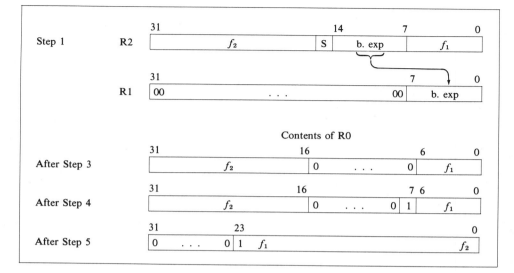

Figure 13.7   Some steps in the conversion from F_floating to integer

1. Extract the biased exponent from bits 14:7 of x into a scratch register.

2. If the exponent of x is not positive, then $|x| < 1$, so $n = 0$. (The exponent is not positive if the biased exponent is ≤ 128). If $n = 0$, set the Z bit in the calling program's PSW (saved on the stack in the call frame). Henceforth we are assuming the exponent is positive.

3. Extract the fraction field, bits $31:16$ and $6:0$, into R0.

4. Set bit 7 of R0, thus inserting the most significant fraction bit that is omitted from the floating point representation.

5. Interchange the two halves of R0 to get the fraction bits in a contiguous string in the proper order.

6. Determine how many positions the fraction bits must be shifted. To do this, observe that if we interpret the contents of R0 as an integer, its value is $1f_1f_2$, or $.1f_1f_2 \times 2^{24}$. The proper value for n is $.1f_1f_2 \times 2^p$, so R0 must be shifted (not rotated) $p - 24$ places. If $p - 24$ is negative, the shift will be to the right, as it should be. If the shift causes overflow, set the V bit in the calling program's PSW.

7. Test the sign, bit 15, of x; if x is negative, negate R0 and set the N bit in the calling program's PSW.

The procedure is shown in Fig. 13.8.

We leave conversion from longword to floating point (without using CVTLF) as an exercise.

```
            .PSECT CVTFL
    ;
    ; FUNCTION CVTFL (ARG)
    ;
    ; This function converts its (single precision) floating point
    ; argument to a longword integer and returns the result in R0.
    ; The conversion truncates the fractional part of the argument.
    ; The condition codes in the stacked calling program's PSW
    ; are set if the result is negative or zero or overflows.
    ;
            .ENTRY CVTFL,^M<R2,R3>
    ;
    ; REGISTER USE:      R0         longword result
    ;                    R1         exponent
    ;                    R2         floating point argument
    ;                    R3         shift count
    ;
            MOVF    @4(AP),R2         ; Get floating pt arg
            BICL3   #^XFFFF807F,R2,R1 ; Extract biased exponent
            ROTL    #-7,R1,R1         ; Exponent in place
            CMPW    R1,#128           ; Determine if exp > 0
            BLEQ    ZERO              ; Exp <= 0, so result = 0
            BICL3   #^X0000FF80,R2,R0 ; Fraction bits in R0
            BISB2   #^X80,R0          ; Insert first fraction bit
            ROTL    #16,R0,R0         ; Fraction bits contiguous
            SUBL3   #152,R1,R3        ; Determine count for shift
            ASHL    R3,R0,R0          ; Shift fraction
            BVC     SIGN              ; Branch if no overflow
            BISB2   #^X02,4(FP)       ; Set V in stacked PSW
    SIGN:   TSTF    R2                ; Test sign
            BGEQ    DONE              ; If non-neg, then done
            MNEGL   R0,R0             ; Negate
            BISB2   #^X08,4(FP)       ; Set N in stacked PSW
    DONE:   RET                       ; Return
    ;
    ZERO:   CLRL    R0                ; Result = 0 if |arg| < 1
            BISB2   #^X04,4(FP)       ; Set Z in stacked PSW
            RET                       ; Return
            .END
```

Figure 13.8 The CVTFL procedure

13.6 PACKED DECIMAL DATA

We have already worked with data in packed decimal format as an intermediate step in conversion between the two's complement integer representation and character code (Section 6.5). In this data type, an integer is represented as a string of from 0 to 31 decimal digits, packed two to a byte, and a sign, occupying the low-order nibble of the last byte in the string. (See Fig. 13.9.) The first (lowest-addressed) byte contains the most significant digit, and the remaining digits follow in natural order. (Alas, now that we have become used to reading memory "backward," i.e.,

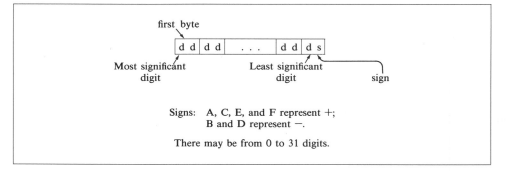

Figure 13.9 Packed decimal string format

showing the lowest-addressed byte at the right in diagrams, the natural left-to-right format of packed decimal may at first be confusing.) The digits are represented in binary, and the sign is represented by the binary patterns 1010–1111—i.e., A through F in hex. A, C, E, and F represent +, and C and D represent −. Signs in decimal strings generated by the CPU as the result of an operation are represented by C (+) or D (−). There are a few examples in Section 6.5.

The VAX, and many large computers, have machine instructions that do arithmetic on packed decimal strings. Since we have a very compact and efficient representation for integers—two's complement—and a compact representation for very large numbers—floating point—it is reasonable to wonder why computer manufacturers would take the trouble to provide another data type and set of instructions for numeric computations. There are two reasons. One is that for some applications, particularly business applications involving amounts of money (e.g., budgeting, accounting), operands may be very large numbers and results must be exact to the penny; neither the integer representation nor the floating point representation may be satisfactory. Amounts in the tens or hundreds of millions of dollars can not be represented in a longword. (We are assuming that the numbers include two decimal places for cents. The decimal point is assumed by the programmer; packed decimal instructions treat the operands as integers.) In many computers, the largest integer data type is a 16-bit word, so not even all five-digit numbers could be represented and efficiently operated on in two's complement. Floating point representation and operations are not satisfactory for such computations because of the accuracy problems described in Section 13.2.

Another reason for the use of packed decimal is that conversions between character code and two's complement (or floating point) for input and output are fairly slow operations. For integer input, for example, the character code is converted first to packed decimal by extracting the low-order nibbles from the character codes, then to two's complement by a Horner's-method computation much as we described in Section 7.4. Although two's complement arithmetic is faster than packed decimal arithmetic, in applications where very few computations and a lot of I/O are done, it may be more efficient to leave the data in packed decimal format. Again, an application area where this phenomenon commonly occurs is business applications. Thus, many COBOL (COmmon Business Oriented Language) compilers use packed decimal as the internal representation for data. The packed decimal data type and instructions are not likely to be used by assembly language programmers.

13.7 PACKED DECIMAL INSTRUCTIONS

Overview

Packed decimal operands acted on by machine instructions must be in memory; they may not be in registers, and they may not be specified as immediate operands. A packed decimal string is specified by the number of digits (not the number of bytes) in the string and the address of its first (lowest-numbered) byte. Since each string requires two instruction operands, some of the packed decimal arithmetic instructions have four-operand and six-operand varieties, depending on whether the result replaces one of the strings or has a distinct destination.

Although many of the usual conventions are followed by the packed decimal instructions, there are several special cases and potential problems to consider. If the number of digits is even, there will be an extra zero digit in the most significant place. If the number of digits is zero, the string occupies one byte containing a zero digit and a plus sign. (Although it is possible to represent −0 as a decimal string, the CPU always produces +0 when the result of an operation is zero and there is no overflow.)

If the result of an operation is smaller than the destination string allotted to it, the most significant digits are filled with zeros. If the result overflows the destination, a decimal overflow fault occurs and a program exception occurs if the decimal overflow trap bit (bit 7) in the PSW is set. This trap bit (like the integer overflow trap bit) is set or cleared on entrance to each procedure, depending on whether or not DV is specified in the register save mask at the procedure's entry point. Program exceptions will occur for reserved operands (a bad nibble in an operand or a number of digits outside the range $0 - 31$) and for division by zero.

Because they work on long strings of bytes in memory (like the MOVC, CMPC, CVTSP, and some other instructions we have seen so far), the decimal instructions use some of the registers for scratch work. They all use R0–R3, and those that have a separate destination operand also use R4 and R5. R0, R2, and R4 (if used) will contain zero after the instruction executes; R1, R3, and R5 (if used) will contain the address of the byte containing the most significant digit of the first, second, and third (if any) decimal operand, respectively. These addresses may be useful to the programmer.

Warning: Unlike most VAX instructions, the six-operand decimal instructions may not work properly if the bytes in memory specified for the destination overlap either of the other decimal string operands.

All the decimal instructions affect the N, Z, and V condition codes in the usual ways. They clear C (with the exception of MOVP, which does not affect C).

Initializing Storage

The .PACKED directive is used to initialize storage with packed decimal constants. Its formats are

.PACKED *decimal_string*
.PACKED *decimal_string, symbol*

The decimal string may have a sign and 0–31 digits. If a symbol is included in the directive, the assembler assigns to it the number of digits in the string; thus the symbol may be used as a literal operand in a decimal instruction to specify the number of digits.

EXAMPLE 13.12: Defining a Decimal String

When the assembler encounters

```
DEC:      .PACKED -2846,DGTS
```

it assembles the constant as 02 84 6D in the bytes beginning at the current location; the value of the location counter is assigned to DEC and the value 4 is assigned to DGTS, which is an absolute symbol.

Note that since on assembly program listings the contents of memory are shown right to left, the bytes containing the packed datum appear backward. For example, if the line containing the above directive were, say, the seventh line in the program section and 26 bytes were used so far, it would appear on a listing as

```
6D 84 02   001A    7 DEC:      .PACKED -2846,DGTS
```

Instructions

The packed decimal arithmetic instructions are

$$\begin{Bmatrix} \text{ADDP} \\ \text{SUBP} \end{Bmatrix} \begin{Bmatrix} 4 \\ 6 \end{Bmatrix} \begin{Bmatrix} num\_dgts\_1,pkd1,num\_dgts\_2,pkd2 \\ num\_dgts\_1,pkd1,num\_dgts\_2,pkd2,num\_dgts\_dest,dest \end{Bmatrix}$$

| MULP | *num_dgts_1,pkd1,num_dgts_2,pkd2,num_dgts_prod,prod* |
| MULP / DIVP | *num_dgts_dvsr,dvsr,num_dgts_dvdd,dvdd,num_dgts_quo,quo* |

In these and all other decimal instructions, the number of digits is specified in a word operand. The DIVP instruction produces an integer quotient; it truncates toward zero, as do the integer DIV instructions. DIVP may use 16 bytes of scratch space on the stack; it will decrement SP to reserve the space and reset SP to release it when it is finished.

EXAMPLE 13.13: *Adding Packed Decimal Strings*

Assume the following memory contents:

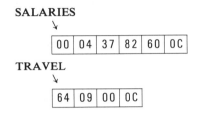

SALARIES

| 00 | 04 | 37 | 82 | 60 | 0C |

TRAVEL

| 64 | 09 | 00 | 0C |

After executing

```
ADDP6   #10,SALARIES,#7,TRAVEL,#12,EXPENDITURES
```

we would have the following result beginning at EXPENDITURES, and the N, Z, V, and C condition codes would be clear.

EXPENDITURES

| 00 | 00 | 05 | 01 | 91 | 60 | 0C |

The MOVP instruction format is

MOVP   *num_dgts,source,dest*

The number of digits for the source and destination is the same.

There are two CMPP instructions because the numbers of digits in the two strings compared may differ. The instructions are

CMPP3   *num_dgts,pkd1,pkd2*

CMPP4   *num_dgts_1,pkd1,num_dgts_2,pkd2*

We described the instructions that convert between packed decimal and two's complement and leading separate numeric in Section 6.5. They are included in the table of decimal instructions in the summary section that follows.

There are no CLR, MOVA, or TST instructions for packed decimal data.

13.8   SUMMARY

The VAX has two standard floating point data types: single precision (type F) in a longword, and double precision (type D) in a quadword, and two optional types: G and H. Floating point numbers on the VAX-11 may be expressed as

$$\pm f \times 2^p$$

where $.5 \le f < 1$ and $-127 \le p \le 127$ (for types F and D)

They are always in normalized form; that is, the first bit after the binary point is a 1; that bit does not appear in the internal representation. The exponent is stored in biased form; that is, the exponent field contains $p + 2^{t-1}$, where t is the number of bits in the exponent field. The formats are shown in Fig. 13.1.

TABLE 13.2   Floating Point Instructions

Instruction		Types	Operation
(All the instructions affect the condition codes in the usual ways.)			
ADDx2	*op1,op2*	x = F, D, G, or H	$op1 + op2 \rightarrow op2$
ADDx3	*op1,op2,dest*	"	$op1 + op2 \rightarrow dest$
SUBx2	*op1,op2*	"	$op2 - op1 \rightarrow op2$
SUBx3	*op1,op2,dest*	"	$op2 - op1 \rightarrow dest$
MULx2	*op1,op2*	"	$op1 * op2 \rightarrow op2$
MULx3	*op1,op2,dest*	"	$op1 * op2 \rightarrow dest$
DIVx2	*op1,op2*	"	$op2/op1 \rightarrow op2$
DIVx3	*op1,op2,dest*	"	$op2/op1 \rightarrow dest$
CLRx	*dest*	"	$0.0 \rightarrow dest$
MOVx	*source,dest*	"	*source* $\rightarrow dest$
MOVAx	*source,dest*	"	*source* address $\rightarrow$ dest
MNEGx	*source,dest*	"	$-source \rightarrow dest$
TSTx	*op*	"	just affect condition
CMPx	*op1,op2*	"	codes
CVTxy	*source,dest*	x = B,W,L,F,D,G,H y = B,W,L,F,D,G,H $x \ne y$, $xy \ne$ DG or GD	*source* (type x) converted to type y $\rightarrow dest$
CVTRxL	*source,dest*	x = F, D, G, H	*source* converted to L, rounded $\rightarrow dest$
ACBx	*limit,incr,index,dest*	x = F, D, G, H	$index + incr \rightarrow index$; branch *to dest* if $incr > 0$ and $index \le limit$, or $incr < 0$ and $index \ge limit$

Because only a finite number of bits are used to store the fraction part of a floating point number, the results of arithmetic operations are not always exact. Unless care is taken in arranging the computation, large errors can result.

Decimal data may be stored in packed decimal string format—i.e., with each decimal digit represented in binary in four bits with a sign in the last nibble of the string. (See Fig. 13.9.) Packed decimal data and instructions are used primarily by high-level language compilers for business applications languages because fairly large integers (up to 31 digits on the VAX) may be stored and operated on with exact accuracy.

Decimal string operands are specified by two instruction operands: the number of digits in the string and the address of its first byte. All the decimal string instructions use R0–R3; the six-operand instructions also use R4 and R5.

The floating point and packed decimal instructions follow the usual conventions about the roles of operands and effects on condition codes. They interpret their operands as being of the type appropriate to the instruction. Program exceptions can occur for overflow, reserved operands, division by zero, and floating point underflow. The programmer has the option of enabling or disabling the decimal overflow and floating underflow traps.

Floating point constants may be assembled using the .*x*_FLOATING directives (for *x* = F, D, G, or H). Certain small floating point constant operands are assembled

TABLE 13.3   Packed Decimal Instructions

Instruction		Operation
(All the instructions affect the condition codes in the usual ways.)		
ADDP4	*num1,pkd1,num2,pkd2*	*pkd1 + pkd2 → pkd2*
ADDP6	*num1,pkd1,num2,pkd2,num_dest,dest*	*pkd1 + pkd2 → dest*
SUBP4	*num1,pkd1,num2,pkd2*	*pkd2 − pkd1 → pkd2*
SUBP6	*num1,pkd1,num2,pkd2,num_dest,dest*	*pkd2 − pkd1 → dest*
MULP	*num1,pkd1,num2,pkd2,num_prod,prod*	*pkd1 * pkd2 → dest*
DIVP	*num1,pkd1,num2,pkd2,num_quo,quo*	*pkd2 / pkd1 → dest*
MOVP	*num,source,dest*	*source → dest*
CMPP3	*num,pkd1,pkd2*	compare *pkd1* and *pkd2;*
CMPP4	*num1,pkd1,num2,pkd2*	affect condition codes.
CVTLP	*long,num,pkd*	*long,* converted from 2's comp to packed → *pkd*
CVTPL	*num,pkd,long*	*pkd,* converted to 2's comp. → *long*
CVTPS	*num_p,pkd,num_s,lsn*	*pkd,* converted to leading sep. numeric → *lsn*
CVTSP	*num_s,lsn,num_p,pkd*	*lsn,* converted to packed → *pkd*

in literal mode. A floating point literal has a three-bit true exponent and three fraction bits. (See Fig. 13.2.) Decimal constants are assembled using the .PACKED directive. Decimal operands may not be used in register, immediate or literal mode.

The instructions described in this chapter are listed in Tables 13.2 (floating point) and 13.3 (packed decimal).

13.9 EXERCISES

1. What floating point number is represented by each of the following data? Show your answers in decimal.

   (a) 0000BFC0   (d) 430047A0
   (b) 8000C40A   (e) 00004080
   (c) 43000041

2. Show the floating point representation (type F) of each of the following:

   (a) 25   (d) ⅝
   (b) −2   (e) 1
   (c) 1048576 (= 2^{20})   (f) $21\frac{3}{16}$

3. Write instructions to compute $7x^2 + 3.8xy - 5.2y^4$, where x and y are floating point numbers (type F) stored at X and Y, respectively.

4. Suppose R5 contains 8A004E14 and R9 contains 06004A31. What will be in R5 and R9, and how will the Z and N condition codes be set after each of the following instructions?

   (a) SUBF2   R9,R5   (b) SUBB2   R9,R5

5. Show the machine code for

           MULD3   #1.5,R5,-(R8)

6. On some computers, any floating point number with zeros in all the fraction bits is interpreted as floating point zero. Why isn't this done on the VAX?

7. We observed that some floating point instructions are identical to the corresponding integer instructions; for example, CLRF is the same instruction as CLRL. Is TSTF the same as TSTL or TSTW? If the instructions are not the same, explain how they differ.

8. What are the differences in the operations of MOVL, MOVW, and MOVF?

9. Write a program segment to estimate the area under the graph of $y = x^2$ by summing the areas of the rectangles shown in Fig. 13.10. Assume that X1, X2, and EPSILON contain floating point numbers (type F). Use the ACBF instruction for loop control.

10. The macros defined in Examples 11.5, 11.6, and 11.12 have an argument TYPE that specifies the data type that the instructions in the macros operate on. Would F, D, G, and H be acceptable values for the TYPE argument in any or all of the macros? Why or why not?

11. Show (in hex) the representation for the smallest and largest positive numbers that can be represented as D_floating numbers.

12. Construct an example to show that the associative law for addition is not always satisfied by floating point arithmetic.

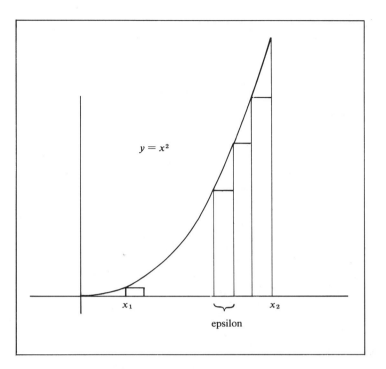

Figure 13.10   Area under the graph of $y = x^2$

13. We showed that, using VAX floating point arithmetic, $a + b = b$ does not imply that $a = 0$ by adding $\frac{1}{2}$ and 2^{24} and getting 2^{24} as the result. Could we have made the same point by adding $\frac{1}{2}$ and 2^{23}? Work out the addition in detail to show why or why not.

14. Suppose two positive floating point numbers are multiplied. What is the maximum number of positions the product may need to be shifted to normalize the result? Why?

15. Outline the steps that would be carried out to convert a type F floating point number to type D without using CVTFD.

16. Write a procedure CVTFD to do the task described in Exercise 15. The procedure should set the condition codes in the calling program's PSW (in the call frame on the stack) in the same ways as the CVTFD instruction does.

17. Outline the steps that would be carried out to convert a type D floating point number to type F without using CVTDF. (The result should be rounded.)

18. Show (in hex representation) a double-precision floating point number that would cause overflow if used as the first operand of CVTDF.

19. Write a procedure CVTDF to do the task described in Exercise 17. The procedure should set the condition codes in the calling program's PSW (in the call frame on the stack) in the same ways as the CVTDF instruction does.

20. Outline the steps that would be carried out to convert a longword integer to floating point (type F) without using CVTLF.

21. Write a procedure CVTLF to do the task described in Exercise 20. The procedure should set the condition codes in the calling program's PSW (in the call frame on the stack) the same way the CVTLF instruction does.

22. Modify the procedure CVTFL in Fig. 13.8 so that it returns a rounded result rather than a truncated one; i.e., it should act like CVTRFL rather than CVTFL.

23. Outline the steps you would use to convert a floating point number to a character string in the following format:

$$.b_1b_2b_3 \ldots b_{22}b_{23}b_{24} \times 2^{\wedge}p$$

where $b_1, \ldots, b_{24}$ are the fraction bits and p is the exponent. Write a procedure that does the conversion. (Of course, there are other formats for the output that would be more natural and more compact, but more work is required to get them. You may want to choose other output formats and write procedures for them.)

24. Show the representation of the decimal number 112,485 in each of the following data types: longword, F_floating, G_floating, leading separate numeric, and packed decimal.

25. Why is it that packed decimal operands can not be specified as immediate operands? (The reason has something to do with the way the operand specifier is treated at execution time.)

26. Write a macro definition for a macro TSTP that acts as a test instruction for packed decimal data. It should have two arguments, NUM_DGTS and PKD, and should set or clear the N and Z condition codes to indicate if the specified decimal string is negative or zero. (If your macro explicitly tests the sign and digits of the decimal string, it will get quite complicated. There is a very short solution.)

27. Write a complete program to read in two numbers from the terminal, convert them to packed decimal, multiply them, and print out the result.

Chapter 14

Character Strings

14.1 OVERVIEW

The VAX has a powerful collection of character string instructions that are useful for, among other things, processing input data and preparing data for output. Some of the instructions are especially helpful for text editing and similar applications where the data operated on are long segments of text. In addition to the MOVC3 and CMPC3 instructions that we have already seen, there are more complex move and compare instructions and instructions to search a string for particular characters or substrings, translate characters, and edit numeric data for output. All these operations could be programmed using other instructions; but having one instruction that performs a complex task simplifies the programmer's job, reduces the likelihood of errors, and makes programs run faster.

A character string is a contiguous string of characters; e.g.,

/CHAPTER 14/

is a character string enclosed between delimiters (the slashes). In the context of character string operations, however, we would define a character string to be a string of character codes (ASCII codes on the VAX) occupying contiguous bytes of memory. (This might more properly be called a *representation* of a character string, but for simplicity of language we won't do so.) For example:

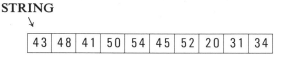

STRING

| 43 | 48 | 41 | 50 | 54 | 45 | 52 | 20 | 31 | 34 |

For the purposes of the character string instructions, this definition is more restrictive than need be. The instructions act on any string of bytes in memory; the bytes may contain any eight-bit patterns, even ones that are not used as ASCII codes. However, the instructions are used most often on bytes that contain character codes.

A character string is specified in an instruction by its length, or number of bytes, and the address of its first byte. (The string can not be in a register or specified as an immediate operand.) In all the character string instructions, the length is a word operand.

As with other string data types on the VAX (e.g., packed decimal and leading separate numeric), what we would naturally consider the first, or leftmost, byte occupies the lowest-addressed byte of the string in memory, and the rest of the characters follow in natural order. Hence, in our diagrams of character strings in memory, we usually show the lowest-addressed byte at the left.

Because the operations carried out by the character string instructions require processing many bytes of operands of varying lengths, the CPU uses some registers for scratch work (for pointers and counters) just as the programmer would if he or she were writing loops to carry out the operations. In many cases the data left in the registers when execution of the instruction is completed are very useful to the programmer. For example, for the instruction, LOCC, that searches a character string for the first instance of a specified character, the CPU uses R1 as a pointer to the byte currently being examined. When the instruction terminates, R1 will contain the address of the byte containing the character sought (if it appears in the string at all). The particular registers used and the data left in them vary with the different instructions, so we provide the details when we present each instruction.

14.2 THE MOVC AND CMPC INSTRUCTIONS

We have already seen and used the MOVC3 and CMPC3 instructions:

> MOVC3   *len,source,dest*
> CMPC3   *len,string1,string2*

MOVC3 copies the string beginning at *source* to the bytes beginning at *dest;* CMPC3 compares the strings beginning at *string1* and *string2*. There is only one length operand because the strings are assumed to be the same length. Both instructions have a variation that allows for strings of different lengths. They are

> MOVC5   *srclen,source,fill,dstlen,dest*
> CMPC5   *len1,string1,fill,len2,string2*

The third operand is a fill character that is used to pad out the shorter string when necessary. All the length operands are word integers, as they are for MOVC3 and CMPC3.

MOVC5—Copy a Character String

For the MOVC5 instruction, if the source length is less than the destination length, the remaining bytes at the end of the destination string are filled with the fill character; if the source length is larger than the destination length, the extra characters at the end of the source string are not copied. Figure 14.1 illustrates these cases. Of course, if the lengths are equal, the source is copied to the destination as it would be by MOVC3.

EXAMPLE 14.1: Copying Character Strings

Suppose BUFFER is an area in memory where we are constructing a line to be printed as part of a table with several columns, each 20 spaces wide. R8 contains the address of the character string that is to appear on the current line in the third column of the table, and R9 contains its length. The item on the previous line may have been longer than the current one, so if we simply moved the new string into the buffer, extraneous characters could appear in the output. The following instruction moves the current string into the buffer and blanks out the extra spaces in the column.

```
MOVC5   R9,(R8),#^A/ /,#20,BUFFER+40
```

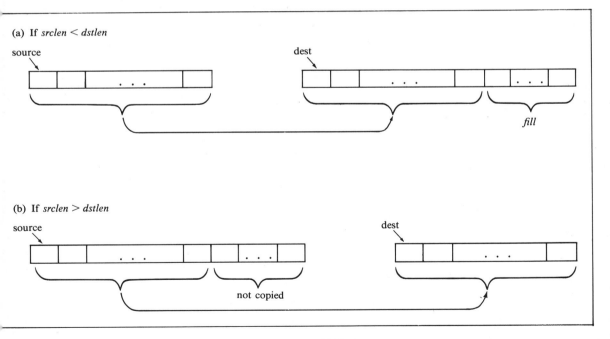

Figure 14.1   What MOVC5 does

EXAMPLE 14.2: Filling a Line with a Character

If the source length in a MOVC5 instruction is zero, the destination string is filled with copies of the fill character. The following instruction creates a line of asterisks in memory beginning at LINE.

```
MOVC5   #0,0,#^A/*/,#80,LINE
```

Note that since the source string has length zero and is not accessed by the CPU, its address can be somewhat arbitrary; we used 0 for simplicity.

The MOVC5 instruction sets the condition codes to indicate the relation between the source length and destination length. Thus, for example, a MOVC5 instruction can be followed by

```
BGTR    TRUNC
```

to take any special action that might be needed if the destination received a truncated copy of the source string. MOVC5, like MOVC3, uses R0–R5. It leaves the following data in these registers:

R0:	the number of bytes in the source string that were not copied to the destination
R1:	the address of the byte following the last one copied
R2:	0
R3:	the address of the byte following the destination string
R4, R5:	0

MOVC5 will work properly even if the source and destination overlap.

EXAMPLE 14.3

Suppose, as in Example 14.1, we move character strings into a buffer to be printed as part of a table, but if a string is too long for its column, we wish to print the rest of it on the next line. If no entries on a line are too long, the line of the table will be followed by a blank line. We assume that no entry needs more than 40 spaces and that BUF2 is available to set up the extra line.

```
        MOVC5   #0,0,#^A/ /,#80,BUF2           ; Blank out BUF2
COL_1:    .
          .
COL_2:    .
          .
          .
COL_3:  MOVC5   R9,(R8),#^A/ /,#20,BUFFER+40   ; Copy string to colm
        BLEQ    COL_4                          ; Branch if item fits
        MOVC5   R0,(R1),#^A/ /,#20,BUF2+40     ; Copy extra bytes
COL_4:    .
          .
          .

        PRINTCHRS BUFFER,#80                   ; Print table line
        PRINTCHRS BUF2,#80                     ; Print extra line
```

Note that if the BLEQ instruction had been omitted, the instruction sequence would still have worked properly; if the item copied by the first MOVC5 instruction were no longer than 20 bytes, R0 would contain 0, so the second MOVC5 instruction would move 20 blanks to BUF2+40.

CMPC5—Compare Character Strings

If the lengths of the strings compared by the CMPC5 instruction are different, the CPU treats the strings as if the shorter one had been padded at the end with copies of the fill character to make it the same length as the longer one. (No changes are actually made to the strings in memory.) CMPC5, like CMPC3, compares the strings byte by byte and stops when the bytes compared are not equal or when the ends of the strings are reached. The condition codes indicate the relation between the last bytes compared; that is, N = 1 if and only if the *string1* byte is less than the *string2* byte (as two's complement integers), Z = 1 if and only if they are equal (i.e., the ends of the strings were reached without encountering bytes that differed), and C = 1 if and only if the *string1* byte is less than the *string2* byte as unsigned integers. (V is cleared.)

CMPC3 and CMPC5 use R0–R3. After either instruction is executed, the contents of these registers will be as follows:

R0: the number of bytes remaining in *string1* (counting the one that terminated the comparison if the strings were unequal, but not counting fill bytes, if any)

R1: the address of the byte in *string1* where the comparison stopped; i.e., the address of the first byte in *string1* that did not match the corresponding byte of *string2*, if there is such a byte, otherwise the address of the byte following the end of *string1*

R2: same as R0, but for *string2*

R3: same as R1, but for *string2*

EXAMPLE 14.4: CMPC5

Suppose R5 contains xxxx0012 and R7 contains xxxx0007 (where the x's indicate data in the registers that are not used), and the bytes of memory beginning at STRING1 and STRING2 are as follows:

When the instruction

```
CMPC5   R5,STRING1,#^A/ /,R7,STRING2
```

is executed, STRING2 will be padded (conceptually) with 11 blanks. The comparison will terminate at the ninth byte, where 62_{16}, the ASCII code for "b" in STRING1, will be compared to 20_{16}, the second padded blank added to STRING2. All four condition codes will be cleared because $62 > 20$, and the contents of R0–R3 will be as follows:

R0:   0000000A   (the number of bytes remaining in STRING1)
R1:   STRING1+8   (the address of the "b")
R2:   00000000   (No bytes remain in STRING2.)
R3:   STRING2+7   (not STRING2+8)

14.3   CHARACTER-SEARCH INSTRUCTIONS

The VAX has five character-search instructions. There are instructions that search for, or skip over, a specified character or any characters in a specified set, and an instruction that searches for a specified substring.

LOCC and SKPC—Find or Skip a Specified Character

The LOCC (LOCate Character) instruction scans a character string for the first instance of a specified character; SKPC (SKiP Character) scans a character string for the first instance of a character *other than* the one specified. The instruction formats are

LOCC   *char,len,string*
SKPC   *char,len,string*

The "result" we would want from these operations is the address of the byte at which the search terminates, but there is no destination operand for this result. LOCC and SKPC use R0 and R1 for a counter and pointer, respectively, while searching the string. The values they leave in these registers and the condition codes when they finish executing are:

R0:   the number of bytes remaining in the string, including the character that was sought, if it was found

R1:   the address of the byte sought, or, if none was found, the address of the byte following the end of the string

Z: cleared if a byte of the desired kind is found, set otherwise

The other condition codes are cleared.

Thus instructions that follow LOCC or SKPC can use R1 as a pointer to the byte sought (after testing Z to make sure one was found). R0 and R1 can be used particularly easily to restart the search in applications where each instance of the character sought, or each segment separated by two of them, must be processed in some way. The next example illustrates this. To focus on the use of R0 and R1, the example does a very simple task of processing the segments: counting them.

EXAMPLE 14.5: Searching for a Character

Suppose a string of text consisting of several substrings separated by slashes is in memory beginning at TEXT, and suppose LEN is a word containing the length of the string. For example, the text might be

```
/October 3/7:30 P.M./AGENDA/
```

The following instructions count the substrings.

```
; REGISTER USE:    R0        length of remaining string
;                  R1        address of remaining string
;                  R5        counter
;
        CLRL       R5                  ; Counter is 0
        MOVAB      TEXT+1,R1           ; Byte after 1st slash
        MOVW       LEN,R0              ; Length of string
;
MSGS:   DECL       R0                  ; Don't count 1st slash
        LOCC       #^A'/',R0,1(R1)     ; Scan for next slash
        BEQL       DONE                ; Branch if no slash
        INCL       R5                  ; Count substring
        BRB        MSGS
DONE:
```

Care must be taken to get the lengths and addresses right to begin each search at the byte after the slash just found, so that the same one won't be found again.

If the processing of each character or segment found using LOCC involves printing or copying the strings, or any other operations that change the contents of R0 and R1 as side effects, then the contents of R0 and R1 must be saved in other registers so that the address and length of the remaining segment of the source are not lost. (The same problem occurs with the other character instructions.)

The SKPC instruction is especially useful for skipping over blanks and finding meaningful, nonblank data in a character string. LOCC and SKPC can be used together very effectively to process free format numerical input. The next example shows how.

EXAMPLE 14.6: Processing Free Format Input

The procedure CVTCL shown in Fig. 14.2 finds the first leading separate numeric string in a character string and converts it to two's complement. It assumes that the character string contains zero or more leading separate numeric strings separated by at least one blank. SKPC is used to skip over blanks and find the beginning of the first lsn string; then LOCC finds a blank at the end of it. CVTCL returns the address of the byte that follows the lsn datum and the length of the remaining part of the character string so that it can be called repeatedly to process each number in the string.

```
        .PSECT  CVTCL
;
;  PROCEDURE CVTCL (STRING, LENGTH, NUMBER, NEXT, NEWLEN)
;
;  This procedure searches a character string for the first
;  instance of a leading separate numeric datum, converts it to
;  a two's complement longword, and returns the address of the
;  next byte of the string and the remaining length. The
;  procedure assumes that the leading separate numeric data in
;  the string are separated by blanks.
;
;  INPUT ARGUMENTS
;
;        STRING   the character string
;        LENGTH   the number of bytes in the string (word)
;
;  OUTPUT ARGUMENTS
;
;        NUMBER   the two's complement representation of the
;                 first number found in the string (longword)
;        NEXT     the address of the byte in the string following
;                 the leading separate numeric string that was
;                 found and converted. (The argument list contains
;                 the address of a longword where this address is
;                 to be stored.)
;        NEWLEN   the number of bytes remaining in the string
;                 (word)
;
;  R0 is used to return a flag to indicate if a number was found
;  in the string. 1 = success; 0 = failure.
;  In the case of failure, no values are stored for the three
;  output arguments.
;
;  No error checking is done for bad characters or too many digits.
;
;  METHOD
;
;     A leading separate numeric string consists of a byte
;  containing a sign (which may be blank) followed by bytes
;  containing digits (all in character code). The conversion
;  instruction requires the address of the string (i.e., its
;  sign byte) and the number of digits.
;     SKPC is used to skip over all leading blanks. It stops at
;  the first non-blank, which may be a sign or the first digit in
;  the case where the sign is a blank. In the latter case, the
;  pointer is decremented by 1. Then LOCC is used to find the
;  blank that follows the leading separate numeric string. Whether
;  a blank is found or the end of the entire character string is
;  reached, R1 will contain the address of the byte following the
;  lsn string.

PKD:    .BLKB  16
```

Figure 14.2   The CVTCL procedure

```
;
; OFFSETS FOR ARGUMENT LIST
;
STRING = 4
LENGTH = 8
NUMBER = 12
NEXT = 16
NEWLEN = 20
;
; REGISTER USE:        R2-R3    used by CVTSP and CVTPL
;                      R5       length of string
;                      R6       address of lsn
;                      R7       number of digits in lsn
;
        .ENTRY  CVTCL,^M<R2,R3,R5,R6,R7>
;
; Find beginning of lsn
;
        MOVW    @LENGTH(AP),R5              ; Get length of string
        BLEQ    NONE                       ; No lsn if len <= 0
        SKPC    #^A/ /,R5,@STRING(AP)      ; Scan for non-blank
        BEQL    NONE                       ; No lsn if all blank
        MOVL    R1,R6                      ; Addr of first non-blank
        CMPB    (R6),#^X30                 ; See if digit
        BLSS    LSN                        ; Branch if non-digit
        DECL    R6                         ; Back up to sign (blank)
;
; Find end of lsn
;
LSN:    LOCC    #^A/ /,R0,(R1)             ; Scan for blank
        MOVL    R1,@NEXT(AP)               ; Store addr of next byte
        MOVL    R0,@NEWLEN(AP)             ; Store remaining length
        SUBL3   R6,R1,R7                   ; Number of bytes in lsn
        DECL    R7                         ; Number of digits
;
; Convert
;
        CVTSP   R7,(R6),R7,PKD
        CVTPL   R7,PKD,@NUMBER(AP)         ; Store 2's comp
;
; Set flag and return
;
        MOVL    #1,R0                      ; Success
        RET                                ; Return
;
NONE:   CLRL    R0                         ; Failure
        RET                                ; Return
        .END
```

Figure 14.2 (Continued)

344

Character Strings / Ch. 14

SCANC and SPANC—Searching for Sets of Characters

SCANC (SCAN Characters) searches a string for any one of a set of characters. SPANC (SPAN Characters) searches for any character not in the specified set. (Clearly, SPANC could be considered superfluous because one could specify the complementary set of characters and use SCANC. Having SPANC just makes things a bit simpler for the programmer.) There are several applications where we want to find any one of a special group of characters. A compiler, for example, may search a program statement for any operator or delimiter. We may want to count the vowels used in a long piece of text. When processing input containing numeric data, SPANC could be used to scan for bad characters—say, anything other than digits, blanks, and signs.

The instruction formats are

SCANC   *len,string,table,mask*
SPANC   *len,string,table,mask*

The table and mask are used to determine which characters are sought. The table is usually 256 bytes long. The contents of a byte, when treated as an unsigned integer, is between 0 and 255. SCANC and SPANC use the contents of each byte

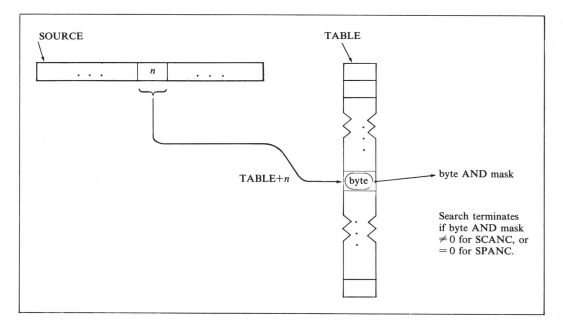

Figure 14.3   Accessing the table in SCANC and SPANC

in the string as an index into the table; that is, if the byte in the string contains the number *n*, then the byte at the table address $+$ *n* is examined to determine if the string byte is in the set desired. A simple way of distinguishing characters not wanted from those that are sought would be to put zero and nonzero entries in the appropriate places in the table. Some large machines have an instruction similar to SCANC that simply scans the string until it reaches a byte whose table entry is nonzero. The VAX instructions are more flexible. A logical AND operation is performed on the table byte and the mask operand specified in the instruction. If the result is nonzero for SCANC, or zero for SPANC, the instruction stops at the current byte. (See Fig. 14.3 for an illustration.) The use of the mask means that one table can be set up to be used with several SCANC and SPANC instructions to search for different sets of characters at different times.

EXAMPLE 14.7: A Table for SCANC and SPANC

One of the tasks done by a compiler, *lexical analysis,* includes finding and extracting the separate items, called *tokens,* that make up a statement. Some examples of tokens are: variable names, operators, and constants. Some of the kinds of entries that we might want to have in a table to be used to extract tokens are:

Character Group	*Table Entry (In Binary)*
Arithmetic operator	00000001
Relational operator	00000010
Statement terminator (e.g., blank or ;)	00000100
Letters (except E)	00010000
E	00110000
Digits	01100000

We are not trying to be complete here and we are ignoring many of the special cases a compiler must handle. The main point is to illustrate how the table entries and the mask can be chosen for flexibility in specifying different sets of characters. Consider the following examples.

If we wish to search for the first arithmetic operator, we could use SCANC with the mask ^X01. We would find the first character of a variable name by scanning for a letter with the mask ^X10. We could find the end of it using SPANC with the mask ^X70 to skip over letters and digits.

Why are two bits set in the entry for digits, and why did we make the entry for E a special case? E could appear as a letter, hence bit 4 is on, but it can also appear in a floating point constant to indicate an exponent. Thus we might want to include E with digits sometimes by using the mask ^X20. The mask ^X40 will distinguish digits from E.

The table could be set up at assembly time as shown below. For simplicity we will fill all bytes in the table not mentioned above with zeros. See the table of ASCII codes in Appendix C to check that the entries are in the right places.

```
TABLE:  .BYTE   0[32]                          ; ASCII special chars
        .BYTE   4,0[9]                         ; Blank & special chars
        .BYTE   1,1,0,1,0,1                    ; * + ' - . /
        .BYTE   ^X60[10]                       ; Digits
        .BYTE   0,4,2,2,2,0,0                  ; : ; < = > ? @
        .BYTE   ^X10[4],^X30,^X10[21]          ; Letters
        .BYTE   0[6]                           ; Miscellaneous
        .BYTE   ^X10[26]                       ; Lower case letters
        .BYTE   0[133]                         ; Misc. and non-ASCII
```

Note that if we were certain that all bytes in the source string contain valid ASCII codes, we could make the table only 128 bytes long, because TABLE+128 through TABLE+255 would not be accessed.

When the SCANC or SPANC instruction finds a byte of the type sought or reaches the end of the string, the following data are left in R0–R3 and the condition codes:

R0:   the number of bytes remaining in the string, including the one that terminated the search if the search terminated because of a table entry

R1:   the address of the byte in the string whose table entry terminated the search, if any; otherwise the address of the byte following the string

R2:   0

R3:   the address of the table

Z: cleared if the search was terminated by a table entry; set otherwise

The other condition codes are cleared.

R0 and R1 may be used as after LOCC and SKPC to process the character found, the segment that precedes it, and the remainder of the string as desired.

MATCHC—Match a Character String

The MATCHC instruction searches for the first instance of a specified substring, rather than a single character, in a character string. The operation it does is sometimes called pattern matching, and the substring sought is called the *pattern* or *object string*. This is an especially powerful instruction that is very useful in text-editing applications. The instruction format is

MATCHC   *patrn_len,pattern,str_len,string*

MATCHC uses R0–R3 and provides information about the results of its search to the program in these registers and the Z condition code as follows:

R0:   0 if a match was found, otherwise the length of the pattern

R1: the address of the byte following the pattern if a match was found, otherwise the address of the pattern

R2: the number of bytes in the string that follow the first instance of the pattern, if any, otherwise 0

R3: the address of the byte following the end of the first instance of the pattern in the string, if any, otherwise the address of the byte following the string

Z: set if a match was found, otherwise cleared

The other condition codes are cleared.

R2 and R3 (and Z) contain the information that is most useful. Subtracting the pattern length from the address in R3 gives the address of the byte where the pattern begins in the string. Note that for the other four instructions described in this section Z is cleared if the search is successful, but for MATCHC, Z is set if the search is successful.

EXAMPLE 14.8: The Effects of MATCHC

Suppose R6 contains xxxx0023, R7 contains xxxx0005, and we have the following strings in memory.

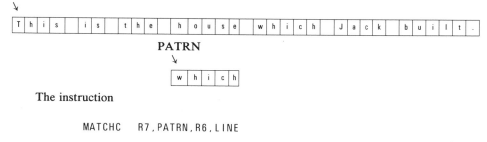

The instruction

```
MATCHC   R7,PATRN,R6,LINE
```

will leave the following data in Z and R0–R3:

Z: 1   (There was a match.)
R0: 00000000   (There was a match.)
R1: PATRN+5   (the address of the byte after the pattern)
R2: 0000000C   (the number of bytes in the string following the match)
R3: LINE+23   (the address of the blank after "which")

EXAMPLE 14.9: Deleting a Substring

The procedure DELETE shown in Fig. 14.4 finds a specified substring in a string and deletes it by moving up all the characters that follow the matched substring. Note that

```
          .PSECT  DELETE
;
; PROCEDURE DELETE (STRING, STR_LEN, PATTERN, PAT_LEN)
;
; This procedure finds the first instance of a pattern in a
; character string and deletes it. The Z condition code in
; the stacked PSW is set if the pattern was found in the
; string and deleted.
;
; INPUT ARGUMENTS
;
;       STRING      a character string
;       STR_LEN     the length of the string (word)
;       PATTERN     a character string to be deleted from STRING
;       PAT_LEN     the length of PATTERN (word)
;
; OUTPUT ARGUMENTS
;
;       STR_LEN     is changed to the new string length after
;                   deleting the pattern.
;
; OFFSETS FOR ARGUMENT LIST
;
STRING = 4
STR_LEN = 8
PATTERN = 12
PAT_LEN = 16
;
; REGISTER USE        R2      length of string segment that
;                             follows pattern
;                     R3      addr of byte after pattern in
;                             string
;                     R4-R5   used by MOVC3
;                     R6      length of string (word)
;                     R7      length of pattern (longword,
;                             used in address computation)
;                     R8      address where pattern starts
;                             in string
;
         .ENTRY  DELETE,^M<R2,R3,R4,R5,R6,R7,R8>
;
         MOVW    @STR_LEN(AP),R6         ; String length
         CVTWL   @PAT_LEN(AP),R7         ; Pattern length
         MATCHC  R7,@PATTERN(AP),R6,@STRING(AP)  ; Find pattern in string
         BNEQ    RETURN                  ; Return if no match
         SUBL3   R7,R3,R8                ; Start of pattern in string
         MOVC3   R2,(R3),(R8)            ; Move up end segment
         SUBW3   R7,R6,@STR_LEN(AP)      ; New string length
         BISB2   #^X04,4(FP)             ; Success flag in Z bit
RETURN:  RET
         .END
```

Figure 14.4 **The procedure DELETE**

the data left in R2 and R3 by the MATCHC instruction are used as operands in the MOVC3 instruction. Also note that although the length operands are words, the pattern length was converted to a longword because it is used in the computation of an address (that of the copy of the pattern in the string).

In Chapter 7 we considered the problem of searching for a particular item in a table. We discussed two algorithms for solving the search problem: sequential search and binary search (which requires that the table be sorted). The operation of the MATCHC instruction is comparable to a sequential search. It (like the other character-string instructions) can be used even if some bytes in the operands do not contain ASCII codes. The next example illustrates the use of MATCHC to find an integer datum, and it illustrates a potential hazard of using MATCHC for this purpose.

EXAMPLE 14.10: Using MATCHC with Noncharacter Data

Suppose a table beginning at TABLE contains 100 entries with 20 bytes each. Each entry begins with a key that is a word integer. We want to find the address of the entry whose key matches the one in KEY. The following instructions could be used:

```
MATCHC  #2,KEY,#2000,TABLE    ; Search for key
BNEQ    NOT_FOUND             ; Branch if no match
SUBL2   #2,R3                 ; Address of entry
```

But will this always work? The problem is that the bytes of the key might happen to match two bytes in some other part of one of the records. Suppose, for example, that each table entry consists of the key, a longword integer, and a 14-byte character string and that we are searching for the entry whose key is 2074_{16}. The segment of the table below shows some of the places where 2074 could be detected—incorrectly in all but the last case. (Because the table contains integer data, the lowest-addressed byte of each entry is shown at the right. The key, or pattern, sought contains 74 in the first byte and 20 in the second byte.)

Characters	Long	Key	first
xxxxxxxxxxxxxxxxxxxxxxxxx	xxxxx20	74xx	← byte
74xxxxxxxxxxxxxxxxxxxxxxx	xx2074xx	xxxx	
xxxxxxxxxxxxxxxxxxxxxxxx20	74xxxxxx	xx20	
xxxxxxxx2074xxxxxxxxxxxxx	xxxxxxxx	xxxx	
xxxxxxxxxxxxxxxxxxxxxxxxx	xxxxxxxx	2074	
xxxxxxxxxxxxxxxxxxxxxxxxx	xxxxxxxx	2074	

To correctly find an entry whose key is 2074, we could test the address in R3 after the last instruction shown above to see if its distance from TABLE was a multiple of the entry size. The MATCHC instruction and the test would be in a loop, so that another scan could begin at the byte following the end of each incorrect instance of the key found. We leave the details to the reader.

14.4 TRANSLATING CHARACTER STRINGS: THE MOVTC AND MOVTUC INSTRUCTIONS

MOVTC—Translating a Character String

The MOVTC (MOVe Translated Characters) instruction translates a string of bytes under the control of a translation table specified as one of the operands of the instruction. It can be used to convert a character string from some other character code (e.g., EBCDIC, another very widely used character code) to ASCII, or vice versa, to change all the lower-case letters to upper case, to change certain special characters, to extract and patch together subfields of a segment of data, and to scramble letters in messages to create cryptograms.

The format of the instruction is

MOVTC   *srclen,source,fill,table,dstlen,dest*

The translation table is usually 256 bytes long and is accessed in the same manner as the table used by a SCANC or SPANC instruction. That is, the contents of each byte in the string is treated as an unsigned binary integer (between 0 and 255) and is used as an index into the table to find the value that is to be substituted for that byte. In other words, a byte containing the number n is translated to the number in the byte whose address is the table address $+ n$. See Fig. 14.5 for an illustration.

As with MOVC5, the fill character is used to pad out the end of the destination if the source length is less than the destination length. If the source is longer than the destination, the extra bytes of the source are simply not translated. The source and destination may overlap (and in many applications where the string being translated is very long, they would occupy the same space). The destination must not overlap the translation table. The condition codes are set to indicate the relation

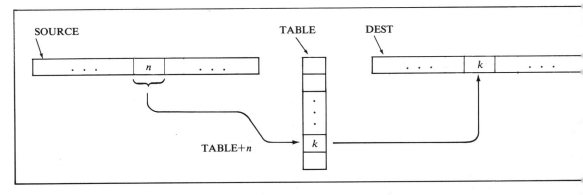

Figure 14.5 Translating a character string

between the source length and destination length. MOVTC uses R0–R5 and leaves the following data in them:

R0:   the number of untranslated bytes remaining in the source string

R1:   the address of the byte following the last translated byte of the source string

R2, R4:   0

R3:   the address of the translation table

R5:   the address of the byte following the end of the destination string

EXAMPLE 14.11: Translating Lower-Case to Upper-Case

Suppose we wish to translate all lower-case letters in a long segment of text to upper-case. Most characters will not be changed. For all entries in the translation table, say TABLE, other than those that correspond to lower-case letters, the contents of TABLE + n will be n. The ASCII codes for lower-case letters are $97–122_{10}$, so TABLE+97 through TABLE+122 are initialized to contain the ASCII codes for the upper-case letters.

```
TABLE:  .BYTE   0,1,2,3,4,5,6,7,8,9,10,11,12,13,14,15,16,17,18,19,20
        .BYTE   21,22,23,24,25,26,27,28,29,30,31,32,33,34,35,36,37,38,39,40
        .BYTE   41,42,43,44,45,46,47,48,49,50,51,52,53,54,55,56,57,58,59,60
        .BYTE   61,62,63,64,65,66,67,68,69,70,71,72,73,74,75,76,77,78,79,80
        .BYTE   81,82,83,84,85,86,87,88,89,90,91,92,93,94,95,96
        .ASCII  /ABCDEFGHIJKLMNOPQRSTUVWXYZ/
        .BYTE   123,124,125,126,127
```

Note that we assumed all bytes in the text contain valid ASCII codes, so we made the table only 128 bytes long.

Suppose the string of text to be translated begins at TEXT and its length is in R8. The following instruction does an "in-place" translation.

```
MOVTC   R8,TEXT,#0,TABLE,R8,TEXT
```

(The fill character would not be used.)

The entries in the translation table in Example 14.11 are in such a simple order that it seems unnecessarily tedious to type out all the numbers as we did in the .BYTE directives. It would be very easy to set up the table in a few simple loops at execution time, but it is inefficient to do work at execution time that can be done at assembly time. The .REPEAT directive described in Chapter 11 can be used outside of macros; it is used in the next example.

A translation table would be constructed at execution time if it depended on execution-time data or computations. A program to generate cryptograms using different permutations of the letters, for example, might generate the permutations with a random number generator and fill the table at execution time.

EXAMPLE 14.12: Setting Up a Table with .REPEAT

The following statements set up the same table as in Example 14.11.

```
TABLE:  .BYTE    0                       ; First table byte
        CODE = 1
        .REPEAT  96                      ; For CODE = 1 to 96
        .BYTE    CODE                    ;     put CODE in TABLE+CODE
        CODE = CODE+1
        .ENDR
        .ASCII   /ABCDEFGHIJKLMNOPQRSTUVWXYZ/
        CODE = 123
        .REPEAT  5                       ; For CODE = 123 to 127
        .BYTE    CODE                    ;     put CODE in TABLE+CODE
        CODE = CODE+1
        .ENDR
```

The MOVTC instruction can be used for purposes other than translation. The next example illustrates one such use.

EXAMPLE 14.13: Extracting Pieces from Records

Suppose we have a collection of records, each say 200 bytes long and each containing a large number of fields. For each record we want to extract the data from several fields and form one string from the pieces extracted. We can do this with the MOVTC instruction with each record playing the role of the translation table. The "string" to be translated is a template containing the position numbers of the bytes to be extracted from the record. The following instructions show how to extract the 18th, third, and 30th five-byte segments, in that order, assuming the address of each record to be processed will be put in R9.

```
TEMPLATE: .BYTE   90,91,92,93,94,15,16,17,18,19,150,151,152,153,154
EXCERPT:  .BLKB   15
            .
            .
            .
          MOVTC   #15,TEMPLATE,#0,(R9),#15,EXCERPT
```

MOVTUC—Translating with an "Escape"

The MOVTUC (MOVe Translated characters Until escape Character found) instruction translates a string of characters Until escape Character found) instruction translates a string of characters using a translation table, as does MOVTC, but it also acts as a character-search instruction. One of its operands is called the "escape" character; MOVTUC will stop translating the source string if it reaches a character in the source that would be translated to the escape character. The format of the MOVTUC instruction is

MOVTUC   *srclen,source,escape,table,dstlen,dest*

The translation proceeds as illustrated in Fig. 14.5 until the translation of a byte encountered in the source is the escape character, or the end of either the source or destination is reached. If the translation completes without an escape and the destination is longer than the source, the extra bytes in the destination are unchanged because there is no fill character operand. The program can determine whether there was an escape and, if so, where it occurred by using the information left in R0–R5 and the values of the condition codes. The registers and condition codes will contain:

R0:   the number of bytes remaining in the source string, including the one that caused the escape if one occurred

R1:   the address of the byte in the source that caused termination of the instruction, either by translating to the escape character or by being beyond the length of the destination string, if termination occurs before the entire source string is translated; otherwise the address of the byte that follows the source string

R2:   0

R3:   the address of the table

R4:   the number of bytes remaining in the destination string, including the one that would have received the escape character, if any

R5:   the address of the first byte of the destination string that did not receive a translated source byte, if any, either because escape occurred or because the source is shorter than the destination; otherwise the address of the byte that follows the destination string

V: set if the instruction was terminated by an escape, otherwise cleared

N, Z, C: indicate the relation between the source and destination lengths

Warning: The effects of MOVTUC are unpredictable if the destination string overlaps the source string or the translation table.

EXAMPLE 14.14: *Translating and Separating Lines*

Suppose BLOCK is the address of a large block of data in EBCDIC consisting of many lines, each terminated by a carriage return character (code 13 in EBCDIC as well as ASCII). We want to translate the characters to ASCII and process the lines one at a time. In a realistic application the processing of the lines would probably include writing them out to a new disk file, but for simplicity in this example the processing will consist of just printing the line. (Only the first 85 characters will be printed if the line is longer.) We assume the length of the entire block of data is in the word BLK_SZ, and the maximum line size in the input block is 150.

The table is constructed so that the entry in TABLE + n is the ASCII code for the character whose EBCDIC code is n. For example, the EBCDIC codes for the digits are 240–249, so the bytes at TABLE+240 through TABLE+249 contain 48 through 57, the ASCII digit codes. (Some EBCDIC codes have no ASCII translation, and some are not used; the table entries for these are zero.) The escape character is the carriage return.

```
CR = 13                                           ; Carriage return
MAX_SZ = 150                                      ; Maximum input line size
TABLE:  .BYTE   0,1,2,3,0,9,0,0,0,0,0,11,12,13,14,15,16,17,18,0,0
        .BYTE   0,8,0,24,25,0,0,0,29,0,31,0,0,28,0,0,10,23,27,0
        .BYTE   0,0,0,0,5,6,7,0,0,0,22,0,0,30,0,0,0,0,0,20
        .BYTE   21,0,26,32,0[9],0,46,60,40,43,0,38,0[9]
        .BYTE   33,36,42,41,59,0,45,47,0[9],44,37,95,62,63,0[9],96
        .BYTE   58,35,64,39,61,34,0,97,98,99,100,101,102,103,104,105
        .BYTE   0[7],106,107,108,109,110,111,112,113,114,0[7]
        .BYTE   126,115,116,117,118,119,120,121,122,0[22],123
        .BYTE   65,66,67,68,69,70,71,72,73,0[6],125
        .BYTE   74,75,76,77,78,79,80,81,82,0[6],92,0
        .BYTE   83,84,85,86,87,88,89,90,0[6]
        .BYTE   48,49,50,51,52,53,54,55,56,57,124,0[5]
LINE:   .BLKB   MAX_SZ
          .
          .
          .
; REGISTER USE:     R0,R10  length of remaining source
;                   R1      address of carriage return in source
;                   R4      number of unused bytes in dest
;                   R6      length of line to be printed
;                   R11     address of remaining source
;
        MOVAB   BLOCK,R11                         ; Addr of source string
        MOVW    BLK_SZ,R10                        ; Length of source
;
NEXT:   MOVTUC  R10,(R11),#CR,TABLE,#MAX_SZ,LINE  ; Translate a line
        BVC     END_OR_ERROR                      ; No CR found
        SUBW3   R4,#MAX_SZ,R6                     ; Compute line size
        SUBL3   #1,R0,R10                         ; Remaining source length
        ADDL3   #1,R1,R11                         ; Addr of remaining source
        PRINTCHRS LINE,R6                         ; Print line
        BRB     NEXT                              ; Get another line
END_OR_ERROR:
        TSTW    R10                               ; Any chars remaining?
        BNEQ    ERROR
END:    ⟨processing completed⟩
```

Note that R10 and R11 would not be needed and the instructions could be simplified somewhat if PRINTCHRS did not use R0 and R1.

14.5 THE EDIT INSTRUCTION

In Chapter 6 we showed how to convert two's complement data to character code for output using the CVTLP and CVTPS instructions. The result of the conversion is a leading separate numeric string—i.e., a sign followed by a certain number of digits (in character code). If the number converted has fewer significant digits than the number of digits specified in the CVTPS instruction, the first few digits of the result will be zeros. For example, if, say, R7 contains FFFFFEBC, the instructions

```
CVTLP   R7,#5,PKD
CVTPS   #5,PKD,#5,LSN
```

produce

where, in this and all other diagrams of memory contents in this section, the first, or lowest-addressed, byte is shown at the left. When LSN is printed, it appears as

$$-00308$$

For most applications, we would prefer that the output appear as

$$-308$$

Using instructions we have covered so far, we can test the string at LSN for zeros, replace them by blanks, and move the sign. This, and any other formatting we might wish to do, would be somewhat tedious and might require a lot of instructions.

Several large computers have an EDIT instruction whose purpose is to format numeric data for output. These instructions convert a packed decimal datum to a character string under the control of a pattern that specifies the format. They may be used by compilers to accomplish the formatting done with a Fortran FORMAT statement or a picture specification in PL/1 or COBOL, etc. Though the details vary with different machines, the tasks that may be accomplished by an EDIT instruction (or made easier for the programmer by it) usually include blank fill for leading zeros, insertion of a sign immediately in front of the first significant digit, and insertion of decimal points, currency symbols, and other special characters.

The VAX EDIT instruction is

EDITPC   num_dgts,pkd,pattern,dest

The first two operands describe the packed decimal datum to be edited. The pattern is a string of bytes in memory that contain "edit pattern operators"—a sequence of editing commands. Many of the operators cause one or more bytes (containing digits, a fill character, a sign, or a special character) to be stored in the next available byte or bytes of the destination. There is no length operand for the pattern in EDITPC; the end of the pattern is marked by a "pattern end" operator—a byte of zeros. There is no length operand specified for the destination because the pattern completely determines the length of the edited character string.

Warning: EDITPC uses R0–R5 for scratch work, destroying the original contents of those registers.

There are 16 different pattern operators, and some of them take operands. Before we describe the details of the operations performed by the operators and the encodings used to specify them in a pattern, we will consider some examples. The point of these examples is to provide motivation for the kinds of operators and features an EDIT instruction should have. We will use symbolic names for the operators. All the names begin with EO$ for Edit Operator. The names are actually system macros that initialize the bytes of the pattern, but for now we need consider them only as abstract names for the pattern operators.

EXAMPLE 14.15: A Simple Editing Pattern for Positive Integers

Suppose PKD contains the packed decimal representation of an integer that we know is positive and has five digits. We want to convert the integer to character code with leading zeros replaced by blanks. EDITPC processes source digits left to right. If the next digit in the packed datum is a zero and no nonzero digits have been encountered so far, we want the fill character (usually a blank) stored in the next byte of the destination. If the next digit is not zero (or is zero but some nonzero digits have already been encountered), the digit must be expanded to its ASCII character code and stored in the next byte of the destination. The EO$MOVE operator acts in this way. It requires an operand, called a repeat count, that tells how many digits it is to operate on. EO$END is the pattern end operator. Thus the pattern commands are

```
EO$MOVE 5
EO$END
```

If PKD contains, say,

```
                          00 70 2C
```

and the pattern is properly encoded in memory at PATRN, the instruction

```
     EDITPC #5,PKD,PATRN,STRING
```

would produce

```
                      20 20 37 30 32
```

beginning at STRING. The first two bytes contain the ASCII code for a blank.

The reader should determine why this pattern is not a good one to use if the integer being edited may be zero.

EXAMPLE 14.16: An Edit Pattern for Signed Integers

Again we assume that the integer to be edited has five digits, but now we make no assumptions about its sign; it may be negative, positive, or zero. The edit pattern described below blanks out leading zeros and puts the sign in front of the first significant digit. For the first four digits we use the EO$FLOAT operator. Like EO$MOVE, it replaces leading zeros with blanks, but it also "floats" the sign across these blanks. When it encounters a nonzero digit in the packed datum, it inserts the sign and the digit (expanded from four bits to the appropriate ASCII character codes) in the next two bytes of the destination. Any subsequent digits encountered by the EO$FLOAT operator will be expanded to character code and stored in the destination. The fifth digit should not be replaced by a blank even if it is a zero; if the integer being edited is zero, we want one zero digit to appear in the output. The EO$END_FLOAT operator sets a flag to indicate that subsequent digits should be treated as significant digits and not replaced by the fill character. It also stores the sign character in the destination if it was not already stored. The EO$MOVE operator stores the ASCII code for the last digit in the destination. Thus the edit pattern consists of the following commands:

```
EO$FLOAT     4
EO$END_FLOAT
EO$MOVE      1
EO$END
```

Note that six bytes must be reserved for the edited result: five for digits or fill and one for the sign, which is inserted by either EO$FLOAT or EO$END_FLOAT. Figure 14.6 shows the steps that would be carried out by the instruction

```
EDITPC  #5,PKD,PATRN,STRING
```

assuming that the edit pattern has been properly encoded in memory beginning at PATRN. The significance flag and the fill and sign characters referred to in the figure are described in more detail below.

The Significance Flag

Examples 14.15 and 14.16 suggest the need for a feature common to editing instructions: a significance flag. When the EO$MOVE and EO$FLOAT operators process a zero digit, they must be able to determine whether to store it in the destination or replace it with a fill character. When EO$FLOAT encounters a nonzero digit, it must be able to determine whether to store just the digit or to also store the sign. In each case, the first option should be chosen if any significant (i.e., nonzero) digits have been encountered so far. The VAX EDITPC instruction uses the C condition code bit as the significance flag. It is cleared when EDITPC begins execution and is automatically set by the EO$MOVE and EO$FLOAT operators when they encounter a nonzero digit. It is set, cleared, and used by several other operators.

The Fill and Sign Characters

As indicated in Examples 14.15 and 14.16, the default value for the fill character—the character that replaces leading zeros—is a blank. Similarly, the default values for the sign character are a blank for positive numbers and a minus sign for negative numbers (determined by the last nibble of the packed source datum). These defaults can be changed by pattern operators. EDITPC initializes a fill register and a sign register (actually, both are parts of R2) to contain the default values. Several operators

(a) Editing the packed datum 00 30 8D

	Fill =^X20 Sign =^X2D	
Operator	*Packed Source*	*Destination*
EO$FLOAT	00 30 8D	20
EO$FLOAT	00 30 8D	20 20
EO$FLOAT	00 30 8D	20 20 2D 33
		sign digit
		Significance flag set
EO$FLOAT	00 30 8D	20 20 2D 33 30
EO$END_FLOAT		No action since signif. flag already set.
EO$MOVE	00 30 8D	20 20 2D 33 30 38
EO$END		

(b) Editing the packed datum 00 00 4C

	Fill =^X20 Sign =^X20	
Operator	*Packed Source*	*Destination*
EO$FLOAT	00 00 4C	20
EO$FLOAT	00 00 4C	20 20
EO$FLOAT	00 00 4C	20 20 20
EO$FLOAT	00 00 4C	20 20 20 20
EO$END_FLOAT		20 20 20 20 20
		sign
		Significance flag set
EO$MOVE	00 00 4C	20 20 20 20 20 34
EO$END		

Figure 14.6 Editing steps for Example 14.16

allow the programmer to load other characters into these registers at any point during the editing. There will be examples below.

Encoding the Pattern Operators

The edit pattern is a string of bytes containing the edit pattern operators and, for some operators, their operands. There are three kinds of operands: repeat counts (used with EO$FLOAT and EO$MOVE in Examples 14.15 and 14.16), characters (alternate fill or sign characters or special characters to be inserted in the output), and lengths. For operators that take a repeat count—a number indicating how many times the operator is to be applied—the operator and the repeat count share a byte. The operator is in bits 7:4 and the repeat count in bits 3:0; thus repeat counts are in the range 1–15. Operators that take no operand or a character or length operand occupy one byte; the operand, if any, is in the next byte.

Table 14.1 lists (alphabetically) all the pattern operators and their encodings and describes the operations they perform. Each operator name is also the name of a system macro that generates the one- or two-byte encoding for the operator and its operand, if any. Although a pattern could be initialized in one line using the .BYTE directive and the encodings described in the table, the use of the names makes the pattern definitions more readable and will minimize errors.

The action and uses of many of the operators will be illustrated below in examples.

EXAMPLE 14.17: The Pattern Used in Example 14.16

Using Table 14.1, we can see that the pattern used by the EDITPC instruction in Example 14.16 should be

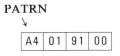

The pattern could be initialized in a program as follows:

```
PATRN:  EO$FLOAT      4
        EO$END_FLOAT
        EO$MOVE       1
        EO$END
```

Examples

As a guide for setting up patterns in the examples below, we will write out format diagrams of the result we want. The diagrams show how many digits there are, where special characters should go, whether or not a sign is included, where the significance flag must be turned on, etc. One of the advantages to using such a diagram

TABLE 14.1   Edit Pattern Operators

Operator	Code (hex)	Operand	Operation
EO$ADJUST_INPUT	47	length	Specifies number of source digits to use, overriding the num_dgts operand. Extra leading zeros in source are ignored or created, as needed.
EO$BLANK_ZERO	45	length	If source = 0, put fill in the last length bytes of the destination.
EO$CLEAR_SIGNIF	02		Clear significance flag.
EO$END	00		End of pattern.
EO$END_FLOAT	01		If significance flag is clear, set it and store sign in destination.
EO$FILL	80+r	repeat count	Store r copies of the fill char. in the destination.
EO$FLOAT	A0+r	repeat count	If signif. is set, store next digit. Else, if digit = 0, store fill. Else, store sign and digit and set signif.
EO$INSERT	44	character	If signif. is set, store char., else store fill.
EO$LOAD_FILL	40	character	Put character in fill register.
EO$LOAD_MINUS	43	character	Put character in sign register if source < 0.
EO$LOAD_PLUS	42	character	Put character in sign register if source > 0.
EO$LOAD_SIGN	41	character	Put character in sign register.
EO$MOVE	90+r	repeat count	If signif. is set, store next digit. Else, if digit = 0, store fill. Else, store digit and set signif.
EO$REPLACE_SIGN	46	length	If source = −0, replace sign with fill.
EO$SET_SIGNIF	03		Set significance flag.
EO$STORE_SIGN	04		Store sign in destination.

is that it helps determine how many characters there will be in the edited result, i.e., how many bytes must be reserved for the destination operand of EDITPC. We will use the letter d to mean a digit or fill character, and the letter s to indicate a sign. The s will be shown in the first position where the sign may appear; in most of our examples the sign will float over leading fill characters and appear in front of the first significant digit. A caret will indicate the position where the significance flag must be set if it was not set earlier.

The format diagram for the simple pattern used in Example 14.15 is

$$d \quad d \quad d \quad d \quad d$$

The diagram for the pattern in Example 14.16 is

$$s \quad d \quad d \quad d \quad d \underset{\wedge}{d}$$

EXAMPLE 14.18: Inserting Special Characters

We want to define a pattern to edit a seven-digit integer with commas following the millions and thousands places. The format diagram is

$$s \quad d \quad , \quad d \quad d \quad d \quad , \quad d \underset{\wedge}{d} \quad d$$

Clearly, we would not want a comma to appear if there is no significant digit to the left of it. The EO$INSERT operator is designed to store the fill character rather than the character specified as its operand if the significance flag is not set. Note that the destination needs ten bytes. The pattern could be set up as follows:

```
PATRN:  EO$FLOAT      1
        EO$INSERT   <,>
        EO$FLOAT      3
        EO$INSERT   <,>
        EO$FLOAT      2
        EO$END_FLOAT
        EO$MOVE       1
        EO$END
```

Note that a comma must be enclosed in angle brackets; if it is not, the assembler interprets it as a separator and generates an error.

The encoding of the pattern is

PATRN
↓

| A1 | 44 | 2C | A3 | 44 | 2C | A2 | 01 | 91 | 00 |

EXAMPLE 14.19: An Alternate Fill Character

For this example we have a positive five-digit integer to be printed with three asterisks before and after the number and with asterisks in place of leading zeros. The format is

$$* \quad * \quad * \quad *$$
$$* \quad * \quad * \quad d \quad d \quad d \quad d \underset{\wedge}{d} \quad * \quad * \quad *$$

where we have shown the alternate fill character over the d's because it is not the usual blank. The pattern is initialized by

```
PATRN:    EO$LOAD_FILL  *
          EO$FILL       3
          EO$MOVE       4
          EO$SET_SIGNIF
          EO$MOVE       1
          EO$FILL       3
          EO$END
```

EXAMPLE 14.20: A Floating Currency Symbol in Place of a Sign

Suppose we are editing a seven-digit number that represents an amount of money. The rightmost two digits are to be preceded by a decimal point, and a dollar sign is to appear in front of the first nonzero digit. The dollar sign will be loaded into the sign register and inserted in the appropriate place by the EO$FLOAT or EO$END_FLOAT operator. There are some problem cases to watch for: if the amount is less than a dollar, the decimal point will not appear because no significant digit precedes it. Thus we must set the significance flag before the decimal point. We will set it so that at least one digit, perhaps a zero, appears before the decimal point. Thus the format is

$$\$ \ d \ d \ , \ d \ d \underset{\wedge}{} d \ . \ d \ d$$

The pattern is initialized by

```
PATRN:    EO$LOAD_SIGN    $
          EO$FLOAT        2
          EO$INSERT      <,>
          EO$FLOAT        2
          EO$END_FLOAT
          EO$MOVE         1
          EO$INSERT        .
          EO$MOVE         2
          EO$END
```

Thus, for example, if **PKD** contains

$$00\ 00\ 00\ 9C$$

the instruction

```
EDITPC  #7,PKD,PATRN,AMOUNT
```

would store the following data, beginning at **AMOUNT**:

$$20\ 20\ 20\ 20\ 20\ 24\ 30\ 2E\ 30\ 39$$

which, when printed, would appear as

$$\$0.09$$

(with five blanks in front of the dollar sign).

EXAMPLE 14.21: *Adjusting Source Length*

Suppose we want to produce a four-digit number. A packed decimal number always has an odd number of digits. The EO$ADJUST_INPUT operator overrides the source length. If, for example, the packed datum has five digits, EO$ADJUST_INPUT with an operand of 4 will cause the EDITPC source pointer to advance one nibble, skipping the first digit. The pattern described below produces an unsigned four-digit integer with leading zeros included, not replaced by fill. The format is

$$\wedge^{d \ d \ d \ d}$$

The pattern is initialized by

```
PATRN:  EO$ADJUST_INPUT 4
        EO$SET_SIGNIF
        EO$MOVE         4
        EO$END
```

Condition Codes and Caveats

The EDITPC instruction affects all the condition codes. As we have seen, the C code is used as the significance flag. The N and Z bits have their usual meanings. N is set if the packed source operand has a negative sign; however, it will be cleared if all digits in the source are zeros, i.e., if the packed operand is -0. The Z bit is set if all digits are zeros. The V bit is set to indicate overflow if the EO$ADJUST_INPUT operator causes any nonzero digits to be discarded. This is the only situation in which overflow can occur. If enough room has not been reserved for the destination, EDITPC will overwrite other data.

Certainly an instruction that does as much as EDITPC has ample opportunity to run into problems. Most of the events that cause faults are reasonable; i.e., they are situations where something is clearly wrong. A reserved operand fault will occur, as always, if the number of digits specified for the packed source datum is outside the range 0–31. The length specified for an EO$ADJUST_INPUT operator must also be in this range. (If the packed datum has a bad nibble, the results will be incorrect but a fault may not occur.) A reserved operand fault occurs if the pattern does not process all the digits in the source or if it attempts to process more digits than there are. A reserved operand fault occurs if the pattern contains an invalid operator code.

WARNING: The results of EDITPC *are unpredictable if the destination overlaps the packed source operand or the pattern.*

14.6 SUMMARY

The VAX has a variety of character string manipulation instructions that are very useful for processing input and output data, for text editing, and for various other applications.

Character strings are specified in machine instructions by their length and the address of their first byte.

All the character string instructions use some of the general registers for scratch work—and for providing information to the program about the results of the operation performed by the instruction.

The EDITPC is the most complex of the character manipulation instructions. It edits a packed decimal datum according to a pattern specified as one of the instruction operands. It can be used to insert special characters, blank out leading zeros, and place a sign (or other character) just in front of the first significant digit. The edit pattern commands are described in Table 14.1.

The instructions described in this chapter are listed in Table 14.2.

TABLE 14.2   Character String Instructions

	Instruction	*Operation*	*Registers Used*
MOVC3	*len,source,dest*	Copy string	R0–R5
MOVC5	*srclen,source,fill,dstlen,dest*	Copy string	R0–R5
CMPC3	*len,string1,string2*	Compare strings	R0–R3
CMPC5	*len1,string1,fill,len2,string2*	Compare strings	R0–R3
LOCC	*char,len,string*	Find first byte containing *char*	R0–R1
SKPC	*char,len,string*	Find first byte not containing *char*	R0–R1
SCANC	*len,string,table,mask*	Find first byte with *table entry* AND	R0–R3
SPANC	*len,string,table,mask*	*mask* ≠ 0 (SCANC) or = 0 (SPANC)	
MATCHC	*patrn_len,pattern,str_len,string*	Find *pattern* in *string*	R0–R3
MOVTC	*srclen,source,fill,table,dstlen,dest*	Translate source	R0–R5
MOVTUC	*srclen,source,escape,table,dstlen,dest*	Translate with escape	R0–R5
EDITPC	*num_dgts,pkd,pattern,dest*	Edit packed datum	R0–R5

14.7 EXERCISES

1. Consider Examples 14.1 and 14.3. Suppose that if the entry for the third column is too large for a column, it is to be printed entirely on the next line beginning where column

3 begins. You may assume that it has at most 40 characters. Write the instructions to copy the string into the proper place and blank out any bytes that need it.

2. What will be in R0, R1, and R3 after the MOVC5 instruction in Example 14.2 is executed? What values will the condition codes have?

3. Using the string and the program segment in Example 14.5, what will be in R0 after the LOCC instruction is executed each time? Why is TEXT + 1 put in R1 initially instead of TEXT?

4. Rewrite the instructions in the loop in the program segment in Example 14.5 so that one instruction can be eliminated. (Make any necessary changes in the initialization so that the segment will still work correctly.)

5. Write a procedure to do the operation done by the SKPC instruction without using any of the character string instructions introduced in this chapter. Assume that CHAR, LEN, and STRING are the arguments, taking the roles of the *char, len,* and *string* operands, respectively. Your procedure should return in R0, R1, and Z the same data that would be left there by SKPC.

6. Write a procedure to count the occurrences of each of the vowels (separate counts for each) in a section of text. The procedure arguments are TEXT, LENGTH, the number of bytes in the text, and a word array VOWELS where the counts should be stored. (You should not have to explicitly test to determine which vowel has been found. Try to find an "automatic" way of incrementing the appropriate counter.)

7. Modify the CVTCL procedure in Fig. 14.2 so that it will work properly even if the input string may have a signed leading separate numeric string immediately following another lsn string without a blank as a separator.

8. Write a procedure REPLACE that finds and replaces the first instance of a specified substring in a string by another substring. REPLACE should have six arguments:

STRING	the string to be modified
STR_LEN	its length
SUB_STR_1	the substring to be replaced
STR_1_LEN	its length
SUB_STR_2	the replacement string
STR_2_LEN	its length

STR_LEN should be changed to the new length of the modified string. You may assume that there is sufficient space after the end of the string to extend it to a total length of 150. If the replacement would cause the length to exceed 150, it should not be done. REPLACE should set a flag in R0 to distinguish among the three cases: successful replacement, pattern not found in string, and replacement would exceed length limit. Your documentation should indicate what values in R0 indicate which cases.

9. Write a program segment that finds the first entry in the table with the format described in Example 14.10 that has a key that matches the one in the word KEY.

10. Devise an algorithm to do the operation of the MATCHC instruction—i.e., to determine if one string appears anywhere in another—given the addresses and lengths of the two strings. Your algorithm should set a variable to the address where the pattern appears in the second string, or to 0 if it does not appear.

11. Considering what is left in the registers when MOVTC completes execution, what do you think is put in R0, R1, R3, and R5 when MOVTC begins?

12. Write a procedure to do the operation of MOVTC without using any of the character string instructions introduced in this chapter. Assume that the arguments SRC_LEN, SOURCE, FILL, TABLE, DEST_LEN, and DEST play the roles of the MOVTC operands. Your procedure should leave in R0–R5 the data that are left in them by MOVTC.

13. Is the second operand specifier in the instruction

```
MOVB    #^A/ /,TABLE+^A/0/
```

valid? Why or why not? What does the instruction do?

14. Write assembler directives to set up a translation table that could be used to replace all square brackets ([ ]) with curly brackets ({ }) and leave all other characters unchanged.

15. The translation table set up in Example 14.11 has only 128 bytes. What errors could occur if the string being translated had a byte containing a number larger than 127?

16. Write instructions to do the operation done in Example 14.13, but without using MOVTC.

17. Write a program that reads in lines of text from the terminal, one at a time, translates them using a table that permutes the letters but leaves punctuation unchanged, and prints out the resulting cryptogram. The program should include a procedure that constructs the permutation in a random way.

18. Do Exercise 42 of Chapter 12 using the MOVTUC instruction.

19. Show the encoding of the edit pattern used in Example 14.15.

20. If PKD contains 00 00 0C and if the EDITPC instruction and pattern in Example 14.15 are used, what will be in the bytes beginning at STRING when the instruction completes executing?

21. Would the pattern generated by the following statements have the same effects as the one in Example 14.16? If so, explain why. If not, give an example of a source string on which they behave differently.

```
PATRN:    EO$FLOAT 4
          EO$SET_SIGNIF
          EO$MOVE 1
          EO$END
```

22. Show the encoding of the pattern in Example 14.19. How many bytes must be reserved for the edited result?

23. Show what would be in the bytes beginning at AMOUNT if the EDITPC instruction and pattern in Example 14.20 were used and PKD contained 04 89 00 1C.

24. Write a sequence of pattern initialization macros for a pattern for a signed six-digit integer.

25. Write a procedure that converts the entries of a longword array to character code (using EDITPC) and prints them with eight numbers on a line. Assume that the array entries have at most six significant digits. The output is to be lined up in columns with a field of ten spaces per entry. The procedure arguments are the array and a longword that contains the number of entries in the array.

26. Write a sequence of pattern initialization macros for output in the format used in Example 14.19, but with the letters CR appearing after the last digit if the number is negative.

27. Write a sequence of pattern initialization macros for output in the format used in Example 14.20, except that an asterisk should be used for the fill character.

28. Write a sequence of pattern initialization macros to edit a three-digit number where, if the number is negative, the minus sign is to appear after the last digit.

29. Write a sequence of pattern initialization macros to edit a five-digit signed integer using blank fill, but where the sign is to appear in the first byte of the output.

30. Write a procedure, *not* using EDITPC, that takes a five-digit packed decimal string and converts it to a character string of length six with leading zeros replaced by blanks and the sign appearing just before the first significant digit.

Chapter 15

Input and Output Using RMS

15.1 INPUT AND OUTPUT

Input and output operations are among the most complex operations in a program. I/O is complex for a number of reasons. The CPU and the main memory of a computer are housed in the computer cabinet and communicate with each other at very high speed. As long as no I/O operations are done, the CPU can continue humming along, manipulating and moving around data in memory, oblivious to the world outside the cabinet unless someone pulls the plug. I/O operations require that the CPU communicate with physical devices of varying speeds and characteristics in the outside world. Some factors that make I/O programming complex are that:

1. The physical I/O devices perform their operations at much slower speeds than the CPU.
2. To avoid wasting CPU time while I/O is being done, the CPU executes part of another program while the program performing I/O is waiting for the operation to complete. CPU and I/O operations are asynchronous; that is, they are not naturally coordinated in time. Thus when the slow I/O operation completes, the CPU is interrupted and must respond appropriately to the event that occurred, then resume executing some program.
3. I/O programs must consider physical problems such as an I/O device being disconnected, a printer out of paper, or a tape drive not turned on.

In a large system shared by many users, the applications program does not directly control the I/O devices—for two reasons. One is that it is much easier for the programmer not to have to learn the many details needed. The more important reason, though, is that the resources of the system can be used much more efficiently (and without conflict between users) if the operating system manages them. Thus instructions in (high-level or assembly language) programs to read or write data are actually requests to the operating system to perform the operation. To learn more about how I/O is actually done, the reader should consult a text on operating systems or the operating system manuals for a particular computer. The *VAX Software Handbook* describes the VAX/VMS operating system and contains some chapters on I/O.

The programmer may think (and program) in terms of *logical files* and *logical I/O operations,* as opposed to physical operations. The operating system will keep track of how and where the actual data are stored and translate the logical operation requested—e.g., input a record—to the physical steps that must be carried out to find and transfer the desired data.

In this chapter we will consider I/O from a high, or logical, level. Our intent here is to give the reader unfamiliar with I/O an introduction to the subject and some familiarity with the kinds of file processing and I/O services available from an operating system. In Section 15.2 we will describe how the programmer may use the VAX-11 Record Management Services (RMS) to describe and manipulate files. The discussion is far from complete. We will cover enough detail to do straightforward I/O with disk files and at the terminal using RMS directly instead of indirectly via the macros introduced in Chapter 5.

15.2 AN INTRODUCTION TO VAX-11 RECORD MANAGEMENT SERVICES

The VAX-11 Record Management Services (RMS) is a collection of macros and procedures that allow the user to process records and files and, in particular, do input and output, by describing the logical, rather than physical, organization of the records and files and by using relatively high-level operations. We will be describing only a small portion of RMS here. For more features and more detail about the features we present, the reader may consult the *VAX-11 Record Management Services Reference Manual.*

A *file* is an organized collection of related data, called *records.* In a text file (for example, a program source file or a data file such as the DATA.DAT file used by the READRCRD macro) each line is a record.

Files are usually stored on a disk or tape, though a program may construct input and output files for a terminal. We will describe those facilities of RMS used for processing relatively simple disk files and I/O files for the terminal. We will examine the I/O macros and routines in IOMAC and IOMOD as illustrations of the use of RMS.

Files may be organized in several ways. The simplest, and the one we use for DATA.DAT and terminal I/O, is *sequential.* That is, records are arranged in a particular sequence and are processed in order. The other forms of file organization are *indexed* and *relative*. In indexed files each record has an identifier, or key, and the particular record desired is specified by its key. In relative files records may be assigned to particular positions in the file and are referred to by position number.

Communicating with RMS

In order to process a file, a program must communicate with RMS. There are two aspects to the necessary communication:

1. The program must contain blocks of data, called control blocks, that describe the files and records being processed. These control blocks are used for two-way communication; that is, the program fills some fields in the blocks with information for RMS to use, and RMS fills some fields to return information to the program.
2. The program must issue specific requests to cause action (e.g., read in a record) whenever it wants such action to occur.

RMS provides macro instructions to make reservation and initialization of the control blocks relatively easy for the programmer. It also provides macro instructions for the various processing actions. We will discuss the control blocks first, but they will be easier to understand if we know some of the terminology for the actions that may be performed on files and records. The following list briefly describes those most commonly used.

Open a file	Check that the file exists.
	Make it available for processing.
Create a file	Initialize a directory entry.
	Open the file.
Get a record	Input a record from a file.
Put a record	Output a record to a file.
Close a file	Terminate processing of the file.

We will describe two kinds of control blocks: file access blocks and record access blocks. Two other kinds of blocks may be used for providing additional information, but they are not needed for the fairly straightforward I/O that we will do.

File Access Blocks (FABs)

A *file access block* (FAB for short) is a block of 80 bytes of information describing a particular file. One file access block is needed for each file accessed in a program. A FAB has 28 fields, each containing a particular item of information.

The $FAB macro may be used to reserve space for a FAB and initialize some of the fields. Some fields are filled by RMS when the file is opened or created. $FAB has 23 arguments, most of which correspond exactly to a field in the FAB. (There are fewer arguments than fields because some fields can't be initialized by the user, and some arguments initialize more than one.) Since RMS fills some of the fields and since many of the arguments have very useful default values, very few of the arguments actually have to be specified unless the file has unusual characteristics.

Note that since the $FAB macro initializes a data area, it should be placed in the storage reservation and initialization portion of a program, not among executable instructions.

The format of the $FAB macro is

label: $FAB   arguments

Because there are so many arguments and most are usually omitted, it is convenient to specify the arguments using keywords. The list below contains the keywords and roles of some of the arguments.

Some $FAB arguments

FNM = File NaMe. The file specification for the file described by this FAB is enclosed in angle brackets.

ORG = file ORGanization. The options are SEQ for sequential, INDX for indexed, or REL for relative. The default is SEQ. This field is initialized by the programmer for a file to be created; for an existing file, RMS will fill the field with the actual file organization when the file is opened.

ALQ = ALlocation Quantity. This is the number of disk blocks to be allocated when this file is created. If the file already exists, RMS will put its actual size in this field when the file is opened.

DEQ = Default file Extension Quantity. This is the number of blocks by which the file is to be extended when space runs out. (ALQ and DEQ have useful defaults and may often be omitted.)

FAC = File ACcess options. The particular kinds of processing that will be done on the file must be specified in advance in the FAC field. Examples of processing action are: GET, PUT, DEL (delete), and UPD (update). If more than one is specified, they are enclosed in pointed brackets—for example:

```
FAC = <GET,UPD>
```

The FAC field contains one bit for each option. By default, when an existing file is opened, the GET bit in the FAB is set, and when a new file is created, the PUT bit is set, so FAC may be omitted for simple I/O.

RFM = Record ForMat. Two of the possibilities are FIX, for fixed size, and VAR, for variable size. The default is VAR.

MRS = Maximum Record Size. This field should be filled by the programmer for a file being created. When an existing file is opened, RMS puts the actual maximum record size in the field.

One important field in the FAB that can not be initialized by the programmer is the completion STatuS code field (STS). RMS fills this field with a success or failure code after attempting to perform an operation on the file. For example, after attempting to open a file, RMS may return the code for "file not found." If an attempt was made to access a file in a way not specified in the FAC field, RMS will return an appropriate error code.

EXAMPLE 15.1: The FAB's for Terminal I/O and DATA.DAT

The file access blocks for the terminal input and output files used by the READLINE, PRINTCHRS, and DUMPLONG macros and the FAB for the DATA.DAT file accessed by the READRCRD macro are defined by

```
INFAB:    $FAB    FNM=<SYS$INPUT>
OUTFAB:   $FAB    FNM=<SYS$OUTPUT>,MRS=85
DISKFAB:  $FAB    FNM=<DATA.DAT>
```

We can rely on the default argument values and the data filled in by RMS at execution time to initialize the other fields. The file names SYS$INPUT and SYS$OUTPUT are logical names that are assigned by default to the user's terminal, but their meaning may be changed when a program is run, so that, for example, the output can be directed to a disk file instead of the terminal. (Note that in the IOMOD module shown in Appendix D, the labels DISKFAB, INFAB, and OUTFAB are followed by two colons to declare them global symbols so that they can be accessed by the I/O macros in the user's program.)

Record Access Blocks (RABs)

A record access block is a block of 68 bytes of data describing the records in a file. Each record access block is associated with a particular file access block. The $RAB macro reserves space for the RAB and does some of the initialization. Some fields may be filled by the program at execution time, and some are filled by RMS after it performs an operation. As with $FAB, $RAB has useful default values for many of its arguments. The format for $RAB is

label: $RAB   *arguments*

Some $RAB arguments

FAB = File Access Block address. This field must contain the address of the FAB for the file containing the records described by this RAB. It is specified by writing the label used on the $FAB macro.

RAC = Record ACcess mode. The record access mode is the way records in the file are accessed or stored. Two of the options are SEQ, for sequential, and KEY. The default is SEQ.

ROP = Record processing OPtions. There are many options that may be selected. For example, some of the options that may be used with a terminal input file and their meanings are:

PMT	A prompt message will be displayed at the terminal when an input line is requested.
CVT	All letters read in from the terminal are to be converted to upper case.
TMO	There will be a time limit on how long RMS waits for input from the terminal.

If several options are specified, they are enclosed in angle brackets. For example:

```
ROP = <PMT,TMO>
```

PBF = Prompt BuFfer. The address of a prompt message to be displayed for terminal input is specified. The user must store the prompt message in memory.

PSZ = Prompt message SiZe. The number of bytes in the prompt message is specified. Note that if PBF and PSZ are used, PMT must be included as an option in the ROP field.

TMO = TiMe Out. This is the maximum number of seconds allowed for completion of an RMS operation. TMO may be at most 255. Note that to use TMO, the TMO option must be included in the ROP field.

UBF = User BuFfer. This is the buffer address for input—i.e., the address of the location in memory where the user wants RMS to put a record read in from a file. This field may be initialized in the $RAB macro if a standard location is used, or the programmer may fill this field before each *get* operation with the location for that particular record.

USZ = User buffer SiZe. This is the length of the user buffer.

RBF = Record BuFfer. This is the buffer address for output—i.e., the address in memory from which RMS is to take the record to be written out to the file. As with UBF, this field may be initialized in $RAB or filled by the program at execution time.

RSZ = Record SiZe. For input, RMS fills this field with the actual number of bytes in the record read in. For output, this field must contain the size of the record to be written out to the file.

Like the FABs, RABs have a completion STatuS code field (STS) that is filled by RMS to report a success or failure completion code after each operation.

*EXAMPLE 15.2: The **RABs** for Terminal I/O and* **DATA.DAT**

The IOMOD module contains the following RABs and related directives:

```
LF = 10                                      ; Line feed
CR = 13                                      ; Carriage return
INRAB:    $RAB    FAB=INFAB,USZ-80,-         ; For terminal input
                  ROP=PMT,PBF=PROMPT,PSZ=5
OUTRAB:   $RAB    FAB=OUTFAB                  ; For terminal output
DISKRAB:  $RAB    FAB=DISKFAB,USZ=80          ; For DATA.DAT
PROMPT:   .ASCII  <LF><CR>/?? /               ; Terminal prompt
```

The buffer fields (UBF for input and RBF for output) will be filled by the I/O macros READRCRD, READLINE, and PRINTCHRS. The input buffer size field USZ is initialized to 80, so no more than 80 bytes will be read in. The RAB for the terminal input file specifies that a prompt of length 5 will be displayed whenever input is requested from the terminal.

We have pointed out that some fields in a RAB may be set by the program at execution time. To do so the programmer must know something about the format of a RAB. To avoid the need to know all the details of the format (and to make it easier to modify if necessary without requiring changes in programs already written), the system provides system-defined symbolic names for the offsets for the fields. The symbolic names use a standardized pattern:

RAB$*type_fieldname*

For example, RAB$L_UBF is the offset from the beginning of a RAB for the longword field containing the address of the user buffer, and RAB$B_PSZ is the offset for the byte field containing the size of the prompt message. We use some of these symbols in the I/O procedures in IOMOD, described in examples below. There are similar system-defined symbolic names for the field offsets for FAB fields.

Processing Macros

The I/O processing macros cause action at execution time. They are used in a program like machine instructions (or the I/O macros presented in Chapter 5); i.e., they are placed at the point in the program where the action is to occur. The processing macros call system procedures to do the actual work.

There are two kinds of processing macros: those that operate on files and those that operate on records. All the processing macros have three arguments:

FAB	address of the FAB for the file being processed, *or*
RAB	address of the RAB for the record being processed;
ERR	entry point of a routine to handle errors,
SUC	entry point of a routine to execute if the operation completes successfully.

The ERR and SUC arguments are optional; if they are omitted, the next instruction executed is the one that follows the macro in the program.

File Processing Macros

The macros for the file operations used most often are

$OPEN	makes an existing file available for processing
$CREATE	creates a new file and opens it
$CLOSE	terminates access to the file

A file must be opened before any processing may be done on it. Files should be closed when the program is finished processing them.

Some other operations available in RMS are

$ERASE	deletes the file and erases its directory entry (The file must be closed before it is erased.)
$EXTEND	increases the space allocated to the file (The file must be open before it is extended.)

Record Processing Macros

The record processing macros perform operations relating to individual records or to record access blocks. The main input and output operations are *get* and *put*. Two operations that need some explanation are *connect* and *disconnect*. Before records are read or written, the record access block to be used must be explicitly "connected" to a file access block. Recall that each RAB has a field, its FAB field, that contains the address of the associated FAB. It is possible for several RABs to specify the same FAB, so a specific RAB is chosen at execution time. (For sequential files, only one RAB may be connected to a particular FAB at one time.)

Some of the record processing macros are

$CONNECT   connects the specified RAB to its FAB, allocates buffers
                for I/O, sets a pointer to the first record in the file
$DISCONNECT   disconnects the RAB from its FAB
$GET   inputs a record. RMS places the record in the area specified
                in the UBF field and puts its length in the RSZ field of
                the RAB. It sets the STS field to indicate if there were
                any errors or unusual conditions (e.g., end-of-file).
$PUT   outputs a record

EXAMPLE 15.3: The BEGIN and EXIT Macros

The BEGIN and EXIT macros in IOMAC do some of the initialization and termination
work needed when using RMS. The macro definitions are

```
.MACRO  BEGIN    NAME
        .ENTRY   NAME,^M<IV,DV>  ; Define entry point
                                 ; Set overflow traps
        $OPEN    FAB=INFAB       ; Open terminal input file
        $CONNECT RAB=INRAB
        $CREATE  FAB=OUTFAB      ; Create terminal output file
        $CONNECT RAB=OUTRAB
        $OPEN    FAB=DISKFAB     ; Open disk input file
        $CONNECT RAB=DISKRAB
.ENDM   BEGIN

.MACRO  EXIT
        $CLOSE   FAB=INFAB       ; Close I/O files
        $CLOSE   FAB=OUTFAB      ;        "
        $CLOSE   FAB=DISKFAB     ;        "
        $EXIT_S                  ; System exit macro
.ENDM   EXIT
```

EXAMPLE 15.4: READLINE

The simplest of the I/O operations in IOMAC and IOMOD is READLINE. The macro,
like READRCRD and PRINTCHRS, calls a procedure that does the work. (This is
to keep the macros fairly short, so that they may be used in loops that use byte displacements for the branch destinations.) The READLINE macro definition is

```
.MACRO  READLINE WHERETO
        PUSHAB   WHERETO         ; Stack user buffer addr.
        CALLS    #1,RDLINE
.ENDM   READLINE
```

The RDLINE procedure is

```
; PROCEDURE RDLINE (WHERETO)
;
; This procedure gets an input line from the terminal. It
; uses the RAB labeled INRAB which causes a prompt to be
; displayed at the terminal. The input record is stored
; in memory at WHERETO, RDLINE's argument. RDLINE returns
; the length of the record in R0.
;
        .ENTRY  RDLINE,0
        MOVL    4(AP),INRAB+RAB$L_UBF    ; Fill UBF field in RAB
        $GET    RAB=INRAB                ; Get record
        CVTWL   INRAB+RAB$W_RSZ,R0       ; Record size to R0
        RET
```

EXAMPLE 15.5: READRCRD

The READRCRD macro definition is

```
        .MACRO  READRCRD WHERETO,?LBL
        PUSHAB  WHERETO                  ; Stack user buffer addr.
        CALLS   #1,RDRCRD                ; Returns length in R0
        BNEQ    LBL                      ; Got a record
        BRW     EOF                      ; End-of-file
LBL:    .ENDM   READRCRD
```

The RDRCRD procedure is

```
; PROCEDURE RDRCRD (WHERETO)
;
; This procedure reads the next record from the DATA.DAT file. If
; there was a record, it is stored in WHERETO and its length is put
; in R0. If there were no more records, the Z bit in the stacked PSW
; is set to indicate end-of-file.
; RDRCRD uses the RAB labeled DISKRAB.
;
        .ENTRY  RDRCRD,0
        MOVL    4(AP),DISKRAB+RAB$L_UBF     ; Fill UBF field in RAB
        $GET    RAB=DISKRAB                 ; Get record
        CMPL    DISKRAB+RAB$_STS,#RMS$_EOF  ; Check STS field for EOF
        BEQL    EOF
        CVTWL   DISKRAB+RAB$W_RSZ,R0        ; Record size to R0
        RET
EOF:    BISB2   #^X04,4(FP)                 ; Set EOF flag
        RET
```

RMS$_EOF is a system-defined symbol whose value is the status code for end-of-file.

For more examples the reader may examine the **PRINTCHRS** macro and **PTCHRS** procedure that appear in Appendix D.

15.3 EXERCISES

The macros in IOMAC are not to be used for any of these exercises.

1. Suppose that a file access block, record access block, and other areas are defined as follows for input from a terminal:

```
LF=10                                    ; Line feed
CR=13                                    ; Carriage return
INFAB:  $FAB    FNM=<SYS$INPUT>
INRAB:  $RAB    FAB=INFAB,UBF=INBUF,USZ=80,-
                ROP=PMT,PBF=MSG,PSZ=8
INBUF:  .BLKB   80
MSG:    .ASCII  <LF><CR>/INPUT:/
LINE:   .BLKB   80
```

   (a) Assuming that the file is already open, write the instruction(s) to read in a line from the terminal and store it in LINE.
   (b) What prompt will appear on the screen to tell the user that input is expected?

2. Suppose a file access block, record access block, and other areas are defined as follows for output to a terminal:

```
LF=10                                    ; Line feed
CR=13                                    ; Carriage return
SPACE=32                                 ; Space
OUTFAB: $FAB    FNM=<SYS$OUTPUT>,MRS=85
OUTRAB: $RAB    FAB=OUTFAB,RBF=OUTBUF,RSZ=85
OUTBUF: .ASCII  <LF><CR>
        .BYTE   SPACE[85]
```

   (a) Assuming that the file is already open, write the instruction(s) needed to print a ten-character message stored in memory at MESSAGE.
   (b) Suppose later in the program a second message is to be printed. It is located at TITLE and has eight characters. Write the instruction(s) needed to print it.

3. Write a program for the following problem. There are two data files on the disk, DATA1.DAT and DATA2.DAT, both containing 80-byte records that start with an eight-character key. Both files are sorted alphabetically by key. The program is to construct one new file, RECS.DAT, that contains all the records in order; i.e., the program is to merge the two files. The program should delete the two input files after merging them. (The program should be modular—i.e., use procedures as appropriate.)

Index of Instructions

In the table below, operands are shown in the format *name.type*. (The type for string operands is given as *b*.) (Adapted with permission from the *VAX-11 Programming Card* published by Digital Equipment Corporation.)

Name	Operands	Operation	Opcode		Page
ACB*x*	*limit.x,incr.x,index.x,dest.*w x = B, W, L, F, D, G, or H	*Add, compare, and* *branch*	ACBB	9D	120,312
			ACBW	3D	
			ACBL	F1	
			ACBF	4F	
			ACBD	6F	
			ACBG	4FFD	
			ACBH	6FFD	
ADD*x*2	*op1.x,op2.x* x = B, W, L, F, D, G, or H	Add	ADDB2	80	73,310
			ADDW2	A0	
			ADDL2	C0	
			ADDF2	40	
			ADDD2	60	
			ADDG2	40FD	
			ADDH2	60FD	
ADD*x*3	*op1.x,op2.x,sum.x* x = B, W, L, F, D, G, or H	Add	ADDB3	81	73,310
			ADDW3	A1	
			ADDL3	C1	
			ADDF3	41	
			ADDD3	61	
			ADDG3	41FD	
			ADDH3	61FD	

Name	Operands	Operation	Opcode		Page
ADDP4[2]	*dgts1*.w,*pkd1*.b,*dgts2*.w,*pkd2*.b	Add packed	20		328
ADDP6[3]	*dgts1*.w,*pkd1*.b,*dgts2*.w,*pkd2*.b,*dgts3*.w,*pkd3*.b		21		328
		Add packed			
ADWC	*op1*.l,*op2*.l	Add with carry	D8		96
AOBLEQ	*limit*.l,*index*.l,*dest*.b	Add 1; branch if ≤ 0	F3		117
AOBLSS	*limit*.l,*index*.l,*dest*.b	Add 1; branch if < 0	F2		117
ASH*x*	*count*.b,*src*.x,*dest*.x	Arithmetic shift	ASHL	78	282
	x = L or Q		ASHQ	79	
ASHP[2]	*count*.b,*srcdgts*.w,*src*.b,*round*.b,*dstdgts*.w,*dest*.b		F8		
		Arithmetic shift and round packed			
BBC	*posn*.l,*base*.b,*dest*.b	Branch if bit clear	E1		
BBCC	*posn*.l,*base*.b,*dest*.b	Branch if bit clear, and clear it	E5		
BBCS	*posn*.l,*base*.b,*dest*.b	Branch if bit clear, and set it	E3		
BBS	*posn*.l,*base*.b,*dest*.b	Branch if bit set	E0		
BBSC	*posn*.l,*base*.b,*dest*.b	Branch if bit set, and clear it	E4		
BBSS	*posn*.l,*base*.b,*dest*.b	Branch if bit set, and set it	E2		
BCC	*dest*.b	Branch if carry clear	1E		101
BCS	*dest*.b	Branch if carry set	1F		101
BEQL	*dest*.b	Branch if equal	13		101
BEQLU	*dest*.b	Branch if equal, unsigned	13		101
BGEQ	*dest*.b	Branch if greater or equal	18		101
BGEQU	*dest*.b	Branch if greater or equal, unsigned	1E		101
BGTR	*dest*.b	Branch if greater	14		101
BGTRU	*dest*.b	Branch if greater, unsigned	1A		101
BIC*x*2	*mask*.x,*dest*.x	Bit clear	BICB2	8A	278
	x = B, W, or L		BICW2	AA	
			BICL2	CA	
BIC*x*3	*mask*.x,*src*.x,*dest*.x	Bit clear	BICB3	8B	278
	x = B, W, or L		BICW3	AB	
			BICL3	CB	
BICPSW	*mask*.w	Bit clear in PSW	B9		163
BIS*x*2	*mask*.x,*dest*.x	Bit set	BISB2	88	278
	x = B, W, or L		BISW2	A8	
			BISL2	C8	
BIS*x*3	*mask*.x,*src*.x,*dest*.x	Bit set	BISB3	89	278
	x = B, W, or L		BISW3	A9	
			BISL3	C9	
BISPSW	*mask*.w	Bit set in PSW	B8		163
BIT*x*	*mask*.x,*src*.x	Bit test	BITB	93	277
	x = B, W, or L		BITW	B3	
			BITL	D3	

Name	Operands	Operation	Opcode		Page
BLBC	*scr*.l,*dest*.b	Branch if low bit clear	E9		101
BLBS	*scr*.l,*dest*.b	Branch if low bit set	E8		101
BLEQ	*dest*.b	Branch if less or equal	15		101
BLEQU	*dest*.b	Branch if less or equal,unsigned	1B		101
BLSS	*dest*.b	Branch if less	19		101
BLSSU	*dest*.b	Branch if less, unsigned	1F		101
BNEQ	*dest*.b	Branch if not equal	12		101
BNEQU	*dest*.b	Branch if not equal, unsigned	12		101
BRB	*dest*.b	Branch, byte displ.	11		101
BRW	*dest*.w	Branch, word displ.	31		101
BSBB	*dest*.b	Branch to subroutine, byte displ.	10		178
BSBW	*dest*.w	Branch to subroutine, word displ.	30		178
BVC	*dest*.b	Branch if overflow clear	1C		101
BVS	*dest*.b	Branch if overflow set	1D		101
CALLG	*arglst*.l,*proc*.b	Call procedure (general argument list)	FA		193
CALLS	*numargs*.l,*proc*.b	Call procedure (argument list on stack)	FB		193
CASE*x*	*selector*.*x*,*base*.*x*,*limit*.*x*,*dstlist*.w *x* = B, W, or L	Case	CASEB CASEW CASEL	8F AF CF	
CLR*x*	*dest*.*x* *x* = B, W, L, Q, O, F, D, G, or H	Clear	CLRB CLRW CLRL =CLRF CLRQ = CLRD =CLRG CLRO =CLRH	94 B4 D4 7C 7CFD	77,311
CMP*x*	*op1*.*x*,*op2*.*x* *x* = B, W, L, F, D, G, or H	Compare	CMPB CMPW CMPL CMPF CMPD CMPG CMPH	91 B1 D1 51 71 51FD 71FD	103,311
CMPC3[2]	*len*.w,*str1*.b,*str2*.b	Compare characters	29		107,336
CMPC5[2]	*len1*.w,*str1*.b,*fill*.b,*len2*.w,*str2*.b	Compare characters	2D		336
CMPP3[2]	*dgts*.w,*pkd1*.b,*pkd2*.b	Compare packed	35		329
CMPP4[2]	*dgts1*.w,*pkd1*.b,*dgts2*.w,*pkd2*.b	Compare packed	37		329
CMPV	*posn*.l,*size*.b,*base*.b,*long*.l	Compare bit field	EC		297
CMPZV	*posn*.l,*size*.b,*base*.b,*long*.l	Compare zero-extended bit field	ED		297

Name	Operands	Operation	Opcode	Page
CVT*xy*	*src.x,dest.y* *xy* may be any of the 40 combinations in the CVT instructions listed below.	Convert		83,311

CVTBW 99	CVTWB 33	CVTLB F6
CVTBL 98	CVTWL 32	CVTLW F7
CVTBF 4C	CVTWF 4D	CVTLF 4E
CVTBD 6C	CVTWD 6D	CVTLD 6E
CVTBG 4CFD	CVTWG 4DFD	CVTLG 4EFD
CVTBH 6CFD	CVTWH 6DFD	CVTLH 6EFD

CVTFB 48	CVTDB 68	CVTGB 48FD	CVTHB 68FD
CVTFW 49	CVTDW 69	CVTGW 49FD	CVTHW 69FD
CVTFL 4A	CVTDL 6A	CVTGL 4AFD	CVTHL 6AFD
CVTFD 56	CVTDF 76	CVTGF 33FD	CVTHF F6FD
CVTFG 99FD			CVTHD F7FD
CVTFH 98FD	CVTDH 32FD	CVTGH 56FD	CVTHG 76FD

Name	Operands	Operation	Opcode		Page
CVTLP[2]	*scr.*l*,dgts.*w*,pkd.*b	Convert long to packed	F9		91
CVTPL[2]	*dgts.*w*,pkd.*b*,dest.*l	Convert packed to long	36		89
CVTPS[2]	*dgts1.*w*,pkd.*b*,dgts2.*w*,lsn.*b	Convert packed to leading separate numeric	08		91
CVTPT[2]	*dgts1.*w*,pkd.*b*,tbl.*b*,dgts2.*w*,trl.*b	Convert packed to trailing	24		
CVTR*x*L	*src.x,dest.*l *x* = F, D, G, or H	Convert rounded to long	CVTRFL	4B	311
			CVTRDL	6B	
			CVTRGL	4BFD	
			CVTRHL	6BFD	
CVTSP[2]	*dgts1.*w*,lsn.*b*,dgts2.*w*,pkd.*b	Convert *lsn* to packed	09		88
CVTTP[2]	*dgts1.*w*,trl.*b*,tbl.*b*,dgts2.*w*,pkd.*b	Convert trailing to packed	26		
DEC*x*	*op.x* *x* = B, W, or L	Decrement	DECB	97	77
			DECW	B7	
			DECL	D7	
DIV*x*2	*dvsr.x,op2.x* *x* = B, W, L, F, D, G, or H	Divide	DIVB2	86	74,310
			DIVW2	A6	
			DIVL2	C6	
			DIVF2	46	
			DIVD2	66	
			DIVG2	46FD	
			DIVH2	66FD	
DIV*x*3	*dvsr.x,dvdd.x,quo.x* *x* = B, W, L, F, D, G, or H	Divide	DIVB3	87	74,310
			DIVW3	A7	
			DIVL3	C7	
			DIVF3	47	
			DIVD3	67	
			DIVG3	47FD	
			DIVH3	67FD	
DIVP[3,4]	*dgts1.*w*,dvsr.*b*,dgts2.*w*,dvdd.*b*,dgts3.*w*,quo.*b	Divide packed	27		329

Name	Operands	Operation	Opcode		Page
EDITPC[3]	dgts.w,pkd.b,patrn.b,dest.b	Edit packed	38		355
EDIV	dvsr.l,dvdd.q,quo.l,rem.l	Extended divide	7B		
EMODx	mulr.x,mulrex.b,muld.x,int.l,frac.x		EMODF	54	309
	x = F or D	Extra precision multiply	EMODD	74	
EMODx	mulr.x,mulrex.w,muld.x,int.l,frac.x		EMODG	54FD	309
	x = G or H		EMODH	74FD	
EMUL	mulr.l,muld.l,add.l,prod.q	Extended multiply	7A		
EXTV	posn.l,size.b,base.b,dest.l	Extract bit field	EE		294
EXTZV	posn.l,size.b,base.b,dest.l	Extract zero-extended bit field	EF		294
FFC	posn.l,size.b,base.b,dest.l	Find first clear bit	EB		291
FFS	posn.l,size.b,base.b,dest.l	Find first set bit	EA		291
INCx	op.x	Increment	INCB	96	77
	x = B, W, or L		INCW	B6	
			INCL	D6	
INDEX	subsc.l,low.l,high.l,size.l,base.l,offset.l		0A		
		Array index computation			
INSQUE	entry.b,addr.l	Insert into queue	0E		
INSV	src.l,posn.l,size.b,base.b	Insert bit field	F0		294
JMP	dest.b	Jump	17		109
JSB	dest.b	Jump to subroutine	16		
LOCC[1]	char.b,len.w,str.b	Locate character	3A		340
MATCHC[2]	len1.w,str1.b,len2.w,str2.b	Match characters	39		346
MCOMx	src.x,dest.x	Move complemented	MCOMB	92	281
	x = B, W, or L		MCOMW	B2	
			MCOML	D2	
MNEGx	src.x,dest.x	Move negated	MNEGB	8E	77,311
	x = B, W, L, F, D, G, or H		MNEGW	AE	
			MNEGL	CE	
			MNEGF	52	
			MNEGD	72	
			MNEGG	52FD	
			MNEGH	72FD	
MOVAx	src.x,dest.l	Move address	MOVAB	9E	79, 84,311
	x = B, W, L, Q, O, F, D, G, or H		MOVAW	3E	
		MOVAL = MOVAF	DE		
		MOVAQ = MOVAD = MOVAG	7E		
		MOVAO = MOVAH	7EFD		
MOVx	src.x,dest.x	Move	MOVB	90	83,311
	x = B, W, L, Q, O, F, D, G, or H		MOVW	B0	
			MOVL	D0	
			MOVQ	7D	
			MOVO	7DFD	
			MOVF	50	
			MOVD	70	
			MOVG	50FD	
			MOVH	70FD	
MOVC3[3]	len.w,str1.b,str2.b	Move characters	28		65,336
MOVC5[3]	len1.w,str1.b,fill.b,len2.w,str2.b	Move characters	2C		336

Name	Operands	Operation	Opcode		Page
MOVP[2]	*dgts*.w,*pkd1*.b,*pkd2*.b	Move packed	34		329
MOVPSL	*dest*.l	Move PSL	DC		303
MOVTC	*srclen*.w,*src*.b,*fill*.b,*tbl*.b,*dstlen*.w,*dest*.b	Move translated characters	2E		350
MOVTUC	*srclen*.w,*src*.b,*escape*.b,*tbl*.b,*dstlen*.w,*dest*.b	Move translated characters until escape	2F		352
MOVZ*xy*	*src.x,dest.y*	Move, zero-extended	MOVZBW	9B	97
	xy = BW, BL, or WL		MOVZBL	9A	
			MOVZWL	3C	
MUL*x*2	*op1.x,op2.x*	Multiply	MULB2	84	73,310
	x = B, W, L, F, D, G, or H		MULW2	A4	
			MULL2	C4	
			MULF2	44	
			MULD2	64	
			MULG2	44FD	
			MULH2	64FD	
MUL*x*3	*mulr.x,muld.x,prod.x*	Multiply	MULB3	85	73,310
	x = B, W, L, F, D, G, or H		MULW3	A5	
			MULL3	C5	
			MULF3	45	
			MULD3	65	
			MULG3	45FD	
			MULH3	65FD	
MULP[3]	*mulrlen*.w,*mulr*.b,*muldlen*.w,*muld*.b,*prodlen*.w,*prod*.b	Multiply packed	25		329
NOP		No operation	01		
POLYF[2]	*arg.f,degree*.w,*coefs*.b	Evaluate polynomial	55		309
POLY*x*3	*arg.x,degree*.w,*coefs*.b	Evaluate polynomial	POLYD	75	309
	x = D, G, or H		POLYG	55FD	
			POLYH	75FD	
POPR	*mask*.w	Pop to registers	BA		258
PUSHA*x*	*op.x*	Push address	PUSHAB	9F	186
	x = B, W, L, Q, O, F, D, G, or H		PUSHAW	3F	
		PUSHAL = PUSHAF	DF		
		PUSHAQ = PUSHAD = PUSHAG	7F		
		PUSHAO = PUSHAH	7FFD		
PUSHL	*long*.l	Push longword	DD		186
PUSHR	*mask*.w	Push registers	BB		258
REMQUE	*entry*.b,*addr*.l	Remove from queue	0F		
RET		Return from procedure	04		196
ROTL	*count*.b,*src*.l,*dest*.l	Rotate	9C		282
RSB		Return from subroutine	05		178
SBWC	*op1*.l,*op2*.l	Subtract with carry	D9		
SCANC[2]	*len*.w,*str*.b,*tbl*.b,*mask*.b	Scan for character	2A		344
SKPC[1]	*char*.b,*len*.w,*str*.b	Skip character	3B		340
SOBGEQ	*index*.l,*dest*.b	Subtract 1; branch if ≥ 0	F4		115

Name	Operands	Operation	Opcode		Page
SOBGTR	*index*.l,*dest*.b	Subtract 1; branch if > 0	F5		78,115
SPANC	*len*.w,*str*.b,*tbl*.b,*mask*.b	Span characters	2B		344
SUB*x*2	*op1.x,op2.x*	Subtract	SUBB2	82	73,310
	x = B, W, L, F, D, G, or H		SUBW2	A2	
			SUBL2	C2	
			SUBF2	42	
			SUBD2	62	
			SUBG2	42FD	
			SUBH2	62FD	
SUB*x*3	*op1.x,op2.x,dif.x*	Subtract	SUBB3	83	73,310
	x = B, W, L, F, D, G, or H		SUBW3	A3	
			SUBL3	C3	
			SUBF3	43	
			SUBD3	63	
			SUBG3	43FD	
			SUBH3	63FD	
SUBP4[2]	*len1*.w,*pkd1*.b,*len2*.w,*pkd2*.b	Subtract packed	22		328
SUBP6[3]	*len1*.w,*pkd1*.b,*len2*.w,*pkd2*.b,*len3*.w,*pkd3*.b		23		328
		Subtract packed			
TST*x*	*op.x*	Test	TSTB	95	103,311
	x = B, W, L, F, D, G, or H		TSTW	B5	
			TSTL	D5	
			TSTF	53	
			TSTD	73	
			TSTG	53FD	
			TSTH	73FD	
XFC	user defined	Extended function	FC		
XOR*x*2	*mask.x,dest.x*	Exclusive or	XORB2	8C	278
	x = B, W, or L		XORW2	AC	
			XORL2	CC	
XOR*x*3	*mask.x,src.x,dest.x*	Exclusive or	XORB3	8D	278
	x = B, W, or L		XORW3	AD	
			XORL3	CD	

Instructions used only or primarily by operating systems programs

ADAWI	*op1*.w,*op2*.w	Add aligned word, interlocked	58		
BBCCI	*posn*.l,*base*.b,*dest*.b	Branch if bit clear and clear, interlocked	E7		
BBSSI	*posn*.l,*base*.b,*dest*.b	Branch if bit set and set, interlocked	E6		
BPT		Break point fault			
CHM*z*	*parameter*.w	Change mode to *z*	CHME	BD	
	z = E (executive), K (kernel),		CHMK	BC	
	S (supervisor), or U (user)		CHMS	BE	
			CHMU	BF	
CRC	*tbl*.b,*initial.1*,*len*.w,*stream*.b,*dest*.l		0B		
		Calculate cyclic redundancy check			

Name	Operands	Operation	Opcode	Page
HALT[5]		Halt	00	
INSQHI	*entry*.b,*header*.q	Insert at head of queue, interlocked	5C	
INSQTI	*entry*.b,*header*.q	Insert at tail of queue, interlocked	5D	
LDPCTX		Load process context	06	
MFPR[5]	*procreg*.l,*dest*.l	Move from process register	DB	
MTPR[5]	*src*.l,*procreg*.l	Move to process register	DA	
PROBER	*mode*.b,*len*.w,*base*.b	Probe read access	0C	
PROBEW	*mode*.b,*len*.w,*base*.b	Probe write access	0D	
REI		Return from exception or interrupt	02	
REMQHI	*header*.q,*addr*.l	Remove entry from head of queue	5E	
REMQTI	*header*.q,*addr*.l	Remove entry from tail of queue	5F	
SVPCTX[5]		Save process context	07	

[1] Uses R0–R1
[2] Uses R0–R3
[3] Uses R0–R5
[4] Uses scratch space on the user stack
[5] May be executed by the operating system kernel only

Appendix B

Hex Conversion Table and Powers of 2

Hex Conversion Table

Position\Digit	*Hex Digit Positional Value*							
	16^7	16^6	16^5	16^4	16^3	16^2	16^1	16^0
0	0	0	0	0	0	0	0	0
1	268,435,456	16,777,216	1,048,576	65,536	4,096	256	16	1
2	536,870,912	33,554,432	2,097,152	131,072	8,192	512	32	2
3	805,306,368	50,331,648	3,145,728	196,608	12,288	768	48	3
4	1,073,741,824	67,108,864	4,194,304	262,144	16,384	1024	64	4
5	1,342,177,280	83,886,080	5,242,880	327,680	20,480	1280	80	5
6	1,610,612,736	100,663,296	6,291,456	393,216	24,576	1536	96	6
7	1,879,048,192	117,440,512	7,340,032	458,752	28,672	1792	112	7
8	2,147,483,648	134,217,728	8,388,608	524,288	32,768	2048	128	8
9	2,415,919,104	150,994,944	9,437,184	589,824	36,864	2304	144	9
A	2,684,354,560	167,772,160	10,485,760	655,360	40,960	2560	160	10
B	2,952,790,016	184,549,376	11,534,336	720,896	45,056	2816	176	11
C	3,221,225,472	201,326,592	12,582,912	786,432	49,152	3072	192	12
D	3,489,660,928	218,103,808	13,631,488	851,968	53,248	3328	208	13
E	3,758,096,384	234,881,024	14,680,064	917,504	57,344	3584	224	14
F	4,026,531,840	251,658,240	15,728,640	983,040	61,440	3840	240	15

Powers of 2

p	2^p	p	2^p	p	2^p	p	2^p
0	1	8	256	16	65,536	24	16,777,216
1	2	9	512	17	131,072	25	33,554,432
2	4	10	1,024	18	262,144	26	67,108,864
3	8	11	2,048	19	524,288	27	134,217,728
4	16	12	4,096	20	1,048,576	28	268,435,456
5	32	13	8,192	21	2,097,152	29	536,870,912
6	64	14	16,384	22	4,194,304	30	1,073,741,824
7	128	15	32,768	23	8,388,608	31	2,147,483,648
						32	4,294,967,296

ASCII Codes

Hex	Dec	ASCII	Hex	Dec	ASCII	Hex	Dec	ASCII	Hex	Dec	ASCII
00	0	NUL	20	32	SP	40	64	@	60	96	`
01	1	SOH	21	33	!	41	65	A	61	97	a
02	2	STX	22	34	"	42	66	B	62	98	b
03	3	ETX	23	35	#	43	67	C	63	99	c
04	4	EOT	24	36	$	44	68	D	64	100	d
05	5	ENQ	25	37	%	45	69	E	65	101	e
06	6	ACK	26	38	&	46	70	F	66	102	f
07	7	BEL	27	39	'	47	71	G	67	103	g
08	8	BS	28	40	(	48	72	H	68	104	h
09	9	HT	29	41	)	49	73	I	69	105	i
0A	10	LF	2A	42	*	4A	74	J	6A	106	j
0B	11	VT	2B	43	+	4B	75	K	6B	107	k
0C	12	FF	2C	44	,	4C	76	L	6C	108	l
0D	13	CR	2D	45	−	4D	77	M	6D	109	m
0E	14	SO	2E	46	.	4E	78	N	6E	110	n
0F	15	SI	2F	47	/	4F	79	O	6F	111	o
10	16	DLE	30	48	0	50	80	P	70	112	p
11	17	DC1	31	49	1	51	81	Q	71	113	q
12	18	DC2	32	50	2	52	82	R	72	114	r
13	19	DC3	33	51	3	53	83	S	73	115	s
14	20	DC4	34	52	4	54	84	T	74	116	t
15	21	NAK	35	53	5	55	85	U	75	117	u
16	22	SYN	36	54	6	56	86	V	76	118	v
17	23	ETB	37	55	7	57	87	W	77	119	w
18	24	CAN	38	56	8	58	88	X	78	120	x
19	25	EM	39	57	9	59	89	Y	79	121	y
1A	26	SUB	3A	58	:	5A	90	Z	7A	122	z
1B	27	ESC	3B	59	;	5B	91	[	7B	123	{
1C	28	FS	3C	60	<	5C	92	\	7C	124	|
1D	29	GS	3D	61	=	5D	93	]	7D	125	}
1E	30	RS	3E	62	>	5E	94	^	7E	126	~
1F	31	US	3F	63	?	5F	95	_	7F	127	DEL

Appendix D

I/O Macro Definitions and Procedures

THE IOMAC FILE

To create the IOMAC macro library, the macro definitions shown below should be put in a file called IOMAC.MAR. The command

```
LIBRARY/CREATE/MACRO IOMAC.MLB IOMAC.MAR
```

will create the library file IOMAC.MLB.

```
        .MACRO  BEGIN       NAME
                .ENTRY      NAME,^M<IV,DV> ; Define entry point
    ;                                      ; Set overflow traps
                $OPEN       FAB=INFAB       ; Open terminal input file
                $CONNECT    RAB=INRAB
                $CREATE     FAB=OUTFAB      ; Create terminal output file
                $CONNECT    RAB=OUTRAB
                $OPEN       FAB=DISKFAB     ; Open disk input file
                $CONNECT    RAB=DISKRAB
        .ENDM   BEGIN
    ;
        .MACRO  READLINE    WHERETO
                PUSHAB      WHERETO         ; Stack user buffer addr.
                CALLS       #1,RDLINE
        .ENDM   READLINE
    ;
        .MACRO  READRCRD    WHERETO,?LBL
                PUSHAB      WHERETO         ; Stack user buffer addr.
                CALLS       #1,RDRCRD       ; Returns length in R0
                BNEQ        LBL             ; Got a record
                BRW         EOF             ; End-of-file
LBL:    .ENDM   READRCRD
```

```
        ;
                .MACRO    PRINTCHRS STRING,LENGTH=#85
                          CVTWL     LENGTH,-(SP)   ; Stack string length
                          PUSHAB    STRING         ; Stack string address
                          CALLS     #2,PTCHRS
                .ENDM     PRINTCHRS
        ;
                .MACRO    DUMPLONG ARG1,ARG2,ARG3,ARG4,ARG5,ARG6-
                          ARG7,ARG8,ARG9,ARG10,ARG11,ARG12
                          CALLS     #0,STARX       ; Print stars
                .IRP      ARG,<ARG1,ARG2,ARG3,ARG4,ARG5,ARG6,-
                          ARG7,ARG8,ARG9,ARG10,ARG11,ARG12>
                .IF       NOT_BLANK  ARG
                          MOVQ      #^A/%EXTRACT(0,8,ARG)/,-(SP)  ; Stack name
                          PUSHL     SP             ; Stack addr of name
                          PUSHL     ARG            ; Stack longword to dump
                          CALLS     #2,CVTPRT
                          ADDL2     #8,SP          ; Pop name
                .ENDC
                .ENDR
                          CALLS     #0,STARX       ; Print stars
                .ENDM     DUMPLONG
        ;
                .MACRO    EXIT
                          $CLOSE    FAB=INFAB      ; Close I/O files
                          $CLOSE    FAB=OUTFAB     ;      "
                          $CLOSE    FAB=DISKFAB    ;      "
                          $EXIT_S                  ; System exit macro
                .ENDM     EXIT
```

THE IOMOD MODULE

The **IOMOD.OBJ** module contains the FABs and RABs used by the I/O macros and the procedures that they call to perform the I/O operations. To construct the file, the **IOMOD.MAR** file should be typed as shown below, and then assembled with the command

```
                    MACRO IOMOD+IOMAC/LIB

        ;
                .PSECT IO_DATA,LONG,NOEXE
        ;
LF = 10                                      ; ASCII line feed
CR = 13                                      ; ASCII carriage return
SPC = 32                                     ; ASCII space
        ;
INFAB::    $FAB  FNM=<SYS$INPUT>             ; Terminal input
OUTFAB::   $FAB  FNM=<SYS$OUTPUT>,MRS=85     ; Terminal output
DISKFAB::  $FAB  FNM=<DATA.DAT>              ; For DATA.DAT file
INRAB::    $RAB  FAB=INFAB,USZ=80,-
                 ROP=PMT,PBF=PROMPT,PSZ=5
OUTRAB::   $RAB  FAB=OUTFAB
DISKRAB::  $RAB  FAB=DISKFAB,USZ=80
PROMPT:    .ASCII <LF><CR>/?? /
```

```
        ;
        ;
        ;         .PSECT    IO_PROCS,NOWRT
        ;
        ; PROCEDURE RDLINE (WHERETO)
        ;
        ; This procedure gets an input line from the terminal.
        ; It uses the RAB labeled INRAB which causes a prompt to be
        ; displayed at the terminal. The input record is stored
        ; in memory at WHERETO, RDLINE's argument. RDLINE returns
        ; the length of the record in R0.
        ;
                  .ENTRY   RDLINE,0
                  MOVL     4(AP),INRAB+RAB$L_UBF    ; Fill UBF field in RAB
                  $GET     RAB=INRAB                ; Get record
                  CVTWL    INRAB+RAB$W_RSZ,R0       ; Record size to R0
                  RET
        ;
        ;
        ; PROCEDURE RDRCRD (WHERETO)
        ;
        ; This procedure reads the next record from the DATA.DAT file.
        ; If there was a record, it is stored in WHERETO and its
        ; length is put in R0. If there were no more records, the Z bit
        ; in the stacked PSW is set to indicate end-of-file.
        ; RDRCRD uses the RAB labeled DISKRAB.
        ;
                  .ENTRY   RDRCRD,0
                  MOVL     4(AP),DISKRAB+RAB$L_UBF ; Fill UBF field in RAB
                  $GET     RAB=DISKRAB              ; Get record
                  CMPL     DISKRAB+RAB$L_STS,#RMS$_EOF   ; CHECK STS field for EOF
                  BEQL     EOF
                  CVTWL    DISKRAB+RAB$W_RSZ,R0    ; Record size to R0
                  RET
        EOF:      BISB2    #^X04,4(FP)             ; Set EOF flag
                  RET
        ;
        ;
        ; PROCEDURE PTCHRS (STRING, MAX_LEN)
        ;
        ; This procedure displays a character string at the terminal.
        ; It sends a carriage return and line feed before the string.
        ;
        ; Input arguments
        ;
        ;     STRING       the string to be displayed
        ;     MAX_LEN      the maximum string length (passed by
        ;                  immediate value).
        ;        At most MAX_LEN characters will be displayed,
        ;        but a byte of 0's is interpreted as a string
        ;        terminator.
        ;
        CR_LF: .BYTE   13,10                        ; Carriage return & line feed
        ;
                  .ENTRY   PTCHRS,0
                  MOVAW    CR_LF,OUTRAB+RAB$L_RBF  ; Set RBF and RSZ fields
                  MOVW     #2,OUTRAB+RAB$W_RSZ     ;    for CR and LF
                  $PUT     RAB=OUTRAB              ; Output CR and LF
```

```
        MOVL      4(AP),OUTRAB+RAB$L_RBF      ; Put STRING addr in RBF field
        LOCC      #0,8(AP),@4(AP)             ; Find 00 byte
        SUBL2     4(AP),R1                    ; Length of string
        MOVW      R1,OUTRAB+RAB$W_RSZ         ; Put length in RSZ field
        $PUT      RAB=OUTRAB                  ; Output string
        RET
;
;
; PROCEDURE STARX
;
; STARX prints 3 stars as header and trailer for DUMPLONG output.
;
STARS:  .ASCIZ  /***/
        .ENTRY  STARX,0
        PRINTCHRS  STARS,#3
        RET
;
;
; PROCEDURE CVTPRT (LONG,NAME)
;
; CVTPRT converts a longword to a hex character string
; and prints it along with its name. The argument list
; contains the longword, passed by immediate value, and
; the address of a character string (of length at most 8)
; that is the name of the longword.
; CVTPRT uses a procedure, OTS$CVT_L_TZ, from the VAX
; Run-time Library to do the conversion.
;
        .PSECT  IO_DATA
LONG:   .BLKL   1
DUMP:   .BLKB   18                          ; For DUMPLONG'S output
;
        .PSECT  IO_PROCS
DESC:   .LONG   ^X010E0008                  ; The library proc. requires
        .ADDRESS DUMP+10                    ;   a string descriptor
ARGS:   .LONG   3                           ; Arglist for library proc.
        .ADDRESS LONG,DESC
        .LONG   8
;
        .ENTRY  CVTPRT,^M<R2,R3,R4,R5>
;
        MOVC5   #0,0,#SPC,#10,DUMP          ; Blank out DUMP buffer
        LOCC    #0,#8,@8(AP)                ; Find end of name string
        SUBL3   R0,#8,R2                    ; Length of name string
        MOVC3   R2,@8(AP),DUMP              ; Move name to DUMP buffer
        MOVL    4(AP),LONG                  ; Addr of longword to arglist
        CALLG   ARGS,G^OTS$CVT_L_TZ         ; Library conversion routine
        PRINTCHRS  DUMP,#18                 ; Output
        RET
;
        .END
```

Appendix E:

Answers to Selected Exercises

CHAPTER 3

1. (a) 10000001000111   (c) 111110101101
2. (a) 1A37CB   (c) 100
3. (a) 2158   (c) 240
4. (a) 50   (c) C03
8. (b) 1DCF
9. (b) 190
13. (a) −1   (c) −8159
14. (a) FDE2   (c) 0100
15. -2^{31}

19. To subtract the two's complement integer x from the two's complement integer y, subtract x from y as unsigned binary numbers. If a "borrow" is needed at the leftmost place, just assume it can be done.

CHAPTER 4

1. MARGIN = 10
2. The location counter is used by the assembler, at assembly time, to keep track of the amount of space used by data and instructions. The PC is used by the CPU at execution time to determine which instruction is to be executed next.
7. (R6) + 16
9. R9 will contain 00000A7A.

13.
```
GRADES:   .BLKW   20
CODES:    .BLKB   13
HEADING:  .BLKB   11
```
14.
```
LINE:     .BLKB   120
COL1 = LINE+10
COL2 = LINE+25
COL3 = LINE+40
```
17. (a) `MPGMSG: .ASCII   '3.785*MILES/LITERS'`

CHAPTER 5

3.
```
MESSAGE:.ASCIZ   /What is today's date?/
INPUT:  .BLKB   80                      ; Input buffer
;
        BEGIN  DATE
;
        PRINTCHRS MESSAGE               ; Print question
        READLINE  INPUT                 ; Get input
        PRINTCHRS INPUT,R0              ; Print input
        EXIT
        .END    DATE
```

6. The same input area may be used several times for input lines of different lengths, so the zeros that were in memory initially may have been overwritten.

CHAPTER 6

1. `DIVW3   #12,EGGS,DOZENS`

8.
```
; Register use          R5,R6  used for scratch work
;
        MULL3   #7,I,R5      ; 7*I
        DIVL3   LL,J,R6      ; J/LL
        ADDL2   R5,R6        ; 7*I+J/LL
        MULL3   R6,R6,K      ; K = (7*I+J/LL)**2
```

10. (a) The word beginning at 184A0 will contain 5B83 and R9 will contain 00148DEA.

(c) The byte at 148DE8 will contain FE.

(e) R7 is unchanged, but the overflow condition code will be set.

14. (a) `ADDW2   #1,R8`

19.
```
; This program segment subtracts 1 from every fourth entry
; in the word array COUNTS, beginning at the fourth entry.
; The number of entries is in the word NUM. (We assume that
; there are at least four entries.)
;
; Register use          R6      array pointer
;                       R7      loop counter
;
        CLRL    R7              ; Loop counter must be longword
        DIVW3   #4,NUM,R7       ; Number of entries to decrement
        MOVAW   COUNTS+6,R6     ; Addr. of first entry affected
;
DECR:   DECW    (R6)            ; Decrement entry
        ADDL2   #8,R6           ; Adjust array pointer
        SOBGTR  R7,DECR         ; Loop control
```

25. (a) R3 will contain 00029A80 and R4 will contain 00029A7C.

29. (a) 2D 33 31 30 35 (with the first byte at the left)

30. (a) 17 0D will be stored beginning at PKD.

35.
```
; This program segment prints out a two-dimensional
; longword array.  The data used are:
;
;         ARRAY    a two dimensional longword array
;         ROWS     the number of rows (longword)
;         COLMS    the number of columns (longword)
;
; It is assumed that the entries have at most five
; significant digits and that there are at most 10 columns.
;
LF = 10                                 ; Line feed
SPACE = 32                              ; Blank
PKD:    .BLKB   3
HDG:    .ASCIZ  <LF>/THE ARRAY/<LF>
LINE:   .BYTE   SPACE[80]
            .
            .
            .
; Register use          R6      array pointer
;                       R7      row counter
;                       R8      column counter
;                       R9      buffer pointer
;
        PRINTCHRS HDG
        MOVAL   ARRAY,R6                ; Initialize array ptr
        MOVL    ROWS,R7                 ; Outer loop counter
;
NEWROW: MOVAB   LINE,R9                 ; Initialize buffer ptr
        MOVL    COLMS,R8                ; Initialize inner loop
;
NEXT:   CVTLP   (R6)+,#5,PKD            ; Convert to packed
        CVTPS   #5,PKD,#5,(R9)          ; Put lsn in line
        ADDL2   #6,R9                   ; Increment line pointer
        MOVB    #SPACE,(R9)+            ; Space to separate entries
        SOBGTR  R8,NEXT                 ; Inner loop control
;
        MOVB    #0,(R9)                 ; Mark end of output string
        PRINTCHRS LINE
        SOBGTR  R7,NEWROW               ; Outer loop control
```

CHAPTER 7

1. (a) N=0, Z=0, V=0, C=1   **(c)** N=0, Z=0, V=0, C=0

2. (a) N=0, Z=0, V=0, C=1   **(c)** N=1, Z=0, V=0, C=0

3. HERE

11.
```
        CMPW    WORD,#-100
        BLSS    NEXT
        CMPW    WORD,#100
        BGTR    NEXT
        CMPB    BYTE,#3
```

```
          BEQL      THERE
          CMPB      BYTE,#4
          BEQL      THERE
NEXT:
```
13.
```
          CMPL      ALPHA+4,BETA+4    ; Compare most signif. part
          BGTR      ABC
          BLSS      NEXT
          CMPL      ALPHA,BETA
          BGTRU     ABC
NEXT:
```

19. The pointer to the byte being examined is incremented after each comparison by the autoincrement in the CMPB instruction, so the address in R6 at the instruction labeled FOUND is the address of the byte following the one that contains the blank. One way to correct the segment is to change the last two lines to

```
NOTFND:   CLRL      LOCBLANK          ; No blank found
          BRB       NEXT
FOUND:    MOVAB     -(R6),LOCBLANK    ; Store address of blank
NEXT:
```

26. **(a)** Sequential search: 64; Binary search: 1.

   (c) Sequential search: 1; Binary search: 7.

28.
```
          ADDW2     #7,R9             ; Increment index
          CMPW      R9,CNT            ; Compare to loop limit
          BGTR      NEXT
          BRW       CHECK             ; ACB uses word displacement
```

CHAPTER 8

For all machine code, the first byte is shown at the right.

1. **(a)** 54 59 58 C1   **(c)** 65 B6

2. **(a)** DIVL2   (R7),R9

4. SOBGTR COUNTER,LOOP

7. MOVL   8(R7),R7

8.
```
          CMPB      4(R8),#20         ; Compare age to 20
          BLSS      NEXT              ; If less, try next person
          CMPB      4(R8),#29         ; Compare age to 29
          BGTR      NEXT              ; If higher, try next
          CMPB      9(R8),#^A/3/      ; Compare Q5 to ASCII 3
          BLSS      NEXT
          INCL      R10               ; Count this person
NEXT:     ADDL2     #12,R8            ; Move ptr to next person
```

12. **(a)** Addresses: 150 14F 14E

   Contents: FF 67 CF

   (c) Addresses: 14F 14E

   Contents: 80 AF

20. **(a)** No error

   (c) The branch destination is too far away for a byte displacement.

27. **(a)** 0C B5

CHAPTER 9

1.
```
    ; PROCEDURE PRINT_STRINGS (STRINGS, NUM)
    ;
    ; This procedure prints out a character string array.
    ;
    ; Input arguments
    ;
    ;       STRINGS         the array
    ;       NUM             the number of entries (longword)
    ;
    ; The length of the strings, SIZE, is defined in this
    ; procedure.
    ;
    SIZE = 12
    ;
            .ENTRY  PRINT_STRINGS,^M<R6,R7>
    ;
    ; Register use        R6      array pointer
    ;                     R7      loop counter
    ;
            MOVL    4(AP),R6            ; Get array pointer
            MOVL    @8(AP),R7           ; Number of entries
    PRINT:  PRINTCHRS (R6),#SIZE        ; Print string
            ADDL2   #SIZE,R6            ; Increment pointer
            SOBGTR  R7,PRINT
            RET
            .END
```

5. (a) Any order is OK.

(c) No; RET wouldn't be able to determine how many registers were saved, so it couldn't find the longword containing the register mask.

8. (a) 0000FF6A

10. (a) MOVL   AP,R10

(c)
```
        MOVL    12(FP),R10      ; Pointer to frame for C
        MOVL    12(R10),R10     ; Pointer to frame for B
        MOVL    12(R10),R10     ; Pointer to frame for A
```

16.
```
        MOVAL   ANSWERS,R6
        MOVAB   GRADES,R7
        MOVL    #NUM_PEOPLE,R8
NEXT:   PUSHAB  (R7)+           ; Address for score
        PUSHAL  KEY             ; Address of KEY
        PUSHAL  (R6)+           ; Addr. of person's answers
        CALLS   #3,SCORE        ; Call SCORE
        SOBGTR  R8,NEXT
```

CHAPTER 10

1. DELTA = 828   IND = 82E   LABEL = 830
TAG = 836   VOLUME = 838   final . = 844

3. All are valid except (d).

4. (a) Valid, relocatable   **(c)** Not valid

5. (a) 36_{16} **(c)** 136_{16} **(e)** 36_{10}

6. (a) 54_{10}, absolute   **(c)** $1C6_{16}$, relocatable

CHAPTER 11

1.
```
        .MACRO  SWITCH  A,B
        MOVL    A,-(SP)                ; Use stack for scratch space
        MOVL    B,A
        MOVL    (SP)+,B
        .ENDM   SWITCH
```

3. Autodecrement, literal

4.
```
        .MACRO  CVTLQ   LONG,QUAD,?LBL
        CLRL    QUAD+4                 ; Sign extension if >=0
        MOVL    LONG,QUAD              ; Sets condition codes
        BGEQ    LBL
        MOVL    #^XFFFFFFFF,QUAD+4     ; Sign extension if <0;
                                       ;   causes N=1, Z=0
LBL:    .ENDM   CVTLQ
```

The actual argument for QUAD must be an expression.

16.
```
        .MACRO  SETREG
        .IRP    N,<0,1,2,3,4,5,6,7,8,9,10>
        MOVL    #N,R'N
        .ENDR
        .ENDM   SETREG
```

CHAPTER 12

1.
```
CLRL    R9
BISL2   #^X00020120,R9
```

7.
```
MNEGL   R8,-(SP)
BICL2   (SP)+,R8
```
Exercise: Explain why this works.

11. (a) 53 59 FF 8F 9C

23. The ASHL instruction will shift left, causing overflow. If the IV trap is disabled, the expected mask (all zeros) will be generated.

24. (a) 00003FFC   **(c)** FE00001F

26.
```
        .MACRO  CVTLQ   LONG,QUAD
        MOVL    LONG,QUAD+4
        ASHQ    #-32,QUAD,QUAD
        .ENDM   CVTLQ
```

29.
```
        .MACRO   UNION  SET1,SET2,DEST,?LOCLBL
        C'LOCLBL=0
        .REPEAT 8
        BISL3    SET1+C'LOCLBL,SET2+C'LOCLBL,DEST+C'LOCLBL
        C'LOCLBL=C'LOCLBL+4
        .ENDR
        .ENDM
```

32. INSV #1,NUMBER,#1,R6

39. (a)
```
        .PSECT  HORIZONTAL_LINE

    ;
    ; PROCEDURE HORIZONTAL_LINE (SCREEN, ROW, RIGHT, LENGTH)
    ;
    ; This procedure "draws" a horizontal line in a bit matrix.
```

```
;
; Input  arguments
;
;
;        SCREEN   the bit matrix (256x8 longwords)
;        ROW      the line's row number (longword)
;        RIGHT    the offset of the right end of the line
;                 from the right end of the screen (longword)
;        LENGTH   the length (in bits) of the line (longword)
;
; It is assumed that the arguments have already been
; checked for validity
;
; The algorithm is:
;
;        posn := row*256 + right;
;        while length >= 32 do
;           begin
;              insert 32 1's beginning at SCREEN + posn;
;              length := length - 32;
;              posn := posn + 32
;           end;
;        insert length 1's beginning at SCREEN + posn.
;
;
; Offsets for argument list
SCREEN = 4
ROW = 8
RIGHT = 12
LENGTH = 20
;
        ENTRY   HORIZONTAL_LINE,^M<R6,R7,R8,R9>
;
; Register use           R6      SCREEN
;                        R7      position
;                        R8      length (loop index)
;
        MOVL    SCREEN(AP),R6          ; SCREEN
        MULL3   @ROW(AP),#256,R7       ; Row number *256
        ADDL2   @RIGHT(AP),R7          ; Posn := row*256 + right
        MOVL    @LENGTH(AP),R8         ; Length
;
        CMPL    R8,#32                 ; Compare length to 32
        BLSS    LAST                   ; Skip loop if less
;
INS:    INSV    #-1,R7,#32,(R6)        ; Insert 1's
        ADDL2   #32,R7                 ; Posn := posn + 32
        ACBL    #32,#-32,R8,INS        ; Decrement & test length
LAST:   INSV    #-1,R7,R8,(R6)         ; Insert remaining 1's
;
        RET
        .END
```

42.   `.PSECT  CVTCB`

```
;
; PROCEDURE CVTCB (STRING, LONG)
;
; THE PROBLEM
;
; This procedure converts the character string STRING to
```

```
; a longword bit pattern and puts the result in LONG.
; The string is assumed to be 8 characters long and should
; contain ASCII codes for hex digits. Thus the string
; "1234ABCD" would be converted to the bit pattern
; ^X1234ABCD.
;
; CVTCB sets the Z condition code in the saved PSW in the
; call frame if the conversion is done successfully.
; If any characters in the string are not valid hex digits,
; Z will not be set and nothing will be stored in LONG.
;
; THE METHOD
;
; Each character is converted to a nibble containing the
; numeric value of the digit. Then the nibble is inserted
; into the right end of the result, and the result is
; shifted left 4 places to make room for the next digit.
; After processing all eight characters, the result must
; be shifted back to the right one nibble because the last
; one inserted did not have to be shifted left.
;
        .ENTRY  CVTCB,^M<R6,R7,R8,R9>
;
; Register use      R6      address of next character
;                   R7      loop counter
;                   R8      binary value of digit
;                   R9      result
;
        MOVL    4(AP),R6            ; Address of STRING
        MOVL    #8,R7              ; Loop counter
        CLRL    R9                 ; Clear for result
DIGIT:  SUBB3   #^X30,(R6)+,R8     ; Get 0-9 ok
        BLSS    RET                ; Char < ^X30
        CMPB    R8,#9
        BLEQ    OK
        SUBB2   #7,R8              ; Get 10-15 ok
        BLSS    RET                ; ^X39 < char < ^X41
        CMPB    R8,#15
        BGTR    RET                ; Char > ^X46
OK:     BISB2   R8,R9              ; Fill nibble
        ROTL    #4,R9,R9           ; Shift left
        SOBGTR  R7,DIGIT
;
        ROTL    #-4,R9,@8(AP)      ; Shift right and store
        BISB2   #^X04,4(FP)        ; Set Z in saved PSW
RET:    RET
;
        .END
```

CHAPTER 13

1. (a) $-3/8$, or -0.375 **(c)** 0.0

2. (a) $000042C8$ **(c)** $00004A80$

7. TSTF tests bit 15 for the sign; TSTL tests bit 31. TSTF tests bits 15:7 to determine if the datum is zero; TSTW tests bits 15:0.

14. One position. Since the factors are each $\geq 1/2$, the product is $\geq 1/4$.

```
26.             .MACRO  TSTP    NUM_DGTS,PKD
                MOVB    #^XOC,-(SP)                 ; Packed zero
                CMPP    NUM_DGTS,PKD,#1,(SP)+       ; Compare to 0
                .ENDM   TSTP
```

CHAPTER 14

2. (R0) = 00000000   (R1) = 00000000   (R3) = LINE+1

6.   .PSECT CNT_VOWELS

```
;
; PROCEDURE CNT_VOWELS (TEXT, LENGTH, VOWELS)
;
; This procedure counts the vowels in a segment of text.
; It counts both capital and lower case letters.
;
; Input arguments
;       TEXT    the text
;       LENGTH  the number of bytes in the text
;
; Output argument
;       VOWELS  counters (word array)
;
; The VOWELS array is not cleared to zeros in this procedure;
; It may be called several times to count all the vowels in
; different segments of text.
;
TABLE:  .BYTE   0[65],1,0[3],2,0[3],3,0[5],4,0[5],5,0[11]
        .BYTE   1,0[3],2,0[3],3,0[5],4,0[5],5,0[10],0[128]
;
; Table entries are indexes of the appropriate counters in
; the VOWELS array.
;
; Offsets for argument list
TEXT = 4
LENGTH = 8
VOWELS = 12
;
        .ENTRY  CNT_VOWELS,^M<R2,R3,R6,R7,R8>
;
; Register use          R0      length of remaining text
;                       R1      address of vowel found
;                       R2-R3   used by SCANC
;                       R6      vowel found
;                       R7      table entry (VOWEL array index)
;                       R8      VOWEL array address
;
        MOVL    TEXT(AP),R1             ; Get TEXT address
        DECL    R1                      ; SCANC uses 1(R1)
        MOVL    @LENGTH(AP),R0          ; Get length
        MOVL    VOWELS(AP),R8           ; Get VOWELS address
        SUBL2   #2,R8                   ; VOWELS-2
;
SCAN:   SCANC   R0,1(R1),TABLE,#^XFF    ; Find vowel
        BEQL    DONE
        CVTBL   (R1),R6                 ; Vowel
        CVTBL   TABLE[R6],R7            ; Table entry
```

```
            INCW      (R8)[R7]              ; Increment counter
            DECL      R0                    ; Remaining length
            BRB       SCAN
    ;
    DONE:   RET
            .END
```

13. It is valid; the operand address is TABLE+^X30, or TABLE+48. The instruction moves the ASCII code for a blank into the position in the table that corresponds to the character "0".

19. First byte $\longrightarrow$ 95 00

26.
```
    EO$LOAD_FILL      *
    EO$FILL           3
    EO$MOVE           4
    EO$SET_SIGNIF
    EO$MOVE           1
    EO$LOAD_PLUS      < >
    EO$LOAD_MINUS     C
    EO$STORE_SIGN
    EO$LOAD_MINUS     R
    EO$STORE_SIGN
    EO$FILL           3
    EO$END
```

CHAPTER 15

1. (a)
```
    $GET    RAB=INRAB
    MOVC3   #80,INBUF,LINE
```
(b) "INPUT:"

INDEX

Abort, 161
Absolute, 230–31, 232, 234
Access violation, 41, 161
Address, 8, 9, 15, 84–85
Addressing modes, 39, 54, 132, 165 (*See also* specific modes)
in macros, 244
Alignment, 10, 221–22
AND macro, 281
Argument list, 180, 183–91, 195–96, 215
Argument pointer (AP), 12, 15, 180, 187, 194–96, 200, 215
Arguments (of procedures), 174 (*See also* Argument list; Macro, arguments)
Arithmetic shift (*See* Shifting)
Array, 43–44, 46, 79–82, 96–97
ASCII, 41, 48–50, 107–8, 124, 353, 356, 389
.ASCII, 48–49, 55
.ASCIZ, 49–50, 55
Assembler, 4, 5 (*See also* VAX-11 MACRO)
Assembler directives, 37, 38 (*See also* specific directives)
Assembly process, 134–35, 141, 143–44, 146–49, 150–51
Assembly time, 6, 134, 261
Associative law, 316
Autodecrement mode, 45, 54, 85, 135, 166
Autoincrement deferred mode, 156, 166

Autoincrement mode, 43–45, 54, 85, 105, 135, 144, 149, 166
Available node list, 202–4

BEGIN, 63–64, 68, 376, 390
Biased exponent, 305–7, 324
Binary number system, 16–21, 26 (*For hex conversions see* Hexadecimal number system)
converting to and from decimal, 20–23
Binary search 110–16
Bit, 5
Bit matrix, 295–96
Bit numbering, 8, 9, 14–15
Bit strings, 276, 297 (*See also* Variable length bit field)
.BLK*x*, 45–47, 55, 233
Boundary, 9, 221
Branch instructions:
conditional, 99–107, 125
unconditional, 100–101, 125
Branch mode, 41–42, 54, 141–43, 166
computation of displacement, 144
Bubble sort, 129–30, 170
Byte, 5, 7, 14, 39, 43
.BYTE, 47, 55, 233

Cache, 7
Call by reference, 184, 198, 215
Call frame, 192–93, 196, 215, 279

CALLG/CALLS flag, 192, 194, 196
CALL macro, 265–66
Central processing unit (CPU), 12–14, 131, 133–34, 136–38, 141–43, 145–46
Character, 8
Character string, 48–50, 55, 65, 86, 94, 191, 234, 335–54
conversion to and from two's complement, 86–92, 122, 124–25
search instructions, 340–49, 364
translation, 350–54, 364
Circular shift (*See* Shifting)
COBOL, 198, 199, 327, 355
Command language, 68
Comment field, 35, 53
COMMON, 226
Comparison instructions, 102–8, 126 (*See also* Floating point; Packed decimal)
character, 107–8, 126
integer, 103, 126
Compiler, 5, 344, 345
Complement, 5, 277 (*See also* Set)
Computer architecture, 4–5, 25
Concatenation, 244–45, 273
Conditional assembly, 261–70, 273
Conditional assembly block directive (*See* .IF)

Condition codes, 72, 99–100, 102, 125, 194, 197, 278, 279, 285, 310, 328, 338, 339, 340, 346–47, 350, 353, 363
Condition handler, 161, 194–95, 217
Control block, 370
Control character, 49
Conversion instructions (*See* specific data types)
Cryptogram, 350, 351
CVTSL macro, 258
CVT2S macro, 264

DATA.DAT, 60, 62, 65, 391
Data types, 11 (*See also* Floating point; Leading separate numeric; Packed decimal; Two's complement)
Datum, 5
Decimal string overflow, 162, 163, 327
Deferred addressing modes, 154–58, 165
Delimiter, 49, 251, 335
Descriptor mechanism, 191, 198
Digital Equipment Corporation (DEC), 1
Direct assignment statement, 37, 53, 54, 230, 233
.DISABLE, 231
Disk map, 292–93
Displacement deferred modes, 155, 166–67, 180, 187
Displacement modes, 135–40, 144, 165, 166, 180, 187
computation of displacement, 145, 147–48
Divide-by-zero trap, 162, 310
.D_FLOATING, 309, 331
DO statement, 119, 120–21
.DOUBLE, 309, 317 (*See also* .D_FLOATING)
DUMPLONG, 63, 68, 391

EBCDIC, 350, 353
Editing numeric data, 354–64
Edit pattern operators, 355–57, 359–60, 364
.END, 52, 55, 181, 220
.ENDM, 241
.ENTRY, 51, 55, 63–64, 68, 181–83, 215, 216, 231
Entry mask (*See* Register mask)
Entry point, 51, 63–64, 68, 182, 230, 231
.ERROR, 269–70
Escape character, 352–53
Exception, 160–62, 167, 217, 310, 331
Executable, 6
Execution of instructions, 133–34, 136–38, 141–43, 145–46, 149–50
Execution time, 6, 134

EXIT, 63–64, 68, 376, 391
$EXIT_S, 52, 55, 63–64, 68
Expression, 226, 228, 234
restrictions, 233
External, 230–31, 234
.EXTERNAL, 231, 232
%EXTRACT, 271–72

FAB (*See* File access block)
Fault, 161
.F_FLOATING, 309, 331
File, 369
indexed, 370, 371
processing macros, 375
relative, 370, 371
sequential, 60, 369, 371
File access block, 370–72, 373
Fill character, 337–38, 355, 357, 360, 361
.FLOAT, 309 (*See also* .F_FLOATING)
Floating point, 8, 9, 39, 40, 43, 304, 326, 330
accuracy, 315–16, 318–23, 331
arithmetic, 310, 313–15, 330–31
comparison, 311
conversion, 311
to and from character code, 312
to and from two's complement, 311, 323–25
double precision (D_floating), 305–6, 308–9, 330
G_floating, 305–6, 330
H_floating, 305–6, 330
overflow, 310, 331
range, 307
representation, 305–6, 330
reserved operand, 310, 331
single precision (F_floating), 305–6, 330
test, 311
underflow, 162, 163, 310, 331
Formal repeat block argument, 264–65, 267
For statement, 119–20, 129
Fortran, 2, 198–99, 226, 322, 355
Fraction (in floating point), 305, 324, 331
Frame pointer (FP), 12, 15, 192, 194–95, 215
Function, 183–84

General register, 12–13, 15
.G_FLOATING, 309, 331
Global, 182, 231, 235
Graphics (*See* Bit matrix)
Guard bits, 314

Header node, 201
Hexadecimal number system, 3, 16–30, 32
arithmetic, 23–25, 32

Hexadecimal number system (cont.)
conversion to and from binary, 17–18, 32
conversion to and from decimal, 19–22, 32, 387
why used, 25–26, 32
.H_FLOATING, 309, 331
Horner's method, 122–25, 326

.IF, 262–64, 270
.IF_FALSE, 264
If statement, 104, 106
.IIF, 263–64
Immediate mode, 40–41, 144, 149–51, 166, 227
FLOATING POINT, 316
Immediate value mechanism, 190–91, 199
Indefinite repeat block directive (*See* .IRP)
Indexed modes, 158–60, 165, 167
Initializing data, 45, 54, 64, 221
address, 184–85, 216
character, 48–50, 55
floating point, 309
integer, 47–48, 55
in a macro, 245
packed decimal, 328
Input and output, 58, 368–78 (*See also* I/O macros)
free format input, 218, 341, 364
Instruction execution (*See* Execution of instructions)
Instruction formats, 131–33
fixed format, 131
flexible format, 131–33
Integer arithmetic, 72–77, 92–93 (*See also* Two's complement)
addition, 73
algorithms, 74–75, 76
conversions, 83–84, 93
decrement, 77–78
division, 74, 92, 285
increment, 77–78
multiplication, 73, 74–75, 76, 285
negation, 77–78
subtraction, 73, 74
Integer overflow trap (IV), 51, 64, 72, 83, 162, 163
Integer representation, 26–32 (*See also* One's complement; Sign-magnitude; Two's complement)
criteria for choosing, 27, 28, 32
range, 92
I/O instructions, 14, 15 (*See also* I/O macros)
side effects, 13
IOMAC, 68–69, 390

I/O macros, 58–63, 237, 238, 372, 374, 390–91
IOMOD, 69–70, 372, 391
.IRP, 262, 264–66
.IRPC, 262, 267

Key, 110

Label, 35, 41, 229 (*See also* Local label)
in macros, 252–53, 267
Label field, 35, 53
Last-in, first-out, 176
Leading separate numeric, 87–92, 94 (*For conversions, see* Two's complement)
%LENGTH, 271, 273
Lexical analysis, 345
LINK command, 69
Linked list, 200–213
Linker, 6, 145, 154, 185, 223, 231, 232, 234, 235
Listing, 5, 6, 66, 67, 151–54, 231, 246–47, 266
Literal mode, 40–41, 54, 140–41, 166, 227
character, 41
floating point, 316, 332
Local, 174
Local label, 252–55, 256, 273
%LOCATE, 272, 273
Location counter, 36, 46, 66, 134, 165, 221, 223, 228, 229, 234
Logical operations, 280–81
Logical shift (*See* Shifting)
.LONG, 47, 55, 233
Longword, 9, 14, 43
Loop instructions, 78–82, 93, 116–21, 125, 312

Machine instructions, 37–38
Machine language (machine code), 1–3, 66, 131–33, 136, 142, 147–54, 157–58, 158–60
Macro, 37–38, 39
arguments, 238, 241, 273
character string, 251
default values, 249–51, 256, 273
keyword, 249–51, 256, 273
positional, 248–49, 273
substitution table, 255
definition, 240, 241, 256
expansion, 237, 246–47
instruction, 237
library, 66, 248
processor, 237, 273
string functions, 271–73
user-friendly, 256–61
.MACRO, 241
MACRO command, 68–69
Mantissa, 304
Mask, 277, 286, 297, 344 (*See also* Register mask)

Mean, 319
Memory, 7–12, 14–15
magnetic core, 7
main, 7
MOS, 7
physical, 7
virtual, 11, 15
.MEXIT, 270
Mode byte, 133, 165
Module, 6
Multiprogramming, 6, 11, 14

Nanosecond, 7
.NARG, 265
Nibble, 5
Node, 200
Normalization, 305, 314–15, 330
.NOSHOW, 248, 265
Null pointer, 200
Numerical analysis, 319

Object program (object module, object file), 5–6, 238, 240
Octal number system, 25
Octaword, 9, 14, 43
One's complement, 27–28, 30–32
Opcode, 131–32, 165
privileged, 160
Opcode reserved to DIGITAL fault, 161
Operand field, 35, 53
Operand specifier, 132, 165, 228
Operating system, 6, 11, 13, 15, 58, 177, 215, 276, 369
VAX/VMS, 6, 369
Operator field, 35, 53
Overflow, 13, 32, 34, 94 (*See also* Floating point; Decimal string overflow; Integer overflow trap)
Overlay, 221, 225

.PACKED, 328, 332
Packed decimal, 87–92, 94, 191, 304, 325–29, 331, 355, 363, 364
arithmetic, 328–29, 331
comparison, 329, 331
representation, 87–88, 325–26, 331
Page, 11, 15
Pascal, 2, 198, 199, 277, 287
Pattern operators (*See* Edit pattern operators)
PDP-11, 5, 306
Pixel, 295
PL/1, 355
Polynomial, 122–23
Pop (a stack), 176, 258
Positional representation, 16–17, 32
PRINTCHRS, 60–62, 68, 391

Procedure, 6, 172, 215, 239 (*See also* Arguments; Argument list; Call frame)
calling, 180, 192–196
returning from, 192–93, 196–97
Procedure calling standard, 175, 179–80, 215, 322
Procedure linkage conventions (*See* Procedure calling standard)
Processor status longword (PSL), 13, 15, 161
Processor status word (PSW), 12–13, 30, 32, 72, 99, 125, 173, 179, 194, 197, 310, 327
Program counter (PC), 12–13, 15, 42, 99–100, 125, 133–34, 144, 165
use in debugging, 163–64
use in execution of instructions, 136–38, 141–43, 145–46, 149–50
Program counter addressing modes, 144, 166 (*See also* Immediate mode; Relative mode)
Program section, 220, 234
attributes, 220–21, 234
default, 223
Prompt, 59, 373
.PSECT, 180, 220, 241
Psect table, 223
Push (on a stack), 176, 258

.QUAD, 48, 55
Quadword, 9, 14, 39, 43
Quadword arithmetic, 96

RAB (*See* Record access block)
Radix, 17, 19, 21, 226
Radix operator, 229, 234
READLINE, 59–60, 66, 376, 390
READRCRD, 60, 68, 197, 377, 390
Record, 369
processing macros, 375–76
Record access block, 370, 372–74
Record Management Services (RMS), 14, 60, 369–77
Register deferred mode, 42–43, 54, 135, 166
Register mask, 180, 182, 194, 196, 227–28, 233, 234, 259, 277
Register mode, 39–40, 54, 135, 166
Relative address, 143, 229
Relative deferred mode, 155–56, 157–58, 167
Relative index mode, 159
Relative mode, 40, 54, 144–49, 166, 232, 235

Relocatable, 229–31, 232, 234
.REPEAT, 262, 267, 351
Repeat-until statement, 117, 118
Repetition factor, 47–48, 233
Reserved addressing mode fault, 161
Reserved operand, 89, 162, 307, 310, 327, 363
Reserving storage, 45–47, 54–55, 64, 221
  in a macro, 245
Return address, 177
Rotate (*See* Shifting)
RUN command, 70
Run-Time Procedure Library (*See* VAX-11 Run-Time Procedure Library)

Saving registers, 181–83
Scientific notation, 304
Search (*See* Binary search; Character string; Sequential search)
Sequential file (*See* File)
Sequential search, 110, 188
Set, 276–77, 287–90, 297, 301
  complement, 288, 301
  empty, 288, 301
  intersection, 287–88, 301
  subset, 288, 301
  union, 287, 301
Shifting, 282, 297
  arithmetic shift, 282, 285–86

Shifting (cont.)
  circular shift (rotate), 282–84
  logical shift, 282
.SHOW, 248, 265
Sign bit, 26, 32
Sign-extension, 83, 94, 294
Significance flag, 357, 360
Sign-magnitude, 26–27, 30–32
Source program (source module, source file), 5
Stack, 175, 177, 180, 186–87, 192–97, 216, 257, 260, 273
Stack alignment bits, 194, 240
Stack frame (*See* Call frame)
Stack pointer (SP), 12, 15, 177, 195–96
Standard deviation, 319
Status flags, 197, 259, 372, 374
Subroutine, 6, 172, 177–79, 216
Symbol, 35–37, 54, 234
  permanent, 35
  user-defined, 35–37, 54
  value of, 36–37, 54
Symbol table, 110, 134–35, 145, 165, 223, 231, 234
Systems programs, 4

Term, 226–28
Test instructions, 102–3, 126
  (*See also* Floating point)
Text editing, 335, 347–48, 364
Textual term, 227, 230
Token, 345
Top (of a stack), 175, 177

Trace trap, 163
Transfer address, 52, 181
Translating character strings (*See* Character string)
Translation table, 350
Trap, 161–63
  enable flags, 182, 195
  enabling and disabling, 161, 163, 228
Two's complement, 26, 28–32, 60, 61, 72, 87, 326
  addition, 29–30, 32
  conversion to and from character code, 86–92, 122, 124–25, 341–43, 354
  multiplication, 74–75, 76
  negation, 29
  subtraction, 34, 74

Unary operator, 226–27

Value parameter, 199
Variable length bit field, 10, 277, 290–98
Variance, 319
VAX-11 MACRO, 1, 226, 228
VAX-11 Run-Time Procedure Library, 198, 199–200
VAX/VMS, 6

While statement, 117, 118
Word, 9, 14, 39, 43
WORD, 47, 55, 233